American Film Musical Themes and Forms

American Film Musical Themes and Forms

MICHAEL DUNNE

McFarland & Company, Inc., Publishers
Jefferson, North Carolina, and London

LIBRARY OF CONGRESS ONLINE CATALOG

Dunne, Michael, 1941–
American film musical themes and forms / Michael Dunne.
p.   cm.
Includes bibliographical references and index.

ISBN-13: 978-0-7864-1877-0
(softcover : 50# alkaline paper) ∞

1. Musical films—United States—History and criticism.
I. Title.
PN1995.9.M86D86   2004   791.43'6—dc22   2004012121

British Library cataloguing data are available

©2004 Michael Dunne. All rights reserved

No part of this book may be reproduced or transmitted in any form or by any means, electronic or mechanical, including photocopying or recording, or by any information storage and retrieval system, without permission in writing from the publisher.

On the front cover: Ginger Rogers and Fred Astaire
perform "Pick Yourself Up" in *Swing Time*

Manufactured in the United States of America

McFarland & Company, Inc., Publishers
Box 611, Jefferson, North Carolina 28640
www.mcfarlandpub.com

Acknowledgments

While I bear full responsibility for the prejudices, misjudgments and just plain errors that appear in this book, I am grateful to many people who have helped me get into the position to make these gaffes. Numerous college friends attended movies with me decades ago when we should have been going to class. Even though the statute of limitations has probably run out on these offenses, I will keep these friends' names secret just in case. Much more recently, Claudia Barnett, Will Brantley and Pete McCluskey helped me by lending me books when I needed them. Will Brantley, Dale Cockrill, Julie Graham, Bob Holtzclaw, Ron Kates, Arthur Knight and David Lavery helped me get hold of videos. Bob Holtzclaw cut out and passed along clippings from various periodicals and also coerced me into buying a used copy of Clive Hirschhorn's invaluable *The Hollywood Musical*. Paul Wells and the staff of the MTSU Center for Popular Music were, as usual, unfailingly helpful and courteous. Jerry Ohlinger helped me locate stills from many of the films I was writing about. The publishers of *Journal of Popular Film & Television* graciously granted permission to revise and reprint material that earlier appeared in their pages. Ray B. Browne provided some helpful and very welcome editorial advice. My wife, Sara, watched countless musicals with me and uncomplainingly listened to Fred Astaire sing (and dance) on vinyl, tape and CD. My gratitude to all of these folks, and especially Sara, goes beyond what my words can express.

Table of Contents

Acknowledgments   v
Introduction   1

1. Hollywood Musicals and the Depression   13
2. Blackface Minstrelsy in Musicals   34
3. Confronting Rock Culture   52
4. Dance as a Narrative Agent   67
5. American Places and Spaces   87
6. Fred and Gene in Never Never Land   107
7. Musical Biopics   126
8. Intertextual Musicals   147
9. Conclusion: "How About a Nice Musical?"   173

Chapter Notes   187
Works Cited   201
Index   209

Introduction

In the introduction to their *Musicals: Hollywood and Beyond*, Bill Marshall and Robynn Stilwell write, "The musical is one of the most popular film genres among both audiences and film scholars, probably for many of the same reasons—the spectacle, the music, the enjoyable predictability of the outcome weighed against the pleasure of the varied details" (1). Their praise of the genre is echoed by many critics, sometimes without even so much acknowledgment of the musical's generic limitations as recognizing "the enjoyable predictability of the outcome." Stephen Citron, for example, simply claims in *The Musical from the Inside Out* that "[t]he musical is the most popular form of entertainment in the world" (14). To reach this conclusion, Citron considers both stage and screen musicals. Focusing more narrowly on films, Jane Feuer makes an equally sweeping claim in her book *The Hollywood Musical*. "The musical is Hollywood writ large," Feuer writes (ix). This is also Liz-Anne Bawden's point in *The Oxford Companion to Film* when she writes that "[t]he history of the screen musical is essentially that of the American musical: the outstanding examples of the genre have been made in Hollywood and only the American industry has consistently produced musicals throughout the sound era" (489). Such testimony concerning the musical itself—and in particular the Hollywood version of the musical—might lead one to conclude that still another book about Hollywood musicals is warranted. At any rate, such criticism has led me to this conclusion—as has my own enthusiasm for Hollywood musicals.

When I was in college, many years ago, there were no videocassettes. Anyone who wanted to see an old movie would have to go to a museum or a revival house. I often went to the latter, to the Thalia and the New Yorker theaters, to see old movies. I saw all of the Marx Brothers' movies this way and most of W. C. Fields's. Most impressive to me, however, was the series of films starring Fred Astaire and Ginger Rogers. I loved those movies when I saw them in a theater in the early 1960s. I loved them later on when I saw them on television, and I loved them when the technology of the videocassette and DVD allowed me to pause, to reverse, to rerun, to appreciate every subtlety of the performances. Of course, other musicals caught my attention along the way: films starring Gene Kelly, and Judy Garland, and Eleanor Powell, and Alice Faye, and a host of others. I also came to relish what the song in *Silk Stockings* (1957) calls "glorious Technicolor, breath-taking CinemaScope, and stereophonic sound"—at least to the extent that they increased the effectiveness of the Hollywood musical.[1]

I became, in short, a Hollywood musicals buff. Several years ago, I even started to teach a course in the subject. Happily, I soon discovered that many students have seen (and loved) musicals—sometimes, even musicals other than *Grease*. Some students have appeared in suitably sanitized high school productions of Broadway musicals. Most have, at one time or another, attended showings of *The Rocky Horror Picture Show*. Following up on these happy experiences, they have been surprised to discover in class the pre–Joseph Breen openness of *Golddiggers of 1933*.[2] They have (almost universally) applauded Donald O'Connor's "Make 'Em Laugh" solo in *Singin' in the Rain*. They have developed discriminating attitudes toward dancers, singers and the directors of musicals. The enthusiasm of these students has also inspired me to write this book.

John Russell Taylor has asserted confidently, "If it is virtually impossible to make the perfect musical, it is also virtually impossible to make a musical which is totally bad" (10). I, naturally, agree, and I invoke for support the testimony of many other critics concerning many Hollywood musicals, both the mostly good and the mostly bad. Examples of either variety can be further classified, according to Christopher Ames, into "the integrated musical, in which the numbers transform the narrative into a world brimming with music, and the show musical, in which the conceit of the show justifies the recurrent emergence of song" (56). Jane Feuer draws the same distinction by invoking the ideas of "the world as a stage" and "the stage as a world" (23–24). In both cases, though, whether we are talking about *Oklahoma!* or *Golddiggers of 1933*, the conceit by which singing and dancing are introduced into a narrative consolidates what Ames calls "the musical's generic tendency toward fantasy" (56). To some viewers, this tendency is enough in itself to moot Taylor's quibble about good and bad musicals. These viewers see themselves as too steely-eyed and realistic to revel in such a self-professed fantasy whether it assumes that the world is a stage or represents a stage that becomes the world to a cast of fictional characters.

As John Mueller observes in *Astaire Dancing*, "Another common observation about these Astaire films, as well as later ones, is that they are 'escapist,' because they have little to say about specific contemporary political and economic ephemera, such as the Great Depression." But, as Mueller cogently continues: "[M]uch the same charge could be leveled against the plays of Shakespeare and the operas of Mozart. Astaire's films are about love, and many of the dances deal profoundly with this distinctly nonephemeral subject" (9). Mark Roth makes the same point about escapism more aggressively by claiming, "But rather than being 'escapist' in any sense it seems to me that the great Warners musicals are essentially political" (55). Welcome as Roth's ringing defense of the genre is, even a confessed Hollywood musicals buff might feel that he is making such claims with insufficient warrant. However, we need not go so far as to attribute political acuity to Busby Berkeley in order to agree with this speculative conjecture by Fredric Jameson: "Is it possible, then, that 'fiction' is what is in question here and that it can be defined essentially as the construction of just such fictive and foreshortened temporalities (whether of film or reading), which are then substituted for a real time we are thereby enabled momentarily to forget?" (74).

Whether "real time" presents us with what Gunnar Myrdal long ago called the "American dilemma" of race,[3] or with wrenching economic crises, or with wrinkle-browed concerns about "kids today," or with just the everyday problems of life, a Hollywood musical can create the kind of emotionally secure environment that a song in *West Side Story* (1961) calls "A Place for Us," a psychological opportunity to reorganize, recharge and "momentarily to forget." And even without being "essentially political," films that can do this deserve our sincere gratitude and appreciation.

The Hollywood musical has been providing these services ever since the advent of sound. As many have observed, the first important Hollywood sound feature, *The Jazz Singer*, starred a fabulously popular musical performer, Al Jolson, and presented many viewers with their first talking picture experience when, on October 6, 1927, Jolson sang a number of songs, including "Toot, Toot, Tootsie," "Blue Skies" and "My Mammy" as parts of the film's narrative.[4] And, as Jolson memorably said, moviegoers hadn't "heard nothin' yet." Soon, everyone seemed to be making talking musical pictures. In his book *The Hollywood Musical*, Clive Hirschhorn discusses the 57 filmed musicals released in America in 1929 and the 77 released in 1930. As James Collins appropriately concludes, "Musicals were among the most popular films of the early sound era since they could show off the new technology to its best advantage" (269). In fact, so many musicals were made so quickly that by the early 1930s viewers began to grow tired of the form.[5] According to Hirschhorn, only ten musicals were released in 1931 and 11 in 1932. Hollywood musicals were coming to seem a flash in the pan.

As the story is usually told, however, the day was saved in 1933 by the Warner Bros. "backstage" musical *42nd Street*, the film that made "putting on a show" the narrative driving the story. In Joan Feuer's formulation, "Over and over again in these backstage films we see the 'kids' triumphing over greed, egotism and all those puritanical forces which would ... conspire against entertainment" (17). All this and singing too! No wonder everyone was delighted! As before in the late '20s (and as so often later on with other popular trends), everyone in Hollywood seemed ready to jump back on the musical bandwagon. Collins continues, "The thirties were perhaps the golden age of the musical since at no other time were they as diversified artistically or as successful with the general public" (270).

This time, however, different studios specialized in different forms of musical. As Rick Altman explains in his introduction to a collection of essays entitled *Genre: The Musical; A Reader*: "The history and theory of the musical have long been tied to a series of separate categories, each teaming one or more names with the studio where they flourished. More than perhaps any other genre, the musical is remembered not film-by-film, but in groups of films sharing a recognizable style: the series of spectaculars which Busby Berkeley choreographed and then directed for Warners in the mid–1930s, the Astaire-Rogers pictures at RKO, the extraordinary sequence of films which Arthur Freed produced for MGM in the post-war years" (2). If we amend Altman's list to include the series of musicals starring — among others — the elfin Shirley Temple, the ice-skating Sonja Henie, the tutti-fruiti hat-wearing Carmen Miranda, the aquatic Esther Williams and the inimitable Elvis Presley, we can see how varied such specialization became.

In the process of becoming specialized, the musical became a popular art form that reached great heights of aesthetic achievement as well as of financial success. The American Film Institute's list of the 100 greatest American movies of all time, for example, contains 11 musicals, including such diverse films as *The Jazz Singer* (1927), *Yankee Doodle Dandy* (1942) and *Singin' in the Rain* (1952)—titles likely to be on any film buff's top 100 list, even if the typical film buff is likely to disagree with the order in which AFI lists the films.[6] Musicals have probably flourished thus in filmgoers' memories because of "the power of dominant cinema's appeal to the emotions, an appeal that addresses itself in a systematic way to basic human needs," as Jane Feuer has written (x). As a result of this power, we can note on the other (financial) side of the ledger, Andrew Bergman's observation in *We're in the Money: Depression America and Its Films* that the "*Motion Picture Herald* listed *Gold Diggers [of 1933]* second and *42nd Street* third in its list of the top moneymakers of 1933" (64). Obviously, 1933 was a banner year for Hollywood musicals, and it was not the only one. According to Feuer, the period of the Hollywood musical's greatest impact extended "from the coming of sound in 1927 to the television era of the mid–1950s" (ix). During these decades, this rich combination of art, appeal to the audience's basic human needs and the economics of the studio system made the Hollywood musical a leading component of the American film industry. As Rick Altman writes in *The American Film Musical*, this success should probably come as no surprise because the Hollywood musical was "the most complex art form ever devised," drawing, in Altman's view, on "painting, theater, opera, ballet, operetta, the music-hall, Tin Pan Alley, vaudeville, [and] television" (ix).

The supposed end of this fabulous success story is easily told, as in this version by John Mueller: "By the mid 1950s the era of the classic Hollywood musical as Astaire had experienced it—indeed, defined it—was coming to an end. Revenues were declining, costs were rising, the studio system was falling apart, competition with television was growing, popular music was moving into the age of rock and roll. Astaire and other products of the classic Hollywood musical, such as Freed and Kelly, were out of business as Hollywood created fewer and fewer musical films, typically extravagant transmutations of Broadway musicals, perfunctory song-and-story vehicles for Elvis Presley or well-scrubbed beach-and-bunny capers aimed at the adolescent crowd" (12–13). Altman's *The American Film Musical* makes the same case statistically:

> To understand the magnitude of the drop-off in production it is perhaps helpful to consider that the production of the war years alone matches the entire production of the last three decades. Or to put it another way, it took just 12 years to produce the first third of the total musical production from 1927 to the present (1927–38 = 457 films). The second third took even less time to produce; by 1947, i.e. in nine years, two-thirds of the total output was history (1939–47 = 462 films). By contrast it has taken the last 37 years to produce the final third of the total production (1948–84 = 466 films). More than any theory or analysis, these figures eloquently explain the debt which the musical owes to Hollywood's assembly-line genre film production system [199].

To be absolutely fair, we should recognize that many musical films achieved success—even popular adulation—during the last third of Altman's historical computation. Turning just to the Academy Awards for Best Picture, we may list many musicals nominated for—and often awarded—Oscars, including: *An American in Paris* (1951), *Seven Brides for Seven Brothers* (1954; nomination), *The King and I* (1956), *Gigi* (1958), *West Side Story* (1961), *The Music Man* (1962; nomination), *My Fair Lady* (1964), *The Sound of Music* (1965), *Oliver!* (1968; nomination), *Hello, Dolly* (1969; nomination), *Fiddler on the Roof* (1971; nomination), *Cabaret* (1972; nomination), *All That Jazz* (1979; nomination) and *Coal Miner's Daughter* (1980; nomination). As is evident, most of these films fall into the category that Mueller describes as "extravagant transmutations of Broadway musicals." Even allowing for the popularity of these pre-sold extravaganzas, the decline of the Hollywood musical must be acknowledged. As Susan Wloszczyna writes in a *USA Today* article about the surprisingly popular success[7] of *Moulin Rouge* (2001), "[W]hen the gritty X-rated drama *Midnight Cowboy* beat *Hello, Dolly!* in the 1969 [Academy Award] race, it was clear the era that embraced swoony fantasy over downbeat naturalism was over" (14D).

At the same time that we recognize both surprising aberrations in popular taste like *Hello, Dolly* and the more general pattern of decline that they defy, we should concede that critics like Mueller are so invested in the kind of musical film epitomized by the work of Fred Astaire, they are perhaps unsuited to appreciate the rock-inflected musicals of the 1960s and '70s[8] or the highly self-referential musicals of the 1980s and beyond. Mueller and his allies are, nevertheless, accurate in their diagnosis of the classic Hollywood musical's decline. Although I will take a back seat to no one in my admiration for Fred Astaire,[9] I am still willing to consider the possibility that interesting and successful Hollywood musicals may have been made in the decades since Astaire ceased to be a significant influence on the genre. Thus, in this book I will discuss later films including *All That Jazz* (1979) and *Pennies from Heaven* (1981) as well as Fred's final musical appearance in *Finian's Rainbow* (1968) and Gene Kelly's swansong in *Xanadu* (1980). It is not my purpose to argue that the Hollywood musical is alive and well today, of course, merely to note that many examples of the genre were produced long after it was supposedly exhausted or dead.[10] At the same time it is only reasonable to concede that a fondness for Hollywood musicals has diminished from the sort of across-the-board interest that Bergman documented in 1933, or even during the heyday of the Freed unit at MGM. In fact, many of the students in my Hollywood musicals course have admitted to a love for musicals in the same hangdog way that they might confess a fondness for large glasses of gin or pipes of crack.

In mentioning later reincarnations of the Hollywood musical, I have perhaps suggested that I intend to pursue my topic historically. This is not my purpose. For one thing, many other writers—most especially, Rick Altman—have already traced what they take to be the historical arc of the Hollywood musical. For another, I am not totally convinced that the issue can best be understood teleologically. I suspect that the Hollywood musical can be productively thought about in ways other than those of its supposed history of production and reception.[11] I am far more interested in thematic patterns than in chronology. I am less interested in how the Hollywood

Jerry Travers (Fred Astaire) and the chorus perform the title tune in *Top Hat*.

musical came about, flourished and fell into decline, than I am in what Hollywood musicals were "about" during this long historical sequence.

One thing Hollywood musicals could be about was the American Depression which was strangling the country during the period in which many early musicals were produced and released. Thus, I have devoted a chapter to how two musicals, *Golddiggers of 1933* (1933) and *Stand Up and Cheer* (1934), deal, or fail to deal, with the realistic economic crises of the Depression. Race is the topic of the succeeding chapter, in which I examine the amazing prevalence of blackface minstrelsy in Hollywood musicals produced in the 1930s and '40s—after minstrelsy had supposedly vanished into oblivion. Actually, the most amazing aspect of this racial phenomenon is the presence of major musical stars—Fred Astaire, Mickey Rooney, Judy Garland

and Bing Crosby—in these films: *Swing Time* (1936), *Babes in Arms* (1939), *Babes on Broadway* (1941), *Holiday Inn* (1942) and *Dixie* (1943). Perhaps someone might be just as amazed to find the American liberal actor Larry Parks impersonating the fabulously successful minstrel performer Al Jolson in *The Jolson Story* (1946). But whether or not one is surprised by this performance, one must attempt to explain the whole blackface development somehow—without succumbing to the hysteria betrayed in Spike Lee's attempted explanation in his satirical film *Bamboozled* (2000).

The third critical issue addressed in this series of thematic chapters is rock and roll culture. Just as the economic struggles of the Depression and the ramifications of racial discrimination bedeviled the popular American mind in the earlier decades of the Hollywood musical's existence, so the coming of rock and roll in the 1950s seemed to cry out for some reassuring response to the threats of juvenile delinquency, teenage sex and rebellion, and a kind of popular music that seemed the very antithesis of well-crafted show tunes. *Girl Crazy* (1943), starring Mickey Rooney and Judy Garland, serves in this chapter to show the picture of youth that some members of the older generation were interested in defending. Four other films show the development of Hollywood's response to the supposedly sad fact that this picture was no longer valid.[12] *Bye Bye Birdie* (1963) attempts to set adults' minds at ease on these issues by dismissing rock and roll culture as something that kids will soon outgrow. *Beach Party* (1963) and *Bikini Beach* (1964) work toward the same goal of reassurance—paradoxically, by embracing youth culture—and flattering the youthful audience at the same time. As the Beach series evolved, however, the importance of adult values markedly declined. By the time that *Grease* was released in 1978, this thematic decline of adult significance was totally institutionalized, and so the co-option of youthful (rock and roll) values by the Hollywood musical was complete. It is perhaps of further interest that, according to most film critics, by the time of *Grease*, the Hollywood musical had actually disappeared.

My next chapter investigates how dance has been used as a narrative agent in Hollywood musicals over many decades. Despite the apparently technical focus of this chapter, the central issue is still what Hollywood musicals are "about." In this chapter, it becomes apparent that in many cases they are about "boy meets girl, boy loses girl, boy and girl get back together for a happy-ever-after conclusion." My argument in the chapter is that dance can further this familiar plot by functioning as a signifier of character, as it does in *Shall We Dance* (1937) and *Dirty Dancing* (1987). Dancing can also function as a plot integer, as in *Top Hat* (1935) and *The King and I* (1956). Finally, dance can reveal deep-rooted psychological drives, as in *Carefree* (1938) and *Oklahoma!* (1955). Like the songs and creative lives that function in other Hollywood musicals as excuses for entertainment, these dance performances both entertain and signify. In the judgment of John Mueller, "The particular glory of the American musical, whether of the Broadway or the Hollywood variety, has been the songs and dances, not the plots" (23). Since the plots of most musicals are somewhat contrived, Mueller is probably justified in estimating the cardinal significance of dance as well as song.

Another thematic agent in the creation of Hollywood musicals is the fictional geography that authorizes musical celebrations of various sorts. *Mississippi* (1935)

Penny Morris (Judy Garland) and Tommy Williams (Mickey Rooney) perform "Hoedown" in *Babes on Broadway.*

and *Li'l Abner* (1959), for example, are about "the South," although this region is very differently defined in the two films. *On the Town* (1949) and *West Side Story* (1961) differ from the first two films in adopting New York for their setting, a locale obviously very much unlike the South constructed by either *Mississippi* or *Li'l Abner. On the Town* and *West Side Story* also differ radically from each other in the sense that the two New Yorks presented in these films authorize vastly different forms of musical celebration. The South and New York are, of course, not the only possible settings for Hollywood musicals. *Carousel* (1956) takes place in Maine, and *The Most Happy Fella* (1980) in California. *Seven Brides for Seven Brothers* (1954) is set in the American West, as are *Girl Crazy* (1943) and *Paint Your Wagon* (1969). Elvis Presley went outside the continental borders of the United States, all the way to Hawaii for *Blue Hawaii* (1961) and *Paradise, Hawaiian Style* (1966) and to Mexico for *Fun in Acapulco* (1963). Richard Rodgers and Oscar Hammerstein II were equally adventurous in *The Sound of Music* (1965), set in Austria, and *South Pacific* (1958), whose location is apparent.

In these and countless other Hollywood musicals, the setting—what the Russian critic Mikhail Bakhtin calls the "chronotope" of the films—permits exotic variations on some familiar plots. Because all things must have some kind of limit, however, I have restricted the further examples in this chapter to two other films, intended to be representative of the whole. The setting of the justly celebrated *Meet Me in St. Louis* (1944) is important not only because Missouri does not appear elsewhere in the discussion, but also because the idealized place and time represented in the film function rhetorically to finesse and redress a real-world context defined by World War II and the familial disruptions caused by this national crisis. *Sun Valley Serenade* (1941) not only features an Idaho location but filters it through the prism created by Sonja Henie's world-class ice skating. St. Louis and Sun Valley are assuredly American locations other than New York and the South, but they are also dramatic chronotopes determining what can happen only in each place and time.

In the next chapter, another deliberately created chronotope, a kind of Never Never Land, is discussed. Of course, any world in which characters frequently dance and sing out loud is somewhat fantastic, but the Never Never Lands created in some musicals are extreme even by the fairly generous understanding of setting common in the genre. This is the kind of fantastic world in which Fred Astaire functions in *Yolanda and the Thief* (1945) and as Gene Kelly does in *Brigadoon* (1954). These two films are connected not only in sharing the same director, Vincente Minnelli, but in also starring the two male dancers that most critics of the Hollywood musical consider to be the very finest practitioners of their craft. The opportunity to write about Fred and Gene is too tempting to resist, and so in this chapter I note their all too infrequent appearances together — in *Ziegfeld Follies* (1946) and *That's Entertainment* (1974). In addition, I discuss their appearances in the two films already mentioned, made when each was at the height of his talent. To balance these two top-of-his-game appearances, moreover, I look at the final significant dancing roles for each in a Hollywood musical: Fred Astaire's title role in *Finian's Rainbow* (1968) and Gene Kelly's role opposite Olivia Newton-John in *Xanadu* (1980). Fantastic chronotopes are the excuse, but genius is the true concern of this chapter.

Another flimsy excuse for making Hollywood musicals is apparent in the musical biopic, the film biography of some significant figure in the history of American musical entertainment. Such films solve the problem of having fictional characters suddenly break into song and dance by making this singing and dancing necessary parts of the famous figures' lives. The musical biographies of Florenz Ziegfeld and George M. Cohan are loosely presented in *The Great Ziegfeld* (1936) and *Yankee Doodle Dandy* (1942), respectively. The biographies of the composing teams of Rodgers & Hart and Kalmer & Ruby are dramatized, very loosely, in *Words and Music* (1948) and *Three Little Words* (1950). *Night and Day* (1946), the fictionalized biography of Cole Porter, and *Till the Clouds Roll By* (1946), the equally fictionalized biography of Jerome Kern, are the last two films discussed in this chapter. In the case of all six films, issues of biographical accuracy take a back seat to the opportunity to present famous songs— what these films are really "about."

Intertextuality is the subject of my final chapter of discussion. Since many Hollywood musicals have been based on Broadway shows, it is likely that some viewers would be in a position to compare the former and the latter. Even those viewers who have not seen the original would be encountering intertextuality, however, since this narrative technique entails the co-presence of two or more artistic elements in the minds of the creators of the principal text, or in the minds of the viewers, or simply in the texts themselves. At times, intertextuality promotes earlier texts—a play of Shakespeare's, for example, or the tradition of Roman New Comedy—into a level of significance competing with the principal diegesis. This is the case with *Kiss Me Kate* (1953), based on William Shakespeare's *The Taming of the Shrew*, and with *A Funny Thing Happened on the Way to the Forum* (1966), based on the plays of Plautus. If the viewers of either film are familiar with its textual antecedents, they can participate fully in an intertextual community, but the intertextual encounters are present whether any single member of the audience is or is not aware of the original(s). *The Band Wagon* (1953) belongs to the category of intertextuality also since this film presents the creation of musical entertainment for the stage as its own form of cinematic entertainment. In films like *The Band Wagon*, the illusion of diegetic representation is often subordinated to a different, self-referential illusion, and both illusions are what these films are "about." This is also true of Bob Fosse's later contribution to this form, *All That Jazz* (1970). The musical shows created in both films must finally stand side by side with the musical films in which they are created. The film that many critics consider the finest of all Hollywood musicals, *Singin' in the Rain* (1952), is also intertextual—perhaps even more so than *The Band Wagon* or *All That Jazz* because the secondary narrative here is also a musical film. Finally, *Pennies from Heaven* (1981) brings matters full circle in that the intertext in this film is the very Depression-era musical films discussed in an earlier chapter. When all is said and done, then, intertextual musicals are musicals about musicals.

In my concluding chapter, I accept the principle enunciated by John Russell Taylor in *The Hollywood Musical*: "[I]f we are content to enjoy whatever is there to be enjoyed, without constantly measuring it against some impossible ideal, we are likely to find the musical the most continually satisfying of all film genres" (11). My principal concern here is how Hollywood musicals can continue to be "satisfying" after the conditions of their production and reception have perceptibly changed. It is clear, for example, from television's attention to musicals in recent years that moviemakers can no longer assume that "a nice musical" is what most filmgoers are looking for. When the whole idea of "All Singing, All Dancing" becomes a topic of controversy in TV shows like *Cop Rock*, *The Simpsons* and *Buffy the Vampire Slayer*, we can see that those sending the entertainment signals as well as those receiving them conceive of the very genre of the Hollywood musical as something of a problem. Even so, films including *Moulin Rouge* (2001) and *Chicago* (2002) have enjoyed considerable success—at least in part because their creators share this assumption about changed conditions of reception. This concluding chapter, then, both recognizes the parlous state of the Hollywood musical and celebrates some of its recent successes.

Earlier in this discussion, I offered testimony that this film genre has been continually satisfying me for many decades. In the course of working on this book, I have realized that this satisfaction has only increased instead of diminishing. It may be, as some would claim, that a new age of the Hollywood musical is dawning, ushered in by music videos, Bollywood musicals,[13] *Moulin Rouge*, and *Chicago*. It may just as likely be that the economics of film production dictate that big-budget musicals will never again be made in large numbers by Hollywood. In a *USA Today* story about the enormous success of *Chicago*, for example, Andy Seiler writes that the film has been "a critical and commercial hit ... a combination no musical has been able to pull off since the 1960s," but he adds, "Whether it could happen again anytime soon is the question on Hollywood's mind" (1D).

Whether or not many — or any — musical blockbusters come along, we are fortunate to have the Hollywood musicals we have already. Even if no other Hollywood musical is ever made, we will still have Gene Kelly's performance of the title song in *Singin' in the Rain*, and Fred and Ginger performing "Isn't It a Lovely Day (To Be Caught in the Rain)?" and "Cheek to Cheek" in *Top Hat*. We will also have Judy Garland's rendition of "The Trolley Song" in *Meet Me in St. Louis* and her performance of "Under the Bamboo Tree" with Margaret O'Brien in the same film. Then there are "The Shadow Waltz" and "Brother Can You Spare a Dime?" in *Golddiggers of 1933*, and "Shall We Dance" in *The King and I*, and too many others to list. As Peter Gammond states, in *The Oxford Companion to Popular Music*, "If, as some might claim, the film musical as such had long passed its peak [by the late 1960s], it hardly mattered as there was such a wealth of nostalgic material to look back on that the world's musical needs could be satisfied forever simply by running through what had been permanently immortalized on film" (406). Over 30 years after the '60s ended, Gammond might say the same thing. During the interim, however, Joel Grey's smarmy master of ceremonies has welcomed viewers into the decadent world of the Kit Kat Klub with the song "Wilkommen" in *Cabaret* (1972); Roy Scheider and Ben Vereen have celebrated Joe Gideon's death with "Bye Bye Life" in *All That Jazz* (1979); and Catherine Zeta-Jones has performed a socko version of "All That Jazz" in *Chicago* (2002). Admittedly, all of these memorable Hollywood musical numbers are associated in some way with one man, Bob Fosse. However, similarly enchanting moments were often associated with one man in earlier days also — sometimes with Busby Berkeley, sometimes with Arthur Freed, sometimes with Gene Kelly, sometimes with Fred Astaire. In earlier times, of course, these film highlights did not focus on such matters as death, genocide, sexual decadence and murder. Even so, and despite the shift in subject matter, there is a clear line of continuity stretching from the early 1930s to the first decade of the twenty-first century, a line consisting of singing, dancing and big production numbers. Who knows what the future will bring?

1

Hollywood Musicals and the Depression

Passages from two presidential addresses perfectly encapsulate the historical paradox implicit in the phrase *Depression Musical Comedies*. In his Second Inaugural Address (January 20, 1937), President Franklin D. Roosevelt memorably described the deplorable economic conditions then ravaging his country:

> In this nation I see tens of millions of its citizens—a substantial part of its whole population—who at this very moment are denied the greater part of what the very lowest standards of today call the necessities of life.
> I see millions of families trying to live on incomes so meager that the pall of family disaster hangs over them day by day.
> I see millions whose daily lives in city and on the farm continue under conditions labeled indecent by a so-called polite society half a century ago.
> I see millions denied education, recreation, and the opportunity to better their lot and the lot of their children.
> I see millions lacking the means to buy the products of farm and factory and by their poverty denying work and productiveness to many other millions.
> I see one-third of a nation ill-housed, ill-clad, ill-nourished [91].

Less famous, but equally revealing, is Will H. Hays' 1934 *President's Report to the Motion Picture Producers and Distributors of America*: "No medium has contributed more greatly than the film to the maintenance of the national morale during a period featured by revolution, riot and political turmoil in other countries. It has been the mission of the screen, without ignoring the serious social problems of the day, to reflect aspiration, optimism, and kindly humor in its entertainment."[1] In his capacity as president of the motion picture industry association, Hays can hardly be considered an objective witness, and yet his biased judgment clearly articulates the key issue in any discussion of Depression musicals. How is it possible to "reflect aspiration, optimism, and kindly humor" in a popular art form without "ignoring the serious social problem" of the millions of Americans unemployed at the time of Roosevelt's first two inaugurations?

The first step toward a workable solution, it would seem, is to associate the logically opposed cinematic elements of realism and escapism with the diegetic or performative settings appropriate to each. As Jane Feuer explains, this is standard practice in the genre, even apart from any historical or economic considerations associated with the Depression: "Musicals are built upon a foundation of dual registers with the contrast between narrative and number defining musical comedy as a form" (68). In other words, a successful Depression musical comedy might be expected to use highly differentiated settings to present the conflicting content of realistic representation and healthy escapism. In the interests of clarification, these radically different settings may be understood as what the Russian critical theorist Mikhail Bakhtin calls "chronotopes." In *The Dialogic Imagination*, Bakhtin writes, "We will give the name *chronotope* (literally, 'time space') to the intrinsic connectedness of temporal and spatial relationships that are artistically expressed in literature." He continues, "The chronotope as a formally constitutive category determines to a significant degree the image of man in literature..." (84–85; Bakhtin's emphasis). In other words, the spatio-temporal parameters established by authors prepare readers for the sorts of actions and characters that may plausibly follow. The chronotope established by the sentence, "Once upon a time there was a worthy man who married for his second wife the haughtiest, proudest woman that had ever been seen," for example, legitimates very different sorts of narrative developments than the chronotopes introduced by either "It is a truth universally acknowledged, that a single man in possession of a good fortune must be in want of a wife" or "You don't know about me, without you have read a book by the name of *The Adventures of Tom Sawyer*, but that ain't no matter."[2] In each case, readers are suitably warned that the fantastic or the realistic, the adventurous or the satiric, is likely to follow. Fictional characters in these highly varied chronotopes are consequently empowered to follow or defy the laws of verisimilitude and to be driven by blinding passions of an operatic sort or to be motivated by the everyday psychological drives that also motivate the reader.

Clearly, the same may be said about "the image of man" on the screen. In film, as in literature, specific chronotopes authorize our expectations of what can and can't happen. Viewers entertain very different expectations about the characters, motivations and actions likely to follow upon shots of a stagecoach frantically crossing Monument Valley, a young girl stepping out of a sepia house into a full-colored Oz or a spaceship approaching the screen at warp speed.[3] Furthermore, when two or more distinctly different chronotopes are developed within the same film, a Bakhtinian encounter may ensue among different modes of representation/presentation. As Bakhtin also says in *The Dialogic Imagination*: "Within the limits of a single work ... we may notice a number of different chronotopes and complex interactions among them.... Chronotopes are mutually inclusive, they co-exist, they may be interwoven with, replace or oppose one another, contradict one another or find themselves in ever more complex relationships.... The general characteristic of these interactions is that they are *dialogical* (in the broadest sense of the word)" (252; Bakhtin's parens. and emphasis). I am assuming that the same may be said of "the image of man" in Depression-era films. This is to say that setting not only determines where fictional characters would live and what they would wear in Depression America but also what they would be likely (and able) to think about sex, God and language. As Bakhtin concludes, "The image of man is always intrinsically chronotopic" (84–85), and so

Feuer's categories of narrative and number clearly require quite different chronotopic contexts if the characters within them are to function effectively on screen.

The apparently irreconcilable difference between the two chronotopes exploited in Depression musicals is apparent in a passage of dialogue quoted by Christopher Ames in *Movies About the Movies*. When John L. Sullivan, a film director in Preston Sturges' *Sullivan's Travels* (1942), says to the studio money men, "I want to hold a mirror up to life. I want this to be a picture with dignity ... a true canvas of the suffering of humanity,"[4] studio executive Hadrian replies, "How about a nice musical?" (82). In "a nice [1930s] musical" entitled *Top Hat*, Mark Sandrich transports Fred Astaire and Ginger Rogers away from any symptoms of economic distress for the film's crucial scenes into a chronotope of pure fantasy, metonymically represented by RKO's "Big White Set."[5] Any mention of the real Depression is limited to Dale Tremont's threat to return to the States and "live on the dole" rather than to wear Alberto Beddini's glamorous clothes. *Golddiggers of 1933* separates the realistic chronotope embracing a narrative about chorus girls struggling to survive in the Depression from production numbers of staggering excess, in large part by having Mervyn LeRoy direct the former, Busby Berkeley the latter. In *Stand Up and Cheer*, the economic Depression familiar to audiences in 1934 drives the plot, and yet all the characters we see in detail have jobs to go to and plenty to eat. In the case of each of these films, the realistic economic pressures of the Depression are depicted in opposition to fantasies of imaginative freedom through obviously conflicting chronotopic representations.

Opposition is, of course, not resolution, and so, in order to negotiate the conflicts between "aspiration, optimism, and kindly humor" and "the serious social problems" of the Depression, a movie musical of the 1930s should ideally be structured so as to harmonize the conflicting chronotopic assumptions about actual human experience and fantastic possibility evident in so many escapist musicals of the 1930s. To use terms from Rick Altman's *The American Film Musical*, the Depression musical must "reduc[e] an unsatisfactory paradox to a more workable configuration, a concordance of opposites" (27). According to Jane Feuer, this synthesis is achieved most often on the level of plot, as the principal singing and dancing lovers find romance and musical success at the same moment when their musical show turns out to be a success.

That Mervyn LeRoy's film *Golddiggers of 1933* can best be characterized taxonomically as a "Depression musical comedy" encapsulates the paradox troubling most of the critics who write about the film. James M. Collins, for example, calls "We're in the Money," the film's opening number, "surely one of the most preposterously optimistic reflections on the depression in screen history," a view shared by *The Motion Picture Guide*, which explains that "no one was in the money, except those people who made these kind of movies" (1052). Collins plausibly continues, "Here the Hollywood musical offers the viewer a saccharine alternative to economic hard times outside the confines of the movie theatre, entertainment as escapism pure and simple..." (272). Richard Dyer agrees with this assessment, writing, in his essay "Entertainment and Utopia" that "[t]he thrust of the narrative is towards seeing the show as a 'solution' to the personal Depression-induced problems of the characters;

Fay Fortune (Ginger Rogers) and Brad Roberts (Dick Powell) in a publicity shot for *Golddiggers of 1933*.

yet the non-realist presentation of the numbers makes it very hard to take this solution seriously. It is 'just' escape, 'merely' utopian" (186). From this highly critical perspective, the *musical comedy* dimension of my original characterization clearly counterbalances the *Depression* side, perhaps fatally trivializing LeRoy's film in the process.

To Stanley Green, however, "[T]he element that distinguishes the 1933 *Golddiggers* from other backstage sagas of the period is that it is the only one showing the influence of the Depression.... [T]he movie not only deals with the problems of raising money to produce a show, but also with the daily financial concerns of aspiring actresses Keeler, Rogers, Joan Blondell, and Aline MacMahon" (23). Such diversity of critical judgment suggests that *Golddiggers* probably creates within itself palpable tensions between its representation of the historical Depression and its presentation of joyful, escapist musical numbers (largely directed by Busby Berkeley). This conflict is implicit in Thomas Schatz's summary judgment in *The Genius of the System: Hollywood Filmmaking in the Studio Era*. Schatz calls "We're in the Money" "A bizarre celebration of capitalism, commercial entertainment, and the commodification of female sexuality," but adds that this number "was also an ideal counter to 'My Forgotten Man,' Berkeley's closing lament for the anonymous victims of World War I and the Depression" (152). Tensions, conflicts and paradoxes abound in these critical judgments and (admittedly) in the film on which they are founded. The final challenge lies in easing these tensions, compromising the conflicts, and resolving the paradoxes.

In *Golddiggers of 1933*, the diegetic treatment of the Depression applauded by Schatz and Green centers on the situation of three impoverished chorines who must steal milk from a neighbor's fire escape to furnish their meager breakfast early in the film and who must pool their few still-presentable garments to equip even one of them to audition for a new show. The personal freedom and optimism identified by Collins and Dyer come primarily from the Busby Berkeley production numbers included in this show.[6] The stylistic dialogue between the chronotope realistically representing the Depression with which the audience is already familiar and the other chronotope legitimating unrealistic production numbers simultaneously recognizes and denies the force of economic circumstance. The result is a dialogical resolution of a seemingly insoluble paradox, as an analysis of several key scenes will reveal.

The first shot of *Golddiggers*, following the opening credits, is a full-screen image of a coin. This coin is succeeded by a full-screen close-up of Ginger Rogers singing "We're in the Money" directly into the camera. As Ginger sings, it becomes apparent that she is wearing a costume supposedly composed of coins like the one in the opening shot. This impression is reinforced as the camera pans to the right away from Ginger to reveal a line of chorus girls wearing similar costumes. All of these women seem to be "in the money" in both a figurative and a literal sense, thereby apparently violating the probable real-life economic situations of viewers in 1933 and their legitimate expectation that some representation of everyday reality will appear on the screen. The chronotopic signals suggest instead that a musical fantasy will follow, a suggestion strengthened when the pan to the right that began with Ginger's face ends with her face also. This must be some sort of theatrical trick, in other words, rather like the visual joke in which a burlesque comic crosses the stage to the left carrying the front of a long ladder and then enters from the right carrying the end of the same ladder.

The next shots serve to confirm this impression as the camera pulls back to reveal the shiny stage on which Ginger and the chorus girls are singing and dancing. The following sequence is not altogether presentational, however, since these shots are inter-cut with shots of a man dressed in everyday clothing who is sitting in a theater seat chomping sourly on a cigar. Past cinematic experience now suggests that the previous singing and dancing are intended to be absorbed into a more realistic chronotope of representation, one in which the man with the cigar is watching the women perform a "number." They are probably not goddesses who are actually clothed in gold, then, but theatrical characters who are wearing costumes while performing in a represented show. When a posse of men dressed in everyday clothes come onstage and interrupt the number because the man with the cigar has not paid his bills, viewers can then expect that the representation embracing all of these constituents will be a realistic diegetic narrative after all; a story about people trying to survive — and perhaps succeed — in show business despite the real-world economic crisis that also involves the viewers.

Soon the three principal female characters in this narrative — now unemployed — are seen in their low-rent apartment bemoaning the Depression that has taken their money, their hopes, and even their desire to get out of bed at 10:30 in the morning. Played by Joan Blondell, Aline MacMahon and Ruby Keeler, these three chorus girls must steal milk from a neighbor's fire escape merely to have breakfast, ignore their landlady's pleading note that they pay even a little bit of their back rent, and pool their clothing to dress even one of them attractively enough to send her off to an audition for a new show produced by the man with the cigar, Barney Hopkins, played by Ned Sparks.

Fortunately, Barney is nearly ready to go into rehearsal for a show that will, as he says, display "the gay side, the hard-boiled side, the cynical and funny side of the Depression." He offers employment to the crowd of chorus girls soon gathered in the trio's apartment and immediately promises the bombshell part to Blondell's character, Carol, and the leading comedy role to MacMahon's character, Trixie. Then, in order to secure the musical score written by Brad Roberts, played by Dick Powell, Barney happily offers another part to Brad's sweetheart, Polly, played by Ruby Keeler.[7] Things are beginning to look up for the central characters until Barney says that his only problem is finding $15,000 to finance the show. Since this is a realistic problem in times of economic distress, Carol responds like a realistic character operating within a realistic Depression chronotope: "You've got your nerve, Barney! What about these girls? They've given up jobs just because you said that.... Oh, you ought to be ashamed of yourself! Gee, it's tough enough without you making mugs of us. We counted on this, all of us!" Even when the apparently impoverished Brad offers to provide backing for the show, the dimensions of realism are maintained because no one except Polly believes that Brad has that much money, and Polly believes Brad primarily because she is in love with him. Surprisingly, however, Brad *does* produce the $15,000 in cash — perhaps threatening to move the narrative outside its realistic chronotope—but Trixie keeps the story within its expected limits by suggesting that Brad may be a Toronto bank robber. That is to say that, despite the theatrical subject matter and the fantastic performance of the opening sequence, the film's realistic Depression chronotope is not seriously compromised up through this point.

Soon, however, Barney's show, *Forgotten Melody,* is ready to open and—as past cinematic experience might lead us to expect—Polly's leading man, Gordon, cannot go on because of an attack of lumbago. After Brad reluctantly agrees to take Gordon's place, the film's chronotope begins to change. The narrative sequence in which Brad agrees to perform in the play concludes with a fade-out on Polly and Brad kissing backstage. The next scene opens on a rising curtain and a shot of a theater orchestra. Then a close-up shows a book cover, *Advice to Those in Love.* Next we see Brad and Polly, dressed in fashionable but everyday clothing, sitting on a bench. Brad begins to sing "Pettin' in the Park," and the camera pulls back to reveal a shiny stage surface. Brad and Polly (or perhaps Dick and Ruby) sing several choruses of the song and dance a little—all presumably as part of Barney's *Forgotten Melody,* and thus they are still somewhat enfolded within the film's realistic diegesis.

After these two exit from the diegetic stage, however, the camera shows a closeup of a box of animal crackers picturing two monkeys in a cage, which dissolves into a shot of actual monkeys in a zoo, shown while a chorus sings "Pettin' in the Park" on the soundtrack. The next shot reveals that this chorus is composed of some policemen who are supposedly working in a large park containing nine spooning couples of various ages, sizes and races, including one couple baby-sitting an infant played by a very young Billy Barty. Everyone in this scene is in love, no one is out of work, no one has been forgotten by the economic system. In this respect, the scene cannot be part of the realistic narrative about Carol, Trixie and Polly's struggles in the New York of the 1930s. On the other hand, this park full of lovers *can* be part of a narrative set in a different chronotope, one in which an equivalent amount of space can contain either a single book cover or three singing cops and 18 lovers on nine benches. Soon Brad and Polly enter this world in a taxi that can comfortably share the space of a proscenium stage with all of the lovers and a much expanded cadre of policemen, now mounted on roller skates.[8] The same visual space then is filled with a roller-skating production number that includes the infant Barty.

Until this point, the film's most striking chronotopic displacements have involved playing with space. As this extended musical sequence designed by Busby Berkeley proceeds, however, time becomes equally elastic. The skating policemen begin to feel autumn winds, and then the stage space is filled with falling snow and couples playing with beach ball–sized snowballs. Space expands and contracts as the camera alternately shows distant shots of the winter crowd and closeups of warmly clad bathing beauties. This episode ends with the infant Barty rolling one of these snowballs toward the camera, and the next episode opens in a warm spring park populated by men in boaters and women in enormous picture hats. All this while, of course, the soundtrack has continued to play "Pettin' in the Park,"[9] a song that is now mixed with thunder as a spring shower begins to fall. This rain drenches everyone's clothes and drives the women from this scene onto a two-level stage set that apparently shares theatrical space with the park in springtime. Behind opaque screens on this set, the women remove their wet clothing. Then the Barty character pulls up the screens, revealing the women now attired in metal bathing suits. In these costumes they rejoin the no-longer-wet men on a series of park benches. When the men's attempts to "pet" are frustrated by the metal garments, the Barty character produces a can opener, and the scene ends with a closeup of Brad's can opener at work on the back of Polly's costume.

At the time of this film's release, a *Variety* reviewer observed in wonder, "As a new medium of musical comedy expression, the screen's latitude permits a liberal interpretation of any productioned [sic] number which no theatre stage, no matter the number of cantilever platforms, could possibly afford" (June 13, 1933). Quite obviously, "Pettin' in the Park" confirms the reviewer's observation. It also proleptically confirms Rick Altman's judgment in *The American Film Musical*: "Busby Berkeley ... alone among the early practitioners of the musical understood the extent to which the audio dissolve liberates the picture plane of all diegetic responsibilities" (70).[10] In more Bakhtinian terms, the sequence demonstrates that a Busby Berkeley production number involves a distinctly different "intrinsic connectedness of temporal and spatial relationships" than does realistic cinematic representation such as the Depression narrative that has previously constituted the film.

The differences in representative modes continue as the diegetic narrative resumes. After the shot of Brad working on the back of Polly's costume, we see the orchestra and curtain again, this time as the curtain descends. A scene in the lobby then represents supposedly realistic theatergoers of 1933, all dressed in evening clothes. The diegetic plot is served as these characters try to figure out who Brad really is, and chronotopic dialogue is served as the realistic Depression begins to take on the properties of the musical-fantasy chronotope of "Pettin' in the Park" through the theatergoers' elegant costumes.

Transformation continues in the next scene when the three chorus girls again settle down to breakfast. Though the activity is the same as in an earlier scene, the scene itself is quite different. Now the three women are living in an incredibly posh hotel suite resembling the ones often occupied by Fred Astaire and Ginger Rogers in other musicals of the era.[11] In this glamorous, art nouveau setting, it is unnecessary to steal milk from a neighbor or worry about overdue rent. The management even slips a complimentary newspaper under the door, with a headline revealing that the struggling song-writer Brad Roberts is actually Robert Trent Bradford, "Scion of an Old Boston Family." In this setting it is easy to assume that only a few minor plot complications now stand between Brad and Polly and the happy ending they deserve. If we can pause at this juncture to recall how these characters were living at the beginning of the picture, we can perhaps realize how implausible such assumptions would have been within that chronotope.

Fantasy continues to be the set decorator in the following scene, which takes place in the University Club, the same sort of imaginary, all-male, stuffed-shirt environment that Fred Astaire scandalizes with his tap-dancing in the beginning of *Top Hat*. In *Golddiggers* this setting is the meeting place for Brad, his older brother J. Lawrence Bradford (Warren William) and Peabody (Guy Kibbee), the family lawyer. The latter two try to persuade Brad to give up Polly and then threaten to cut off his income when he refuses to cooperate. The significant degree to which "chronotope ... determines ... the image of man" is apparent when Brad immediately repudiates his inheritance in favor of marrying Polly. Of course, the conventions of romantic comedy for centuries have emphasized the principle that John Dryden called "All for Love."[12] In this case especially, the chronotopic elisions from the depths of the Depression through "Pettin' in the Park," and then through the elegant hotel suite to the University Club have naturalized these conventions and authenticated a new "image of man" as an active practitioner of romantic freedom rather than as a passive victim of economic circumstance.

This image predominates through several subsequent narrative sequences—all developed within rich, glamorous settings. The anticipated impediments to Brad and Polly's immediate happiness are represented by J. Lawrence and Peabody, who determine to break up the couple, first by trying to buy off what they assume to be a conniving little golddigger, and then by deviously trying to transfer her affections from Brad to J. Lawrence. In these plans, they are opposed by Trixie and Carol (they erroneously assume the latter to be Polly). The comic/romantic developments of this case of mistaken identity begin in the women's plush hotel suite, progress in an enormous and equally plush speakeasy, develop further at a night club even larger than the speakeasy and also featuring a large roof garden, and conclude back at the plush hotel. During this sequence, the men from Boston unhesitatingly spend enormous amounts of money on champagne, flowers and gifts for Carol and Trixie; they stay for a week or so at an equally grand hotel; and they dress consistently either in evening clothes or in Savile Row suits.

Although these events are diegetic consequences of the film's opening scenes, there is no recognition between "Pettin' in the Park" and the next musical production number that anyone in America is out of work or stealing milk from a neighbor's fire escape. This absolute transformation of the film's chronotope is made clear when Carol, who has earlier confessed to accepting large sums of money from rich men, rejects J. Lawrence's peace offering of $10,000. Like Brad, Carol has been converted to the "all for love" motto; she wants J. Lawrence, not his money. This is just as well, since J. Lawrence is now also in love with Carol, as Peabody is in love with Trixie, and vice versa. Comedic closure is apparently just around the corner. This happy narrative sequence ends with only a slight cloud of uncertainty hanging over Brad and Polly's future. Will they be restored to the good graces of the Bradford family and—incidentally—to Brad's inheritance? Or will they have to struggle along on their salaries as successful Broadway performers, the kind of salary that has previously allowed the three former chorus girls to afford a suite in a hotel like the Ritz or the Plaza?

Transition between the diegetic world in which these questions remain unanswered and the totally fantastic world of Busby Berkeley begins with shots of female hands reaching for hoop skirts in a frantic backstage dressing scene. Then a rising stage curtain once again signals the beginning of a production number. Brad is revealed wearing white evening clothes. He begins to sing "The Shadow Waltz." Polly is revealed in a blonde wig and spangles, staring at him in rapt wonder. As in "Pettin' in the Park," the song is presented in full by the two principals before the camera angle widens to include the vast numbers of singers and dancers we expect from Berkeley. In this case, the vast numbers constitute a chorus of women, all dressed like Polly and all carrying a white violin like hers.

As the principals and chorus sing, dance, and act out "The Shadow Waltz," space is once again defined in very different terms than those observed in the represented narrative. J. Lawrence and Peabody may have spent fantastic sums of money in the diegetic story, but they have maintained constant physical proportionality to their settings. In "The Shadow Waltz," the space of the screen is sometimes filled with the well-lighted face of a single beautiful dancer, sometimes with an overhead shot of dozens of dancers forming geometric patterns in a dark setting illuminated only by their neon violins. Spatial conflicts notwithstanding, a chronotope in which dozens of identically dressed women simulate playing white violins outlined with neon is a very different chronotope than one in which three women in ratty clothing worry about where their next meal is coming from.

This escape from the restraints of chronotopic realism continues through the end of the number. In a closeup, Brad kisses Polly, who drops a flower into a pool of water. The last shot in this sequence shows ripples spreading out from this flower. After the fact, we may wonder how members of the diegetic audience were supposed to see these ripples, or the overhead shots of the violins, or the faces of the beautiful dancers reflected in the pool. Perhaps we may even wonder what any of this has to do with a show about "the gay side, the hard-boiled side, the cynical and funny side of the Depression." Even if we think of these questions, a falling curtain once again signals that a fantastic sequence is ending and that the chronotope is consequently about to shift back to what remains of the realistic.

The only realistic setting left is, ironically enough, the back stage. Here, the six possible lovers meet and arrive at a happy ending. Significantly, Brad, Polly, Carol and Trixie are dressed in their costumes from *Forgotten Melody*, and J. Lawrence and Peabody are dressed in the elegant suits they have habitually worn — as much an element of fantastic costuming in 1933 as Trixie's cop uniform or Carol's apache outfit. That is to say, the romantic couples are suspended somewhere between realism and fantasy, a situation chronotopically validated by the liminality of the backstage setting.[13] Another noteworthy element of this liminality is a sense of pending finality. This awareness is signaled by backstage shouts of "Forgotten Man Number" and by the orchestra's repeated playing of the theme. Calling what is likely to follow a "number" surely creates possibilities to violate the principles of realism and the restrictions that might be imposed by a realistic chronotope. At the same time, the sense of an ending to this film as well as to the diegetic narrative leads us to expect some sort of closure to the long-deferred issues of the Depression and its "forgotten" victims.

The next scene immediately suggests that these expectations will be fulfilled. This production number opens not on the stage lovers, Brad and Polly, but on a patently theatrical rendering of a realistic street scene. On this stage, a down-and-out man picks up a cigarette butt and encounters Carol, dressed in the beret, tight skirt and striped top that she wore in the previous scene. Now, however, she is clearly playing a role in the show rather than working out details of her life with J. Lawrence. In this role, she sympathizes with the man, offers him a fresh cigarette and, as he walks sadly away, begins a recitative about "My Forgotten Man." Realistic Depression motifs are struck by the song's references to World War I and agricultural failures. Carol's recitation is followed by a soulful rendition sung by Etta Moten while shots of several other actresses in other parts of this stage suggest WPA photographs of the poor and suffering. The sequence concludes with a tableau in which a cop hassles an apparent bum who turns out to be a veteran decorated for bravery, as we can see when Carol pulls back his shabby lapel to reveal a combat medal.

The whole sequence obviously suggests that women's hearts are more capable of comprehending the horrors of the Depression than are the male rules and regulations personified by the cop. The sequence also suggests, however, that even the Depression can best be understood in terms of love and romance. In addition to mentioning the war and the decline of American labor, the song lyric definitely affirms that a woman has to have a man. Such a woman empathizes with the forgotten man's perceptions of social injustice, but she also experiences first-hand the effects of his feelings of impotence. The most affecting part of the lyric — at least the part most stressed by both Joan Blondell and Etta Moten — emphasizes that the forgotten man used to love his woman back when he had some sense of worth. That's when she was happy. This is not to suggest that "My Forgotten Man" is merely an escapist fantasy but rather to note another way in which categories of thought and experience are elided through this film's slippery use of chronotopes.

As we might expect on the basis of the film's earlier musical productions, the "Forgotten Man" number soon transcends realistic categories of time and space. Just after we — and presumably the theater audience — see the man's combat medal in closeup, the screen fades to black and re-opens on lines of soldiers marching in a victory parade through showers of confetti. Since this parade is shown from both a stage level and from overhead, realistic space is clearly not a significant element of this chronotope. Apparently, neither is time, because it now begins to rain, just as it rained in the park during an earlier number. In this case, the soldiers march opposite to an equally long line of wounded, who can also be seen in closeups because of the unconfined tracking of the camera. Another fade to black erases the soldiers from what is supposed to be the stage of a theater and replaces them with men grimly lining up at a soup kitchen. Closeups of the men's faces show the misery and humiliation of their situation at the expense of any realistic perspectivity.[14]

After another fade to black, the screen re-opens on a multi-leveled stage set. Soldiers march in counter directions on all levels of this set as a swelling chorus sings the lyric. A line of male civilians, perhaps intended to represent various professions, walk down a flight of steps in unison and then part to reveal Carol, who sings the lyric again with choral background. During this stirring rendition, the camera shoots sometimes from in front and sometimes from above the performers, thus certifying cinematic space rather than the theatrical space dictated by the realistic chronotope. This chronotopic reference is recovered in the film's final shots, however, as the camera pulls back from the stage full of singers to frame the whole shot in the looped curtains of a proscenium stage. This is, apparently, the chronotope in which the six principal diegetic characters will live happily and wealthily ever after.

The contemporary reviewer in *Variety* wrote that this final sequence provided "A bing-bang build-up that'll have The American Legion proclaiming paens of endorsement for the flicker" (June 13, 1933). This judgment seems to me both right and wrong. There are assuredly flags and marching men signifying patriotic motifs in this climactic production number. There is also a sense that gloomy characterizations of America's economic plight are misplaced, or, as Ginger Rogers sang in the opening number, "We never see a headline about a breadline today," because "Old Man Depression" is "through." On the other hand, the final scenes have called up haunting images of war, pain, poverty and human suffering. Richard Fehr and Frederick G. Vogel write in *Lullabies of Hollywood* that this final production number "crusades against a perceived social injustice" in a style that "is both poignant and powerful, yet delivered as an appeal to conscience rather than as a clarion call to revolution" (103). Ironically enough, however, these ideologically realistic effects have been produced within the chronotopic parameters originally designed to authorize the romantic fantasies of Berkeleyesque production numbers.

Given what Bakhtin would characterize as "monologic" definitions of organic consistency, this "Forgotten Man" number — and *Golddiggers of 1933* more generally — might seem to go beyond thematic richness into the kind of aesthetic contradiction identified by James M. Collins and Richard Dyer. Such negative judgments can also be explained in Bakhtinian terms. As Bakhtin explains in his *Problems of Dostoevsky's Poetics*, "Raised on monologic forms of artistic visualization, thoroughly steeped in them, aesthetic thought tends to absolutize those forms and not see their boundaries" (271). From such a monologic perspective, we might be inclined to agree not only with Collins and Dyer but also with the previously quoted *Variety* reviewer that the film is narratively flawed by its many "script inconsistencies." By recognizing the animating force of Bakhtinian dialogue, however, we might be able to comprehend the concept, also articulated in *Problems*, that "[t]he idea is a *live event*, played out at the point of dialogic meeting between two or several consciousnesses" (88; Bakhtin's emphasis). In the case of *Golddiggers* in particular, we might be able to comprehend that ideas are cinematically rooted in chronotopic specificity and that juxtaposing such radically different chronotopes can create ideological dialogue between such radically different ideas as social representation and romantic escapism.

The critical challenge in accepting this dialogical resolution lies in the fact that, as Bakhtin explains, "[T]his dialogue cannot enter into the world represented in it; it is outside the world represented, although not outside the work as a whole. [This dialogue] enters the world of the author, of the performer, and the world of the listeners and readers" (*Dialogic Imagination* 252; Bakhtin's parens.). In other words, the task of resolving the paradoxes posed by *Golddiggers of 1933* falls to the viewer and critic because resolution cannot be fully attained within the textual limits of the film.[15] As Bakhtin goes on to affirm, "[T]he listeners or readers who recreate and in so doing renew the text ... participate equally in the creation of the represented world in the text" (253). Thus, while it is perfectly understandable that some viewers committed to absolutely organic aesthetics might fault *Golddiggers* for certain narrative and/or ideological inconsistencies, other viewers committed to a Bakhtinian aesthetic might praise the film equally for its dialogical resolution of chronotopic tensions.

In this last respect, *Golddiggers of 1933* can be seen as exemplary of a quality that, in *The American Film Musical*, Rick Altman takes to be crucial to the musical genre: "By recognizing terms previously seen as mutually exclusive, the musical succeeds in reducing an unsatisfactory paradox to a more workable configuration, a concordance of opposites" (27). Or, we might say with Barney Hopkins that it is possible to depict "the gay side, the hard-boiled side, the cynical and funny side of the Depression" in a musical comedy so long as members of the viewing audience are willing to participate in the dialogical process. Even to raise such possibilities in connection with *Golddiggers* is to second a proposition advanced by *The Motion Picture Guide*: "If you have but one 1930s Warner Bros. musical to see, make it this one" (1052).[16] Going beyond the recommendation of *The Motion Picture Guide*, however, we might wish to invoke Bakhtin one more time to add: "The work and the world represented in it enter the real world and enrich it, and the real world enters the work and its world as part of the process of its creation, as well as part of its subsequent life, in a communal renewing of the work through the creative perception of listeners and readers" (*Dialogic Imagination* 254). To rephrase Bakhtin, musical films at their best — including *Golddiggers of 1933* — can succeed, with the viewers' "creative perception," in "dialogizing the paradox."

In confronting the task of structural reconciliation posed by the subgenre "Depression musical comedies," Hamilton MacFadden's 1934 film *Stand Up and Cheer* also solves the problem through a dialogic encounter of realistic and fantastic chronotopes, and — significantly — adds liminal settings to the mix. As we have seen, according to Bakhtin's *The Dialogic Imagination*, this sort of harmonious resolution is only to be expected: "Within the limits of a single work ... we may notice a number of different chronotopes and complex interactions among them.... Chronotopes are mutually inclusive, they co-exist, they may be interwoven with, replace or oppose one another, contradict one another or find themselves in ever more complex relationships" (252). In *Stand Up and Cheer*, these relationships are very complex indeed.

Based on a story idea provided by Will Rogers and Philip Klein, and released by Fox, *Stand Up and Cheer* addresses the contemporary economic crisis in terms both absurd and realistically plausible. Realistically, the unnamed, but F.D.R.–like, President of the United States proposes still another federal project aimed at eliminating the Depression. Absurdly, the project involves establishing the cabinet-level post of Secretary of Amusement. As the President explains to future Secretary Lawrence Cromwell (Warner Baxter):

> Mr. Cromwell, our country is gravely passing through a serious crisis. Many of our people's affairs are in the red and, figuratively, their nerves are in the red. But, thanks to ingrained sturdiness, their faith is not in the red. Any people blessed with a sense of humor can achieve success and victory. We are endeavoring to pilot the ship past the most treacherous of all rocks, fear. The government now proposes to dissolve that destructive rock in a gale of laughter. To that end, it has created a new cabinet office, that of Secretary of Amusement, whose duty it shall be to amuse and entertain the people, to make them forget their troubles. Mr. Cromwell, we are drafting you and your splendid talents into public service. And it is with great confidence and pleasure that I offer you the cabinet position of Secretary of Amusement.

As the *Variety* reviewer discretely noted at the time (April 24, 1934), "The idea ... is open to debate." On the other hand, Mordaunt Hall proposed in the *New York Times* (April 20, 1934) that the film based on this highly disputable premise "often comes close to a conception of what a modern Gilbert and Sullivan opus might be" (1051). Music, laughter, political satire, witty dialogue—all the Gilbert and Sullivan ingredients were present in *Stand Up and Cheer*, in Hall's view. To the *Variety* reviewer, however, the film was "all thin and sporadic," prompting the suggestion that it might be renamed *Fox Follies*.[17] More than six decades later, both critics' positions make sense—another apparent contradiction—but once again the problem can be solved by examining the film's ingenious use of chronotopes.

One striking example occurs quite early in the film. Shortly after Cromwell has settled into his official position, he tells his assistant for children's entertainment, Mary Adams (Madge Evans), that the department's initial effect on public morale has been all that anyone could ask. "Why, they're laughing from the Atlantic to the Pacific," he tells her in a voiceover, as the screen fills with a newspaper featuring his photograph and a front page headline containing the same news—all elements rooted in the realistic chronotope of government bureaucracy. Then Nick Foran breaks through the photograph, dressed in a proletarian costume to sing that he's laughing even though he hasn't anything much to laugh about. If he can sing and shout under these adverse circumstances, then the listener can too. A performative chronotope of great optimism has obviously supplanted the realistic one. The scene is thus mildly challenging to the audience and gives evidence of greater challenges to come. As Foran sings the main line of the song, the screen is successively filled with other groups who, in an example of what Jane Feuer calls a "passed-along song," sing that they have adopted the same optimistic philosophy as Foran. Feuer also explains that montage is this sort of number's most common visual equivalent (16), and Mac-Fadden follows this strategy here. First a stereotypical Irish washerwoman laughs despite her struggles to feed 12 children, and then two toothless hillbillies in a horse-drawn wagon laugh in the face of their heavy mortgages. Jewish women with their noses economically chained to their sewing machines in a sweatshop sing that this life is not easy, but they are upbeat even so (despite the possible anti–Semitic stereotype implicit in the song lyric). Then cops out in the rain, construction workers on skyscraper scaffolding, chorus girls, street cleaners and blacksmiths happily join in the song. The sequence ends with Aunt Jemima (Tess Gardella) singing the same song in an African-American meeting hall (perhaps a church). The screen then fills with a close-up of her laughing face before a complete fade. In this number, a wide variety of representative Americans dressed in realistic costumes participate in a fantastic performance. Inclusiveness—of gender, geography, race and occupation—is a large part of the message of this presentational sequence.[18]

Another large part of the message involves a '30s sense of solid working-class values: Everyone seems to have a job. Even the Irish woman may be doing someone else's laundry for pay. Unlike "The Forgotten Man" hymned in *Golddiggers of 1933*, these laughing Americans do not have to stand in line for free soup. This theme is clearly epitomized later on when Jimmy Dugan (James Dunn) seeks an interview with Cromwell on behalf of his little daughter, Shirley (Shirley Temple). Contrary to what we might expect from having seen other Depression musicals, Dugan is not exploiting his charming offspring to gain employment. As Dugan says, he is "booked solid for 40 weeks," and so he is merely seeking to appeal Cromwell's edict that children under seven years of age cannot appear on the professional stage. Perhaps some members of the Republican opposition might see Cromwell's policy as a predictable bureaucratic snafu, but it is easily manageable in this film, as breadlines would not be (as they are not easily manageable in the finale of *Golddiggers*, for example). The inclusive, upbeat, performative chronotope of the "I'm Laughin'" number — which originally derives from a newspaper in Cromwell's office — has created the distinct impression that the problems of the Depression are *all* manageable if people will only start thinking about them in the right way, the actuating principle of Cromwell's government agency.

This is even the conviction of Cromwell's antagonists back in the realistic chronotope, a cartel of tycoons who want the Depression to continue because the national lack of economic confidence has allowed them to reap such obscene profits. As their spokesman declares, "If the mood and temperament of the people become optimistic, prosperity will arrive with a bang, and that will ruin us." In addition to re-enforcing the common Hollywood disposition to represent economic forces in personal terms,[19] this plot turn introduces a realistic setting with strong ideological significance. Not only do these tycoons dress differently from the laughing workers in the earlier musical number, they also spend their time in a different kind of environment: a well-appointed board room. Leather chairs, polished tables, cigar smoke — these are the markers of anti-proletarian privilege in the board rooms and Senate chambers of *Stand Up and Cheer*, as the furnishings of exclusive men's clubs are in other Depression musicals like *Golddiggers* and *Top Hat*. In these environs, plots can be hatched to sabotage Cromwell's (and the President's) plans for national recovery. As the principal tycoon continues: "The world is full of pussyfoots, blue-noses and killjoys. Laughter and gaiety are their arch-enemies. It shouldn't be hard to make them see the hand of the Devil in Cromwell's program of national nonsense. We'll put up millions [for] a campaign of ridicule" and misinformation. Here a narrative complication to MacFadden's realistic Depression narrative is authorized by a setting consistent with chronotopic realism.

Because of the audience's negative associations with this setting signifying business privilege, another scene that soon follows also seems likely to portend trouble for the Department of Amusement. Immediately following the tycoon conspiracy, a sequence is devoted to Jimmy and Shirley Dugan, first seen in Cromwell's government offices and then on stage. After the sequence closes with a full-screen close-up of Jimmy and Shirley beaming at the conclusion of "Baby, Take a Bow," a group of well-dressed white men are shown sitting around a conference table. If viewers think the plot has returned to the conspirators' world after a musical interlude, their mistake is understandable, but these men are United States Senators, not tycoons, and this setting is a Senate meeting room not the tycoons' boardroom. At the outset, the tone of the meeting is equally anti–Department of Amusement, and so viewers may think they are not so mistaken in their suspicions after all. The purpose of this meeting is to investigate how the public's money is being spent (or misspent) a clear threat to the party of hope with whom viewers are probably allied by this point. The Senate spokesman introduces a realistic diegetic complication when he reasonably announces, "Gentlemen, a sense of humor cannot assert itself upon an empty stomach." Viewers soon learn that investigating such reasonable objections is not the real purpose of this scene, however, because the Senator's subsequent words—"nor can a nation endure on hollow laughter"—are not merely pompous, they are delivered with a bogus Shakespearean trill on the Senator's R's. Clearly the man is a pompous windbag, a precursor of Fred Allen's comic associate, Senator Claghorn. On the other hand, the Senator did make a good point about humor and hunger, and he does dress and sound like the corporate conspirators. In this realistic setting entailing realistic attitudes toward money and society, perhaps the party of hope may really be in trouble!

The next sequence proves otherwise when Senators Danforth and Short, who have been dispatched by the Senate committee to perform an on-site inspection, turn out to be vaudevillians Mitchell and Durant. In Cromwell's office, the two engage in obviously scripted old jokes rather than in diegetic dialogue that might pose an actual threat to Cromwell's programs. The two supposed Senators also slap each other broadly and take elaborate falls, as they have obviously done hundreds of times before. In any event, their activities function apart from the diegetic narrative about the Depression, so much so that the *Variety* reviewer apparently thought that no mention of these performers was necessary. In the *Times*, on the other hand, Mordaunt Hall considered Mitchell and Durant's turn one of the film's high points. Notwithstanding these reviewers' conflicting preferences, this scene involving Senators Danforth and Short can be seen as significant in that it temporarily moves the narrative outside the bounds of chronotopic realism represented by the boardroom setting and converts Cromwell's office into a liminal performative site.[20]

As a result, this office space can later be used for the same purposes by Stepin Fetchit (born Lincoln Theodore Perry). Just as Mordaunt Hall admired Mitchell and Durant's act, he was greatly impressed by Perry's performance. Viewers today are probably less comfortable with Perry's personification of what Donald Bogle calls "the lazy, dimwitted Negro servant (a walking windup toy for the amusement of whites)."[21] For these reasons, such viewers perhaps cannot see how consistent Perry's performance is with other aspects of the "Fox Follies." In terms of how setting is used to achieve chronotopic resolution, moreover, it is highly significant that Stepin Fetchit's entire performance takes place inside Cromwell's office. On his first appearance, Stepin Fetchit is looking for work, presumably as a dancer since he has brought his practice board along. Unlike Jimmy Dugan, he is not booked solid and so is willing to accept a job as Cromwell's gatekeeper despite the latter's genial racism. Stepin Fetchit has been admitted to the office in the first place under a misapprehension since he shares the famous name George Bernard Shaw. When Cromwell discovers the mistake, he smilingly says to Shaw/Fetchit/Perry, "You're a little sunburned, aren't you?" and the apparently unfazable Stepin Fetchit answers, "Yessuh! But see, Ah's an outdoor man." In the diegetic world of the Depression plot, this exchange is nearly senseless. In the actual world of today's America, the dialogue is also racially offensive.[22] In the liminal setting of Cromwell's office, however, this exchange relates cinematically to Mitchell and Durant's routine as well as to Stepin Fetchit's main scene, in which he interacts comically but subserviently with a talking penguin.

Also singled out for special mention by the *Times*, this later routine is praised even by the reviewer in *Variety* who says that "Fetchit clicks on the comedy" and continues, "[T]here has been nothing funnier on the screen than the penguin who does a Jimmie Durante (...Broadway insiders recognize Lew Brown doing the off-screen gabbing and the Schnozzola routine)." On the way to eliciting these rave reviews, Stepin Fetchit consistently calls the talking penguin "Mr. Jimmy" and plunges ineptly into a large fish tank seeking halibut for the comically disgruntled bird. Viewers today, who are less amused by Durante impressions and by Sambo acting, might be inclined to see this scene as gratuitous and/or diegetically intrusive. In terms of the settings used in *Stand Up and Cheer*, however, we should recognize that Stepin Fetchit's penguin scene is related to other non-diegetic scenes that take place in Cromwell's office in the sense that the office establishes a liminal environment in which the realistic chronotope of the Department of Amusement and the fantastic chronotope of the "Fox Follies" can interact. It is also probable that Stepin Fetchit's vaudeville turns are intended, along with other performative elements of the film, to serve the thematic issue of democratic inclusiveness.

During the "I'm Laughin'" production number early in the film, for example, race is introduced as a constituent of the American melting pot by Aunt Jemima, whose solo is the longest segment of this sequence apart from Foran's opening scene. Also included in the mix are the two comic country bumpkins, stereotypical toothless hillbillies with their pipes, dilapidated hats and cargo of farm livestock. Just as the Irish washerwoman and the Jewish seamstresses are introduced by brief orchestral allusions to their ethnic music, so the hillbillies' entrance is initially signaled by a fiddled "Turkey in the Straw." In the setting that authorizes this production number, ex-centric rustics are as welcome under the umbrella of economic optimism as cops, African-American tap dancers, chorus girls and sweatshop workers, even if they might be excluded from a realistic cinematic representation of the American Depression produced in 1934.

Later on, countryness gets a more extended treatment in the production number "Broadway's Gone Hillbilly." Sylvia Froos initiates this sequence with a recitative about "mountain songs," a category that includes both country and western music. The western side of the country-western equation is established by Froos' glittery Broadway cowgirl costume and by the gorgeous chorus girls' twirling of crepe paper lariats. The country side is suggested largely by the lazy affect and exaggerated rural accents adopted by the singers as well as by background fiddle music. Grafting these geographical markers of the outlands onto the structure of a Broadway production number re-enforces the concept of inclusiveness. Froos' song says that Broadway is getting "moody" because singing stars like Bing Crosby and Rudy Vallee insist on singing songs about doggies and roundups. Though outwardly inclusive, the lyric is also condescending toward non-urban outsiders in the same way that the stereotyping of "I'm Laughin'" and the Stepin Fetchit numbers are to other less-privileged groups.[23] While these "Fox Follies" numbers were probably designed to show that all class, racial and geographical distinctions are insignificant to Americans who want to pull together, to audiences looking back today, the lessons seem more probably to be that the world of lavish entertainment may be the only one in which such distinctions are likely to be ignored and that a chronotope legitimating fantastic production numbers may be the only time and place for this happy resolution.

Living in a pre-multicultural age, audiences in the 1930s would probably be less disposed toward such cynical suggestions. They would not, however, be indifferent to the "complicated visual-narrative style" of the "Broadway's Gone Hillbilly" production number.[24] This style becomes especially complicated as the number builds to a stupendous finish. Along the way, as chorus after chorus of the "passed-along" song is sung by various groups, the scenery has shifted from a proscenium stage (ostensibly on Broadway), to a nightclub, to movie sets, to Manhattan streets full of taxi cabs, and back to the stage, suggesting that Hamilton MacFadden has learned something from the cinematic exuberance of Busby Berkeley.[25] Just before the camera returns to the original stage set, four cowboys rear their white horses on the roof of a Manhattan building. When these same cowboys ride toward the camera through the lariat-twirling chorus girls in the closing shots, they are presented as film images on top of the represented stage performers. Furthermore, this whole melange is accompanied by shots derived from earlier stages of the number, creating a visual reprise as well as a purely fantastic mode of representation. When such varied modes of representation exist simultaneously, they are probably intended to suggest that a similarly harmonious dialogue can take place among varied groups of Depression Americans.

This is certainly the message of the film's closing sequence. First comes a minor plot wrinkle in which Cromwell decides to scrap the highly successful children's division supervised by his true love, Mary Adams. Fortunately, an especially opportune telephone call from the President helps Cromwell to see that Mary is crucial to the national program as well as to his own romantic future. Then, as things are definitely beginning to look up, Jimmy Dugan bursts in on the two lovebirds shouting, "Mr. Cromwell, I've got great news for ya. The Depression's over!" Cromwell and Mary—and probably the audience—look delighted as Jimmy concludes: "There is no unemployment! Fear has been banished! Confidence is reborn! Poverty has been wiped out! Laughter resounds throughout the nation! The people are happy again! We're out of the red!" It seems that the President, Mary Adams, Lawrence Cromwell—even the tycoon conspirators—have been right all along. Public confidence is powerful enough on its own to bring an end to the Depression, to convert the socio-economic "real" world of America into the fantastic world of musical film.

The closing sequence brings this conviction directly to the screen while mixing the realistic and fantastic chronotopes exploited earlier in the film. As in "I'm Laughin'" earlier on, the liminal setting of Cromwell's office metamorphoses into the theatrically presentational as Jimmy Dugan is replaced by Nick Foran. This time Foran is dressed in a quasi-Revolutionary War costume, and he rides a horse through the clouds like a proletarian Paul Revere singing, "We're Out of the Red." As we might expect in a production number that begins with a singer riding through the clouds, "time nor space—distance avails not," as Walt Whitman claims in "Crossing Brooklyn Ferry."[26] Instead, a chronotope of presentational freedom avails and prevails. Foran and his horse gallop above jubilant Civilian Conservation Corps workers, miners, farmers, office workers and stevedores. Bells and whistles sound. The soundtrack music briefly alludes to "San Francisco, Here I Come," "Chicago," "Give My Regards to Broadway." Set back in New York after a lightning cross-country trip, the production number presents lines of people marching though what looks like Washington Square Arch. In orderly lines, large groups of typical Americans—rigidly segregated by craft and costume—join in the celebratory parade.

Even 1930s German audiences accustomed to such carefully orchestrated public events would have to be impressed by the turn-out. Chorus girls with drums march into the camera, followed by forest rangers, sailors, nurses, milk men, office workers, locomotive oilers, farmers, policemen, miners, housewives, chefs, school girls in uniform, street cleaners, doormen, Scots in kilts, soldiers, Marines (accompanied by "La Marseillaise"), mailmen (accompanied by "Rule Britannia"), Shirley Temple dressed as a drum majorette, train porters (led by Stepin Fetchit in top hat and tails) and Boy Scouts (accompanied by "Columbia, the Gem of the Ocean").[27] The screen then fills with cheering multitudes who surround the open car containing Mary Adams and Lawrence Cromwell. Then the sequence fades to black on the picture of this savior amid his grateful masses, bringing an end to all the diegetic conflicts caused by the Depression.

Whether or not viewers harbor political reservations about how desirable deliverance by such a savior might be, "We're Out of the Red" concludes *Stand Up and Cheer* by providing a resolution of the paradox embracing "the serious social problems of the day" and "aspiration, optimism and kindly humor." Throughout the film, this paradoxical resolution has been established by allotting appropriate spatio-temporal settings to each half of the tension between realistic representation and escapism, but the primary solution has been achieved by creating a liminal space that permits passage between the two poles of this tension. The sets representing the President's office, the tycoons' meeting room and the accommodations of Cromwell's bureaucracy realistically situate the Depression narrative in familiar terms even if they pay scant attention to bread lines and Hooverville shanties. Within this chronotope, plot and class conflicts including massive unemployment, the tycoons' conspiracy and Cromwell's self-doubts are permitted realistic expression. The extravagant production numbers—principally "I'm Laughin'" and "Broadway's Gone Hillbilly"—situate the fantastic side of the cinematic opposition by ignoring not only all realistic conceptions of time and space, but also all realistic distinctions of region, race and economic inequity. Within this setting, perfect national unity is possible. Finally, Cromwell's office, which originally enters the film's discourse as part of the diegetic plot, operates as a third sort of setting, the liminal site of transition from the realistic to the fantastic. The cinematic utility of this liminal setting is evident early in the film in the cut from the newspaper photograph of Cromwell, to Nick Foran, to "I'm Laughin'," and later on by the Mitchell and Durant and Stepin Fetchit comic turns. However grandiosely conceived and executed, then, "We're Out of the Red" merely conforms to the chronotopic freedom afforded by this liminal setting.

Getting "out of the red" just by going to the movies—more than seven years before the outbreak of World War II—is in itself an achievement worthy of note.

Nick Foran (Dick Foran) holds Shirley Dugan (Shirley Temple) in a publicity shot for *Stand Up and Cheer.*

Coordinating an uplifting dramatization of fictional characters using mere willpower to overcome the rigors of the Depression with individual performances by Aunt Jemima, Sylvia Froos, Stepin Fetchit, Mitchell and Durant and the other performers uninvolved in this diegetic narrative is still another noteworthy cinematic feat. Resolving all of these issues without making the romance between Cromwell and Mary Adams the only avenue to closure is—from the perspective of movie genres—still a third. None of this would be possible, however, without Lawrence Cromwell's office, a cinematic rabbit hole diegetically authenticated by the Depression chronotope but still imaginatively open to any fantastic performance that might, in the words of the fictional President, "amuse and entertain the people, to make them forget their troubles." Clearly Hamilton MacFadden and Fox intended to do the President one better by seeing these "people" as the ones sitting in a movie theater watching

Stand Up and Cheer instead of merely those living somewhere out in what Nick Carraway calls "the dark fields of the republic."[28] Even today, we may agree that — despite our more "advanced" notions of race, region and gender — the moviemakers were correct in their intentions. At least for the length of a single viewing, *Stand Up and Cheer* seems deliberately and successfully to fulfill Will Hays' program for the Depression cinema by absorbing Americans of all genders, races, regions and occupations into seamless web of fantastic optimism. In this respect, *Stand Up and Cheer*–like *Golddiggers of 1933*— succeeds in resolving a very troubling paradox.

2

Blackface Minstrelsy in Musicals

Black-white race relations have historically been one of the central cruxes of American cultural experience, and so we might naturally expect the Hollywood musical to address these issues in a variety of ways. Curiously, one of the most frequent means by which these problems have been addressed in musical films is through the use of blackface minstrelsy, "a form of stage entertainment," according to Nick Tosches, "in which men blackened their faces, burlesqued the demeanor and behavior of Southern blacks, and performed what were presented as the songs and music of those blacks" (9). Tosches and most other contemporary commentators are understandably amazed and abashed that, as Gary Giddins writes in *Bing Crosby: A Pocket Full of Dreams, The Early Years, 1903–1940*, "[t]he importance of minstrelsy in the development of America's popular arts can hardly be overstated..." (78). This is also Michael Rogin's point when he writes in his *Black Face, White Noise: Jewish Immigrants in the Hollywood Melting Pot* that "[m]instrelsy was the first and most popular form of mass culture in the nineteenth-century United States. Blackface provided the new country with a distinctive national identity in the age of slavery and presided over melting-pot culture in the period of mass European immigration" (5). By the time that the Hollywood musical was at its apex, however, we might expect that the cultural significance of minstrelsy would have dissipated and that blackface musical numbers would not be significant elements of major musical films. Apparently such an expectation would be invalid because, as Arthur Knight has established, "at least seventy-two Hollywood movies containing self-conscious blackface, that is, blackface that draws attention to itself as a mask" (30), were released after Al Jolson's *Big Boy* in 1930.

This popularity of "self-conscious blackface" is amazing because, although blackface minstrelsy flourished in the United States—and not only in the American South—throughout much of the nineteenth century, most historians of the genre would agree with Bill Barlow's judgment, in the *Encyclopedia of Southern Culture*, that "[w]ith the advent of the 20th century, minstrelsy ... went into a slow but steady decline" (1019).[1] It is therefore surprising indeed that major white Hollywood stars performed blackface minstrel numbers in highly successful musical films of the late 1930s and early '40s. Specifically, Fred Astaire performed in blackface in *Swing Time* in 1936, Mickey Rooney and Judy Garland did it in *Babes in Arms* (1939) and *Babes* on *Broadway* (1941), and Bing Crosby did it in *Holiday Inn* (1942). We might expect that performances featuring such outrageous and offensive racial stereotyping many decades after the supposed decline of minstrelsy would have elicited reams of critical commentary, but once again we would be mistaken.² Even most of the standard sources are silent. William J. Mahar mentions none of these films even in passing in his *Behind the Burnt Cork Mask*. In *Toms, Coons, Mulattoes, Mammies, & Bucks* (1990), Donald Bogle also discusses none of them. In his *Blacks in American Films and Television: An Illustrated Encyclopedia*, Bogle touches only on *Holiday Inn* among these films, and he does so only in order to note Louise Beavers' dissatisfaction with still another Mammy role as Crosby's warm-hearted maid and factotum. Spike Lee's social satire *Bamboozled* (2000) does show brief clips from *Babes in Arms* and *Holiday Inn* as part of a closing montage intended to represent the ubiquity of stereotypical Sambo images, but Lee's viewers are left to draw their own conclusions about how these images should be historically construed.³ Michael Rogin discusses *Swing Time*, *Babes in Arms* and *Holiday Inn* in his *Blackface, White Noise*, but his discussion is so acrimonious that it provides no explanation of why anyone not totally sunk in reactionary prejudices might ever have found any of these movies even marginally entertaining. Arthur Knight's *Disintegrating the Musical: Black Performance and the American Musical Film* (2002) finally addresses some of these issues calmly and insightfully and helps us understand the rhetorical situation of performers and audience more clearly. Nevertheless, the profusion of blackface performances in the Hollywood musicals in question still cries out for decisive comment. Unfortunately, looking closely at the situation may still leave one with more questions than answers.

The search for answers must begin with a description of the blackface numbers in question, and — as is historically appropriate — it is best to begin with Fred Astaire. In *Swing Time*, the blackface number occurs just after a sequence in which the romance between Fred and Ginger Rogers— whose interruption was signaled by "A Fine Romance"— temporarily reaches a happy resolution. This resolution is signified by a kiss between the two lovers that is screened from the viewer by an open dressing room door. Since Mrs. Astaire objected to Fred's involvement in any onscreen smooching, the obscured kiss makes biographical sense.⁴ It makes sense for my purposes, too, since Fred emerges from the kiss covered with Ginger's lipstick, thus revealing a slight physical change in his very familiar appearance. Then, because the proprietor of the night club in which Fred and Ginger are performing has already said that Fred is due on stage in five minutes, he appropriately sits down at his dressing table and begins to apply face black over the lipstick, as he sings the song, "Bojangles of Harlem."

The next scene opens with an orchestra playing an instrumental version of this song underscored with beating tom toms. Twenty-four white female dancers dressed in either all-black or all-white costumes— with at least some obviously wearing sepia makeup — perform a Busby Berkeley–esque dance as the curtains open on a huge black construction with a cartoon face. Today many viewers might be reminded of Mr. Potato-head, but in this film the construction turns out to be giant, overlapping shoes. These separate to reveal two immensely long — perhaps symbolically phallic — legs, at the crotch of which sits Fred Astaire in blackface. The costume that Fred is

Penny Carroll (Ginger Rogers) and Lucky Garrett (Fred Astaire) perform "Pick Yourself Up" in *Swing Time*.

wearing is not the black tie and tails that we expect of him — and that he wears in the film's next dance number, "Never Gonna Dance" — but rather a more minstrel-like derby hat, polka dot jacket, white gloves and spats. The dance he then performs is not especially minstrel-like, however, except for some gloved hand patting, *à la* Eddie Cantor, and an occasional open-armed, white-gloved appeal to the audience. In fact, putting aside the fact that Fred is performing in blackface, the overall effect of the number is a sense of pretty impressive hoofing. As in the "Top Hat" number from the film of the same title, Fred dances in the foreground to a background of male dancers. Here, however, the dancers are three giant shadows of himself. This is the Fred Astaire of legend, in other words—except perhaps for the gloved hand claps and "man-oh-man" aura of his exit from the scene.

During the following scene, in which some gamblers and Fred's fiancée from back home again disrupt the central romance between Fred and Ginger, Fred is still wearing his Bojangles makeup. He thus looks as out of place in this scene as he did with lipstick smeared all over him in the earlier one. Like lipstick, blackface is definitely all on the surface with Fred. The question obviously is, then, why did he do the number in the first place? Arlene Croce says that the dance is "not the homage of one white to one black man, but of one great artist to another," in other words, of Fred Astaire to Bill Bojangles Robinson (107). Thomas Cripps apparently agrees in *Slow Fade to Black: The Negro in American Film, 1900–1942* when he says that "Fred Astaire paid touching homage to 'Bojangles' in *Swingtime*" (256).[5] While conceding that "the number could even be seen as a homage to Robinson," John Mueller points out that "Astaire was not particularly impressed by Robinson as a dancer, and tended to regard him as a one-trick artist who mainly tapped up and down stairs" (108). Questions thus multiply. Richard Dyer puts the matter most cogently by writing, in his essay "The Colour of Entertainment," that the supposed homage was "[g]enerously meant, no doubt," but adding that "the use of blackface cannot help but be disturbing (even if it is far from the grotesqueries of minstrelsy)," and asking finally, "wouldn't it have been better if Astaire had used his influence to get Robinson himself on screen?" (29). Dyer's point is well taken. Bill Robinson was hardly a Hollywood star in 1936, although he did the choreography for Shirley Temple's *Dimples* that same year. The fact that Robinson was unbilled in *Dimples* is probably as significant as his later stereotyped roles as an affable, elderly, sexless dance partner for the lovable moppet.[6] *Stormy Weather*, in which Robinson played the romantic lead opposite Lena Horne, was still seven years in the future in 1936. I guess if we were going to see Bojangles in a major production number in a Hollywood musical at that time, it would have to be as filtered through Fred Astaire in blackface.

The next case is equally problematic. In *Babes in Arms*, Mickey Rooney and Judy Garland, in the roles of Mickey Moran and Patsy Barton, are intent on proving to their faded vaudevillian parents that kids like them have the talent to provide Broadway audiences with what they are crying out for in the grip of the Great Depression. Much of the film is devoted to planning and rehearsing the show that is intended to prove this, and so the climax in terms of plot should occur when the no-longer babes in arms finally get to strut their stuff on stage for a preview audience of Broadway bigwigs. Even though we have seen several other numbers being rehearsed during the course of the film, what we see on the opening night at an outdoor theater is a blackface number.

Judy, as the definitely Caucasian Patsy, opens the number by standing in front of the curtain and singing a song that declares her minstrel heritage. Her daddy, she sings, performed in minstrel shows back when minstrelsy was "the thing." The lyric is accurate historically in the sense that minstrels are no longer "the thing" in the late 1930s—in vaudeville, on Broadway or elsewhere in America. The lyric is also accurate diegetically, since Patsy's vaudevillian mother has told her in an earlier backstage scene:

Mickey Moran (Mickey Rooney) and Patsy Barton (Judy Garland) perform for their parents in *Babes in Arms*.

"Your daddy was a minstrel man. So was his daddy. They did plenty of crazy things, but they never walked out on a show." Minstrelsy and nostalgia thus combine, and as Jane Feuer writes in *The Hollywood Musical*, nostalgia is best understood as "remystification in a sentimental vein" (91). That is to say, according to Feuer, that "[m]instrel shows ... evoke an even earlier and folksier entertainment era" than the cinematic present (95)—presumably for white audiences. Thus, Patsy's schmaltzy lyric goes on to invoke the legendary Mr. Bones, Eddie Leonard and Primrose in order to lead us down Memory Lane with an old fashioned minstrel show. Her plaintive recitative is followed by the entry of the entire cast — including little children in blackface — in an up-tempo parade set to the tune "Camptown Races."[7] Judy and Mickey then appear onstage in blackface dressed in matching minstrel costumes to sing "Oh Susannah." Mickey engages in exaggerated eye-rolling during this number and in the following exchange of jokes with Mr. Interlocutor, played without blackface by Douglas McPhail. Mickey's minstrel persona during this sequence is crudely comic and drenched in Negro dialect. In the same scenes, Judy's persona is cool and sexy despite her costume. As the minstrel show proceeds, Mickey does an Eddie Leonard impression without using black dialect, but with a mouth exaggerated by makeup and with way-too-short pants. Judy then reappears in sepia makeup and a revealing skirt to sing "I'm Just Wild About Harry." Two racial stereotypes interact as Mickey continues to clown broadly in polka-dotted pants and Judy vamps around showing lots of leg. Then the clouds suddenly open, and a torrential rain drenches the outdoor stage and the audience. Whether or not audiences today might see this downpour as retribution from a just and angry god, Mickey's character stands in the rain with blackface makeup streaking down his cheek, futilely begging the audience to stay for the rest of the show.

Plot is served when a member of this drenched audience turns out to be producer Harry Maddox, who has been so impressed by what he has seen that he determines to bring this show to Broadway. Maddox feels very optimistic because, as he says, "Old-fashioned sentiment's not taboo any more." Then, despite his fondness for things "old-fashioned" and despite the show's exploitation of minstrelsy as an agent of nostalgia, Maddox paradoxically avers that *Babes in Arms* is "as fresh and sparkling as anything that's ever hit Broadway." We are spared a "fresh and sparkling" reprise of the minstrel show, however, because the next production number we see is "God's Country," a patriotic finale to the show and the film that is obviously intended to counteract the threat of European fascism rampant in 1939.[8] In fact, this Arlen-Harburg song even goes so far as to say that in "God's Country," the U. S. A., everyone can be his or her own dictator because our freedoms are so much greater. In case someone might still be in doubt about this production number's message, the lyric's rhyme goes on to privilege Garbo and Norma Shearer over any old duce or führer. Clearly the number is a paean to all that made America great on the eve of World War II. Just as clearly, these patriotic values are seen as compatible with gross racial and ethnic stereotyping. Thus, the number ends with a melting-pot chorus of ethnic stereotypes—including comic Indians—supporting the four principal babes in arms in their anthem to "God's Country."

In *Babes on Broadway*, the minstrel number does not precede a patriotic finale; it *is* the finale. The premise here is that, once again, Mickey and Judy's characters, Tommy Williams and Penny Morris, want to put on a show to demonstrate to a Broadway producer—here Thornton Reed (James Gleason)—what they have to offer the Great White Way. Various plot exigencies determine that, when it comes down to it, they can show Thornton only one number. This turns out to be a production number in which the six principal babes try to decide what kind of show to put on. After a ballet, a circus, a Brazilian number and an aquacade are rejected as theatrical possibilities, Judy/Penny proposes that they do something tried and true. Mickey/Tommy suggests that a minstrel show would be just the thing. The next scene shows the six applying blackface in front of three mirrors. The song they sing mixes historical references by suggesting that it is okay to black up at a time when there are likely to be blackouts. That is to say, the old minstrel tradition is still relevant in times of aerial warfare. Reed is as impressed by this youthful minstrelsy as Harry Maddox was in *Babes in Arms*, and so the next shot is of title cards announcing, "Thornton Reed Presents Babes on Broadway." A minstrel number follows as part of Reed's show, with scores of dancers, brilliant costumes, imaginative crane shots and the kind of full-scale Busby Berkeley treatment that film audiences might expect—all presented against an art-nouveau background of the New York skyline.[9]

As in *Babes in Arms*, Mickey's minstrel character is broader than Judy's. When the number concludes with "Waiting for the Robert E. Lee," Judy is once again sexy in sepia and a revealing gown while Mickey is once again an over-the-top Sambo. Before this conclusion, however, Judy has played Mr. Tambo with exaggerated lips and darkly sooty makeup to balance Mickey's Mr. Bones. The minstrel songs included in the earlier stages of this sequence are mostly old favorites — "By the Light of the Silvery Moon," "Swanee River," "Alabamy Bound" — but a new piece, "Franklin D. Roosevelt Jones" by Harold Rome, is also inserted. The lyric to this song asserts that a newborn baby boy with such a name is destined for greatness but, since Judy performs the song in her Tambo costume and makeup, viewers might be forgiven for assuming that such grandiose naming is merely a joke at the expense of African Americans, especially since one of the minstrel dancers elsewhere in this long sequence is named Mr. Rufus Rastus Jefferson Davis Brown. There are, by the way, no actual black performers visible in this minstrel scene — or elsewhere in the picture.[10] The elaborately named Rufus Brown is played by the very white Ray McDonald, and his tap dance is as hot as Berkeley allows the number to get, unless we count Mickey and Judy's performance in "Waiting for the Robert E. Lee."[11] During this last song, most of the minstrel performers are dressed in (perhaps parodic) evening dress. The screen then fills with the six leading characters, including Tommy/Mickey, in evening dress but out of blackface, singing "Babes on Broadway" against the New York skyline backdrop. A closeup of Mickey and Judy actually concludes the number and the film, but the minstrel show surely leaves a more lasting impression.

The patriotic motif so apparent in *Babes in Arms* is not absent in *Babes on Broadway*, however. About halfway through the film, Penny sings "Chin Up! Cheerio! Carry On!" to inspire the besieged English parents of the children who have fled to America to escape the Blitz. Berkeley's camera lingers lovingly on the faces of these irresistible, super-white moppets before, during and after the song, and he intercuts scenes of the London we recall so well from earlier, pre–World War II films with closeups of the inspirational Penny. Other elements from the earlier film also function intertextually: the principal stars, for example, as well as the basic plot and the title.[12] In addition, regular film goers would surely be reminded of the Dead End Kids by the poor children of the Dorman Street Settlement House, whom Penny hopes to help get into the open air of the country and whom Tommy hopes to exploit in order to get his big break on Broadway. Another clear echo is of Carmen Miranda's performance in *Down Argentine Way* (1940), via "Bombshell From Brazil," Tommy's drag performance in a show that was canceled just before Thornton Reed's appearance. Then again, minstrelsy is probably another likely form of continuity — at least for Mickey and Judy.

Minstrelsy is equally accepted, and equally anomalous, in *Holiday Inn*. As most fans of Hollywood musicals probably know, the plot of this film revolves around an inn operated by Bing Crosby that is open to the public on only the 15 days each year designated as significant holidays. In the practical operation of the inn, Bing, in the role of Jim Hardy, is aided by Louise Beavers, in the role of Mamie, a mammy with a heart of gold and two cute little children. In the grand entertainment that is themed to go along with each holiday, Bing is aided by Marjorie Reynolds, in the role of Linda Mason, a singer-dancer who is also pursued by Jim's old song-and-dance partner, Ted

An uncomfortable Jim Hardy (Bing Crosby) plays while Linda Mason (Marjorie Reynolds) dances with Ted Hanover (Fred Astaire) in *Holiday Inn*.

Hanover, played by Fred Astaire. When Fred/Ted shows up at the inn on February 12 searching for Marjorie/Linda, Bing/Jim proposes that they do their Lincoln's Birthday tribute in blackface, ostensibly to make the number more authentic, but actually to hide Linda from Ted by means of disguise. Linda is at first put off at the prospect of donning blackface but only because she has dreamed for a month and a half about how pretty she will look on stage and because she doesn't even know how to put on black makeup. Jim tells her not to worry, that he "broke in as a bootblack," and that if she cooperates they will have a beautiful future together. As when Fred Astaire dons blackface in his dressing room in *Swing Time*, and when the potential Babes on Broadway sit before mirrors preparing for their socko minstrel number, we see Marjorie Reynolds only partly blacked-up during this love scene.[13]

Once again, the black is only on the outside, but in *Holiday Inn*, the outside is far more clownish and stereotypical than in *Swing Time*. Bing is white-whiskered and tottery, leaning on a cane, during the "Abraham" number that follows, even though he sings the lyric in his usual der Bingle fashion. Marjorie Reynolds is a total Mandy, however, with huge lips and rag-wrapped pigtails.[14] The effect of the two principals' minstrel-like appearance is reinforced by Louise Beavers and her kids. These three take up the second chorus of "Abraham" offstage when Mamie asks in song who freed the "darkies," and her children sing, "Abraham," with the wide-eyed, affectless aura patented by Buckwheat in the *Our Gang* comedies. Jim and Linda are also backed in this number by the waiters and waitresses of Holiday Inn, who are all dressed for minstrelsy as well, including blackface makeup — perhaps more exactly, sepia makeup for the girls. To conclude this outrage, the camera moves in on an image of Abraham Lincoln — appropriately enough the one on the five-dollar bill.

What this all goes to show, of course, remains problematic. If it is true, as Richard Dyer says, that Fred Astaire's Bojangles number "cannot help but be disturbing (even if it is far from the grotesqueries of minstrelsy)," what can we say about Bing Crosby and Marjorie Reynolds' performance in *Holiday Inn*— to say nothing of the scenes involving Louise Beavers? In 1942, *Variety* had plenty to say, and most of it was highly complimentary. In fact, the *Variety* reviewer singles out this number for particular praise: "With Louise Beavers as his housekeeper and her two cullud [sic!] kids, Shelby Bacon and Joan Arnold, for comedy assists, the Abraham Lincoln motif keys a corking 'Abraham' spiritual which Crosby croons to wow effect" (June 17, 1942). Probably most readers today would be astonished by this reviewer's response, as they would be astonished by producer Harry Maddox's judgment that the minstrel show in *Babes in Arms* was "as fresh and sparkling as anything that's ever hit Broadway" or by the suggestion that building a theatrical tunnel of long legs leading toward Fred Astaire in blackface might function as an homage to Bill Robinson.[15] The cinematic world in which all of these events occurred was, however, the same cultural environment in which the ultimate radio minstrel show, *Amos 'n' Andy*, was variously attacked as a stereotypical degradation of African American culture and defended as the only venue in which the virtuous activities of a struggling black family man like Amos might be represented to a mass audience.[16] Perhaps in keeping with such cultural ambivalence, minstrel scenes in these films fulfill widely different functions. At least in *Holiday Inn*, there is the flimsy narrative justification of disguise for donning minstrel makeup. Jim even proposes donning cork for Valentine's Day in hopes of fooling Ted! In *Swing Time*, *Babes in Arms* and *Babes on Broadway*, on the other hand, the blackface numbers could just as easily have been replaced with performances keyed to the stars' stage personae. Jerome Kern and Dorothy Fields produced "The Way You Look Tonight" and "A Fine Romance" for *Swing Time*. Surely they could have written something other than "Bojangles of Harlem," just as the many composers who contributed songs like "Where or When," "Broadway Rhythm" and "I Cried for You" to *Babes in Arms* could have been exploited for something more appropriate than the minstrel number. Ralph Reed and Burton Lane contributed "How About You?" to *Babes on Broadway*. So, a lack of suitable songs is not the problem. Then, what is it?

Clearly, some element of racism must be acknowledged to be at work here. This is, after all, Spike Lee's point in *Bamboozled*. Even without Lee's prodding, however, most viewers today — black and white — must be made slightly uncomfortable by Louise Beavers' performance in *Holiday Inn* and by the delight with which the various babes in arms fasten upon a minstrel show as the solution to all their theatrical problems.[17] In *Redefining Black Film*, Mark A. Reid observes that "[e]ven the denotation of 'blackface' emphasizes the importance of race in the construction of this comic form" (19). In consequence, as he goes on to argue from a Freudian perspective: "The constructive properties of blackface minstrelsy include an addresser, an imaginary 'black' object of ridicule, and an interested spectator. These three properties make blackface minstrelsy similar in textual construction to the tendentious joke. Both forms require an addresser, an object of ridicule, and a viewer-listener. In a tendentious joke, the ridiculed object has a similar function as African-Americans in blackface humor and women in pornography, since blacks and women are objectified for the pleasure of whites in one instance and men in the other instance" (20). So, there is definitely a sense in which the white singers and dancers performing minstrelsy in the films under consideration are addressing white viewers over the heads of the stereotyped characters they are portraying and over the heads of actual African Americans to whom these stereotypes may refer. But, as Reid also argues, "[R]eception is not constructed so simply. Audiences have the ability to overlook the obvious racism and seize the humane properties of the overtly racist discourse" (21). In the case of blackface minstrelsy, white cinema audiences of the 1930s and '40s surely were appropriating this "overtly racist discourse" through some sort of nostalgia, another thematic element of the Hollywood musical.[18]

This is Jane Feuer's point when she writes about minstrel shows' "evok[ing] an ... earlier and folksier entertainment era" (95). In *Babes on Broadway*, for example, the nostalgic appeal of "something old, something tried and true" (minstrelsy) is reinforced by the production number "Hoedown," which is introduced by asserting that if it was good enough for Grandma and Grandpa, it's good enough for Tommy. Another nostalgic note is struck in this film by the extended sequence in which Tommy and Penny visit an old theater and impersonate famous actors from the past. These famous actors—Richard Mansfield (b. 1857) in *Cyrano de Bergerac*, Fay Templeton (b. 1865) in *Forty-Five Minutes to Broadway*, Harry Lauder (b. 1870) singing "Daisy," Blanche Ring (b. 1877) singing "Rings on My Fingers," Sarah Bernhardt (b. 1844) performing as Joan of Arc—all serve to distance the diegetic narrative from the contemporary environment marked by the end of the Depression and the coming of World War II. In *Babes in Arms*, the audience is also led into nostalgic affirmation by a trip down Memory Lane with an old-fashioned minstrel show. The "Abraham" number in *Holiday Inn* needs no sentimental narrative bridge to contextualize it as part of the past, but this absence of narrative continuity should probably come as no surprise because, as Arthur Knight explains, "[B]lackface is most frequently left out of the narrative chain of cause and effect" (52). Instead, temporal dislocation is established merely through the costumes and minstrel makeup on Jim and Linda. Thus, although the diegetic narrative of *Holiday Inn* is firmly rooted in the present, this minstrel number can be seen as an appeal to an earlier, supposedly "simpler" and more "innocent" period of American entertainment history. Fred Astaire's testimonial to Bill Robinson in *Swing Time* similarly evokes the past simply through Fred's wearing of blackface, something that major white entertainers were not usually doing in 1936. Why this form of racial recidivism should appeal to white audiences in 1936 or at any time on up through 1942 is, of course, another matter.

One likely answer is simple escapism, an always promising explanation for popular cultural successes. As John Cawelti explains in *Adventure, Mystery, and Romance*, most of us "seek escape from our consciousness of the ultimate insecurities and ambiguities that afflict even the most secure sort of life: death, the failure of love, our inability to accomplish all we had hoped for..." (16). In keeping with Cawelti's analysis, we might note that between 1936 and 1942 the highly popular film version (1937) of James Hilton's best-selling novel *Lost Horizon* (1933) appeared, with Ronald Colman in the starring role. Surely, American audiences beset by economic Depression at home and ominous rumblings of war abroad might be forgiven for dreaming of a romantic Shangri-La in which no one was hungry or frightened and everyone who deserved to be happy was. This happy escapism was the key also to the series of Andy Hardy films which began during this same era and extended through 15 slight variations. The Carvel in which the Hardys lived was obviously designed by Louis B. Mayer to offer an affirmative alternative to the social and political disruptions of real-life America, and perhaps for this reason the series received a special Oscar in 1942 for "furthering the American way of life." Partway through the Hardy series, another escapist fantasy appealed to hard-pressed Americans when *The Wizard of Oz* appeared in 1939.

These suggestions about the nostalgic appeal of cinematic minstrelsy are born out by two other films produced slightly later in the 1940s, the highly fictionalized biopics *Dixie* (1943) starring Bing Crosby and *The Jolson Story* (1946) starring Larry Parks. Michael Rogin explains that "[m]ost musicals using blackface in the 1930s and 1940s fall into two subcategories, both derived from *The Jazz Singer*: they are either backstage musicals about putting on a show or biographies of the central figures in the history of American popular music" (167). *Babes in Arms*, *Babes on Broadway* and *Holiday Inn* obviously belong to Rogin's first group. Just as obviously, *Dixie* and *the Jolson Story* fall into the latter category. In *Dixie*, Bing Crosby takes on the role of Daniel Decatur Emmett (1815–1904), the noted minstrel who composed the famous title tune and Southern battle cry, and *The Jolson Story* purports, as the title indicates, to represent the life of the legendary entertainer (1886–1950) who starred in the first significant talking picture, *The Jazz Singer*, and who is remembered as well for his legendary blackface performances.[19] Both of these men, then, had much to do with the popularity of blackface minstrelsy on stage — and in the Hollywood musical.

Peter Gammond has written in *The Oxford Companion to Popular Music*, "It is impossible to overrate Bing Crosby's influence" (139). If anyone might suspect that Gammond might be overstating the case, Gary Giddins' recent best-selling biography of the crooner should resolve any debate about Crosby's importance as a recording giant, radio personality and movie star. In Giddins' words: "Harry Lillis Crosby was the most influential and successful popular performer in the first half of the twentieth century" (4). It is probable, therefore, that Crosby's appearances in musical films featuring minstrel performances—such as *Holiday Inn* and *Dixie*— might be a reliable measurement of how Hollywood developed these popular racial images during the period of Bing's cinematic ascendancy. In and out of blackface in *Dixie*, Bing sings, acts, and — in company with Billy De Wolfe —clowns his way to a happy movie ending, once again in the arms of Marjorie Reynolds. As in the films discussed earlier, everyone who deserves to be happy ends up in *Dixie* with more or less what he or she desires, despite any temporary inconveniences or minor setbacks. Economic

Depression, racial discrimination, World War II — the more disturbing elements of the outer, off-screen world — do not trouble Bing Crosby and the other (white) inhabitants of this cinematic blackface culture.

In addition to its claims of biographical validity, *Dixie* is undeniably a narrative romance and a Hollywood musical. As biography, the film has been justifiably indicted as inaccurate. Emmett was actually a native of Mount Vernon, Ohio, and he first successfully performed "Dixie" at the Bowery Amphitheater in New York City on February 6, 1843.[20] For reasons of narrative effect, most of these facts were changed in *Dixie*. As Michael Rogin points out, for example, "To hide minstrelsy's roots in northern, proslavery idealizations of the South, which it was repeating, Paramount moved Dan Emmett from New York to New Orleans for *Dixie*" (179). Furthermore, the plot provides Emmett's character with a behavioral forgetfulness about laying down his still-smoking pipes in order to set up the finale in which his debut performance of the tune "Dixie" in New Orleans must be speeded up to its current lively tempo because his discarded pipe has set the backstage on fire. To develop this narrative thread, Emmett accidentally burns down the family home of his fiancée Jean Mason, played by Marjorie Reynolds, early in the film; later on, Millie Cook, played by Dorothy Lamour, barely avoids another disastrous fire when she snatches up Emmett's smoldering pipe in the theatrical boarding house that she runs with her father in New Orleans. Not too long after this, Emmett's discarded pipe destroys the theater in which his new minstrel act is on its way to becoming a phenomenal success. As so often is the case in musical biopics, the available historical facts are subsumed by the narrative exigencies of the genre.

The biographical shades into the romantic when we notice that — as in *Mississippi* (1935) — Crosby's character is embroiled in the conflict between the dark (Millie Cook) and light (Marjorie Reynolds) maidens much discussed by critics of nineteenth-century American literary romance.[21] The conventional triumph of the light over the dark maiden is further complicated in this case by the fact that Jean Mason has been stricken with what her father calls "the paralyzing sickness," so that Bing's choice of the light maiden results from honor as well as from literary precedent.[22] In fact, everyone involved in the romantic triangle is noble. Emmett marries Jean despite his established — and perfectly understandable — preference for Millie because he feels that doing otherwise would break Jean's heart now that she is crippled. Jean is initially ready to give Dan Emmett up because she doesn't want to saddle him with a wife who can't walk, and later, after their marriage and move to New York, she encourages a return to New Orleans even though she understands that Millie is there. Millie is furious with Dan for breaking their engagement until she realizes that Jean is crippled, and then the two women become best friends, nobly committed to each other's happiness. Since Dan has already won Jean's heart when the film opens, all these complications are required to keep the plot running long enough to absorb all the musical numbers.

These are of a fairly high order and are mostly written by James Van Heusen and Johnny Burke. The film opens with Emmett singing the Burke–Van Heusen ballad "Sunday, Monday, or Always" to Jean Mason. Soon, after accidentally burning down the Masons' house, Emmett joins the black deckhands on a riverboat in the traditional spiritual "Swing Low, Sweet Chariot." As soon as Emmett joins in, everyone else recedes into the chorus. In Arthur Knight's acerbic account: "The laborers, awestruck, stop singing and look around for this unfamiliar voice; they all end up looking heavenward since, as it turns out, Crosby stands on a deck high above them. Once they have found him, the laborers resume singing — now as an earthly choir in support of their godlike soloist" (87). Most of the rest of the songs, original and traditional,[23] are performed in blackface to illustrate Emmett's progress in his minstrel career. Emmett/Crosby croons "The Last Rose of Summer," "She's from Missouri," "A Horse That Knows His Way Back Home," a reprise of "Sunday, Monday, or Always" and "Dixie" in blackface makeup on the minstrel stage. Out of blackface, he sings "If You Please" to his wife Jean during their sojourn in New York. In addition, there are minstrel production numbers of various sizes involving groups ranging from Emmett's initial troupe of four (Crosby, Billy De Wolfe, Lynne Overman and Eddie Foy, Jr.) to 40 (the Virginia Minstrels). As this list of musical performances suggests, race plays an important part in *Dixie* no matter where we plug into the inquiry.

Race is a problematic issue in *Dixie* since Emmett is a minstrel man as well as a white man. Atmospheric black characters abound in the film: as deckhands aboard the riverboat, for example, and as ushers in New Orleans theaters—although not as pedestrians on New Orleans streets. In the uncredited role of Lucius the servant, George Reed gets to push Marjorie Reynolds around in a wheelchair; in the also uncredited role of a steward aboard the steamboat, Willie Best[24] gets to show Dan Emmett how Mr. Bones (De Wolfe) has cheated him at cards. All of these atmospheric roles fulfill Thomas Cripps' claim in *Making Movies Black* that whenever African American characters appeared at all in Hollywood films of that day, they usually functioned as "conservative memory banks of painless nostalgia" (4). The black servants in *Gone with the Wind* (1939) immediately spring to mind as further corroboration of Cripps' point, as does Louise Beavers' Mamie.

But, of course, the most striking manifestation of racial presence in *Dixie* has to be the minstrel performances of Bing Crosby and the other important white actors. Significantly, both Marjorie Reynolds and Bing Crosby had appeared in blackface during the previous year in *Holiday Inn* when the plot required a disguise to keep Fred Astaire from recognizing Reynolds. In *Dixie*, the plot agent is a fistfight with restaurant employees that leaves Emmett and Mr. Bones with black eyes. Millie Cook saves the day when she says, in Dorothy Lamour's best Southern accent, "What're you gonna do about those black eyes? Makeup won't cover those.... I know what you can do. You can't change the color of your eyes, but you can make your faces up to match them. Go as darkies!" The rest, as they say, is history. Abetted by Lynne Overman and Eddie Foy, Jr., Crosby and De Wolfe form the original minstrel act, and go over like a house afire, perhaps because, as a member of the first-night audience points out, "They aren't darkies. They're white men blacked up." This racial discrepancy is apparent from the outset. During the performance in which the four minstrels first stumble upon their winning formula, their makeup, in addition to burnt-cork skin, features enormous mouths and three-pointed fright wigs. (In fact, a photo of Bing Crosby in this outfit accompanied the *New York Times* review of the film.)[25] As the troupe becomes even more successful, their stage set at the Maxwell

Theater features a huge Sambo backdrop through whose grinning mouth the minstrels cakewalk onto the stage.[26]

Minstrelsy combines with the syntax of the Hollywood musical at the close of the film when Emmett's rousing rendition of "Dixie" brings the whole audience together. Until this point, the formally dressed members of the audience at the New Orleans Opera House have — perhaps correctly — considered the antics of the Virginia Minstrels boorish and in "bad taste." Emmett's up-tempo version of "Dixie" begins to break the ice and to build toward the unified celebration that we have come to expect at the conclusion of a Hollywood musical. Before this point is reached, Emmett is forced to whip up enthusiasm by asking the audience, "What's wrong with you out there? This is Dixie...." Rebel yells, group singing and dancing in the aisles follow. Millie and Jean embrace each other. The whole Virginia Minstrels chorus joins in while cakewalking in line behind Emmett. Even the (exclusively white) stagehands sing along backstage. Group unity is achieved in the film's finale, as it is in the concluding number of *Babes in Arms*, by asserting a common (white) experience of entertainment.[27] The title card at the beginning of the film claims that *Dixie* is the story of Dan Emmett, "who donned burnt cork and sang his way into the heart of a nation with his immortal song 'Dixie.'" This closing sequence demonstrates just what the card claims— at least as far as white audiences are concerned.

The shared experience of entertainment is also at the heart of *The Jolson Story*. Although there is no title card at the beginning of the film to establish Jolson's importance to the development of American popular entertainment — perhaps none was required in 1946 — it is clear that the film's purpose is to explain how Jolson's eminence was achieved, providing familiar musical moments along the way. Clive Hirschhorn is only one of many to question the biographical accuracy of the film. In Hirschhorn's words, "Of course, it wasn't like that in real life" (274). Doug McClelland explains why this was so in his book *Blackface to Blacklist*: "The authors of the screenplay were encouraged to make the story work first, then (if at all) worry about whether the material was totally factual" (45–46). Even so, McClelland quotes a contemporaneous *Look* review that calls *The Jolson Story* "backstage biography at its best" and continues, "Its semi-fictional account of the singer's life and loves varies little from a familiar film pattern, but the expert treatment keeps it fresh and exciting..." (94). This "familiar pattern" is evident in the early part of Jolson's life (when Al was still Asa Yoelson), for example, where his life story is borrowed from *The Jazz Singer* in the sense that Asa would rather sing popular songs in the theater than perform in his father's synagogue choir. This alteration is probably forgivable since a young boy's rebellion against his father's more traditional form of music is a staple narrative element of the genre[28] and since the generational contrast also provides an opportunity to demonstrate throughout the film the ease with which non–native-born Americans like Jolson's parents (Ludwig Donath and Tamara Shayne) can be incorporated into the greater body of the American mass audience.[29] Whether Jolson's musical comedy star wife should be Julie Benson (Evelyn Keyes), as in this film, or Ruby Keeler, as in Jolson's life, is perhaps less easily settled. Since most critics note Keeler's opposition to her actual depiction in the film,[30] Julie Benson is probably the best that we can expect. It is likely in any case that Benson is more generous and understanding toward her success-driven husband than any actual wife—Keeler or otherwise—could manage to be.[31] Whatever the biographical and narrative questions, the real justification for the film has to be Jolson's signature tunes, performed in and out of blackface.

During the early sequences, the young Jolson (Scotty Beckett) sings familiar old songs—"On the Banks of the Wabash," "By the Light of the Silvery Moon"—from the audience as part of Steve Martin's (William Demarest) burlesque act, wearing appropriate dress for a young boy of the day and without blackface makeup. After Beckett turns into Larry Parks, the young Jolson continues to sing and whistle songs from the audience in the same way until one night in Louisville, Kentucky, when blackface singer Tom Baron (Bill Goodwin) is too drunk to go on, and Jolson dons cork makeup to sing and dance "Ma Blushin' Rosie" in Baron's place. This substitution is effective dramatically because young Al has been trying for some time to move Martin's act in a more spontaneous, emotional direction. His performance as Tom Baron apparently fulfills these artistic goals temporarily because Lew Dockstader (John Alexander), who is in the audience because of the Kentucky Derby, invites Jolson to join Dockstader's Minstrels. In the Dockstader show, Jolson is forced to perform "I Want a Girl Just Like the Girl That Married Dear Old Dad" in blackface for over a year—as part of a chorus, in a quartet, and then in a duet. This enforced continuity is fine with Dockstader, who tells the impatient Jolson, "It's a matter of tradition.... Minstrels have been doing fine for 50 years, and we take pride in doing it like it's always been done."[32] Jolson is dissatisfied nevertheless until he stumbles upon a Dixieland band performing in New Orleans and recognizes the music that he has been searching for all along.[33] While lost in this soulful music, Jolson forgets about a performance of the Dockstader Minstrels, just as he forgot about singing in the synagogue choir earlier in the film. In the earlier case, everything worked out for the best, and we may assume that the same will be true again.

When Dockstader fires Jolson in the subsequent sequence, the fundamental nature of blackface performance is highlighted. Jolson is in his street clothes and without makeup; Dockstader is in blackface and dressed in an absurd minstrel costume. The fact—frequently observed in this chapter—that cinematic blackface is all on the white surface is nowhere more patently demonstrated. When the two characters shake hands at parting, it might be assumed that Jolson is moving past blackface toward a more authentic form of expression. This turns out not to be the case, however. Almost at once, through the efforts of Tom Baron and Steve Martin, Jolson gets a chance to play the Winter Garden Theatre in New York. A false crisis arises when the Winter Garden Show, *Vera Violetta*, seems to be running long, and Jolson's number is about to be cut. Instead, Jolson defies the director and the stage manager, shoves his blacked-up face through the closed curtains and tells the audience, "You ain't heard nothin' yet." The version of "My Mammy" that follows is almost entirely presentational, composed of closeups of Larry Parks's corked-up face except for some brief shots of Steve Martin beaming in the audience. Since Jolson dubbed the singing in this number, and in most of the others, viewers can experience the full–Jolson, an example of what Hirschhorn calls "an unashamedly entertaining wallow" (274). Like most viewers, the first-night audience is totally won over,

2. Blackface Minstrelsy in Musicals 49

and so the newspaper headline the next day says, "Al Jolson, Mammy Singer, Surprise Smash."

In narrative terms, the film might end here, but there are a lot of famous songs still to be sung by Jolson and lip-synched by Larry Parks. In the immediately following montage of numbers, Jolson performs "I'm Sitting on Top of the World," "You Made Me Love You" and "Swanee" in blackface. "The Spaniard Who Blighted My Life" shows us Parks in appropriate costume for *The Honeymoon Express* but without blackface makeup, and this continues to be the pattern for the rest of the film. Jolson's Sunday evening concerts are performed without blackface, and it is diegetically appropriate that he sing "Lisa" as himself on Julie Benson's opening night in *Show Girl*. While we hear "There's a Rainbow Round My Shoulder" on the soundtrack when the Jolsons go to the opening night of *The Jazz Singer*, we do not see the film, and so no one is wearing blackface. Jolson sings "The Anniversary Song" privately to his parents, and so everyone is white, as usual. This is also the case when the anniversary party moves to a Hollywood nightclub and Jolson is coaxed up on stage to sing "Waiting for the Robert E. Lee," "Rock-A-Bye Your Baby with a Dixie Melody" and "April Showers." In other words, once Jolson has been established as a blackface success, he no longer needs to perform in blackface. Nick Tosches claims biographical accuracy for this development: "As Jolson the stylist overtook the song, he was beheld no longer as merely a minstrel or a blackface showman, but as an embodiment of the age, a jazz singer" (189).

Aside from the biographical dimensions of Jolson's own reliance on minstrelsy, it might be assumed that the decline of blackface performances as the film progresses was owing to Larry Parks's liberal political discomfort at performing in blackface.[34] Clearly, Parks' political career must be linked to his career in films, as the title of Doug McClelland's study establishes: *Blackface to Blacklist: Al Jolson, Larry Parks, and "The Jolson Story."* As McClelland writes about Parks, "He ... had joined [the Communist Party] because it was the 'most liberal' of the political parties but had left because of 'lack of interest — of not finding things I thought I would'" (119). Larry Caplair and Steven Englund provide a similar account in *The Inquisition in Hollywood: Politics in the Film Community 1930–1960* when they write about those Hollywood figures required to testify, as Parks was, in the "second round" of HUAC hearings in 1951: "Whatever the American Party had since become in their eyes, or whatever crimes and errors they now believed the Soviet Union had committed in the name of communism, these former Reds asserted over and over that *their* personal reasons for remaining Communists were idealistic, not revolutionary or subversive — i.e., as Communists they wished to fight injustice and social evil and help to bring about a better world" (37). In a *Newsweek* account of Parks's HUAC testimony (April 2, 1951), it emerges that Parks joined the Party in 1941 but had severed his affiliation by 1945 — before his appearance in *The Jolson Story*. No matter what his convictions were at the time of filming, it is certain that Parks' Party membership led to his blacklisting (and that of his wife, Betty Garrett) and the end of his motion picture career.[35] It is also clear that, whatever his political convictions, Parks threw himself into the Jolson role with great enthusiasm. Thus, we may be hearing Jolson singing on the soundtrack, but it is Larry Parks mugging in blackface for the camera. In some respects, then, we would seem to be left with as many questions after all this discussion as before it.

The briar patch created by minstrel numbers performed by white actors in Hollywood musicals ensnares even those professionally committed to honoring the memories of these white performers. Gary Giddins, for example, goes to some lengths to deflect charges of racism from his subject in *Bing Crosby: A Pocket Full of Dreams, The Early Years, 1903–1940*, as when he argues that Crosby "encouraged and pioneered racial integration on stage, radio, and records and in movies; in 1936, after winning the contractual right to produce his own pictures, he hired Louis Armstrong and gave him star billing, a Hollywood first for a black entertainer" (10). Despite these exemplary later actions, Giddins is forced to admit Crosby's involvement in earlier minstrel performances, as in this account of his appearance in a college production: "Though it surely stretched Gonzaga's notion of credible theater, Bing, Corkery, and a few friends offered a minstrel burlesque of Shakespeare, depicting Caesar as a 'dark-skinned bone artist'" (66–67). That this was not Bing's only appearance in blackface—aside from *Dixie* and *Holiday Inn*—emerges when Giddins writes, "Shortly before the semester ended, he again appeared in blackface, for Gonzaga University Glee Club's minstrel show *A Study in Tone and Color*" (77). To put these performances in the context of Crosby's long career, Giddins explains, "Whatever appeal blackface had for the other end men (among them Leo Lynn), for Bing it represented a bond with the mighty Al Jolson, whose talents he broadly emulated" (77). As we might imagine, then, explaining Jolson's blackface career to contemporary readers is an even more difficult undertaking. Doug McClelland, for example, first essays the position that there is really nothing to apologize about. As he says mockingly about critics of *The Jolson Story*, "The blackface portions have clearly offended some raised consciousnesses..." (vii). Eventually, though, McClelland must admit that the film poses some problems for its defenders: "Even some of the film's publicity, which would be considered insensitive if not downright racist today, was naïve" (259). The problem—for McClelland, and Giddins, and others writing about these performers—is that "raised consciousnesses" are found just about everywhere these days.

For example, McClelland quotes this extended passage from a *Portland Oregonian* account of negative local responses to the 1968 re-release of *The Jolson Story*: "*The Al Jolson Story* [sic] today is an anachronism, a rather mediocre film biography of one who was a great entertainer in an era now irrevocably past. We cannot unwrite history, so there is no point in pretending it didn't happen: not so many decades ago singers and actors did blacken their faces and audiences were amused by it. But the reaction to the re-run of *The Al Jolson Story* is proof enough that it can't happen in America any more. The owners of the film may as well put it back in the vault to stay" (257). The passage seems noteworthy to me because it takes account of the audience's involvement in both the earlier popularity and the later reprehension of blackface minstrelsy in Hollywood musicals. Arthur Knight writes about these evolving attitudes from the perspective of the black American film audience: "The last blackface Hollywood films were made in 1953. In combination with mass mediation, however, blackface had done its critical work for African Americans, who had forsaken blackface as a black performance tradition and who, at least judging from the printed record, had lost interest in Jolson and white blackface in general" (91). The passage that McClelland quotes from *The Portland Oregonian* is evidence — even if we discount our own discomfort when we view the "Abraham" or "Bojangles of Harlem" numbers — that this lack of interest is very widely dispersed in the culture. Thus, although we cannot "un-write history," we can confidently assume that history will not repeat itself.

Before we congratulate ourselves too enthusiastically, however, we might consider Constance Rourke's remark in *American Humor: A Study of the National Character*: "The appeal of minstrelsy was insistent and enduring..." (103). Larry Parks' performance in *The Jolson Story* might be seen to illustrate Rourke's claim, as might Mark Twain's testimony in his *Autobiography*: "But if I could have the nigger show back again in its pristine purity and perfection I should have but little further use for opera. It seems to me that to the elevated mind and the sensitive spirit the hand organ and nigger show are a standard and a summit to whose rarified altitude the other forms of musical art may not hope to reach" (59). If we need further support for this claim of the historic (white) fondness for minstrelsy, we might consult Nick Tosches' report that — in addition to Fred Astaire, Mickey Rooney, Judy Garland, Bing Crosby, Marjorie Reynolds, Al Jolson and Larry Parks — Jimmie Rodgers, Bob Wills and Gene Autry all performed in blackface (66–67, 168). That this should not have been so is a conclusion that might make sense to just about anybody. That it distinctly was so is a conclusion equally clear. While we might wish that Fred and Bing and Judy and Mickey and Larry Parks had not appeared in blackface on screen, the facts are that they did so, that a mass audience of largely white film viewers found these performances acceptable — even if questionable for reasons of social justice or just plain good manners — and that all of this is a part of the story of the Hollywood musical.

3

Confronting Rock Culture

According to John Cawelti in *Adventure, Mystery, and Romance*, the popular cultural phenomena that he calls "formula stories" "resolve tensions and ambiguities resulting from the conflicting interests of different groups within the culture or from ambiguous attitudes toward particular values" (35). Admittedly, this may seem to be a grand claim, and yet Cawelti is convinced that cultural dilemmas are often figured forth more effectively in such popular forms than in more sophisticated hieratic forms. In light of these premises, we can see that the Hollywood musical has often attempted to resolve critical issues resulting from pressing social problems. *Golddiggers of 1933* (1933) and *Stand Up and Cheer* (1934), for example, took on the American Depression of the 1930s. Later on, *South Pacific* (1958) addressed racial prejudice—through the mitigating filter of Polynesia—and *West Side Story* (1961) did the same for Anglos and Puerto Ricans, with juvenile delinquency and gang violence thrown in for lagniappe. It is only to be expected, then, that adults disturbed by the coming of rock and roll culture in the 1950s would look to the Hollywood musical for explanations and solutions. Ed Ward describes this parental concern in *Rock of Ages: The* Rolling Stone *History of Rock & Roll* when he recalls "public fears of 'juvenile delinquency' the disease that had teens committing senseless crimes, indulging in alcohol and cigarettes and premarital sex, riding motorcycles or driving hopped-up cars, and listening to rock and roll" (106). Most readers of a certain age can illustrate these parental fears with memories of newsreel footage showing preachers burning rock and roll records or film images of raucous rock-and-roll-listening students terrorizing their teacher in *Blackboard Jungle* (1955).

The likelihood that the Hollywood musical would somehow have to confront rock and roll is increased by the fact that this same rock and roll culture threatened the existence of the very genre itself. As we have seen in the introductory chapter, James T. Maher explains in his introduction to Alec Wilder's *American Popular Song* that the beginning of "the rock era" in the years following World War II can be understood as signaling the end not only of the kind of well-crafted Rodgers & Hart or Cole Porter songs that interested Wilder, but also of the entertainment genres that showcased such songs—specifically big dance bands and musicals of the stage and screen varieties. As we have also seen there, John Mueller substantially agrees with Maher:

By the mid 1950s the era of the classic Hollywood musical as Astaire had experienced it — indeed, defined it — was coming to an end. Revenues were declining, costs were rising, the studio system was falling apart, competition with television was growing, popular music was moving into the age of rock and roll. Astaire and other products of the classic Hollywood musical, such as Freed and Kelly, were out of business as Hollywood created fewer and fewer musical films, typically extravagant transmutations of Broadway musicals, perfunctory song-and-story vehicles for Elvis Presley, or well-scrubbed beach-and-bunny capers aimed at the adolescent crowd [12–13].

Or, as Denny Martin Flinn states the problem somewhat more sympathetically: "[P]opular American music would henceforth be divided into Before and After Chuck Berry. This pulled a once-substantial commercial rug out from under Broadway musicals" (315). It was therefore incumbent on the Hollywood musical to find ways to make rock and roll seem less threatening to those worried both about their children and about the future of this film genre, to finesse the challenge posed by rock culture as other musicals had finessed racism and economic hardship.

Just how much of a problem rock culture posed is apparent if we consider a musical film about young people made not long before the advent of rock and roll, *Girl Crazy* (1943), directed by Norman Taurog. Based on the 1930 Broadway musical with songs by George and Ira Gershwin, *Girl Crazy* is focused on Danny Churchill, Jr. (Mickey Rooney), a young man afflicted with the mania denoted by the title. A youth-oriented rock musical — perhaps an Elvis Presley vehicle — could easily share the title *Girl Crazy*, and some elements of the 1943 film point to the college-age status of the central couple. Danny uses slang expressions like *snerpy*, *dilljo* and *loogan*, for example; his love interest Ginger (Judy Garland) often wears slacks instead of demure dresses. However, this film usually represents young people as apprentice adults, folks with tastes and modes of behavior not very different from those of their elders. Since *Girl Crazy* is a romantic comedy, we cannot be surprised that Danny and Ginger eventually end up together in what promises to be a happily-ever-after future of the sort endorsed by their elders. Coming from the perspective of today's America, however, we might be surprised to see this couple and their peers dressing like their elders and sharing their elders' musical tastes.

The film opens with Danny riding in the back seat of an open convertible driven by two very stylish young women. Despite his age and educational situation as a Yale student, Danny is wearing top hat, white tie and tails, and the young women are wearing fur. When Danny is taken out of Yale by his father shortly afterwards and sent "out West" to Cody College of Mines and Agriculture, he arrives in Codyville wearing a suit, tie and hat. Nothing so clearly illustrates Denny Martin Flinn's distinction between "Before and After Chuck Berry" (315) as Danny's sartorial contrast to the way Bobby Rydell or Frankie Avalon will soon dress on screen. Danny's hat later becomes a plot agent when Ginger throws it out of her old jalopy in order to instigate the duet "Could You Use Me?" When Ginger has a birthday party, the all-male student body of Cody turns out dressed in either white dinner jackets with dark trousers or dark jackets with white pants. No one in the whole college is coatless or tieless despite the school's location in the desert. Later on, at a dance to crown the rodeo queen, the whole student body is rigged out in white dinner jackets. They may be college men, but they dress like members of the country club where Fred and Ginger dance in *Carefree*.

Costumes for female performers are equally adult. After some early scenes in which she wears stylish trousers, Ginger is usually attired in an evening dress, since there always seems to be some sort of formal affair going on in this film. When her friend Polly Williams (Nancy Walker) shows up at Cody, Polly is wearing a tailored suit and hat. Ginger wears a similar outfit when she goes with Danny to beg the Governor (Howard Freeman) to spare Cody from a political order to shut down. Danny is wearing a pin-striped suit for this interview, a garment that we would never expect to see on *American Bandstand* or *Grease*. Danny also sports a white pocket handkerchief and has a billfold full of business cards in his inside pocket, along with a fountain pen. The importance of this grown-up suit is underscored when Danny demurs about attending a party for the Governor's daughter since he has nothing to wear but "this pin-striped suit." The Governor tells Danny that his suit will do just fine, and so Danny gets to meet several college-age women in evening gowns at this elegant party, one of whom (Frances Rafferty) will provide a temporary threat to the Danny-Ginger romance.

Also at this dance — and at the nightclub in the opening sequence — are Tommy Dorsey and his orchestra. At the Governor's party, Dorsey and company play their own special arrangement of George Gershwin's "Fascinating Rhythm," complete with musical references to "Rhapsody in Blue." Despite the high tone affected in this musical performance, everyone at the party, young and old, is enchanted, especially when Danny sits in on piano.[1] In the opening sequence the orchestra plays "Treat Me Rough," a solo for June Allyson, and Danny once again joins in. Being "girl crazy" apparently also means being crazy about "a Gershwin tune." In the grandiose finale of the film, directed by Busby Berkeley, the Dorsey band resurfaces in cowboy outfits to play "I Got Rhythm." Everybody in the band looks pretty silly dressed this way, but Tommy Dorsey is probably the most unlikely cowboy, perhaps because of his glasses. Nevertheless, everyone in the huge crowd, irrespective of age, is once more delighted by the band's music, and Cody College is saved.

In less obvious ways, too, the young people in this film act like older people. Thus, no one is likely to ask, "What's the matter with kids today?" about these young Americans. For example, Danny is the only one to question why students have to rise at 5:45 A.M. at Cody. Obviously, all the other young men assume that rules are made to be obeyed, not questioned. Even Danny recognizes the force of authority, though, when he and Ginger finally get in to see the Governor. After pretending that one of Danny's business cards is really his father's, Danny is tongue-tied in the Governor's presence, all brashness silenced by the majesty of political office. One can hardly imagine James Dean or the young Marlon Brando being similarly intimidated by authority. While waiting to deceive the Governor through the business card ruse, Danny entertains Ginger with some impressions: of the announcer at a tennis match, of Clem McCarthy, and of Joe Louis. These are references spread across the culture, directed to viewers of all ages; there is nothing particularly youthful about them. The same might be said of Ginger's other suitor, Henry Lathrop (Robert E. Strickland).

For reasons of plot development, Henry must come across as less attractive than Danny, but this plot contingency is handled by making Henry hopelessly stodgy, like the doomed rivals of Henry Fonda and Cary Grant. There are all sorts of ways to make a young male suitor unattractive. To make him act like an old fogy is an odd choice, however — although perhaps not so odd, given the more mature inflection of this film.

In *Girl Crazy*, as in countless other films starring Mickey Rooney and Judy Garland, these lovable youngsters triumph in the end. Their youth is probably responsible for their enthusiasm, and–given our national preoccupation with aging — their youth is probably what makes them acceptable — then and now — as lovers. Even so, Mickey and Judy are not teenagers as we later have come to understand the term, nor are they college students of the sort we might expect to see frolicking on the beach at spring break. In the "Before Chuck Berry" era, the "problem" resulting from some people just being young is less troubling to makers and viewers of musical films. Rock and roll makes all the difference, even though some film makers try to act as if this is not so.

Bye Bye Birdie (1963), directed by George Sidney, is just one film that tries to dodge these issues, as a brief summary should make clear. Like most musicals, *Bye Bye Birdie*, based on the 1960 Broadway musical of the same title, focuses on romance. The primary romance involves aspiring songwriter Albert Peterson, played by Dick Van Dyke, and his secretary Rosie DeLeon, played by Janet Leigh. The supporting romantic couple are two high school kids, Kim McAfee and Hugo Peabody, played by Ann-Margret and Bobby Rydell. The film's title and plot are generated by an Elvis Presley figure named Conrad Birdie, played by Jesse Pearson. Birdie is scheduled to sing one song (written by Albert) and kiss one faithful fan (Kim) during his last appearance on *The Ed Sullivan Show* prior to being drafted into the army, as Elvis was drafted in 1958. After suitable confusion, comedy, singing and dancing, Birdie goes off to the Army and the couples end up happily together.

It is significant, first of all, that the central characters in *Bye Bye Birdie* are adults. The male love interest, Albert Peterson, has been struggling for years to write a successful song, and he is equipped by his college education to be a biochemist. Moreover, the actor who plays Albert, Dick Van Dyke, had not only already enjoyed a successful run on Broadway in *Bye Bye Birdie* but was starring at the time in his own highly rated TV sitcom (1961–66). By the same token, Rosie DeLeon has been out on her own long enough to be worried about becoming an old maid, and Janet Leigh had recently enjoyed success in *Psycho* (1960) and *The Manchurian Candidate* (1962). Moreover, Kim's father, Harry, played by the incomparable Paul Lynde, gets to solo on two highly effective songs, "Kids" and "Hymn for a Sunday Evening." Ann-Margret and Bobby Rydell are certainly attractive eye candy, but in 1963 they must take a back seat to the grownups both in terms of the plot and in actual screen time. So, although one can legitimately call *Bye Bye Birdie* a Hollywood musical about rock and roll, its narrative is definitely skewed toward a mature audience.

Costuming establishes the same generational values. The 21-year-old Ann-Margret is a sexy knockout when performing the title song solo at the beginning, and especially the end, of *Bye Bye Birdie*.[2] Diegetically, however, her costuming seems

Conrad Birdie (Jesse Pearson) knocks the ladies of Sweet Apple cold with his version of "Honestly Sincere" in *Bye Bye Birdie*.

designed to de-emphasize — even to mock — her sexuality. Especially while performing the number "How Lovely to Be a Woman," Ann-Margret is costumed so as to reassure adults that sex is the last thing on her character's mind. In this scene, Kim changes clothes in front of the camera while modestly covered up in a huge, baggy sweater. The actress has certainly been hired for her sex appeal, a fact signaled by an occasional bare leg and by her erotic shimmy into a pair of too-tight jeans, but the 15-year-old character is presented as childish and pre-sexual. This sexual innocence is signaled by the décor of Kim's bedroom, especially by her Flintstones dolls, and by the fuzzy bedroom slippers and cutely askew ballcap with which she finishes off her outfit. If this is her idea of what it means to be a woman, then her parents — and the parents in the audience — have nothing to worry about "kids today," despite their professed fondness for rock and roll music. Bobby Rydell's costuming coordinates well with Kim's. Hugo and the other teenage boys at Sweet Apple High tend toward clean tennis shoes and cardigan sweaters, usually displaying the school's name. It is probably unsurprising in light of this costuming that when Kim and Hugo kiss during the "One Boy" number, they pretty obviously keep their mouths closed.

Rob Burt accurately identifies a wide spread social concern in the world into which *Bye Bye Birdie* was released when he writes in *Rock and Roll: The Movies* that "[j]uvenile delinquency and mixed-up kids kept the Fifties press turning with sensational reports of rock 'n' roll revolts and general teenage unrest — a blanket coverage from Boston to Bolton, with most of the blame put squarely at the feet of rock movies" (6). And yet, it is apparent even from these few summary notes that teenage angst and teenage delinquency hardly amount to crippling concerns in *Bye Bye Birdie*. This is due, at least in part, to the fact that the semantics of rock and roll culture have been studiously co-opted in the film to serve the interests of the older generation. Even rock and roll itself is tamed and toothless. Generally speaking, little of the music from *Bye Bye Birdie* is even mildly rocking. Nor does it aspire to be. Albert's candidate for a Conrad Birdie hit song early in the film is entitled "Mumbo Jumbo Gooey Gumbo." So much for rock and roll! Later on, Kim's "How Lovely to Be a Woman" is not a rock song but an act of self-mockery, as much because of the pizzicato strings in the background as the naïve lyrics. "One Boy," performed by Kim and Hugo, sounds like something out of the remake of *State Fair*, released the previous year, rather than something by Mickey and Sylvia or Paul and Paula. Since Ann-Margret appeared in *State Fair* as a temptress with a heart of gold — along with the more saccharine Pat Boone and Pamela Tiffin — we are probably safe in assuming that "One Boy" was intended as the kind of unthreatening, white-bread pop tune favored by the powers that be. "Put on a Happy Face," the hit song from *Bye Bye Birdie*, receives clownish choreography and mugging from Dick Van Dyke as well as a trombone and wood block arrangement from the soundtrack. Only Conrad Birdie's "Honestly Sincere" and "I've Got a Lot of Livin' to Do" rock, and they do so, as it were, in italics. Birdie's Elvis-like glittery costuming, his absurd Conway Twitty–like name and his exaggerated pelvis gyrating — all serve to frame Jesse Pearson's numbers as mildly comic rather than as truly threatening to the status quo. After one of Birdie's performances, Albert says, "He might make a terrific soldier. Turn him loose and the enemy'll twitch itself to death," and Harry McAfee sputters, "My daughter is not going to be publicly kissed by that, that wriggler." Conrad is thus perceived not as the anti–Christ indicted in fundamentalist pulpits but as something of a joke, at least to men of mature years. For this reason, whenever Birdie performs, the women of Sweet Apple, young and old, convey their sexual arousal by fainting rather than in the ways common in other hit movies of 1963, such as *The L-Shaped Room*, *Hud*, *Cleopatra* and *Tom Jones*. Sure, kids may scream at Conrad and Elvis, this movie says, but they screamed at Frank Sinatra[3] and Harry James, didn't they? And they — by which we mean *we*— turned out all right, didn't we? To support the same point, Conrad's motorcycle spends more time in the McAfee's living room than it does following the Steppenwolf's advice to get out on the highway.[4]

In other words, *Bye Bye Birdie* handles the threatening aspects of rock and roll by absorbing them harmlessly into the fabric of mature, mainstream, white-middle-class culture. This is Robert Mitchell's point in a review essay written for *Magill's Survey of the Cinema* almost two decades after the film's release: "The film, like the play, is an exceedingly pleasant burlesque — satire is too strong a term — of pop Americana in the relatively innocent years of the early 1960's. Set during the Kennedy

Administration, *Bye Bye Birdie* is nevertheless redolent of the ambience that has come to be associated with the Eisenhower era: the nuclear family reigned supreme and unquestioned; only teenagers cared about rock and roll; and everything ground to a halt on Sunday evening when *The Ed Sullivan Show* appeared on television" (375). As Mitchell implies, the values that an older generation might be presumed to endorse may be detected throughout *Bye Bye Birdie*. The mature Rosie DeLeon, for example, assures Kim that she is still a virgin, "a good girl," despite all her years out there looking for a husband. After Rosie and Albert finally come together in order to conclude their part of the romantic narrative, we see them the next morning wearing pajamas but emerging from separate rooms. Furthermore, the song that seals their love, "Everything Is Rosie," is performed first as a soft-shoe number by Albert and Rosie before it is taken up in a similar arrangement by the happily reunited Kim and Hugo. True rock and roll culture plays little part in any of this. The same may be said of *The Ed Sullivan Show*, despite the much-advertised guest appearances by famous rock and rollers on that show. Significantly, when *Bye Bye Birdie* was originally screened at Radio City Music Hall in Easter 1963, the *New York Times* reviewer listed the full entertainment bill available: "The Music Hall is presenting the annual Glory of Easter pageant, in addition to Francois Szony, Nancy Claire, Pinky and Porky, the Choraleers, Mary Beth Old, the Rockettes and the Corps de Ballet." If this sounds like a line-up for *The Ed Sullivan Show*, it probably should. Thus, the rapturous number "Hymn for a Sunday Evening," performed by the McAfee family in choir robes, can be contextualized as only mildly satirical. By the same token, the theme song of the Conrad Birdie fan club, "We Love You Conrad," also receives choir-like presentation even if the girls do not wear robes. Just as *Your Hit Parade* and the major television variety shows of the time attempted to contain rock and roll music and culture within the established limits of popular music, so *Bye Bye Birdie* attempts to absorb Conrad Birdie, Bobby Rydell and Ann-Margret within the limits of suburban middle-class culture. The dominant values in this adult-oriented narrative are epitomized by the supposedly critical, but actually indulgent, song "Kids." When Paul Lynde foolishly proposes in the song that kids should swing and sway with Sammy Kaye instead of listening to Conrad Birdie, it should be apparent that no one is really being critical. There is really nothing wrong with "kids today" apart from their ages.

American International Pictures' *Beach Party* (1963) loudly agrees that "There's nothing wrong with kids today!" Directed by William Asher, and starring Annette Funicello and Frankie Avalon, this film initiates a series of "beach movies" in which the values of teenagers gain clear ascendancy over the values of the older generation — even while mounting no serious criticism of the established culture or offering any viable alterative to it beyond the presentation of what R. L. Rutsky describes as "the comic and romantic escapades of white suburban teenagers having good clean fun at the beach" (12). As in *Bye Bye Birdie*, then, the Hollywood musical succeeds in co-opting rock culture even while seeming to adopt a different set of values than the *Father Knows Best* ideology of *Bye Bye Birdie*. The result is a series of films that succeed, in the words of Thomas Doherty, in "[f]ulfilling the best hopes of the older generation" (qtd. in Rutsky 12). That is to say that despite their weird slang and un–Sammy Kaye-like music, these young people are merely going through a harmless

Dolores (Annette Funicello) and Frankie (Frankie Avalon) head for fun at the beach in *Beach Party*.

stage on their way to responsible adulthood. As the series develops, however, slight changes in emphasis suggest that the forces of youth are gaining the upper hand.

In *Beach Party*, for example, Bob Cummings and Dorothy Malone, who fulfill the dramatic function of the older romantic couple familiar from *Bye Bye Birdie*, rate top billing over Frankie and Annette. By the time of *Bikini Beach*, released the following year, Frankie and Annette appear above the title, with the older couple, Keenan Wynn and Martha Hyer, getting second billing. To some degree, the shift represents smart marketing on the part of American International. If the series is working, why not take advantage of its built-in advertising appeal?[5] In another sense, the demotion of older, more established actors to the status represented by secondary billing indicates the diminishing importance of their characters' narrative significance. Bob Cummings' character in *Beach Party*, Prof. Robert O. Sutwell, functions diegetically as a mild threat to the happiness of the story's young surfers. At the same time, he also acts as a romantic alternative to Frankie Avalon's character, Frankie. Keenan Wynn's Harvey Huntington Honeywagon merely poses a mild threat to the surfers in *Bikini Beach* and never acts as a rival to Frankie. Other older recognizable actors, such as Morey Amsterdam and Don Rickles, merely provide professional backup for the charming but inexperienced pop stars. In this sense, the films reproduce the more general experiences of the teenagers in the audience: adults exist somewhere in the background to supply money, meals and housing, and although they can often be annoying, they don't really matter in the way that teenage acquaintances do. According to Mark McGee. such an orientation on youth was viewed as dramatically unwise by many, including the *New York Times* reviewer of *Beach Party*: "The real trouble is that almost the entire cast emerges as the dullest bunch of meatballs ever, with the old folks even sillier than the kids ... Jody McCrea, Harvey Lembeck, and Morey Amsterdam, as sideline comics, are downright embarrassing. Mr. Cummings has to be seen to be believed..." (qtd. in McGee 229). Wise or not, *Beach Party* definitely marks an acceleration of trends in the Hollywood rock musical already at work in *Bye Bye Birdie*.

Beach Party opens with antic bongo drums, a sure sign that the film hasn't settled on rock and roll as its musical identity. Bongos signify beatniks rather than teenage rockers, a signification touched on elsewhere in the film by the meditating girls in black leotards glimpsed repeatedly in Big Daddy's lounge, by the parodic beatnik poem recited by Cappy (Morey Amsterdam), and by the cameo appearance of American International staple Vincent Price as Big Daddy himself, guru to Cappy, the three girls, and an undeveloped tribe of beach dwellers. All of these references are largely unrelated to rock culture, but they fall under the heading of things that sensible adults like Harry McAfee find ridiculous, and so they can find a place in *Beach Party*. Sensible adults do like beautiful scenery, however, and William Asher is careful to introduce each significant narrative sequence in *Beach Party* with eye-catching, nature-documentary shots of sky, sand and surf. The film's values may be youth-oriented, then, but the overall cinematic package caters to adult viewers also. This appeal to the older set can be the only possible reason for Bob Cummings' presence. The *New York Times* reviewer is surely not the only viewer likely to find Cummings' performance anomalous. At one point, for example, we are asked to believe that shaving off his beard makes Prof. Sutwell look like a plausible lover for Annette. Since Cummings was born in 1908 and looks every day of it, believing this involves quite a stretch. It is supposed to be a joke on Annette's naivete that she is willing to believe that the Professor saw action as a pilot in World War I, but his service in World War II makes him equally implausible as Frankie's rival.

The film does establish youthful values by embracing surfing culture. Bill Ogersby is surely correct when he argues, in his *Playboys in Paradise: Masculinity, Youth and Leisure-style in Modern America*, that "[s]hifts in the texture of youth culture are impossible to pinpoint with temporal precision, but by the beginning of the 1960s a recognizable surfing subculture existed among (mainly middle-class) Southern California youngsters" (104). Thus, rock culture does not have to come to town in *Beach Party* as it does in *Bye Bye Birdie*; it is already here, as Frankie and Annette testify in the film's opening number, "Beach Party," which follows the slightly misleading bongo introduction. Process shots of surfing by Frankie and Professor Sutwell alternate with actual surfing film of the sort that will make the *Endless Summer* documentary a huge box office success in 1966. Perhaps as a result, the professor is quickly won over to this youthful surf culture — instead of having the young people choose to become junior adults, as they do in *Bye Bye Birdie*.

Musically as well, this film represents a step toward becoming a rock and roll musical. "Beach Party," the duet that sets the film's tone, is a rock song, even if we can't imagine Chuck Berry singing it. Two songs performed by Dick Dale and the Del Tones, "Secret Surfin' Spot" and "Surfin' and a-Swingin,'" are just as clearly authentic examples of beach music. Frankie's solo, "Don't Stop Now," and Annette's, "Treat Him Nicely,"[6] are not Broadway show tunes even if they are not Top 40 rockers. The possible exception is "Promise Me Anything (But Give Me Love)," performed by Dorothy Malone, a fine actress — as *Written on the Wind* (1956) and *Too Much, Too Soon* (1958) attest — but just as clearly no singer. At least Bob Cummings doesn't sing! On a related note, we might observe that when Frankie dances with Eva Six to "Don't Stop Now," he is usually filmed from the waist — or the pelvis — up rather than from his feet up, as Fred Astaire would have been. The Beach series' departure from the traditional, non-rock musical is nowhere more evident.

Bikini Beach closely follows the pattern set by *Beach Party*, even while accelerating the switch in emphasis toward youth that we have already noted. For one thing, the male half of the older couple, Harvey Huntington Honeywagon (Keenan Wynn), operates a retirement home called Sea-Esta by the Sea and wishes to buy the kids' surfing spot to develop an even grander establishment. This generational contrast is made explicit when a group of elderly women from Honeywagon's retirement home are seen going off on a bird walk just before the camera pans to Candy Johnson shaking her fringed behind in a wild version of the Watusi. Thus, Honeywagon's generational values are established as diegetically opposite to those embraced by the rock and roll surfers. In *Beach Party*, Prof. Sutwell's initially condescending distance from rock and roll culture was signified by the title of his proposed book, "The Behavior Patterns of the Young Adult and its [*sic!*] Relation to Primitive Tribes." In *Bikini Beach*, Honeywagon's similarly critical initial position is indicated by his statement, "I am determined to prove that you young people are borderline cases leaning toward feeble-mindedness, with an abnormal preoccupation with sex." Like Sutwell, Honeywagon will eventually come to realize that "the kids are all right." Unlike Sutwell, Honeywagon will confine his romantic engagement to a member of his own generation, whom he eventually marries—Vivian Clements, played by Martha Hyer.[7]

By 1964, a new factor has entered the rock and roll equation with the coming of Beatlemania to America, and so *Bikini Beach* adds a comic English rocker called Potato Bug (also played, with a bogus accent, by Frankie Avalon) to the conflict generated by the generation gap. Annette — here called Dee Dee — is mildly attracted to Potato Bug, as she was mildly attracted to Prof. Sutwell in the earlier film. As we might expect, however, Frankie and Annette end up together, and Potato Bug ends up with his French assistant, played by Danielle Aubry. In fact, there is a general tidying up of loose romantic threads at the end of *Bikini Beach*. Honeywagon and Vivian marry long before the film's climax. Even Honeywagon's trained chimp, Clyde, hooks up, across species lines, with a trained bird belonging to Big Drag (Don Rickles). Potato Bug does get to perform a Beatle-like "How About You" in the film, but Frankie soon picks up the lyric and gets the camera back on the real Frankie Avalon. So much for Beatlemania!

The familiar semantic elements of the series are present despite these minor variations. For one thing, most of the actors wear bathing suits most of the time, and, as R. L. Rutsky observes, "In setting rock-and-roll music and dancing on the beach, where the participants could dance in bikinis and swim trunks, these films often heightened the sexuality and sense of freedom associated with teens and rock-and-roll" (18). In this film, the erotic potential of beach wear is accentuated during the opening scene when the camera tracks an eye-catching female bikini bottom as it causes mayhem all along the beach *à la The Girl Can't Help It* (1956). There is still a real rock band in the film although Dick Dale and the Del Tones are replaced by the Pyramids. The American International Pictures cameo is taken by Boris Karloff in *Bikini Beach*, but he does refer to Vincent Price along the way. The role of the understanding, mildly comic, older outsider, played by Morey Amsterdam in *Beach Party*, is here filled by Don Rickles, whose character is an abstract expressionist painter as well as a drag race proprietor. As a result of Rickles/Big Drag's preoccupation, there is exciting film of drag racing in *Bikini Beach* as well as film of surfing. Eric Von Zipper (Harvey Lembeck) and his motorcycle gang of Ratz and Mice are once again in evidence. What with their black leather jackets, their motorcycles and their anti-social attitudes, Von Zipper's gang might function as a threatening alternative to the clean-cut surfers of the beach tribe. Echoes of *The Wild One* (1954) are almost unavoidable. In actual fact, though, these echoes are turned into harmless fun. Von Zipper is never much of a threat to anyone, as his name surely suggests. In Rutsky's formulation, "The Ratz ... are ... clearly older than the teen surfing crew, [and so] their age only makes them more ridiculous" (16). At the end of *Beach Party*, the members of the Ratz motorcycle gang are pelted with cream pies. In *Bikini Beach*, they are splashed with paint, and some of them are slugged by Harvey Huntington Honeywagon, others by Frankie and Potato Bug, who are now friends. Since Von Zipper can be paralyzed by touching a forefinger — even his own — to his temple, he offers little threat to anyone. Like Conrad Birdie's motorcycle in *Bye Bye Birdie*, signifiers of youthful rebellion, even of juvenile delinquency, are thus co-opted in these Beach movies into signs of good clean fun.

The final feel-good element in the film is a guest appearance by Little Stevie Wonder, whose up-tempo climactic number is a great success. Potato Bug dances along with Stevie and the band, as do Honeywagon and his bride Vivian. The old women from the retirement home also join in, along with the unstoppable Candy Johnson. As the confirming sign that rock and roll has bridged the generation gap, Candy shimmies frantically across the closing credits and is joined by another female dancer playing the part of a retiree. The song on the soundtrack is "I Got You Where I Want You," a sentiment that these credits attribute to people of all ages.

Stevie Wonder's appearance brings up another element of these Beach films, the co-option of actual rock-and-roll performers to serve the values of white middle-class entertainment. In "Beach Blanket Bimbo from Outer Space," the celebrated *Saturday Night Live* parody of these Beach movies, first broadcast on November 18, 1978, Garrett Morris plays the part of Chubby Checker and gets to deliver the sketch's most satiric speech by telling the fictional teenagers that there is nothing he likes better than playing his music for a bunch of rich white kids. Co-optation has seldom been more accurately explained. In this *SNL* sketch, Carrie Fisher reprises her *Star Wars* role as Princess Leia, a "teenager from outer space" who has been plunked down in the middle of a Beach movie.[8] John Belushi plays Eric Von Zipper, Bill Murray is Frankie Avalon and Gilda Radner gets to introduce herself to the Princess by saying, famously, "I'm Annette, and these are my breasts." Dan Aykroyd's Vincent Price is a bit more ostentatiously gay than the cameo figure in the beach movies, but the exaggeration does little to damage the parody's accuracy. It is, of course, significant that the Beach movies should be well enough remembered more than a decade after their initial releases to make this parody possible, accurate or not. The reasons seem to me not far to seek. Frankie and Annette are charming in a squeaky clean way. The beaches are gorgeous. The music is pleasant, if forgettable. And these movies are intended for young people, not for old people who look down their noses at "kids today!"[9] In his history of American International Pictures, Mark Thomas McGee quotes Sam Arkoff, founder of the company with Jim Nicholson, "We did make pictures that appealed to youth, and in doing so we took a different position from other producers and didn't moralize" (218). The effect was to move the counter significantly further along the board toward the imaginary space marked "Rock and Roll Musical."

In the years following the release of *Bikini Beach*, an audience habituated to listening to rock and roll could grow to appreciate a parody like "Beach Blanket Bimbo from Outer Space." In addition, the popular success of rock-inflected films including *A Hard Day's Night* (1964), *The Graduate* (1967), *American Graffiti* (1973) and *Saturday Night Fever* (1977) necessarily altered mainstream perceptions of rock culture's threatening qualities. Therefore, in the 15 years between the releases of *Bye Bye Birdie* (1963) and *Grease* (1978), rock music could be taken more for granted as an ingredient of Hollywood musicals. Significantly, however, rock culture continued to be co-opted — in *Grease* through the totalizing irony of nostalgia rather than through the narrowly targeted generational irony of *Bye Bye Birdie*.

Like *Bye Bye Birdie*—and, importantly, unlike the Beach movies—*Grease* was based on a successful Broadway show (1972). As Denny Martin Flinn points out, however, "Much is in place, but played straight it's a Frankie and Annette film instead of a farcical spoof. This successful film has, unfortunately, almost totally obscured the hilarious original stage version, so that high schools (and Broadway revivals) now perform this charmer by taking the fifties seriously!" (508). It may seem to be an historical irony that a film released in the late 1970s should take the teen culture of the 1950s more "seriously" than *Bye Bye Birdie* did in 1963. And yet, such attention is not incompatible with a considerable measure of condescension. This is Robert Mitchell's argument in his essay review of *Grease* written for *Magill's Survey of Cinema*: "[T]he film was written from the perspective of a decade that was (or at least felt itself to be) considerably hipper than the 1950's ever pretended to be. *Grease* laughs at, as well as with, the 1950's..." (922). The key to resolving these potentially conflicting views, according to Vincent Canby, can be found in the concept of nostalgia. In his *New York Times* review of *Grease*, Canby maintains that the "time and place"—what I have been calling the *chronotope*—created in *Grease* has "less to do with any real 50's than with a kind of show business that is both timeless and old-fashioned, both sentimental and wise" (June 16, 1978). In this sense, *Grease*, even while it seems to valorize rock and roll culture semantically, distances this culture through a filter of adult irony that renders its potentially threatening qualities harmless.

As in the American International beach movies, the principal romance in *Grease* involves two high school students, Danny Zuko, played by John Travolta, and Sandy Olsen, played by Olivia Newton-John. The supporting couple are not second-billed older actors but two other teenagers: Kenickie, played by Jeff Conaway, and Rizzo, played by Stockard Channing. Insofar as *Grease* has a plot, it follows the usual musical comedy of errors dating back to the Greeks—unless Rizzo's pregnancy alarm can be considered a true exception to the rule. In any case, everyone is suitably paired up at the end. Even from this brief summary, it should be obvious that *Bye Bye Birdie* and *Grease* share elements of characterization and plotting, and yet the differences between them clearly show how America absorbed rock culture in the years between 1963 and 1978.

For one thing, in *Grease*, adults exist only to provide a comic context, more in the manner of *Bikini Beach* than of *Bye Bye Birdie*. Eve Arden handles her role as Principal McGee with as much brio as Paul Lynde, but she is consigned to the margins by the plot and by her time on the screen clock. The same should be said about Sid Caesar's Coach Calhoun and Joan Blondell's character Vi, the understanding waitress at the Frosty Palace malt shop. The names of these grownup professionals may give additional resonance to the cast list, but throughout the film the camera focuses lingeringly on the supposed teenagers.[10] It is therefore appropriate that the kind of show-stopping solos given to Paul Lynde in the earlier movie will here be given to Stockard Channing. Channing's Rizzo is consequently featured, very effectively, in "Look at Me, I'm Sandra Dee" and "There Are Worse Things I Could Do." In these and other ways, *Grease* shows approval of what these teenagers are doing at the malt shop and elsewhere just as much as *Bye Bye Birdie* affirms the values of the older generation.

The semantics of dress also mark the evolution of the rock musical. In *Grease*, the T-birds and the Pink Ladies dress in gang clothes, as the title of the film indirectly promises. Even when Danny dons a letter sweater toward the close of the film, as Bobby Rydell might have done in *Bye Bye Birdie,* Danny is looked on as freakish by the other leather-clad members of his gang. Therefore, he soon rips off this sweater to dance to "You're the One That I Want" in his signature black t-shirt. In this sense, the semantics of teen rebellion derived from *The Wild One* are more apparently echoed in *Grease* than in any of the other films considered so far in this chapter. Appropriately, in terms of such costuming, there is a distinct sexual aura to the characters' behavior in *Grease*. When Danny alternates choruses of "Summer Nights" with Sandy early in the film, her friends ask about romance while Danny's friends ask "how far" he got with her, all the while simulating hot petting. When Danny then sings, "We made out under the dock," he thrusts out his pelvis provocatively. Later on, Rizzo and Kenickie discuss condoms while parked in lovers' lane; then Rizzo ends up thinking that she is pregnant — she claims by someone other than Kenickie. Even Frankie and Annette always stopped short of actual intercourse, as Prof. Sutwell and Harvey Honeywagon discover voyeuristically. Since all this sexuality is pretty much what many concerned moralists had warned would follow in the wake of rock and roll, *Grease* can in one sense be seen as a confirmation of adult fears about rock culture, just as *Bye Bye Birdie* and the Beach movies can be seen to calm these fears.

But this perception of sexual liberation is accurate only in that one sense. Sandy's rhyming answer to Danny's boast about making out is that they stayed out until ten o'clock, a line that echoes the "kids are all right" message of *Bye Bye Birdie*, especially the exchange in which Kim tells Hugo that she is allowed to stay out until ten o'clock and he replies that he has to be in by nine. That is to say that, despite the cooler costuming and the suggestive sexual aura with which *Grease* addresses its younger audience, this Hollywood musical seeks to reassure its mature audience that everything is safely under control as far as rock culture goes.

The key to this reassurance, as Flinn argues in his book *Musical! A Grand Tour*, is nostalgia. Confirmation of Flynn's view abounds throughout the film. The opening sequence is shot at the beach under the 1955 hit song "Love is a Many Splendored Thing." If this opening reminds viewers of William Asher beach movies like *Beach Party* and *Bikini Beach*, then all the better! Having one of Danny's fellow gang members refer to "Annette's jugs" during the "Summer Nights" number crudely confirms this nostalgic reference. Later on, at the Frosty Palace, the kids from Rydell High listen to the original recordings of "La Bamba" (1958) and "Whole Lot of Shakin' Going On" (1957). This rock nostalgia should probably come as no surprise since these teenagers attend a high school named after the singing idol who played opposite Ann-Margret in *Bye Bye Birdie*. Other voices from the rock and roll past belong to Annette's co-star in the Beach movies, Frankie Avalon, who is called upon to perform the fantasy number "Beauty School Drop-out," and Edd "Kookie" Byrnes, who plays a Dick Clark–style television deejay named Vince Fontaine. In the 1972 Broadway show, the rock and roll past of the 1950s was introduced through a flashback from a high school reunion set in the present. In the 1978 film, the past is more immediately accessible because the film's backward look merely assumes that everything worked out just fine, despite hysterical fears to the contrary.

Grease authorizes these self-satisfied conclusions through nostalgia. By collapsing musical and historical categories, the film equates actual rock performers like Ritchie Valens and Jerry Lee Lewis with rock re-enactors like Sha-Na-Na. In this way, the film is able to view the rock and roll culture of the past as an undifferentiated lump, as something that we all got through safely some time ago. Toward this end, the opening credits of *Grease* quick-cut among historical icons: Elvis, Davy Crockett, Groucho, Marilyn, Jackie Gleason, Ike, Josef Stalin, a Jules Feiffer cartoon, *Mad* magazine, *Playboy*. What is signified by the accumulation of these signifiers is "somewhere back in the past," a chronotope not much more specific than the Lone Ranger's "thrilling days of yesteryear." Because of this historical indeterminacy, Olivia Newton John's favorite songwriter, John Farrar, can interpolate "Hopelessly Devoted to You," a late–70s, country-inflected song, into *Grease* and still come up with a surefire hit. By the same historical latitude, the big event of a rock and roll movie released in 1978 turns out to be a dance contest at which most of the boys are wearing jackets and ties. Never mind the war in Vietnam! Never mind the assassination of one president and the resignation of another! As Don Henley would later complain about another dance-crazy partner: Nothing else matters; she just wants to dance![11]

Then, again, that's what other characters did when confronted by the Depression, by racism, by gang warfare, by World War II. It's what you do when faced by a crisis in a Hollywood musical.

4

Dance as a Narrative Agent

In the theme song for the movie-clips film *That's Dancing* (1985), the lyric asks why dancing is so important and answers its own question by affirming that there is no better way to get from here to there. The images on screen while this lyric is being sung make clear that "here to there" refers to a physical area involving space on the set, how to get from upstage left to downstage right, for example. However, it is not stretching matters too far to say that in Hollywood musicals dancing also helps us get from "here to there" in terms of plot. In an essay entitled "The Concept of Plot and the Plot of *Tom Jones*," R. S. Crane proposes that we think of plot in narrative as "the particular temporal synthesis effected by the writer of the elements of action, character, and thought that constitute the matter of his invention" (66). This explanation of Crane's suggests the three subcategories of narrative plotting — action, character and thought — that I investigate in this chapter. More specifically, it may be that the two central lovers in the musical just can't seem to get together through the ordinary cinematic devices of dialogue and action, but when they dance together the romantic impasse can be resolved.[1] Or it may be that some emotion deeply concealed within one of the lovers cannot be made manifest through conventional dramatic avenues, but this emotion can be expressed in a dream dance, most likely a dream ballet. Dancing can come to the rescue in these and other cases by letting the potential lovers discover their true feelings while dancing, or by revealing through the imaginative projection of a dance number what a character is secretly desiring or fearing.

Hollywood musicals resemble other narrative forms in their reliance on the six conventional structural elements identified by Aristotle in his *Poetics*.[2] That is to say that Hollywood musicals resemble novels and dramatic tragedies in being composed — literally or figuratively — of plot, character, diction, thought, song and spectacle.[3] They differ from other narrative modes in that the narrative agents of action, dialogue and song are often enhanced by the additional agency of dance. In some musicals—*Shall We Dance* and *Dirty Dancing*, for example — the principal characters are dancers, so that dancing becomes an agent of narrative simply as an extension of their characterizations. In other musicals—*Top Hat* and *The King and I*, for example — dancing together develops the action of the plot in terms of the principal characters' romantic involvement. In still other musicals—*Carefree* and *Oklahoma!*, for example — dancing reveals subconscious elements of a character's personality, what Aristotle calls that character's "thought." In the terms that Crane supplies, the plots of musicals may be advanced in terms of action, character and thought through dancing. In the terms that I have chosen to use here, dancing may be seen in all these cases to be a significant narrative agent.

It will be apparent to many that the films I have chosen to illustrate my argument are heavily weighted toward the dancing of Fred Astaire. The personal rationalization for this choice is that Fred is simply my favorite dancer. The theoretical justification is that I am not alone in my preference. John Mueller, for instance, begins his book *Astaire Dancing* by noting that George Balanchine, Merce Cunningham, Rudolf Nureyev and Mikhail Baryshnikov have all publicly testified in favor of Astaire's premier terpsichorean genius (3). Thus, I have selected one of Fred's films to illustrate each of the three narrative subcategories I intend to investigate. In each case I have also chosen a non–Astaire film to make the same points. Of course I hope that the categories can stand on their own, but I am happy to think and talk about Fred's films in any case.

In a slight violation of Aristotle's recommended schema,[4] we might begin by considering the ways in which plot is affected by dancing as a function of character.[5] In *Shall We Dance* (1937), Fred Astaire plays Peter P. Peters, a plain old American from Philadelphia who is dancing in Paris as Petrov, star of the Russian ballet. After seeing a flip book of photos of Linda Keene, an American dancer played by Ginger Rogers, Petrov tells Jeffrey Baird, his impresario, that he intends to marry Linda, whom he has yet to meet. The plot of a typical romantic comedy is thereby launched. Since Petrov's declaration occurs quite early in the film, plot requires that a number of complications interfere before the romance is finally concluded in the film's last sequence. There is really nothing surprising about this narrative exigency. Katherine and Petruchio, Scarlet and Rhett, Mickey and Judy[6]— all encounter similar obstacles to romantic happiness, but their problems usually have little or nothing to do with dancing. In *Shall We Dance*, the generic narrative necessity that the lovers' happiness be delayed for an hour or so is inflected through the characters' roles as dancers, particularly in the sense that one apparent obstacle to their happiness lies in the differing dancing styles pursued by Petrov and Linda.[7] The film opens with shots of the female dancers from the Russian ballet *en pointe*, and soon the camera tracks to a painting of Petrov in a definitely Russian ballet costume.[8] Fred Astaire's character is thus clearly marked as a ballet dancer from the start. We first see Linda, on the other hand, by means of the flip book of photos showing her dancing on stage in a patently popular style. When this shot segues into Linda's live version of the same dance with the same partner, we know for sure that she is a stage entertainer, not a ballerina.[9] Petrov's impresario, played by Edward Everett Horton, considers Linda's form of popular dancing low-class and common, and this judgment spells trouble for the lovers. Then, when Pete Peters finally meets Linda, he affects a bogus Petrovian Russian demeanor, leading Linda to consider him an arrogant phony — another potential problem. Since dancing initially signifies the lovers' distance from each other, we may logically assume that dancing will also point to a happy resolution.

This eventuality is indicated by the scene midway through the film, in which

Petrov and Linda do an improvised dance together at a swanky rooftop nightclub to the delightful Gershwin tune "They All Laughed." First Linda is called up to sing, then the orchestra leader announces that she will dance with Petrov, and then the two lovers reveal their compatibility by following each other's leads despite their different dancing styles. As Arlene Croce describes this number: "[Fred] swoops importantly around her in *grands ronds de jambe* and other nonsense. She counters with a burst of tap. He imitates this haltingly, then snaps to. The orchestra begins a vamp and they sail away. The number has everything — games, jokes, hard tap, cool tap, a lovely series of ballet finger turns, and two white pianos to jump onto" (121). In addition to all the virtues that Croce identifies, the number also serves as a narrative indicator that these two talented dancers obviously belong together off as well as on stage.

A series of complications predictably delays the lovers' ultimate union: Linda's rich but boring fiancé, scandalous rumors in the press, a former ballerina who is still pursuing Pete, the interference of Jeffrey Baird and Linda's manager, Arthur Miller. These are perhaps common enough events in a romantic comedy. That they are all here subordinated to dancing may be indicated by the newspaper headlines used to represent public opinion about Pete and Linda. "Secret Marriage of Dance Stars Revealed" and "Broadway and Ballet Merge" are the two most pertinent. Pete and Linda may be temporarily star-crossed lovers, in other words, but they are also— and significantly — dancers.

The final resolution follows a consistent narrative strategy. In the climax of the show that Pete agrees to do for the now-affiliated Jeffrey Baird and Arthur Miller, ballet dancers first appear *en pointe* to accompany the oh-so-bizarre Harriet Hoctor, who is temporarily filling the role of Pete's dance partner.[10] Then Pete solos in white tie and tails, a signature Astaire number obviously intended for a popular audience rather than the ballet stage. Linda resurfaces, and the two destined lovers dance happily together to a reprise of "They All Laughed." A happy ending is what we expect from a romantic comedy, and so at the end of *Shall We Dance* we find ourselves in approximately the same place as we find ourselves at the end of *It Happened One Night* (1934) or *His Brother's Wife* (1936). The principal difference lies in the fact that so much of the plot of *Shall We Dance* revolves around dancing. As the title song advises, we would be wise to dance any and every time we possibly can.

This sentiment certainly would win the endorsement of Johnny Castle (Patrick Swayze) and Baby Houseman (Jennifer Grey), the central lovers in *Dirty Dancing* (1987). Although Johnny is the only professional dancer in this couple, dancing can be understood as an extension of character here as it is in *Shall We Dance*. A reverse Cinderella romance between a wealthy woman and a poorer man has many cinematic antecedents including, most notably, Douglas Sirk's *All That Heaven Allows* (1955), starring Jane Wyman and Rock Hudson. The striking difference in this case is that Johnny Castle is not a gardener but an Arthur Murray dance instructor who works during the summer at Kellerman's resort where Baby and her sister and parents (her father is a doctor) have come for their family vacation. As such, he represents erotic possibility to the intelligent but sexually inexperienced Baby as well as access to a new type of dance music unfamiliar to Baby's family and the other guests at Kellerman's. As Timothy Shary writes in *Generational Multiplex*, "[Baby's] eventual mastery of dance techniques through Johnny's training becomes her ascension to sexualized womanhood, literally and figuratively..." (91). Johnny could do something else for a living and still play his part in a romantic screen comedy, but that film could not be called *Dirty Dancing*.

As in *Shall We Dance*, a difference in dance styles figures significantly in the plot. Kellerman's summer resort encourages its patrons to engage in what one character calls the "family foxtrot," occasionally mixed with the sort of Latin dancing that can be mastered by taking lessons—a realistic circumstance for a film set in the America of 1963.[11] Off duty, Johnny and the rest of the entertainment staff at Kellerman's engage in their own mode of improvisational dancing set to rock music and styled "dirty" in opposition to the culturally approved ballroom alternative—another realistic possibility for the times.[12] These free-spirited dancers are seen in black-and-white under the opening credits dancing to the Ronettes' recording of "Be My Baby," and the scene is reprised in color when Baby first crashes a staff dance. Interestingly enough, on its second appearance, this dirty dancing is backed by the Contours' version of "Do You Love Me," an even more appropriate diegetic musical context because the lyric qualifies the title question by saying that the singer is now able to dance as well as sing. As we might expect in a Hollywood musical, somebody does love somebody else: Baby loves Johnny, whom she has been unable to take her eyes off. When Johnny briefly dances with her on this occasion, the connection between love and dancing is firmly established—at least for Baby.

Penny Johnson (Cynthia Rhodes) and Johnny Castle (Patrick Swayze) demonstrate some steps to the customers at Kellerman's Resort in *Dirty Dancing*.

Since this film is a romantic comedy, temporary obstacles must delay the total fulfillment of this love. A false problem arises when Baby initially assumes that Johnny is in love with his regular dance partner, Penny Johnson. After Baby learns that Johnny and Penny can dance together with convincing eroticism even while keeping their hearts to themselves, everything begins to look up, but it is still early in the picture. The lovers are thus harassed by troubling issues of class and wealth involving Baby's father, Penny's unexpected pregnancy, a heartless Yale medical school student and Baby's awkwardness on the dance floor. As Baby laments, she "can't even do the merengue." This last seems to be the most serious problem of all because the trajectory of their romance requires that Baby perform a mambo with Johnny at the Sheldrake hotel while Penny is taken to an abortionist in another town.

Therefore, the most memorable section of the film is the subsequent sequence in which Johnny teaches the dance intended for the Sheldrake to Baby — on the dance floor where Baby learns to follow Johnny's lead, on a log bridge where Baby learns balance (to Bruce Channel's version of "Hey Baby") and in a lake where Baby learns how to do leaps— and the two clearly fall in love. The ensuing dance at the Sheldrake, like the dance at the rooftop supper club in *Shall We Dance*, provides an advance glimpse of the happy ending that we may now anticipate.

Dirty Dancing differs from *Shall We Dance* in the fact that in 1987 dancing can lead to on-screen sex. In the earlier film, the possibility that the two dancers might not actually be married leads the manger of their hotel (Eric Blore) to change the lock on the door connecting their suites as part of a comic subplot that the audience of 1937 can easily recognize and appreciate. The 1987 audience, on the other hand, can be considered either more broad-minded or more blasé. In any event, Baby goes to Johnny's cabin after he has been demeaned by her father and asks him to dance privately with her. As in many other scenes, Johnny is shirtless here, demonstrating that Patrick Swayze and not Jennifer Grey is the usual object of the viewer's gaze.[13] As they dance, Johnny removes Baby's blouse, and their protracted dancing becomes increasingly erotic. The following scene in Johnny's bed is quite brief, however, leaving us with a definite sense that the dancing was the truly sexy part.[14] Later on, brief scenes of the two in Johnny's bed on other occasions primarily serve to advance the plot through the accompanying dialogue.

This connection of dancing to the overall romantic plot of the film is confirmed in a sequence that begins with Stan, a hotel employee played by Wayne Knight, leading hotel guests through a ridiculous group dance that involves a lot of hopping around. The music behind this scene is "Love Is Strange" by Mickey and Sylvia, a song that continues to play as the scene shifts to the dance studio where Baby and Johnny are dancing and clowning around together; they even lip-synch the Mickey and Sylvia parts. Baby and Johnny are not only lovers and dance partners, in other words, but well-matched friends. The film could be structured to end here with the principal romantic characters living happily ever after.

Instead, more socioeconomic prejudices and problems intrude, and so we approach the concluding musical sequence of the film with Johnny nowhere in sight. This sequence begins with '50s pop and foxtrot dancing very much in the ascendancy, with Johnny driven away, and Baby sitting disconsolately in a corner with her disappointed parents. All of the forces of hypocrisy and snobbery that we have learned to repudiate during the film seem mustered onstage to sing the Kellerman anthem to the tune of the Cornell fight song. Then Johnny suddenly reappears and grabs the microphone. "I always do the last dance of the summer," he says, "So I'm going to do my kind of dancin' with a great partner." We hardly need add that the partner is Baby and that she and Johnny dance beautifully together to "The Time of My Life" by Bill Medley and Jennifer Warnes. In fact, they dance so effectively that the assembled audience — staff and patrons, young and old, even Baby's parents— join in and do what looks more like dirty dancing than the family foxtrot. Baby and Johnny share a close-up kiss as part of this sequence, but the film doesn't end with the kiss. Instead, everyone goes on dancing, the film changes to black-and-white and we see more dirty dancing under the closing credits— this time with Baby and Johnny as part of the group.

As I have noted, there are significant differences between *Dirty Dancing* and *Shall We Dance*, many of which can be explained by the 50 years that elapsed between their dates of release. One film is (mostly) in color, and the other is in black-and-white. Jennifer Grey and Patrick Swayze are not well known partners in a series of films as Fred and Ginger were.[15] There is sex and nakedness in *Dirty Dancing*. The later film also exploits the same rock music that earlier musicals such as *Bye Bye Birdie* treated as a potential threat to the very genre of the Hollywood musical. When Baby hears "Do You Love Me" blaring out at the staff dance party, she knows that she is in a freer, less controlled, more erotic environment than she has been familiar with at home and on the dance floor at Kellerman's. When members of the audience hear this song — and others including "Be My Baby," "Stay" and "Will You Love Me Tomorrow"— they are encouraged to bring their own rock and roll memories to bear on the present case of Baby's sexual (and perhaps social) awakening.[16] Viewers today may also have personal associations with "They Can't Take That Away from Me" and other fine Gershwin songs from *Shall We Dance*, but these songs were brand new to moviegoers in 1937. Most of the songs quoted in *Dirty Dancing*, on the other hand, might be assumed in 1987 to constitute part of most viewers' pasts, either from their original releases—"Do You Love Me" (1962), "Be My Baby" (1963), "Stay" (1960), "Hey Baby" (1962), "Will You Love Me Tomorrow" (1960)— or from their recycling on oldies radio stations. Despite these very real differences, however, *Shall We Dance* and *Dirty Dancing* may be fruitfully viewed as similar because of the ways they use dancing as a function of character to advance their narrative plots.

In *Top Hat* (1935), Fred Astaire's character, Jerry Travers, is also an American dancer. In fact, Arlene Croce goes so far as to say that "*Top Hat* gives us Astaire in the best role ever written for a dancer in a movie; the dance technique is an element of the characterization" (57). Much of what Jerry Travers does in the film, then, can be seen as an extension of his professional character, and yet my purpose in introducing *Top Hat* at this point is not so much to illustrate how dancing can serve to develop character in Hollywood musicals as to emphasize another way in which dancing can function as a narrative element — by forwarding the action of the plot. Croce would probably be comfortable with this strategy also since she claims that "[c]ontemporary reviewers of *Top Hat* praised ... its smooth integration of plot and musical numbers" (56). Specifically, I wish to focus on the ways in which the central romantic plot in *Top Hat* is forwarded by two dance numbers: "Isn't This a Lovely Day (To Be Caught in the Rain)" and "Cheek to Cheek." While it is certainly true that dancing serves to signify the love felt by the principal couples in *Shall We Dance* and *Dirty Dancing*, my earlier discussion highlighted the dance numbers' relations to the fictional dancers' characters.

In *Top Hat*, as in *Dirty Dancing*, only the male half of the couple is a professional dancer. Ginger Rogers' character, Dale Tremont, is a model hired to show off the fashion designs of Alberto Beddini (Erik Rhodes). As is appropriate in a romantic comedy, Jerry is attracted to Dale from early in the film. While dancing noisily in the hotel suite of his friend, Horace Hardwick (once again Edward Everett Horton), Jerry accidentally awakens Dale, who is trying to sleep in the suite below. When Dale comes up to complain, Jerry is hooked. As is also appropriate, Dale is at first reluctant to return Jerry's love, finding him too noisy and pushy, an impression initially strengthened when Jerry takes the place of the horse-cab driver taking Dale to the park on the next morning. Soon, however, we learn that things will work out fine for Dale and Jerry because they reveal their mutual love in a dance.

After arriving at the park, Dale is driven by a rainstorm to take shelter in a gazebo. As is consistent with her initial resistance to Jerry, Dale turns down his offer to rescue her, claiming that she prefers "being in distress." An opportune burst of thunder drives Dale into Jerry's arms, however, and soon provides him the opportunity to explain thunder and lightning in terms of the encounters between a "clumsy cloud and a fluffy little cloud." Dale is still suspicious of Jerry but somewhat charmed by his story, and so Jerry is encouraged enough to sing, "Isn't This a Lovely Day (To Be Caught in the Rain)." The lyric is followed by Jerry's beginning a walking dance while Dale whistles the tune. Soon the two are trading fairly complicated dance steps set to varying tempos, but without touching. Another burst of thunder causes the two to dance in each other's arms, so happily and appropriately that they forget about the rain and briefly exit from the gazebo. After feeling raindrops, they return to the shelter, sit cross-legged side by side and shake hands. Apparently, this match has been signed, sealed and delivered quite early in the film. In terms of plot, we have learned through this dance that Dale and Jerry can be friends and lovers. If the narrative were to end here, the plot would have been completed through a dance. But, of course, the narrative can't end here.

Even so, this impression of lovers united carries through to the following sequence, which begins with Dale singing the opening lines from "Isn't This a Lovely Day." As the orchestral soundtrack takes up the tune, however, Dale is led to believe that Jerry, whose name she doesn't know, is actually Horace, the husband of her friend Madge (Helen Broderick). The specific token of misidentification in this scene is a brief case, but comic writers going back to the days of Plautus and Terence have used dozens of other tokens to work dozens of variations on the same plot complication.[17] In order to keep Dale and Jerry apart until the end of the film, Dale must continue to think Jerry is Horace through a whole series of plot complications. John Mueller is only one of those critics who believe that this plot element is a bit strained: "This confusion is maintained at great length through airy artifice — we are asked to believe Astaire has met, become enamored of, chased, sung to, danced with, won the love of, and proposed marriage to Rogers without once telling her either his first or his last name" (77). Whether or not we believe all this, Dale and Jerry are kept apart during the following sequence in the film.

Then things seem to turn in Jerry's favor. Beddini wants Dale to wear his fashions someplace where rich women can view them. Madge wants to bring Dale and Jerry together for matchmaking purposes. Jerry, who does know Dale's name, learns through a telegram from Madge that Dale will be staying with her in Italy. So, everyone quickly ends up on the Lido. Plot is twisted when Dale pretends to be a French fortune hunter in order to teach Horace a lesson. Since Jerry is on the receiving end of the lesson, he is surprised by Dale's behavior, but he is undeterred in his love for her. In fact, this plot sequence ends with Jerry telling Horace that he intends to marry Dale. Significantly, Dale and Jerry have maintained their essential characters through this whole series of lies, pretenses, masquerades and confusions.[18] Plot demands that something hold the two apart, but their love can survive any plot twists that the scriptwriters—Dwight Taylor and Allan Scott—can throw at them.

The most significant event in terms of plot then occurs when Dale and Jerry dance together to Irving Berlin's "Cheek to Cheek." The sequence begins with Dale and Madge sitting at an outdoor table, both still convinced that it is Horace who has been romancing Dale. When Jerry then comes up to their table, Madge is happy to see him because her matchmaking plans seem to be working so smoothly. Jerry is delighted by any opportunity to see the woman he loves. Since Dale still doesn't know Jerry's name, she naturally assumes that a husband and wife are meeting and speaking congenially to each other. Dale is therefore surprised when Madge encourages her to dance with the man she believes to be Madge's husband. Madge says, "You two run along and dance and don't give me another thought," and Dale replies, "That's what I'm afraid of." The confusion over identities that has blocked the lovers' happiness is thus still fully functioning as far as plot is concerned. As soon as Dale and Jerry begin to dance, though, it is clear that they are as attracted to each other as they were during the "Isn't This a Lovely Day" dance number. Therefore, when Madge encourages them to dance closer, Dale says, "Well, if Madge doesn't care, I certainly don't." That is to say, Dale's love seems stronger than her reluctance to violate her friend's marriage vows. But this can hardly be the happy ending that moviegoers would anticipate in 1935. Jerry saves the day by raising the action from the diegetic plot to a dance number. After Dale says that she doesn't care what happens, Jerry responds, "Neither do I. All I know is"— and he begins to sing "Cheek to Cheek." This great Irving Berlin song and the dance that follows guarantee the happy ending that the film's dialogue and action alone have been unable to deliver. John Mueller contrasts this dance with "Isn't This a Lovely Day": "In this duet they are no longer flirting — they are in love. But Rogers feels guilty and deceived and is trying to avoid Astaire's advances, seeking to fall out of love with him. Consequently, Astaire's objective in this number is to get her to forget her misgivings (which he doesn't understand) and to get her to yield to him" (83). Astaire/Jerry succeeds brilliantly, and so Rogers/Dale confesses her love for him. Jerry is ecstatic: "She loves me!" This dance, in other words, has brought closure to the romance that underlies this film's narrative.[19]

A sign of unresolved plot complications can be glimpsed in Dale's confession of love: "How could I have fallen in love with anyone as low as you?" We thus must expect further developments in the confused-identity plot even though the true Dale-and-Jerry plot has been satisfactorily concluded. Croce puts the matter succinctly: "The first hour of *Top Hat* is unqualified joy; only after 'Cheek to Cheek' does the film drop off into a desert of talk..." (57). Dale decides to marry Beddini. Beddini promises to kill Horace: "For the woman, the kiss; for the man, the sword." Jerry dances noisily on the floor above Dale and Beddini's honeymoon suite. Horace's manservant Bates (Eric Blore again) gets arrested. Jerry tells Dale his real name. The marriage between Beddini and Dale is exposed as bogus. And all of this occurs after "Cheek to Cheek" has tied up all the loose ends that really matter! As if to atone for maintaining the plot beyond its natural span of life, director Mark Sandrich concludes the film with a short sequence of Dale and Jerry dancing outdoors—to an up-tempo version of "The Piccolino." Then an instrumental version of "Cheek to Cheek" plays behind a title card that says "THE END." As Arlene Croce—among others—has observed, the plot of *Top Hat* is full of holes. What coherence there is, though, can easily be understood to result from the two dance numbers—"Isn't This a Lovely Day (To Be Caught in the Rain)" and "Cheek to Cheek"—by means of which the narrative's plot is advanced.

Dance is an equally significant element of the romantic plot in Rodgers and Hammerstein's *The King and I* (1956). Despite the political and ethnographic dimensions of the plot, *The King and I* is definitely a romantic narrative. Early in the film, it is evident to the viewer that King Mongkut of Siam (Yul Brynner) is the only available romantic partner for Anna Leonowens (Deborah Kerr), the English widow hired to teach western forms of behavior to the royal wives and children. Capt. Orton, who brings Anna to Siam, and the Kralahome or prime minister, who greets her on her arrival, are obviously unsuitable romantic partners because of their ages and physical appearance. The significance of this romantic focus on the King becomes evident when we recall that in *Anna and the King of Siam*, the book by Margaret Landon on which the Broadway musical and Hollywood film are based, Capt. Orton proposes marriage to Anna before she steps ashore (3), and the Kralahome appears as an impressive erotic object. On Anna's first meeting with the Kralahome, for example, we read: "Although he was half naked and without any emblem to denote his rank, Anna knew that this Siamese noble compelled respect. There was about him an air of command and latent power oddly at variance with his attire" (25). Under other circumstances, this passage alone would be enough to signal to the reader that a romance between Anna and the prime minister will soon develop. Written confirmation of this intimation soon follows. When Anna has an official meeting with the Kralahome, "She found herself unable to think clearly. Then too, she was uncomfortably aware of his naked torso. She had never before done business with a half-clothed man" (33). This sexual tension between Anna and the Kralahome is reinforced by Anna's perception of the monarch as "this withered grasshopper of a King" (60). But, of course, *The King and I* has a different focus than *Anna and the King of Siam*, as its more intimate title suggests. Yul Brynner is consequently no withered grasshopper, and the Kralahome (Martin Benson) is sent to the margins of the film by the

The King (Yul Brynner) says something outrageous, as usual, to Mrs. Anna (Deborah Kerr) in *The King and I*.

plot and by the camera. It seems likely, in fact, that the attractive qualities of the Kralahome in the book (including his naked torso) have been transferred to the King.

Substantial barriers stand between Anna and the King, however, and frustrate the lovers' destined mating, even more so than in *Top Hat*. He is a king, after all, and she is merely a teacher. He is Siamese, and she is English. He is the polygamous father of 106 children, and she is a Victorian widow. Were two lovers ever so star-crossed?[20] To bring these two successfully together will require considerable narrative ingenuity — or at least a well-placed dance number.

Until that time, sexual tension is signaled whenever Anna and the King come together on screen by the sort of competitive-but-smitten carping that Fred and Ginger raised to an art form.[21] Anna keeps insisting on the private brick home she has been promised in her written contract. The King insists that no one's head can be higher than his, even when he is reclining on the floor. The King is high-handed, arrogant and tyrannical. Anna is self-reliant and fiercely independent, a true offspring of Katharine Hepburn. Sparks expectedly fly, but we know from the many other romantic comedies we have seen that it should all work out somehow in the end. This expectation is confirmed even at their first on-screen meeting when the King says to Anna, "You are not afraid of King.... Not to be afraid is good thing in scientific mind." When the King summons Anna at 2:00 A.M. to dictate a letter to President Abraham Lincoln, she is amused at his plan to send couples of male elephants to the United States for breeding purposes, but she does not correct him directly. Even so, he says to her, "You are very difficult woman...." This is the kind of sparring between lovers that all movie goers have grown accustomed to. And yet, problems still impede a happy resolution of the plot. Class and caste barriers remain, and there is still the polygamy problem.

Matters seem to have reached a low point during a shouting match in the schoolroom that leads to the King's troubled frown and to Anna's sad resolve to return to England. Oddly enough, a partial resolution occurs as a result of the troubling issue of polygamy. Lady Thiang, one of the King's wives and mother to the crown prince, intervenes at this especially difficult plot juncture to ask Anna to advise the King on a political matter without letting him know that he is being advised. Anna is first of all bent on returning to England and thus reluctant to get sucked back into her troubled relationship with the King, and she is naturally surprised that a woman who, in terms of plot, might be considered her rival for the King's affections should make such a request. By singing the song, "Something Wonderful," Lady Thiang effectively moots the issue of the King's polygamy and also establishes the common ground on which she and "Mrs. Anna" can both love the King. In the song's lyric, the King is described as a man who thinks with his heart and not his head and so a man who will always need a woman's love. Such a man might well deserve the love of two— or many—women. In any event, Anna is won over and so agrees to try to advise the King undetected. In terms of plot, this agreement is significant because it keeps Anna in the royal palace in Siam rather than sending her back to England.

The political issue that baffles the King involves a charge by some English diplomats that he is a "barbarian" and that Siam is consequently a candidate for English colonization.[22] Anna's role is to get the King into a position to rebut the charge without letting him see that he is being manipulated. Of course, he does see this—in so far as an absolute monarch can ever see such things—but he blusters on as if every one of Anna's suggestions is actually his own. It is thus decided to give a Western-style banquet for the English Ambassador and all of Bangkok's Western residents. Significantly, during the personal negotiations that lead to this resolution, Deborah Kerr and Yul Brynner engage in repeated side glances and smiles intended to let viewers know that both lovers realize what is going on. Their mutual recognition is sealed when, at the end of this scene, the King grabs Anna's hand and pulls her off to a giant statue of Buddha to pray for success in their diplomatic adventure. As in *Oklahoma!*, the characters realize that their hands feel grand when they are intertwined. During prayers, the King plays his old "whose head is higher" game, and Anna participates with more smiles and sidelong glances. It is unsurprising, therefore, that this sequence includes the King's agreement finally to give Anna her own house. As in an ideal romantic coupling, each side seems to be winning.

The banquet itself provides many opportunities for East-West humor as well as for further signals of the principal characters' love for each other. The King feels, for example, that Anna's off-the shoulder evening gown is too revealing. While dancing with her old suitor, Sir Edward Ramsey, Anna tells him that her "heart is very much alive," and she keeps glancing away to see what the King is up to. The King's looks reveal that he is jealous even so. He thus insists that he, rather than Ramsey, will take

Anna's arm to lead her into the banquet. The title *The King and I* seems especially apt during this sequence — and even more so during the following sequence, in which dancing becomes an agent of plot as it does in *Top Hat*.

The dance number "Shall We Dance" not only echoes the title of an earlier Astaire–Rogers film, it functions as one of the major icons of the screen musical. Any advertisement designed to make people want to buy videocassettes or DVDs of Hollywood musicals will contain — in addition to a Busby Berkeley production number, Gene Kelly "singing and dancing in the rain" and Fred in top hat and tails— shots of Anna and the King's animated dance, and no wonder! The scene is powerful and exciting, and it is also the apex of this film. Following the successful banquet, the King and Anna luxuriate in their social success like an American couple who have just given a successful party. The King gives Anna a valuable ring as a sign of his gratitude, and she looks lovingly at him as the soundtrack plays "Something Wonderful." The stage is definitely set for a climax of some sort when the King asks, "Everything going well with us?" and Anna repeats his words affirmatively. To confirm this dialogue, Anna soon begins a recitation about a young girl's first dance, which leads to her singing of "Shall We Dance" and to dancing by herself in definitely English ballroom style. The King is captivated, watching her with approval and singing along. Inevitably, he asks to dance in this fashion, and Anna teaches him. The scene contrasts East and West in the principals' costumes, in their discussions about Siamese and English sexuality and in their versions of English — the King says, "[A]fter each little star have leave the sky...." The scene also confirms the principals' suitability as cinematic lovers. All anyone needs to know about Anna and the King comes across clearly as they dance.[23]

As in *Top Hat*, however, the plot does not conclude with this episode. Moreover, there are clear signs that subsequent events may not lead to the kind of resolution that happily concludes *Top Hat*. As soon as Anna and the King have breathlessly stopped dancing, it immediately emerges that the King's new concubine, Tuptim, has been captured after an attempted escape with her young lover. When the King orders Tuptim whipped, Anna intervenes and cries that the King has "never loved anyone." Taking the whip into his own hands, the absolute monarch looks into Anna's face and finds that he is unable to punish the girl. Anna is appalled even so and returns the King's ring. The scene epitomizes the problems that forbid a conventional happy ending. Instead of straightening out misperceptions and confusion in order to bring about a perfect reconciliation between lovers, subsequent events lead to the King's death.

Once again Lady Thiang asks Anna to go to the King, but this time it is to his deathbed. As Anna reads the King's farewell letter, "Something Wonderful" again plays in the background, and so she naturally agrees to go to him. Her feelings for the King are thus apparent. At the same time, it is suggested that the King is dying of a broken heart, unable to reconcile his royal inheritance with his love for this English woman. Anna thus says about the dying King, "We can't hurt each other any more." This leads her son, Louis, to inquire, "You really like him, don't you, Mother?" and Anna to answer, "Yes, Louis, I like him very much, very much indeed." It is therefore appropriate for Anna — rather than Lady Thiang or Tuptim — to rest her cheek on the dead King's hand as "Something Wonderful" plays in the background. The overall plot therefore has not resulted in the happy union of lovers that usually seals a romantic narrative. However, as John Cawelti writes in *Adventure, Mystery, and Romance*, the death of one or both lovers need not be taken as a repudiation of the narrative formula: "The moral fantasy of the romance is that of love triumphant and permanent, overcoming all obstacles and difficulties. Though the usual outcome is a permanently happy marriage, more sophisticated types of love story sometimes end in the death of one or both lovers, but always in such a way as to suggest that the love relation has been of lasting and permanent impact" (41–42). The realistic socio-political issues dividing East and West in *The King and I* require that this musical take on the shape of the "more sophisticated types of love story" and keep Anna and the King permanently apart. For a few minutes while they are dancing onscreen, however, these realistic barriers disappear, and the "Shall We Dance" number completes the romantic plot in a manner that the design of the overall film narrative cannot provide.

The third way in which dancing can serve as a narrative agent in Hollywood musicals is, as I have written above, to reveal subconscious elements of a character's personality, what Aristotle calls that character's "thought." As Joseph Andrew Casper has observed, "[T]here are times when only dance can say what must be said. Certain states of soul or emotions, certain moods are difficult, well-nigh impossible to articulate without bodily movement" (148). *Carefree* (1938), another Fred Astaire–Ginger Rogers film, demonstrates this concept vividly. At the beginning of the film, Ginger's character, Amanda Cooper, a radio singer, is slated to marry Stephen Arden (Ralph Bellamy) but is reluctant to go through with the marriage. Stephen asks his psychiatrist friend Dr. Tony Flagg — played, oddly enough, by Fred Astaire — to help Amanda get in touch with her true feelings, which Stephen mistakenly believes will result in her choosing to marry him. Everyone in the audience must know that Fred and Ginger will end up together at the end of the picture, but how they will be brought together in view of the story's basic premises remains to be seen. Somehow the expected feelings of love must develop between Amanda and Tony (Ginger and Fred) despite the presence of Stephen and despite the professional restrictions on wooing imposed by Tony's role as a psychiatrist. Plot manipulation is thus crucial to the narrative's ultimate success,[24] but so too is "thought." In a reverse on the usual pattern, Ginger falls in love with Fred first in this romantic narrative, and he doesn't know it. What Amanda feels deep down must therefore be considered central to the plot.

As most viewers would also be aware — in 1938 or today — the romance between Fred and Ginger usually begins with some sort of tension, and the plot typically develops so that the tension can be eliminated in favor of a happily-ever-after romantic resolution. In this case, the initial tension between Fred and Ginger is, as is often the case, based on a misunderstanding. At the beginning of the film, Tony seems uninterested in Amanda, considering her "one of those dizzy, silly, maladjusted females who can't make up her mind." Furthermore, Tony believes that Amanda should marry his good friend Stephen. Since Amanda hears all of Tony's negative opinions on a tape recording, she naturally finds him condescending and obnoxious. Everything thus gets going according to the usual plan — demonstrated, let's say, in

Amanda Cooper (Ginger Rogers) and Dr. Tony Flagg (Fred Astaire) show their romantic compatibility by dancing together in *Carefree*.

Top Hat and *Shall We Dance*. On the basis of past experience, what we would expect is for Fred/Tony to lose his heart and spend the next 30 or 40 minutes trying to correct the misunderstanding and break down Ginger/Amanda's reserve. Things begin to tilt in this direction as Tony shows off for Amanda in "Since They Turned 'Loch Lomond' into Swing." Amanda initially seems pleased with Tony's efforts, and he looks up for her approval after he has demonstrated his skill at playing the harmonica, dancing and driving golf balls. But, she has already left the scene by the time he finishes his demonstrations, and Tony merely smiles at her departure instead of expressing a lover's frustration. Things are therefore not proceeding as normal. When Tony crashes his bicycle during the next major scene, Amanda seems to soften toward him even more, for reasons that John Mueller explains: "[Tony] again meets his discomfort with amusement—a trait [Amanda] apparently finds admirable" (143). In an Astaire–Rogers plot based on other premises, Tony and Amanda would soon dance together and discover that they were truly in love. In this story, only Amanda realizes this, and she does so because she dreams of dancing with Tony rather than because an actual dance fulfills their relationship. Tony still assumes that she belongs with Stephen.

In order to bring Amanda's amorous feelings to the surface—and perhaps to help the audience adjust to this variation on one of their favorite themes— Amanda dreams that she is romantically dancing with Tony in a dreamy setting and that the dance ends with the sort of movie kiss that usually signals that the two kissing lovers will live happily ever after. Mueller calls it a "full-out, no-kidding kiss," and admits that it runs counter to the no-kissing-allowed rule that controlled the pair's earlier films. Mueller stresses, though, that "it is *Rogers* who consummates the kiss.... In languorous slow motion, she reaches upward, wraps her arms around his neck, and then gradually pulls her body up until her face meets his" (144; Mueller's emphasis). This critical analysis definitely suggests that something different from the usual is at work in *Carefree*, and we may assume that different narrative exigencies call for different narrative strategies. In this case, the reversal that has Ginger chasing Fred requires a dance number that will reveal her inner feelings in a fashion that the outer action cannot make manifest.

The dance number "I Used to Be Color Blind" definitely fulfills these functions. As Arlene Croce explains, after consuming "a large meal of bizarre dishes that will induce [her] to dream[, Amanda] dreams a slow-motion duet with the doctor ... and wakes up in love with him" (140). Mueller's explanation of the number's function is similar: "This duet is of particular interest because it may well be the first 'dream ballet' in American musical comedy and, unlike its more famous counterpart in *Oklahoma!* (created five years later), it advances the plot: as a result of the dance, Rogers comes to realize she is in love with Astaire..." (143). The terms used by these critics—*slow-motion, dream ballet*—clearly suggest that the action represented by this dance occurs outside the causally interrelated series of actions that typically constitutes a film's narrative. Astaire dancing in slow motion is a definite sign that something unusual is occurring on the screen.[25] Costuming plays a part too. Amanda's white gown suggests a wedding fantasy, as does Tony's morning coat. The scarf that floats like gossamer from Amanda's wrist also indicates that the dance is occurring in some realm other than the diegetic here-and-now. The setting is also other-worldly, with huge artificial flowers and floating dance floors.[26] There is, in short, no doubt that when Amanda and Tony dance together so lovingly, this dance occurs in a dream. In fact, Amanda tells her Aunt Cora (Luella Gear) the next morning, "In my dream I was with the most wonderful man." Then, when Aunt Cora asks, "I wonder if it's possible to fall in love with a man you dream about?," Amanda answers, "Oh, I'm positive." Amanda is in love, and we have seen her dance with the man she is in love with. The only real problem remaining is to get this man to recognize his role in the romance and accept it.

Plot complications delay this recognition. Tony assumes that Amanda has merely experienced a "transference," as a result of which she mistakenly assumes that she is in love with her therapist. When he hypnotizes her into believing that she loves Stephen and hates Tony, Amanda accepts the suggestion even though it runs contrary to the inner feelings that everyone but Tony knows about. Eventually, Tony realizes that he loves Amanda and removes the hypnotic suggestions. Then they can marry and live happily ever after, as Amanda anticipated in her dream dance earlier in the film. Significantly, the two lovers are united by walking down the marriage

Curly (Gordon MacRae) sings to Laurie (Shirley Jones) about what a beautiful morning it is in *Oklahoma!*

aisle rather than in a grand dance duet. However, this dance duet has already taken place in Amanda's dream. It is perhaps ironic that a narrative that relies so heavily on the importance of dreams should so systematically satirize the field of psychiatry. It would take a foolish theory like analysand transference, we are led to believe, to convince a male lover that the woman for whom he is destined really should marry another man. Even Tony's subconscious, captured in a mirror, chides him: "If you doctors weren't such wise guys, you'd forget your textbooks once in a while." On the other hand, if it weren't for psychoanalysis, the plot variation that requires Ginger to dream of her happy ending with Fred would not have occurred in the first place. What the dream ballet accomplishes is to get feelings that cannot be made manifest in the usual cinematic ways up there on the screen.

In Rodgers and Hammerstein's *Oklahoma!* (1955), by the same token, the mixed feelings that trouble Laurey (Shirley Jones) concerning marriage, maturity and sexuality find expression through a dance number rather than through expository dialogue or through action. At the point in the narrative when this dance number occurs, Laurey has found the conventional tensions between herself and her ideal lover, Curly (Gordon MacRae), complicated by the intervention of the malign and unconventional Jud Fry (Rod Steiger). While the Laurey–Curly romance functions safely within the expected limits of romantic comedy — and thus provides the opportunity for songs like "People Will Say We're in Love" — Steiger's Jud introduces elements of sensuality and violence more to be expected in realistic films like *On the Waterfront* (1954) than in Hollywood musicals. No wonder Laurey is disturbed! In addition, Laurey is beset by doubts about leaving the protected world of rural adolescence to enter the adult world of love and marriage. As Laurey says to Aunt Eller (Charlotte Greenwood) shortly before the significant dance sequence, she "want[s] everything to stay just as it is," with "everything" defined by Laurey's natural surroundings on the farm and her untroubled life with Aunt Eller.[27]

This narrative crux is solved when Laurey goes out on the porch to sit in a rocking chair and inhale the supposedly magic "Elixir of Egypt" that she has bought from the peddler Ali Hakim (Eddie Albert). Laurey sniffs the bottle, closes her eyes and prays, "Elixir of Egypt, make up my mind for me. I'm waiting for an answer." The musical cue, "Out of My Dreams," then leads Laurey to imagine herself as the similar, but by no means identical, dancer Bambi Linn and to sing the full lyric. At the end of the song, Laurey walks toward Linn, touches her hand and imagines that *she* is now dancing out her psychological dilemma. In *The Hollywood Musical*, Jane Feuer uses the ensuing dance to epitomize a narrative trope popular throughout musical films of the 1940s and '50s: "Although not every dream sequence uses ballet in the strict choreographic sense, it's natural to refer to such interludes as dream ballets, since most of them do employ a narrative style of dance" (73). What is narrated here through the dream ballet is everything that Laurey is trying to work out for herself in the plot.

At the beginning of the dream ballet, choreographed by Agnes de Mille, Laurey (Linn) sees Curly (James Mitchell) and runs toward him, just as one side of the diegetic Laurey wishes to do. During the *pas de deux* that follows, it is evident that this dream ballet couple belong together as surely as the diegetic lovers who have been foolishly approaching and withdrawing from one another in the central plot. Then, just when a happy ending to the dance seems imminent, Linn turns perky and quirky, prolonging the dance sequence and representing another dimension of Laurey's deeply mixed feelings. Appropriately the music underlying the dancing elides at this point from "Out of My Dreams" to "Oh What a Beautiful Mornin'" and "Surrey with the Fringe on Top," two songs used earlier in the film to underscore the approaches and withdrawals of the central couple. In the dream ballet — and, we may anticipate, in the overall narrative — the Laurey character quickly abandons her coy behavior, and the ballet builds toward a wedding. Other, female, dancers join Linn and Mitchell, representing community sentiment by applauding the couple's decision to marry. These female dancers are soon augmented by male dancers who dance to "Surrey with the Fringe on Top" in the style of de Mille's earlier ballet, *Rodeo* (1942), another diegetically appropriate touch for a community settled in Oklahoma at the turn of the century. This segment of the dream ballet ends as Mitchell/Curly lifts Linn/Laurey's wedding veil, only to turn into Jud Fry.

The music turns movie-ominous, as a frightened Laurey hides her face and runs from Jud. Even when Laurey finds Curly again, Curly withdraws— probably revealing one of the diegetic Laurey's fears—and Jud forces Laurey into a cattle pen that opens into a brothel. All of Laurey's fears of change and adulthood are acted out in the ensuing segment in which female dancers enact bare-shouldered sexuality to the tune "I'm Just a Girl Who Can't Say No." Laurey finds herself trapped with no place to turn; the male dancers look on her plight, unaffected; and Jud looms ominously. Soon Jud grabs Laurey and briefly dances with her to a snatch of ragtime music, only to be quickly distracted by another female dancer. Sexuality abounds as the corps of female dancers shake their skirts provocatively, and the male dancers beat their arms like roosters. Laurey is frightened and confused, as the musical mixture of "Out of My Dreams" and "Can't Say No" vividly shows. In her confusion, Laurey joins the other dancers in a chorus line to indicate her partial embrace of mature sexuality and then flees up a flight of stairs that lead nowhere to indicate her desire to escape from Jud's form of animalistic sexuality. As in so many cinematic dreams, a hotel corridor dotted with closed doors then appears at the top of the stairs in order to symbolize Laurey's mental confusion.

At the end of this corridor, Lurey rushes out into a stormy version of the open skies that framed the opening segments of the ballet. Winds blow and a painted tornado cloud hangs on the horizon. In this ominous environment, Curly and Jud fight, with Curly revealing great bravery and determination to defend the woman he loves but Jud proving impervious to Curly's bullets. Perhaps unsurprisingly, Jud eventually kills Curly and drops his body at the feet of a stricken Laurey. The ballet then ends with Jud carrying Laurey off amid a great blast of stage fog. This dance sequence is both long and complex, and it has a decidedly unhappy ending. Even so, it serves effectively to advance the film's narrative. As Feuer also says, "Yet there is always traffic between dream and reality" in such dance sequences (70). Laurey is thus awakened from her dream by Jud's voice telling her to get ready for the party he is escorting her to.

Going to a party with Jud is thereby revealed to be the fix that Laurey has gotten herself into by playing too skittish and hard-to-get with Curly.[28] Even though Laurey may have had reason to object to Jud as an escort earlier in the film, her dream has revealed to her how truly dangerous and repugnant he is. The dream ballet has also revealed that Curly truly loves and respects her, that he would protect her even at the risk of his own life, and that Laurey and Curly should get married, despite her maidenly reluctance. Since everything turns out in the directions that the dream suggests, it should be apparent how essential to the overall narrative of *Oklahoma!* this dream ballet is. Jud tries unsuccessfully to kill Curly and Laurey, they get married, and the whole community of Oklahoma absorbs them happily into its fabric. In a sense all of these developments — with the possible exception of Jud's murder attempt — might have been predicted from the opening scenes in which we first see Curly and Laurey meeting on screen. After all, as Northrop Frye explains, that's what romantic comedy is all about. On the other hand, it can definitely be seen that this variation on the familiar plot has set the two lovers at crossed purposes in ways that cannot be easily adjusted through dramatic action or dialogue, especially when Jud Fry is thrown into the mix. Laurey's dream ballet thus solves a narrative problem by leaping across these difficulties by means of a dance.

In his *Recent Theories of Narrative*, Wallace Martin writes, "We need not go to school to understand the importance of narrative in our lives" (7). I hope that the examples cited in this chapter will make clear that we can also go to the movies to gain this knowledge. The six Hollywood musicals discussed here share the same basic plot in which lovers use dance somehow to advance the resolution implicit in their narrative situations as lovers in romantic comedies. The lovers in *Shall We Dance, Dirty Dancing* and — to a lesser extent — *Top Hat* dance because they are dancers by vocation so that dancing is an extension of their very nature as fictional characters. For this reason, their most successful interactions take place on the dance floor. In *Top Hat* and *The King and I*, the lovers cannot proceed with their romances through the normal dramatic agencies of action and dialogue, and so they dance to advance the romantic situation that is, after all, their excuse for being on the screen in the first place. In *Carefree* and *Oklahoma!*, on the other hand, the problems keeping the lovers from their destined happy ending are apparently too complex to be solved simply by dancing together. The problems must therefore be exposed by means of a dream ballet so that the diegetic plot can absorb and transcend these problems. In all of these cases, dancing functions as a narrative agent in order to help bring the romantic plot to its destined end.

Dance can often be a crucial element in the construction of musical film narratives because, as Joseph Andrew Casper writes, in *Vincente Minnelli and the Musical Film*, "Dance ... is a perfect medium to represent the subliminal self, festivity, and performance since it is coalescent movement, a harmony of disparate energies, directions, and contours, a movement that is elevated and extraordinary as these spheres of being are" (147). The values of dancing to the Hollywood musical have long been discussed in a variety of critical assessments. Elizabeth Dempster, for example, writes somewhat defensively that "[d]ance has been represented as a secondary, derivative, diversionary and minor art, an art which does not generate its own meanings" (24). To Leo Braudy, on the other hand, "The essence of the musical is the potential of the individual to free himself from inhibition at the same time that he retains a sense of limit and propriety in the very form of the liberating dance" (140). Despite their differing orientations, both Dempster and Braudy clearly feel that dancing should be integral to a musical narrative.

Since my discussion in this chapter argues for an understanding of how dance functions integrally within some film narratives, I am disposed to agree partially with both critics. As we began this discussion of plot with Aristotle, we may conclude with him also, in particular with his assumption, also in Chapter 26 of his *Poetics*, that "each art ought to produce, not any chance pleasure, but the pleasure proper to it" (46). In the case of the Hollywood musical, this pleasure quite obviously consists, in many cases, of understanding how there is no better way to get from here to there than through dancing.

5

American Places and Spaces

In their invaluable reference work *A Handbook to Literature*, William Harmon and C. Hugh Holman define *setting* as "the background against which action takes place," and they go on to explain that "[t]he elements that go to make up setting are: (1) the actual geographic location...; (2) the occupations and daily manner of living of the characters; (3) the time or period in which the action takes place, for example, epoch in history or season of the year; (4) the general environment of the characters, for example, religious, mental, moral, social, and emotional conditions" (469–70). To movie makers intent on wringing some sort of novelty out of a film genre as frequently abused as the Hollywood musical, it is only too probable that exploiting a new setting might seem to provide easy access to a much-needed novelty.[1] Representing characters who wear different clothes, speak with a different accent, engage in different "occupations and daily manner[s] of living" or who experience different "religious, mental, moral, social, and emotional conditions" than the characters obsessed with putting on one more Broadway show might seem just the ticket for a genre mired in familiarity. A quick scroll through the index of Clive Hirschhorn's *The Hollywood Musical* shows just how appealing this option has been historically—and geographically. Just about every section of the United States has been used as the setting for a Hollywood musical. Consider (alphabetically): *The Belle of New York* (1952); *California Holiday* (1966); *Carolina Blues* (1944); *Coney Island* (1943); *The Duchess of Idaho* (1950); *Greenwich Village* (1944); *Honolulu* (1939); *In Old Chicago* (1938); *It Happened in Brooklyn* (1947); *Kansas City Kitty* (1944); *Kentucky Moonshine* (1938); *Lake Placid Serenade* (1944); *Las Vegas Nights* (1941); *Louisiana Purchase* (1942); *Manhattan Parade* (1932); *Montana Moon* (1930); *Moonlight in Vermont* (1943); *New Orleans* (1947); *Palm Springs* (1936); *San Antonio Rose* (1941); *Springtime in the Rockies* (1942); *Texas Carnival* (1951); *Those Redheads from Seattle* (1953); *Two Sisters from Boston* (1946); *Wabash Avenue* (1950). As far as the geographical setting of a Hollywood musical is concerned, apparently anything goes.

It would be unproductive—and very tedious—however, to examine every possible American geographical and historical setting. For purposes of convenience, therefore, I am confining myself in this chapter to six films and (approximately) four settings.[2] First of all, I will look at turn-of-the-century family life in St. Louis in Vincente Minnelli's *Meet Me in St. Louis*, staring Judy Garland. Then a pre–World War

II winter vacation site provides a setting for Sonja Henie's skating and the music of the Glenn Miller Orchestra in *Sun Valley Serenade*. The South is the setting for the next two films, *Mississippi* and *Li'l Abner*, but the dreamy antebellum atmosphere of *Mississippi* is so different from that of Al Capp's Dogpatch that, even without the historical and economic contrasts that define the plots of the two films, they end up being "about" vastly different settings. Something similar might be said concerning the last two films discussed in this chapter, *On the Town* and *West Side Story*, two musicals set in New York City. Once again the directors have such different intentions that the New York depicted in one film might as well be in a different state or country from the other.

Meet Me in St. Louis (1944) is, first of all, one of the most admired of Hollywood musicals. In Hirschhorn's representative observation, the film is "113 minutes of unalloyed delight" (248). And, it is assuredly set in an actual geographical location. St. Louis, Missouri, is a place that many of us have visited and some of us live in. However, the film is equally rooted in what Harmon and Holman call "the time or period in which the action takes place." In 1944, most movie goers would be affected by the familial dislocations brought on by World War II. Many men were away in the armed forces. Many women were working outside the home. Many families were living away from their original places of origin. In the St. Louis of Minnelli's film, on the other hand, three — or four — generations of the same family live under one roof, Mother stays at home and Father rules the roost ... or thinks he does. Moreover, the two marriageable daughters in the family maintain chaste relations with their suitors until a sincere marriage proposal is secured. No quicky marriages with servicemen for Rose (Lucille Bremer) and Esther (Judy Garland) Smith! As Rick Altman writes in *The American Film Musical*, *Meet Me in St. Louis* provides a "family album of the American heritage" (78) rather than a picture of the war-torn America of 1944 — and this is a large part of the film's appeal.

Minnelli frames the story with period postcards of the four seasons, intended — as is the typeface of the opening credits— to recall an earlier time. The Smith house also signifies the past in its furnishings and kitchen appliances. In keeping with this turn-of-the-century locale, Esther regards her sister's marriage prospects as the only important factor in Rose's life. As Esther tells Katie the maid (Marjorie Main), "Although we love Rose, the brutal fact is that she isn't getting any younger." Since Rose is a mere senior in high school at this time, viewers can only chuckle indulgently at Esther's old-fashioned ideas. Esther feels this way about her own life, too, as she reveals in the number "The Boy Next Door," based on her crush on John Truett (Tom Drake). When John attends a going-away party for Esther's brother Lon (Henry H. Daniels, Jr.), Esther's romance progresses satisfactorily toward marriage, even though the two potential lovers begin by calling each other "Miss Smith" and "Mr. Truett." When leaving, John also tells Esther that the party has been "ginger peachy." These genteel usages are intended to be historically charming — and they are — as are the supposedly amateur musical entertainments at the party, including the sensational "Under the Bamboo Tree," performed by Esther and her little sister Tootie (Margaret O'Brien).

While pining for the boy next door and dancing with Tootie, Esther is dressed modestly in period costume with her newly washed hair appropriately draped down her back. Later on, Esther is painfully laced into a corset by Rose for the big St. Louis Christmas dinner dance. Perhaps the scene recalls Scarlett being laced into a corset by Mammy in *Gone with the Wind* (1939) for some viewers. Whatever the case, all viewers must see the scene as a signifier of those remote days when girls wore corsets instead of bobby socks. This is also the message sent by the film's final action sequence in which the whole family, including the happily paired-off sisters, head off for the 1904 World's Fair that has bracketed many previous plot developments. All of the female family members, including Tootie and Agnes (Joan Carroll), are dressed in white with the kind of enormous picture hats that most movie goers have seen only in old photos or in films about those good old days when, as Esther says at one point, "You can't get a good maid for less than $12 a month."

But St. Louis is also a place. When Tootie first enters the film, she tells Mr. Neely the iceman (Chill Wills) that St. Louis "isn't a town.... It's a city. It's the only city that has the World's Fair, my favorite." Then she asks, "Wasn't I lucky to be born in my favorite city?" Tootie's older sisters feel the same way at the end of the film. Rose says about the Fair, "We didn't have to come here on a train or stay in a hotel. It's

Esther Smith (Judy Garland) and her little sister Tootie (Margaret O'Brien) perform "Under the Bamboo Tree" in *Meet Me in St. Louis.*

right in our own home town," and Esther agrees: "I can't believe it, right here where we live, right here in St. Louis."³ Since Esther's speech is the last in the film, we may assume that it carries considerable thematic import and, in fact, St. Louis functions throughout as a plot agent. As many readers probably know, the plot of *Meet Me in St. Louis* turns on the possibility that the Smith family may move from St. Louis to New York.

During the Fall section of the film, Alonzo Smith, Sr. (Leon Ames), tells the assembled family that Fenton, Rayburn and Co. is "sending [him] to New York for good to be head of the New York office." All of the family members are stunned by his announcement. Mrs. Smith (Mary Astor) says, "New York is a big city. Not that St. Louis isn't big, but it doesn't seem big out here where we live." Rose is equally distressed because she knows that in New York only "rich people have houses. People like us live in flats, hundreds of flats in one building." Tootie adds, "I'd rather be poor if only we could stay here." Mr. Smith can only conclude, "I'm wrecking everybody's life." This is still the dominant impression when Tootie later complains to Esther, "You can't do anything [in New York] like you do in St. Louis." Although her complaint specifically refers to building snow people in the backyard, it obviously extends more broadly, since Mr. Smith quickly concludes that the family will not be moving to New York after all. Significantly, his epiphany arrives as the soundtrack plays the title tune, "Meet Me in St. Louis." In keeping with the film's genial satire of paternal authority, Mr. Smith then begins to boost the virtues of St. Louis—"New York hasn't got a copyright on opportunity. Why, St. Louis is headed for a boom that will make your head spin. This is a great town"—finally endorsing what the other family members have felt all along. To seal the thematic significance of this turnaround, we see that Mrs. Smith is too touched by her husband's announcement to respond in words; we see only that her eyes are shining with tears at the prospect of remaining in St. Louis.

Of course, the Smith family and the setting in which they function are, as Altman writes, "all too perfect" (78). When Tootie smashes her snow people, Esther—who has already sung her the song "Have Yourself a Merry Little Christmas"—tries to reassure her little sister by explaining, "The main thing, Tootie, is that we're all going to be together, just like we've always been. That's what really counts. We could be happy anywhere as long as we're together." Later, after her father has rescinded his decision to move, Esther says, "Oh, Papa, you've given us the nicest Christmas present anybody could ask for." This is some nice high school girl! Then, again, Judy Garland is the star of the film, and so we would expect her to be superhumanly charming. All the Smiths are like that, however. Early in the film, everyone, including Katie the maid, conspires to fool Mr. Smith so that Rose can receive a long-distance phone call from her prospective husband (Robert Sully). When Lon has no date for the Christmas dance, his sister Rose agrees to go with him. When Esther finds herself in the same situation, her grandfather (Harry Davenport) becomes her escort. Even though she is deeply disturbed about the potential move to New York, Mrs. Smith plays the piano so that her husband can sing "You and I" in order to console him after his announcement has been greeted by such hostility. Young St. Louis residents beyond the Smith family are also incredibly sweet and charming. When the young people in the cast gather for the famous "Trolley Song" number, one of the Clinton Badgers proudly invokes his father's inside information that the Fair is going to cost "a cool 50 million" to impress the others. Everyone is duly impressed, demonstrating that parental authority is more respected in 1903 than in 1944. Along the same lines, John Truett is more than happy to wear his father's tuxedo to the big Christmas dance. Things were apparently better then and there than they are here and now, and this is what *Meet Me in St. Louis* is all about.

Although critics are unlikely to accord *Sun Valley Serenade* (1941) the same sort of adulation usually heaped on *Meet Me in St. Louis*, both films rely heavily on setting to achieve their desired effects. Like Minnelli's famous film, *Sun Valley*, directed by H. Bruce Humberstone, uses setting to distract viewers from real-life problems. Released just before the outbreak of World War II, Humberstone's movie confronts the last days of the Depression in the manner pioneered by *Top Hat* (1935), that is, by largely ignoring the whole issue. Early in the film, Nifty Allen (Milton Berle), manager of the Phil Corey (Glenn Miller) Orchestra, is shown with a hole in the sole of his shoe as he tries to inveigle an advance from Jack Murray (William B. Davidson) for the out-of work musicians. Nifty succeeds, Murray gives him $500, and that is the last time that lack of money plays any part in the story. During the film's final production number, for example, a brief cut to Nifty shows him dressed in evening clothes, happily smoking a big fat cigar. Along these same escapist economic lines, just after the band has been booked, Ted Scott (John Payne), the band's piano player, tells his refugee ward Karen Benson (Sonja Henie) that she should feel free to order anything she wants from room service at their very comfortable hotel. When the orchestra moves to Sun Valley, Idaho, to play at Murray's hotel, Nifty and Karen both have fur coats to wear, and Ted and Karen wear stylish ski clothing whenever they go out on the slopes. The Depression causes these characters no serious problems in Sun Valley or in New York. Neither does the threat of war. Although Karen is a refugee from Norway, she seems to feel no traumatic aftereffects from her European experiences and so can quickly turn her attention to trapping Ted into marriage. When a government official comes looking for Ted just after the band has been booked, Phil Corey briefly touches on historical reality by asking Ted, "Did you forget to register for the draft?" However, the looming threat of the draft disappears when it turns out that the government man is from the Department of Immigration and that he only wants to alert Ted and the rest of the band that Karen is on her way to America.[4] The setting of this film thus functions to afford relief from the real-life problems confronting a film audience in 1941.

Other forms of escape also come along with this setting. For one thing, Sonja Henie gets to ice skate. An ice skating gold medallist in the 1928, 1932 and 1936 Olympics, the Norwegian blonde was a hot film property in the late 1930s in American films including *One in a Million* (1936), *Thin Ice* (1937), *Happy Landing* (1938), *My Lucky Star* (1938), *Second Fiddle* (1939) and *Everything Happens at Night* (1939). The narrative challenge in all of these movies—as some of the titles probably attest—was how to get Henie onto the ice, as other film writers faced the challenge of how to get Esther Williams into the water.[5] Sun Valley comes to the rescue here because the resort exists primarily to provide opportunities for ice skating and skiing. Henie therefore performs an appropriate solo on ice about halfway into the film while the soundtrack plays "I Know Why and So Do You." The climactic production number, choreographed by Hermes Pan, also features Henie and a cast of back-up skaters performing to a medley of (once again) "I Know Why and So Do You" and "At Last." As Hirschhorn explains, though, this breathtaking number was truncated when Henie took a nasty fall on the ice and studio head Darryl F. Zanuck refused to allow for another day of shooting (194). The film thus ends with shots of Karen and Ted skiing down a mountain instead of kissing — on or off the ice.[6] Since there have been many earlier shots of these two happily schussing downhill, the equation that involves Sun Valley, winter sports and the absence of all care is confirmed.

Another escape from the humdrum world of 1941 is provided by the Glenn Miller Orchestra. In fact, early in the film a viewer might be forgiven for thinking that *Sun Valley Serenade* would be, like *Orchestra Wives* (1942), a Hollywood musical about a big band rather than about a Norwegian ice skater and her husband-to-be. This impression is created because the film opens with Vivian Dawn (Lynn Bari) singing "It Happened in Sun Valley" with an orchestra. When she demands that this orchestra be replaced, the Miller Orchestra (here called the Phil Corey Orchestra) steps in to back her. First, though, the band plays its famous theme song, "Moonlight Serenade." This unmistakable tune is followed by Vivian's version of "I Know Why and So Do You" (dubbed by Pat Friday) with the full orchestra, including the Modernaires, and with Ted Scott/John Payne on piano and vocals. Since there are as many close ups of Miller as there are of Payne, one might well question whose story this is anyhow. Soon the band is playing "In the Mood" in a New York hotel ballroom, with Payne once more pretending to play piano. In Idaho, when Ted is late for a rehearsal, the Miller Orchestra performs "Chattanooga Choo Choo" with the Modernaires and Tex Beneke.[7] The diegetic premise is that the band must kill time until Ted arrives, but the real purpose obviously is to give movie goers a chance to see and hear the hottest dance band in American perform. The band reappears during the final production number, this time dressed in evening clothes and enhanced with strings, in order to furnish skating music for Sonja Henie. Although the Miller Orchestra could probably be worked into almost any kind of setting, Sun Valley seems to provide the kind of isolation necessary to let them function as just ordinary guys who make music instead of as the superstars who had already achieved unprecedented success with "Tuxedo Junction," "In the Mood," "Pennsylvania 6-5000" and "Moonlight Serenade."

While Sonja Henie and the Glenn Miller Orchestra may set *Sun Valley Serenade* apart from other Hollywood musicals we have been discussing, other elements of the film suggest continuities. The plot, for one thing, should be familiar to most viewers. When the blonde Karen and the dark-haired Vivian compete for the hand of Ted Scott, it should come as no surprise — even ignoring Sonja Henie's prominent place in the credits — that Karen emerges victorious. Then, too, the way that the Karen-Ted romance flirts with and runs away from sexuality should seem familiar to viewers accustomed to Hays Office romance. Part of the film's comic side emerges when it first develops that the Norwegian refugee is a marriageable young woman rather than a child. Under these circumstances, the little girl's room that has been prepared for her seems inappropriate. Inappropriate, too, is the notion that the handsome Ted Scott can be entrusted with such a vivacious blonde ward. At least that is what the hired nurse (Almira Sessions) believes, and so she resigns in a righteous huff. We all know that nothing untoward will take place between Ted and Karen, but it is part of the allowable sexual frisson of 1941 that we temporarily contemplate this remote contingency. This is also the tone later on in the film when Karen tricks Ted into spending the evening alone with her in a remote ski cabin. Typical cinematic male annoyance on Ted's part leads to his comic discomfort while trying to sleep on two chairs. He is angry that Karen has tricked him and determined that no sexual impropriety lessen his anger or destroy his relationship with Vivian. The temper of the times ruled by the Hays Code is epitomized both by Nifty's later suspicion that Karen has been "compromised" and by our knowledge that his suspicions are groundless. After all, we have been there in the cabin with Ted and Karen all along! In the same way it is predictable that Ted and Karen will end up happily together despite his earlier annoyance, despite Nifty's suspicions, and despite Karen's underhanded behavior intended to snare Ted.[8] The only thing missing is the final full-screen kiss, and if Henie hadn't fallen on the ice, we would have it.

Also predictable, but much less acceptable, is the film's treatment of African American performers. As part of the "Chattanooga Choo Choo" production number, Dorothy Dandridge and the Nicholas Brothers perform together. First the three sing a chorus. Then Dandridge exits into a cartoon train set, and the Nicholas Brothers perform their spectacular flash act, complete with flying leaps and splits. There's nothing else like it in the film — not even Sonja Henie's manic twirling and spinning on ice. This fact was recognized at the time of the film's release by the *Newsweek* reviewer who wrote that "the Nicholas Brothers stand out in their staccato dance routine…" (49–50). However, the Nicholas Brothers' part of the number is filmed apart from the rest of the diegetic rehearsal so that we never see the Glenn Miller Orchestra, Nifty, Vivian or any other white cast member in the same shot as Dandridge or the Nicholas Brothers. There is not even a cut away to Nifty, as there is in most other numbers by the band.[9] This cinematic segregation would make it easy to cut the performance for showings in racially hostile environments. That this is reprehensible is obvious; that it was a common practice in Hollywood musicals is undeniable.

The first song in the film is "It Happened in Sun Valley," and the song is reprised in various forms throughout the movie. Clearly, we are supposed to assume that it could *only* happen in Sun Valley. Such assumptions are validated even outside the film. When the Phil Corey band arrives at the Sun Valley train station, the sign also reads "Ketchum," most likely reminding many viewers today of Ketchum's most famous citizen, Ernest Hemingway. Hemingway finally moved to Ketchum in the fall of 1958 and lived there until his death in 1961, and so the location figures prominently in the writing of Hemingway's biographers. Carlos Baker, for example, writes about Hemingway's first visit to the location in 1939: "Sun Valley was the name of a complete small village near the old mining town of Ketchum. It had been built in the midst of the Depression by Averell Harriman and the Union Pacific railroad for the express purpose of making America ski-conscious. A publicity campaign was still in progress to celebrate its virtues as a year-round resort, with skiing and skating in the winter, and fishing and hunting in the summer and fall" (342). A.E. Hotchner adds that when Hemingway lived near Sun Valley, "It was easier to go to Hong Kong than to Ketchum" (190). Romantic excitement and remoteness clearly figure in the constructed perception of this region—and for others as well as for Ernest Hemingway. At the time of the film's release, the *Newsweek* reviewer quoted above noted that "[t]he famous Idaho winter resort sets the picturesque background for a frothy story..." (49). Bosley Crowther makes the point even more explicitly in his *New York Times* review, writing, "For those who may never get to Sun Valley, Idaho, and may never have the pleasure of racing madly down its white ski slopes or partaking of the many other luxuries of one of the world's most magnificent winter resorts, Twentieth Century–Fox has well provided a poor man's substitute" (6 Sept. 1941). It is no wonder, then, that when Phil Corey, Nifty Allen, Ted Scott and Karen Benson arrive in Sun Valley, they can happily ski, skate, play music, sing and fall in love. Significantly, all of this happens "far from the madding crowd" in a setting that is almost too good to be true—except that it actually can be found on the map.

Viewers of *Mississippi* (1935) are thrust into a similarly paradoxical situation. Before the Civil War there was definitely an American river of that name, and steamboats, including showboats like the one commanded by Commodore Jackson (W.C. Fields), could navigate the river. There was also a state of the same name that would eventually join the Confederacy. Even so, what happens in *Mississippi* has a life apart from any real place and time. *Mississippi* is really set in the "South" described in W.J. Cash's classic study *The Mind of the South* (1941): "What the Old South of the legend in its classical form was like is more or less familiar to everyone. It was a sort of stage piece out of the eighteenth century, wherein gesturing gentlemen move softspokenly against a background of rose gardens and dueling grounds, through always gallant deeds, and lovely ladies, in farthingales, never for a moment lost that exquisite remoteness which has been the dream of all men and the possession of none" (ix). Charles P. Roland agrees that this mythic South has been the creation of imagination rather than fact: "The legendary Old South became an idyllic land of kind and gracious masters and obedient and happy slaves. According to the late-nineteenth-century Virginia novelist Thomas Nelson Page, the society of antebellum Virginia was the noblest that ever lived. He believed even the moonlight shone brighter on it" (20). This Mississippi and this American South, rather than any actual geographic location, are the setting for this Hollywood musical.

In the film, Bing Crosby appears as Tom Grayson, a Quaker from Philadelphia whose engagement to marry Elvira Rumford (Gail Patrick) is signaled by his singing the Rodgers and Hart ballad "Soon." When Tom refuses to fight a duel with Elvira's former suitor Major Patterson (John Miljan), Elvira's father (Claude Gillingwater) orders him to leave the plantation in disgrace. Elvira, her father and the Major all think that Tom is a coward. Only Elvira's younger sister Lucy (Joan Bennett) admires Tom's pacifist principles, and she is secretly in love with Tom anyhow.[10] Soon, though, under the tutelage of Commodore Jackson, Grayson accidentally kills Capt. Blackie (Fred Kohler) and assumes the title of the "Singing Killer." By this time Elvira has married Major Patterson, and so—once Tom has straightened out some easily resolved confusion — he is free to accept Lucy's love. The film ends with Tom singing "Soon" to Lucy as a sign that they will live happily ever after.

The other musical numbers are equally well suited to the setting. Early in the film, the field hands gathered outside the French doors leading from the Rumfords' elegant ballroom begin to sing "Swanee River," and Elvira urges Tom to join in. Soon Crosby is singing lead as the African Americans happily retreat to the status of chorus.[11] Later on, Lucy recalls the scene as she stares tearily into the fire at her all-girls boarding school. Tom also croons "Down by the River" for the all-white audience on Commodore Jackson's boat, even interrupting the number for a violent scuffle with Capt. Blackie. Later on in the film, and sporting a very unconvincing moustache, he sings "It's Easy to Remember" for a large — also all-white — outdoor Fourth of July gathering. Alabam' (Queenie Smith), the leading female member of Commodore Jackson's troupe, sings "Roll Mississippi" with the assistance of five African American children billed only as the Cabin Kids. While Alabam' struts onstage in full costume, the Cabin Kids, dressed in ragged clothing, pop up out of a trunk. The Cabin Kids also perform "Little David" at the Rumford plantation after Commodore Jackson introduces them as "five of the little pickaninnies who work for me on the showboat."

As the music is suited to the setting, so are the other elements of the film's ambience, a credit to the director, A. Edward Sutherland. Elvira and Lucy wear eye-catching gowns, especially for Elvira's engagement party. The men usually wear top hats and cravats. Long shots of Commodore Jackson's boat steaming along the river provide a sense of spaciousness and leisure. The Rumford plantation is an imposing two-story structure, and its furnishings are very grand indeed! Even the establishing shots for Miss Perkins [sic] Seminary for Young Gentlewomen and Nadrick's Hotel Catering to the Flower of the South are framed with attractive flowers. W.J. Cash mocked the stereotypical version of the American South imbedded in the popular imagination as a "Cloud-Cuckoo-Land ... Perpetually suspended in the great haze of memory, ... poised, somewhere between earth and sky, colossal, shining, and incomparably lovely ... wherein life would move always in stately and noble measure through scenery out of Watteau" (124). Cash notwithstanding, this is the South that serves as the setting for *Mississippi*— a veritable fairyland.

Another element of the represented setting involves accents. Gen. Rumford is played by Claude Gillingwater, an actor whose long career stretching back to silent days often cast him in Southern roles, a fact that should not surprise us given the actor's striking physical resemblance to Mark Twain, especially when he is made up as Gen. Rumford. His daughter Elvira essays something of a Southern accent, as may be appropriate given her name. Joan Bennett makes no efforts along those lines, though, and so her Lucy sounds very much like Alabam', who sounds as if she would be right at home in other musicals of the day like *42nd Street* or *Golddiggers of 1933*. Bennett's Lucy seems equally equipped by accent to be a Broadway baby rather than a Southern belle. W.C. Fields has no Southern accent even though he pilots a boat on the Mississippi, but his passengers often simulate a Southern drawl. It probably should go without saying that Bing is not Southern for a moment, even when singing "Swanee River." But, one might object, accents are to a large degree functions of actors' mastery of their craft. There surely must be more to all this simulation of the South than the accents. Of course there is more to it, and — as we might expect — it has to do with race. African American characters appear frequently in *Mississippi*— lighting chandeliers, carrying boxes, bowing and scraping, in other words, as primarily atmospheric markers of the narrative's chronotope.

Dismissive racial attitudes are characteristic of *Mississippi*. Commodore Jackson is often attended by a black servant named Moses (John Larkin), whose usual function is to hand Fields his trademark glasses of whiskey. At one point, however, Larkin's character must act as coachman when the Commodore's troupe comes to entertain at the Rumford plantation. In this scene, the Commodore gets to heap familiar Fieldsian abuse on his servant, and he also gets to call him a "Senagambian." Race is also the stimulus for a famous Fields line when he says that the shortest of the Cabin Kids has a "head like a rocky ford cantaloupe." Since it is apparent that the child has been deliberately given the shaved haircut that makes this joke possible, his function as racial window dressing is patent. Slightly more influential in *Mississippi* is the Rumfords' family servant Lavinia, played by Libby Taylor. On the plantation, Lavinia gets to swoon over Tom Grayson's rendition of "Swanee River." Off the plantation, she gets to fuss over Lucy's dress before Lucy is reunited with Tom and to call Lucy "honey chile" in the bargain. A little later, Lavinia writes an ungrammatical, misspelled letter to Tom urging him to come back to the plantation to save Lucy from marrying Joe Patterson. Since this letter is actually shown in closeup onscreen, we can only conclude that its semi-literacy is as significant as its role as an agent of plot. Native American references also abound. Throughout the film, Fields repeats a tall tale about his exploits as an Indian fighter. In every case, he delivers the line, "I hacked a path through a wall of human flesh, dragging my canoe behind me." This braggadocio is exploded late in the film when the Commodore is frightened by three cigar store Indians carved in threatening postures.

What all this goes to show is assuredly problematic. The South represented as the setting for *Mississippi* is open to indictment as racially offensive as well as historically unrealistic. To see these debilitating effects as deliberate on the part of the filmmakers, however, is probably just as unrealistic as the setting is. The purpose of popular art is to please as broad an audience as possible. Sutherland and the other powers behind *Mississippi* must have assumed that the South depicted in their film would have this effect. But, what could they have been thinking? One clue to an answer is suggested when Patrick Gerster and Nicholas Cords write in the *Encyclopedia of Southern Culture*: "[H]istorians have not cultivated enough of a national perspective on the role the Yankee has played in both the original creation and the tenacious upholding of the South's legendary past. Studies of Southern myths have too often failed to explore how regional myths attracted a national audience" (1115).[12] W.J. Cash agrees that America — and "I include Yankeedom in the allegation"— has often been "not only ready but eager to believe in the Southern legend — that it fell with a certain distinct gladness on this last purely agricultural land of the West as a sort of projection ground for its own dreams of a vanished golden time" (62). Thus, A.E. Sutherland of London, Bing Crosby of Tacoma, Washington, W.C. Fields of Philadelphia and Richard Rodgers & Lorenz Hart of New York City could become what Gerster and Cords call "copartners in the creation of a regional pseudopast" (1116), filled with happy darkies and scary redskins, as the setting for *Mississippi*.

Dogpatch, the southern setting of *Li'l Abner* (1959), is as mythical as the setting of *Mississippi*, but the mythic imagery in Melvin Frank's film is almost totally opposed to that of Sutherland's earlier work. Whereas the Rumford plantation was unrealistically stylish and well appointed, the dwellings in Dogpatch are disreputable and subhuman. The Southern land that lovingly encased the principal actors in *Mississippi* was consistently filmed so as to whet the viewer's desire to live there. On the other hand, Dogpatch is, as Senator Jack S. Phogbound (Ted Thurston) says, "obscure, unknown, [and] poverty stricken." In what another character, Earthquake McGoon (Bern Hoffman), calls "this miserable pesthole," poverty, laziness, filth and ignorance seem universal. In *Mississippi* the gentlemen consistently dressed in top hats and silk cravats, and they carried elegant walking sticks or pistols. In *Li'l Abner* the men all wear tattered clothing, usually with an obvious patch on the seat of their ill-fitting trousers. The young women in *Mississippi* are pure and virginal, as is perhaps typified by the scene set in Miss Perkins Seminary for Young Gentlewomen where the female pride of the Southland are all attired in snow white nightgowns. The young women of Dogpatch are patently erotic, bare-footed, attired in scooped-neck tops and short shorts, and panting to get the males of the community carnally engaged.

This erotic disposition points to another contrast between the two films. The atmosphere of *Mississippi* is definitely male. Gen. Rumford, Commodore Jackson, Major Patterson and the hero, Tom Grayson, engage in "manly" activities like poker and dueling, and they make all the important decisions. Women are mere window dressing in this Southern world. In *Li'l Abner*, on the other hand, Pansy Yokum (Billie Hayes) is the most powerful figure in the community, and Daisy Mae (Leslie Parrish) is the one who figures out how to save Dogpatch from atomic destruction and how to save Li'l Abner (Peter Palmer) from being murdered by Gen. Bullmoose (Howard St. John). Furthermore, marriage is the principal concern of the story. Therefore, the lazy, unwashed, uneducated male figures assume second place in this story, despite the prominently announced name of the hero in the title.[13] Some things remain the same, however. The code duello of *Mississippi* is no more stringent than "the code of the hills" where "a promise is a promise" in *Li'l Abner*. And both films end with the central lovers happily locked in each other's arms. When all is said and done, Abner and Daisy Mae are as destined for each other by the narrative arc of the plot as Tom and Lucy are in *Mississippi*. Thus, both the (few) similarities and the (many) differences in these two films demonstrate how variously a setting can be developed to accord with different intentions on the part of filmmakers.

In an example of Jack Nachbar and Kevin Lause's formula of "convention plus invention," the plot of *Li'l Abner* follows a familiar pattern with some minor twists. Daisy Mae wants to catch Abner as her husband in the Sadie Hawkins Day race held annually in Dogpatch. However, the United States Government has decided to destroy Dogpatch with nuclear weapons because there is absolutely nothing of value there. Seeing her chance to snare Abner evaporating, Daisy Mae proposes that the community can be saved if anything unique and valuable can be found in Dogpatch. For

Stupefyin' Jones (Julie Newmar) and some male rustics cavort in *Li'l Abner*.

much of the film it seems that Mammy's Yokumberry tonic will be the valuable asset because it can turn scrawny, spavined hillbilly men into gorgeous hunks. Under this assumption, Gen. Bullmoose conspires to get hold of the formula for the tonic through community property rights by getting Abner to marry Appassionata Von Climax (Stella Stevens). Conspiracy is necessary because Abner has never shown any interest in Appassionata or in any other member of the opposite sex. Thus, it will be necessary for the General to use the services of Evil Eye Kleagle (Al Nesor) to stun Abner long enough for Appassionata to catch him. Everything goes according to the General's plan, and it seems for awhile that Abner will marry Appasionata, that Daisy Mae will marry Earthquake McGoon, and that the film will not end happily. Instead, the tonic turns out to be a libido killer, and so the government decides to go ahead and bomb Dogpatch. At the last minute, it turns out that the statue of the community's worthless founder, Jubilation T. Cornpone, conceals an actual message from Abraham Lincoln. This makes Dogpatch worth saving, and it also indirectly paves the way for Abner and Daisy Mae to marry and live happily ever after.

According to the opening credits, *Li'l Abner* is "based on the characters created by Al Capp"[14] in his long-running (1934–77) syndicated comic strip. From the success of the strip, it might therefore be assumed that viewers of either the Broadway show (1956–58) or of the film would arrive at the theater with pictures already in their minds of what Dogpatch, Abner, Daisy Mae and Mammy Yokum should look like. *Li'l Abner* responds to this situation by combining live action and cartoon-like sets — in the fashion later to be copied by Robert Altman in *Popeye* (1980) — to create a Southern setting that resembles a comic strip.[15] The houses, costumes, cars and stage props in *Li'l Abner* look as much like their comic strip originals as their creators could manage.[16] Live actors play the roles, however, and live chickens walk through the sets. As in *Finian's Rainbow* (1968), some chronotopic tension therefore results.[17] Thus, no matter how well Billie Hayes, Leslie Parrish and Peter Palmer act their parts, viewers might be forgiven for feeling that their own mental versions of Mammy, Daisy Mae and Abner might be closer to Capp's cartoon originals.[18]

Having recognized an important difference between *Mississippi* and *Li'l Abner* occasioned by the latter's previous existence as a comic strip, we might go on to note the difference between broad comedy and sentimental nostalgia. As has already been hinted, *Li'l Abner* resonates with a sexual emphasis entirely absent from *Mississippi*, and this contrast does not result merely from the quarter century that elapsed between the two films' releases. Capp's strip was famous for its satiric edge. As M. Thomas Inge remarks in *Comics as Culture*, "Al Capp's hillbilly comedy ... evolved into an influential forum for ridiculing the hypocrisies and absurdities of the larger social and political trends of the nation" (10). Edwin T. Arnold adds, in his "Al, Abner, and Appalachia," "Like Swift in *Gulliver's Travels*, Capp used the grotesque, the ugly, the absurd, and the outrageous to marvelous satirical purpose" (274). The film based on the strip therefore satirizes institutions and social practices with a brio impossible in *Mississippi*. *Li'l Abner* criticizes the United States government's fondness for nuclear weapons. Abner and Marryin' Sam (Stubby Kaye) perform "The Country's in the Very Best of Hands" to mock the government's tax-and-spend policies. Senator Phogbound is venality personified, and so it is no surprise that he is in the pocket of Gen. Bullmoose, whose goal is to corner all the money in the world before he dies. The Senator is also willing to offer Dogpatch as a site for radioactive waste[19] in order to protect the more valuable property of Las Vegas.

Capp-like satire also extends to America's obsession with sex so that the world of *Li'l Abner* more closely resembles that of *God's Little Acre* than of *Gone with the Wind*. Among the film's characters, for example, are Appassionata Von Climax — whose very name would bar her from *Mississippi* — and Stupefyin' Jones (Julie Newmar), who can paralyze men just by shaking her very statuesque body. Even Daisy Mae is repeatedly complimented on her remarkable build. It is apparent that *Li'l Abner* was released in an America defined by *Playboy* rather than by magazines popular in 1935, like *The Woman's Home Companion*. This sexual aura also embraces the plot development in which Yokumberry tonic turns several Dogpatch husbands into physically gorgeous hunks with no interest in conjugal relations. The men's wives perform "Put 'Em Back the Way They Wuz" as a sign of their own sexual hankerings, and Pappy Yokum (Joe E. Marks) recommends "Cornpone's Powerfully Potent Perpetually Passionizing and Romanticizing Potion" as an antidote. There may be a number of jokes about Commodore Jackson's fondness for alcohol in *Mississippi*, but neither the Commodore nor any other character in that film can be thought of in connection with an aphrodisiac. Those were, apparently, very different times Down South, as both Capp's comic strip and the Hollywood musical based upon it testify.

The difference can be figured, finally, in terms of choreography. When Tom Grayson sings "It's Easy to Remember" in *Mississippi*, he is backed by a female chorus from the riverboat who gracefully twirl large fans in unison while dressed in long gowns. The dancing in *Li'l Abner*, choreographed by Michael Kidd, is designed to suggest anything but grace. "Don't That Take the Rag Off'n the Bush" is an ensemble number early in the film intended to establish the rusticity of the citizens of Dogpatch. Foot-stomping, knee-slapping dance steps signify that these folks are awkward hicks, not Hollywood dancers. Since they are in fact Hollywood dancers—no more hicks than the chorus girls in *Mississippi* are riverboat performers—it can only be that this choreography is intended to function as an adjunct to the setting.[20] The principal dance number for the big Sadie Hawkins Day race features the same kind of dancing stretched over a longer period of time. Everything about these Southern rubes is funny, apparently, including the way they dance.[21] During a scene set in Gen. Bullmoose's mansion, the contrast of rural clodhopping and refined dancing is obvious, but because of the film's broad satirical intentions, neither side of the contrast is privileged. In comparison to the Southern world represented in *Mississippi*, however, the point of the contrast is much clearer. We need only recall W.J. Cash's arch description of the legendary South "wherein life would move always in stately and noble measure through scenery out of Watteau" to see how different this legendary South is from the equally unrealistic world in which Earthquake McGoon, Pappy Yokum and Moonbeam McSwine (Carmen Alvarez) stomp, clomp, scratch and spit up there on the screen. Setting is, obviously, far more than a matter of geography.

The New York of *On the Town* (1949) has more in common with the setting of *Mississippi* than with that of *Li'l Abner* because this New York is not, and never was, a real place. In the words of Albert Auster, the setting of *On the Town* is "a buoyant metropolitan utopia" (288). In such a location, three ordinary sailors on leave might very well find love and happiness-ever-after—and that is what Hollywood musicals are all about in the first place. Even so, many critics have found this variation on a familiar narrative situation far better than most films like it. Clive Hirschhorn, for example, calls *On the Town* "the freshest, most invigorating and innovative screen musical of the decade" (308). A *Newsweek* reviewer calls the film "a picture that achieves the rare virtue of being pure musical comedy instead of just another story with music tacked on" (Dec. 19, 1949). In the *New York Times*, the film's pre–Christmas release at Radio City Music Hall is noted in Bosley Crowther's observation, "The holidays should be nicer for having *On the Town* around" (Dec. 9, 1949). Some of the appeal surely results from the use by the directors (Gene Kelly and Stanley Donen) of actual New York settings to "open out" the film.²² Part of the appeal must be owing to the three male (Kelly, Frank Sinatra and Jules Munshin)²³ and female (Vera-Ellen, Betty Garrett and Ann Miller) leads. If we add a score by Leonard Bernstein (with contributions by Roger Edens) and book and lyrics by Betty Comden and Adolph Green, the critical enthusiasm for this film seems even more plausible. It seems to me, however, that to a great degree the appeal of *On the Town* lies in its presentation of a "utopian," post war New York City.²⁴

In a representative scene, the six principal lovers are filmed atop the Empire State Building at 8:30 in the evening. For singing and dancing purposes, it is convenient that there are no tourists present, and this despite frequent comments by these characters concerning the enormous human population of the city. Nor is there any hint of inclement weather at the top of the Empire State Building or any of the dirt and grime common in such urban locations. The sailors can therefore sit anywhere they wish and even slide across the floor on their knees without worrying about getting stains on their white sailor uniforms. Their dates don't worry about their nice dresses either as the six principals dance all around this set. When their antagonists — several cops and a professor from the Museum of Anthropological History — show up, these narrative agents pose no more real difficulties for the central characters than the possibility of soiling their costumes did. Although the sets are "realistic," then, the film gives us reality heightened and transformed.

Actually, all of the normal agents of stress and strain in any large city are no problem in *On the Town*. Hildy (Garrett) is able to avoid a massive police chase in her cab merely through slick driving, and the cops are the chief facilitators in getting the three couples back together at the end of the film. Everybody in New York is friendly and helpful. Merchants on the street give the sailors slices of fruit, subway riders give them directions, a cab driver gives them free rides. All this friendliness is filmed, moreover — especially during the production number "New York, New York"— against a montage of familiar tourist sights: the Statue of Liberty, the famous skyline, the El, Washington Square, Grant's Tomb, Central Park, Rockefeller Center and the Empire State Building. In this (all-white, all–English-speaking) New York City, it should come as no surprise that everything works out for the best for these deserving kids. John Lahr wrote in his obituary notice for Adolph Green in *The New Yorker*, "Green loved the city, and co-wrote one of its most celebrated anthems ['New York, New York']" (49). This film shows how completely Green incorporated this love in his writing.

There are, of course, other elements in *On the Town*. It is notable, for example, that everyone in New York is white — in the park, on the streets, on the subways. Then again, Hollywood featured this sort of casting in 1949. In keeping with this middle–American world view, when the sailors go to the Metropolitan Museum of Art, Ozzie (Munshin) turns a painting upside down. Apparently everyone has been looking at this painting the wrong way — or maybe not! Modern art is laughable in either case. So are foreigners. When the sailors and Hildy go to the Museum of Anthropological History, they meet Claire (Miller), a budding anthropologist and tap dancer. These five then do a spirited "Pearl of the Persian Sea" number in which the supporting dancers don Pacific Island masks and costumes and beat on native drums while Miller taps her solo. Although there is great energy on screen, there is also a clear sense that all of these ethnic props are comical—and probably that studying something like anthropology is pretty silly in any case. So is studying ballet. That is why Madame Dilyovska (Florence Bates), the ballet teacher of Ivy Smith (Vera-Ellen), is a drunk and a blackmailer. Significantly, even while valorizing middle–American values over those of foreigners, intellectuals and aesthetes, *On the Town* develops a setting in which ordinary people are free to handle the merchandise at New York museums.

Lest we lose sight of the fact, *On the Town* is also a first-rate musical. Both "New York, New York" by Bernstein, Comden and Green and "On the Town" by Edens, Comden, and Green are spirited ensemble numbers designed to showcase the talents of several talented performers. The same may be said for "You Can Count on Me," in which Alice Pearce replaces Vera-Ellen for reasons of plot development. "Main Street," with Kelly and Vera-Ellen, and "You're Awful," with Sinatra and Garrett, are witty duets in the famous Comden and Green idiom. Ann Miller's dance feature at the museum has already been mentioned, but there are also major modern dance production numbers featuring Vera-Ellen ("Miss Turnstiles" ballet) and Kelly ("A Day in New York" ballet). In these latter numbers, the influence of *Fancy Free*, Jerome Robbins' original ballet version of the story, is especially obvious, but

Frank Sinatra, Betty Garrett, Jules Munshin, Ann Miller, Gene Kelly and Vera-Ellen enjoy the sidewalks of New York in *On the Town*.

it is the songs—and especially "New York, New York"—that set this Hollywood musical apart.

To return to where we began, however, we should probably say that it is the setting that especially distinguishes *On the Town*. Even the subways are neat and clean, so that a sailor from Indiana might be forgiven for thinking that Miss Turnstiles is what he elsewhere calls "a real New York glamour girl."[25] And Vera-Ellen's Ivy seems to fit the part of New York glamour girl even if she is a Coney Island hootchy-cootchy girl at night. Betty Garrett's Hildy also looks and dresses the part—surprisingly, since she earns her living as a taxi driver. Ann Miller's character, Claire, is just plain rich, and so we might expect her to be rather elegant in dress and manner. Discovering such blessings in their recently acquired lovers understandably leads the sailors to propose a toast—"Let's drink to New York"—during a night of club-hopping. New York responds to this good will by overlooking all their violations of city regulations, by raising money for their taxi fare, and by enthusiastically cheering for them. And so, when the film ends with a pan of the skyline and a chorus singing that New York, New York, is "a wonderful town," viewers cannot help but agree. New York looks absolutely great in this film, as great as the legendary South of *Mississippi*, and just as unreal.

This New York is echoed—and then repudiated—in the opening scenes of *West Side Story* (1961), directed by Robert Wise and Jerome Robbins. The film opens with the (1957) Broadway show's overture over a puzzling graphic design. Gradually it becomes apparent that the design is based on the famous Manhattan skyline. Once this skyline becomes clear on screen, the camera then tracks from the harbor, past expressways, Central Park, skyscrapers, Grant's Tomb, Yankee Stadium and other sights familiar to film goers from documentaries and movies like *On the Town*. The sequence ends with tenements and a playground on the far upper West Side. This film is also set in New York City, apparently, but we are led from the beginning to assume that we will not be getting another version of the roseate hue familiar from earlier musicals about New York—or about St. Louis or Sun Valley. At the same time, this grittier New York setting authorizes action different from a romp in the Museum of Anthropological History or the St. Louis Christmas dance.

This expectation of different action is reinforced by the introduction of different kinds of actors—members of the Jets and Sharks street gangs. The film's first production number involves carefully choreographed street violence between the two factions in which teenagers are nearly beaten and rumbles nearly develop. Despite these ominous possibilities, there is a definite sense of joyous rhythm to the dancing that represents these developments. The diegetic narrative may focus on gang violence, in other words, but the surrounding film is, after all, a Hollywood musical. Thus, when Tony (Richard Beymer) and Maria (Natalie Wood) first meet at a dance, they are surrounded by members of the warring gangs, but special effects allow the camera to focus on only the two central lovers.[26] The climactic battle in which Tony kills Maria's brother Nardo (George Chakiris) also mixes these two ingredients. Nardo most definitely dies in this scene, but the site for the mortal battle, under the highway, is as clean as a Hollywood soundstage. The fighting, furthermore, is obviously choreographed. That the rumble and Nardo's death are mere plot developments is clear because the preceding and following scenes are set in Maria's bedroom, a free romantic zone related to the song "Somewhere" rather than a locale for urban discord. In this respect, the New York of *West Side Story* is a different, edgier setting than the ones we have seen already, but it is a setting used to authorize very similar plot developments.

The original elements of this setting go beyond its function as a context for warring — albeit artfully choreographed — street gangs. When the police come along to chase the Jets home after an encounter with the Sharks, Riff (Russ Tamblyn) tells Police Lt. Schrank that such outdoor activity "keeps us deprived children off the foul city streets." The speech demonstrates, first, that the Jets are not intimidated by the police and, second, that social theories about ghetto youth are vulnerable to satire. These points are made more emphatically in the production number "Gee, Officer Krupke." Jumping off from Riff's premise that the "cops ... believe everything they read in the papers about us cruddy j.d.'s," this song ridicules psychiatry, social work and the entire criminal justice system. While any of these forces might be ridiculed in a typical musical, it is unexpected that the specific details of the ridicule should candidly identify controversial social problems: physical abuse, narcotics addiction, gender ambiguity. This number alone testifies to how far *West Side Story* departs

The sidewalks of New York are less hospitable to George Chakiris and the other Sharks in *West Side Story*.

ideologically from *On the Town* and *Meet Me in St. Louis*. In "America" another social issue receives attention when Nardo sings about resident American prejudice against Puerto Rican immigrants. Anita (Rita Moreno) sings that in America a person is free to achieve any dream. Nardo realistically responds that immigrants are truly free only to wait tables and shine shoes. If we merely recall how delighted servants were to serve white Americans in earlier Hollywood musicals, Nardo's musical critique acquires even more social impact.

Not all of the film's politically shocking moments occur during songs, however. As a contemporaneous reviewer observed in *Variety* (Sept. 27, 1961), the film effectively captures "the brutality of the juve gangs which vent upon each other the hatred they feel against the world." Thus, at various points in the film, tabooed terms such as *wop*, *spic*, *mick* and *polack* are used by members of the rival gangs. Lt. Schrank says that tolerance of Puerto Ricans will "turn this whole town into a stinking pigsty." To balance the scales, he also condemns the Jets and "the tinhorn immigrant scum you come from." Because of Schrank's reprehensible attitudes, attention is diverted from the ethnic hatred displayed by the juvenile delinquents to the various forms of hatred tolerated in the adult community that is so critical of them. Doc (Ned Glass) says, "When do you kids stop? You make the world lousy." One of the Jets, Action (Tony Mordente), responds, "We didn't make it, Doc." Action, the other Jets and the Sharks are obviously less infatuated with New York than Tootie is with St. Louis. Perhaps for this reason, it is Action and the other Jets who nearly rape Anita in Doc's store, thereby setting up the bloody conclusion in which Tony is shot to death. Society is thus indicted in the film, but so are the individual characters involved in the plot. Only the central lovers are exempt from this criticism, as is appropriate in a Hollywood musical.

It is apparent, then, that *West Side Story* both follows and departs from some generic patterns established by other Hollywood musicals. It is also apparent that the departures are largely justified by the film's setting. This is a New York of mean streets, tenements and back alleys rather than of pristine landmarks and sunny afternoons. And yet, because *West Side Story* is a Hollywood musical, the sordidness is carefully contained. As Howard H. Prouty observes in *Magill's Survey of Cinema*: "[A]lthough much was made at the time about the film being shot on location 'in the streets,' in fact most of the film is quite obviously studio based..." (1828). When the Sharks and their girls climb tenement stairs to the roof in order to perform "America," for example, there is the occasional graffito on the wall, but there is no garbage in the stairwell. Then, too, the roof is highly stylized, an appropriate setting for a musical production number rather than a squalid dumping ground for anything that can't be contained on the crowded floors below. The alley in which Tony seeks for Maria's apartment is also stylized rather than "realistic." Atmospheric laundry sways above ground level. There is an occasional box to signify trash. But, there is no real garbage, there are no rats, and no Sharks appear, even though Maria lives right in the heart of their territory. Even when Maria cradles Tony's head in her lap after he has been shot to death at the end of the film, the ground of the playground shines in places, as if with rainwater, but there is no real dirt of any kind in this poverty-stricken environment. Perhaps the most revealing scene involves Tony's solo "Maria." This number begins in the gym where Tony has just met his love and expands out to include the whole neighborhood. Tall tenements stretch toward the sky, a word is chalked here and there on a sidewalk or fence, streetlights throw shadows, but there is no threat of urban violence anywhere. Even the playground looks nice and safe — at nearly midnight. Significantly, the camera frequently cuts from these markers of the story's urban setting to extended close ups of Tony's face. The scene suggests that Tony is both inextricably part of this setting because of his diegetic character and still apart from it because of his role in the romantic plot.

Other elements of the film point toward the same conclusions. When Maria sings "I Feel Pretty" in the dress shop where she works, a few exposed bricks serve to establish that this shop is not on Fifth Avenue, that it is not the sort of place where Claire would buy her dresses in *On the Town*. Only a few shots dwell on this fact, however, and only a trilled *R* here and there suggests that Maria and the other dancers are new immigrants to America. Maria's bedroom also contains hints that she is not as flush as the showgirls in *Golddiggers of 1933*. When she sings the duet "A Boy Like That" and "I Have a Love" with Anita, however, this room becomes an "anywhere" in which musical performances of a high order can be filmed. Since we have already accepted this bedroom as a refuge for Maria and Tony in earlier scenes, we are probably ready to accept the room as a purely musical space even if it is in the midst of a violent, impoverished setting. For me, this dual focus is epitomized by the closing credits, in which the names of the professional movie people who have brought *West Side Story* to the screen appear as if chalked on a graffiti-filled fence. In probably the unique instance in which this has ever been true, none of the graffiti is obscene. One is stumped to think of another instance of this in the whole history of graffiti extending back to Pompeii. *Just enough* hard-core realism is how much Robert Wise and Jerome Robbins wanted for *West Side Story*, and that is how much we get.

Examining the settings of these six Hollywood musicals validates Mikhail Bakhtin's observation, in *The Dialogic Imagination*: "The chronotope as a formally constitutive category determines to a significant degree the image of man in literature.... The image of man is always intrinsically chronotopic" (84–85). The characters in these films cannot exist in any other spatio-temporal environments. The sailors from *On the Town* cannot go on liberty in Sun Valley. The Sharks and the Jets cannot live in the antebellum South. The inhabitants of Dogpatch cannot move to New York.[27] Moving to New York is considered a potential disaster for the Smith family of St. Louis. Despite these strikingly conflicting settings, however, characters in these films sing, dance, fall in love and — with the exception of poor Tony and Maria — live happily ever after. That is to say, they act like characters in a Hollywood musical.

6

Fred and Gene in Never Never Land

Motion pictures have long been regarded with suspicion by some cultural critics on the ground that they reproduce illusions and dreams instead of recording what these disgruntled critics think of as "reality." According to Robert Sklar's *Movie-Made America: A Cultural History of American Movies*: "This is the principal reason why the message of the movie image was described as myth or dream. In ordinary language, myths and dreams are falsehoods—fantasies, fictions, imaginary tales" (195). Steely-eyed critics of the movies could easily argue that there is no hard evidence that a gangster like Rico Bandello ever repented as he lay dying in an alley as Edward G. Robinson does in Mervyn LeRoy's *Little Caesar* (1930), or that Robin Hood robbed from the rich and gave to the poor as Michael Curtiz and William Keighley have Errol Flynn do in *The Adventures of Robin Hood* (1938), or that Rick actually told Ilsa to get on the plane to Lisbon as he does in *Casablanca* (1942), directed by Michael Curtiz. While William H. Phillips concedes in his *Film: An Introduction* that "[m]ovies have been dismissed as 'ribbons of dreams' and Hollywood as a 'dream factory,'" he adds, counter to critics of film's lack of realism, that "[n]o one questions the entertainment value of movies: the proof is in the huge number of people who watch them...." (2). Thus, even if films technically represent myths or dreams, many viewers applaud them enthusiastically.

Whether or not we accept Phillips' ad hoc argument based on films' popularity, we can easily imagine how much more strident the realists' criticism would become when cowboys, or baseball players, or street gang members begin to sing and dance spontaneously as they go about their business.[1] This stridency might be countered by Rick Altman's observation in *The American Film Musical*: "Overall, the musical is marked by a process according to which the spectator's reality is opposed to the ideal image which the film represents (the musical being the quintessential product of Hollywood's 'dream factory')" (185).[2] Again, dreams seem to be a problem for no one but the reality police. And then fantasy is another generic step away from the realistic, whether travelers cross a Tibetan mountain into Shangri-La as they do in *Lost Horizon* (1937), directed by Frank Capra; or star warriors elude the agents of the evil empire by shifting into hyperspace as they do in *Star Wars* (1977), directed by George Lucas; or a hero is able to return from the dead because he loves his Buttercup so deeply, as happens in *The Princess Bride* (1987), directed by Rob Reiner. Perhaps

Phillips can be called upon for another extenuating answer: "Fantasies show life as large audiences wish it to be. These films are not mirrors of life outside theaters but fun-house mirrors that briefly entertain viewers, often by showing them characters and situations that they can identify with and that make them feel heroic, powerful, rich, romantically desirable..." (429). In other words, if we are willing to set questions of realism or verisimilitude temporarily aside, we can see that all these forms of film narrative satisfy some cravings of some of their viewers.

This is especially true of what is probably the ultimate cinematic insult to partisans of the "real world"—the fantasy musical in which the implausibilities of *The Princess Bride* or *Lost Horizon* are yoked to the semantic and syntactic properties of the movie musical.[3] As Rick Altman has demonstrated in *The American Film Musical* (131–141), the musical fantasy was an early, and has continued to be a popular, staple of the genre, especially what he calls the "Ruritanian" fantasy in which student princes in uniform and princesses disguised as peasant girls can sing and dance their way to romantic fulfillment without any interference from the forces of "reality." Of equal significance, though, is the musical fantasy adjusted to American proportions. As Joseph Andrew Casper explains, "America is the theatrical and film musical comedy's idiom.... If the situation is placed elsewhere ... the piece is either about Americans or their presence is strongly felt" (73). Two well-known Hollywood musicals that fit this pattern snugly are *Yolanda and the Thief* (1945), starring Fred Astaire, and *Brigadoon* (1954), starring Gene Kelly.

Yolanda is supposedly set in the South American country of Patria, and *Brigadoon* is supposedly set in the place identified in the title. Both films were directed by Vincente Minnelli, and as Casper maintains, "[M]any of Minnelli's musicals as a whole ... function as fantasies, counterpointing the world on the screen with that in the darkness" (40). Patria and Brigadoon are both locations more compatible with the characters' desires and those of their audiences than is the "real" world in which these audiences actually live. In this regard, these two films directed by Minnelli epitomize everything that some critics object to in the fantasy musical. From a more sympathetic direction, we might consider James Naremore's rendering of Minnelli's directorial credo: "[A]n unbridgeable gulf separates art from life. Life is cruel, messy, and brief, whereas art, which is determined by life, is pleasurable, coherent, and outside time" (126). That Minnelli directs in these two films what most Hollywood musicals buffs consider to be the two finest male dancers ever to work in films pretty much guarantees that the whole cinematic experience will be "pleasurable, coherent, and outside time."

Fantasy is still in the ascendancy in *Finian's Rainbow* (1968), directed by Francis Ford Coppola, and *Xanadu* (1980), directed by Robert Greenwald. However, Fred Astaire was approaching 70 years of age when he made the former film, and Gene Kelly was very little younger when he starred opposite Olivia Newton-John in *Xanadu*. As many have argued, furthermore, the Hollywood musical was hardly enjoying its very best health at the time both films were made. Finally, neither film was directed with Minnelli's genius, especially his professional gift for working within a fantastic chronotope.[4] Investigating two films made while Fred and Gene were at their professional best and two containing the final significant singing and dancing roles for each should provide us with an opportunity to consider what makes these two dancers the great masters of the genre and also with further information about what Hollywood musicals can be "about."

Comparison/contrasts of major figures in any art form seem inevitable: Shakespeare versus Dryden, Bach versus Mozart, Willie Mays versus Mickey Mantle, Fred Astaire versus Gene Kelly. As John Russell Taylor, asserts, "The only real competition the cinema has ever offered [Fred Astaire] is Gene Kelly, and there the competition is only on the most superficial level of standing; in every other respect their personalities, aims and styles are so different there is little useful point in trying to compare them" (64). It is possible, that is to say, that the Hollywood musical features two best dancers, not just one. Gene Kelly makes this point coyly in *That's Entertainment* (1974) when he says that, despite the claims of Rita Hayworth, Vera-Ellen, Leslie Caron and other gorgeous on-screen dance partners, Fred Astaire is "the greatest partner I ever danced with." In support of this claim, an edited clip from *Ziegfeld Follies* (1946) follows. In this scene, "the only time we had a chance to work together" before 1974, Kelly and Astaire dance together to the Gershwin tune "The Babbitt and the Bromide." The diegetic reason for this unprecedented duet is that Florenz Ziegfeld (William Powell), now in Heaven, gets to put on just one more show. Naturally, everything must be only the best. Esther Williams performs a "water ballet." Fanny Bryce and Red Skelton do comedy numbers. Judy Garland and Lena Horne sing. Fred Astaire does two dance numbers with Lucille Bremer. And Fred and Gene dance together. In *Ziegfeld Follies*, the two premiere dancers also sing Ira Gershwin's lyrics about two men (Babbitts) who have nothing worthwhile to say to each other (Bromides), on Earth or in Heaven. In *That's Entertainment*, the singing is cut, but most of the dance remains. Because of showbiz customs familiar at that time (1946)—Bob Hope versus Bing Crosby, for example, or W. C. Fields versus Charley McCarthy—the dance duet sometimes suggests a feud between the two stars: Fred seems not to recognize Gene at the beginning of the number, Gene knocks off Fred's hat, and so forth. Perhaps the mock feuding also insulates the pair from any hint of homosexuality when they dance together. Viewers can only be impressed by the dancing, in any case, whether they encounter "The Babbitt and the Bromide" in *Ziegfeld Follies* or in *That's Entertainment*. As Kelly attests in the latter film, "When you dance with Fred Astaire, you really have to be on your toes." They both are on their toes in this number, and we can only be grateful.

Kelly and Astaire dance together again in *That's Entertainment, Part II*. This film even seems to draw on "The Babbitt and the Bromide" for cinematic structure. *Part II* opens with historical film intended to illustrate the development of the American cinema. Since this film is intercut with photos of Astaire and Kelly, from babyhood on up, it is apparent that the two premiere dancers are intended to be seen as pillars of the medium. The final, autographed photos of the two serve as their credits in this film, the first in a series of clever credit titles, featuring falling dominoes, burning brands, cash register plates, filing labels, messages in a bottle and so forth. The title song, taken from Astaire's film *The Band Wagon*, follows, sung first in clips from that film and then by Gene and Fred. Then the two dance—not as well as in *Ziegfeld Follies*, but not badly considering that Astaire was over 70 and Kelly was nearly eligible for Social Security. Throughout the film, Fred and Gene are heard in voiceovers introducing the film clips—not confined to musicals this time around. They also sing verses of "Be a Clown" and "That's Entertainment" with lyrics updated to introduce other film clips. In the film's finale, however, the two famous old hoofers actually dance again, with considerable animation and panache, finishing up with a handshake intended to echo the conclusion of "The Babbitt and the Bromide." Surely all fans of the Hollywood musical must be reassured to see that these two can still do it, despite their ages, that these two dancers are still number one simply because they are who they are. John Russell Taylor writes that "[t]here is one great divide [within the basic requirements of the (musical) medium], though ... every now and then mixed and mingled: between the singer's musical and the dancer's musical. Most real *aficionados* tend to prefer the dancer's musical..." (12). Cleary *Yolanda*, starring one of these dancers, and *Brigadoon*, starring the other, are prime examples of "the dancer's musical."[5] By the same token, it should be clear to anyone that these two films occur within totally fantastic chronotopes.

Yolanda and the Thief opens on a patently theatrical studio set depicting an Edenic landscape in which a kindly old schoolteacher (Ludwig Stossel), with a llama in tow, first forgives two charming moppets for their tardiness and then provides a geography lesson that definitely situates the narrative in an unrealistic chronotope: "This is a land which you can see is warmed by the sun and cooled by the benevolent wind. Here life is pleasant, because people are good. It is a fact that jails are empty and the churches are filled. Over us is the Patria sky, which is the color of Heaven; and around us are the fields of flowers, and the cool streams, full of friendly fish...."[6] Then the schoolmaster leads the whole class in singing the national anthem of Patria—oddly enough entitled "This is the Day for Love." The Never-Never-Land aura of this school is continued in the next sequence in the convent that has served until today as the home of the film's female lead, Yolanda Aquaviva (Lucille Bremer). Not only is everyone in the convent warm and friendly, everyone is dressed to take advantage of the film's Technicolor. The convent girls are all in red, the nuns in blue. These unrealistic details are, of course, purely intentional on Minnelli's part and perfectly in keeping with the children's fantasy by Ludwig Bemelmans (1898–1962) that supplied the original story for the film. As Minnelli observes in his autobiography: "I tried to get the quality of Bemelmans's books and illustrations, a curious mixture of worldliness in high places and a primitive naiveté, using his sometimes crude prism colors right out of a child's paint box and combining them with beautifully subtle monotones" (156). "Crude prism colors right out of a child's paint box" continue to define the chronotope throughout the film.

In a scene cut from the final print, Yolanda was to have witnessed a puppet show mounted to celebrate her eighteenth birthday and her emergence from the convent. All that we learn in the existing film is the subject of the puppet show: the importance of guardian angels. Eventually we will come to realize that this is a promise of things to come, a fact confirmed when the scene immediately cuts to Johnny Parkson Riggs (Fred Astaire) on a train entering Patria. We learn at this point that Johnny is planning to steal some of Yolanda's vast fortune with the aid of his partner, Victor Budlow Trout (Frank Morgan). Such dishonesty would ordinarily conflict with the fairy tale atmosphere of the narrative to this point. However, in another hint of the plot's future, Mr. Candle (Leon Ames), an actual guardian angel, is also seen on the train. It is clear even at this point in the film that Johnny and Yolanda must end up together, and so his dishonesty must be somehow subsumed into the fantasy environment first established by the schoolmaster and the Mother Superior (Jane Green) at the convent. It seems probable, moreover, that this resolution will somehow involve guardian angels.

The fantastic setting of the opening scenes is extended when Yolanda arrives home from the convent. The first sign is the completely cloudless sky—"the color of Heaven" identified by the schoolmaster. Then, a combination of vaguely South American costumes on Yolanda's servants and the baroque architecture of her mansion signal that we are surely not in Kansas any more, or any place else in the real world! In another film, this air of unreality might be upset when Yolanda's Aunt Amarilla (Mildred Natwick) boasts nostalgically that the family's servants are "born here and live their lives here," and she is contradicted by several of them. But even this slight air of realism is soon mooted when Johnny and Victor pull up to Yolanda's palatial home in a picturesque taxi, and we see that the mansion and its surroundings is an obvious sound stage set. Part of this Never-Never-Land environment is a sunken garden, complete with grazing does, in which Yolanda prays for practical guidance in front of a statue of a guardian angel. Strings play in the background during the scene, and Johnny eavesdrops from a tree. Having heard Yolanda's prayer, Johnny decides to impersonate her guardian angel in order to relieve her of her fortune. Again, we might otherwise discern a conflict between this confidence game and the otherworldly setting of the film. In terms of the film's overall plot trajectory, however, this potential conflict is immediately resolved when Mr. Candle comes along and helps Johnny out of the tree. While Johnny (and perhaps some especially trusting members of the audience) believe that Candle is another confidence man, it seems unlikely that Leon Ames would stoop to such dastardly behavior after his heartwarming performance in *Meet Me in St. Louis*. Approaching this plot crisis from another direction, it would be hard for *anyone* to believe that Fred Astaire would steal that nice young woman's money.

In the next sequence a mild note of eroticism is introduced as Yolanda luxuriates in a fantastic bathtub. But, like Johnny's criminal intent, the erotic cannot be allowed to compromise this film's fantastic chronotope. Yolanda is covered up with bubbles, except for her head and naked shoulders, and so whatever titillation this scene provides will have to occur within the viewer's imagination rather than on screen—as in an earlier scene in which the convent girls frolic in the shower while covered up with long robes. Even so, this erotic suggestion probably seeps over into the next sequence in which Johnny pretends to be Yolanda's guardian angel when she visits him in the lobby of the Hotel Esperado—which is unaccountably (in 1945) full of customers of both sexes. During this encounter, Johnny still seems to be engaged in bilking Yolanda of her fortune even though he says that she is "pure of heart," a quality she illustrates by kissing his hand and giving him a white flower. Although Yolanda thinks at this point that Johnny is an angel, and although Johnny thinks he is interested only in Yolanda's money, there is a definite romantic charge between them.

In the next scene, Johnny is going to bed in the hotel room he shares with Victor, obviously touched by Yolanda's behavior in the lobby. Johnny is sleepless, clearly disturbed, by his mixed feelings toward Yolanda. After crushing out a cigarette, Johnny prepares for sleep in his very fashionable Chinese pajamas. String music signals that all may not be what it seems, however, and so Johnny picks up a (now red) carnation associated with Yolanda in the previous scene, lights another cigarette, grabs his clothes and hurries outside, where marimba music is playing. Within the narrative proper, any or all of these actions might seem appropriate, and yet there are soon signals that Johnny is not really acting within the narrative proper.[7] To blur the line between the dream ballet and the diegetic narrative, Johnny repeats all of his actions from an earlier scene in which he walked out of the hotel into the town, but these actions are now obliquely accented. A man who borrows a cigarette from Johnny, as he did in the earlier scene, for example, now has multiple arms, like an Asian statue. A clarinet on the soundtrack signals that this kind of character is acceptable in a dream, even if not in reality, and Astaire/Johnny begins to walk in dance steps rather than in a normal gait. Soon he is surrounded by symbols of his mental confusion: a rain of coins representing Yolanda's wealth,[8] beautiful female dancers representing the romantic opportunities offered by other women, constricting blue veils representing the confines of monogamy. The scenery shifts symbolically, too, as in a dreamscape: multiple yellow brick roads (appropriately enough in light of Frank Morgan's earlier role as the Wizard of Oz), Daliesque white sets with surreal outcroppings, suggestive winds. This portion of the dance reaches a sort of climax as Johnny pulls the veils from a mysterious female figure and discovers that she is Yolanda herself. If Johnny's feelings were less complicated, the dance could end here with the central romantic couple dancing together to a full orchestra. When Yolanda sings the Freed-Warren song "Will You Marry Me,"[9] however, the dance and the plot become appropriately complicated. A tom-tom beat introduces other female dancers as a sign of the erotic opportunities that must be sacrificed if Johnny marries Yolanda, and then male dancers join in, bringing with them echoes of the sporting life that Johnny will also leave behind if he marries a girl raised in a convent. Throughout this segment, however, Johnny repeatedly pulls out his empty pockets to signify his impoverished condition and his inability to share the sensuous life of the dream dancers. The dance suggests that Johnny desires all of these physical pleasures even while realizing that marriage to the virtuous Yolanda is his most likely economic opportunity to attain them. As Minnelli explains in his autobiography: "Since Astaire has a horror of legitimacy and marriage, the fantasy ballet sequence evolves as greed fights it out with the mating instinct" (156). When he dances with Yolanda again in this dream, Johnny seems to be in the position of having his cake and eating it. Yolanda is gorgeous and clearly in love with him, and they dance together beautifully.[10] It is only when the female dancers return and bind Johnny with gossamer blue veils that he recalls the restrictive dimensions of marriage to Yolanda. The dream ends with Johnny all tied up in his bed sheets and Victor standing by with a pitcher of water ready to awaken Johnny from his nightmare. And a nightmare it finally seems. "Oh, what a jam I was in!" he says to Victor Trout on awaking.

Johnny's psychological dilemma is made clear by the dream ballet but the final resolution of this narrative dilemma is not yet clear.[11] Perhaps some of this narrative indeterminacy results from the film's overall chronotope of fantasy. The dream ballet in *Carefree* is offset and balanced by a country club that suitably affluent people might belong to. Dr. Flagg's office in that film is no more fantastic than the doctors' offices in other romantic comedies. In *Oklahoma!*, Aunt Eller's farm may be obviously stylized, but it is just as obviously supposed to be somewhere out west. When characters in these films perform dream ballets, therefore, the chronotopic contrast of dreaming and waking is apparent. In *Yolanda and the Thief*, this contrast is absent because the waking world of Patria is so fantastic. Therefore, some other plot device will have to clear up Johnny's ambivalence and bring a happy ending to the romantic narrative.

The plot proceeds when Johnny, in the persona of Mr. Brown the angel, comes to Yolanda's house to get her power of attorney and thus control of her vast fortune. In keeping with the film's fantastic chronotope, Aunt Amarilla asks Mr. Brown the very pertinent question, what brought him to "an out of the way place like Patria?" Plot is then served when Yolanda signs over her money and Johnny hurls a bag full of negotiable bonds out the window to Victor. Musical fantasy is served when it turns out that Johnny can play the harp, which he does while serenading Yolanda with her namesake song. The number is mostly song rather than dance, and the camera is usually on Yolanda rather than Johnny. Things are moving right along toward a happy resolution, however, since Mr. Candle retrieves the bonds even as Yolanda and Johnny are obviously falling more deeply in love.

Minor plot complications aside, the next important sequence in the film takes place at the Patrian national carnival, a perfect opportunity for Minnelli to do what he does best. As Rick Altman writes in *The American Film Musical*, "Minnelli's film is perhaps the first simultaneously to place heavy emphasis on the visual delights of a foreign land and to distance itself from that emphasis. Much of this distancing grows out of Minnelli's developing passion for saturated, garish colors which seem to draw attention to themselves..." (187–88). Carnival costumes are a natural illustration of Altman's point, as are the bizarrely costumed dancers and jugglers who fill the screen. Eventually Yolanda and Johnny dance together to "Coffee Time," once more showing on the dance floor the compatibility that should help them to live happily ever after.

Since it is too early to end the film, Johnny continues to feel guilty about his underhanded methods and decides to leave Patria and Yolanda even if it means going to jail somewhere else. On the train out of the country, Candle finally reveals to Johnny and Victor that he actually is an angel, that he has been managing events up until this point according to his own plans, and that he wants Johnny to return and marry Yolanda. The next sequence, set at the very colorful convent, has Johnny and Yolanda happily married. Candle shows up and gives Johnny a photograph showing the newly married couple five years hence. In the photo, they are the parents of four children, and so Johnny looks seriously perplexed. Yolanda, on the other hand, observes, "It's impossible but it is rather sweet." In a sense, the same might be said about *Yolanda and the Thief*.

In an essay review for *Magill's Survey of Cinema*, Carl Macek quotes Vincente

Tommy Albright (Gene Kelly) and Fiona Campbell (Cyd Charisse) dance amidst the heather in *Brigadoon*.

Minnelli's description of *Yolanda* as "a fantasy film that just didn't perfectly come off" (2733). Viewers might be tempted either to agree or disagree with Minnelli's judgment of his own film. When he expresses such extreme dissatisfaction with *Brigadoon*, however, I am disposed to disagree. Minnelli recalls in his autobiography (279–81) that *Brigadoon* was mostly an opportunity to experiment with CinemaScope. "The wider screen might capture the breadth of the Scottish moors," he recalls, "but it didn't help the more intimate aspects of the story" (280). Clive Hirschhorn agrees with Minnelli, writing in *The Hollywood Musical* that this "whimsical fantasy …

in which two Americans from Manhattan stumble across the fairytale village of Brigadoon while out grouse-shooting and learn that it only materializes out of the highland mists once every 100 years, needed either the stylized limitations imposed on it by the theatre or the spaciousness of the real outdoors, but not the compromise offered by MGM" (343). It seems to me, on the contrary, that, while not up to the standards set earlier by *Singin' in the Rain* (1952) and *The Band Wagon* (1953), *Brigadoon* (1954) is surely more than a technological experiment. With Gene Kelly, Cyd Charisse and a score by Alan Jay Lerner and Frederick Loewe, the film would logically have to have some remarkable aspects. As Hirschhorn's plot summary indicates, though, *Brigadoon* is at least another fine example of a Hollywood musical based on a fantastic chronotope.

As in *Yolanda and the Thief*, the film's opening shots signal fantasy. The Highlands in which Tommy Albright (Gene Kelly) and Jeff Douglas (Van Johnson) are hunting at the beginning of *Brigadoon* are obviously located not in Scotland but in a Hollywood studio. This fantastic impression is reinforced as light gradually illuminates the village of Brigadoon and a chorus sings "Brigadoon" in the background. The villagers of Brigadoon are costumed as colorfully as the inhabitants of Patria, and they have the added distancing provided by antiquity. That is to say, they look charming and very old-fashioned at once, an effect deepened by their tools and occupations. Tommy and Jeff are costumed as contemporary sportsmen from the 1950s, and their hunting rifles are apparently up-to-date. The inhabitants of Brigadoon wear kilts and shawls, they use horses to pull wagons full of rustic produce and they engage in forms of commerce familiar to most viewers only from history books or crafts fairs. It is no wonder, then, that Tommy observes, "Funny clothing they wear around here." This remark takes on thematic significance when we see Tommy and Fiona Campbell (Cyd Charisse) together in a single shot. Tommy's sporty clothes show that he definitely comes from a different world than Fiona's, signified brilliantly by her bright yellow shawl.

The historical contrast signified by costuming is temporarily elided in an ensuing production number, "I'll Go Home with Bonnie Jean," as Charlie Dalrymple (Jimmy Thompson) allows Tommy and Jeff to join in the bachelor dance celebrating his upcoming wedding to Fiona's sister (Virginia Bosler). A spirit of jubilant, transhistorical, male camaraderie results on screen, at least in part because the nature of the CinemaScope camera encourages the kind of across-the-screen dancing best suited to Kelly's style. Hands are clasped behind the dancers' backs, another Kelly trademark, and — most characteristic of all — Kelly beams into the camera throughout the dance with a full-toothed smile. As Rick Altman observes in *The American Film Musical*, "For Kelly dance is ... a silly, clowning, childish activity, an expression of the eternal youth which seems even today to be fixed in Kelly's smile" (57).[12] (Another fine illustration of Altman's characterization will appear later in the film in Kelly's solo, "Almost Like Being in Love.") Shortly after the "Bonnie Jean" number, however, Kelly dances a duet with Cyd Charisse, "The Heather on the Hill," and his smile is once more on display, even though this number requires ranging over the stage set in several directions instead of just gliding smoothly from side to side. In this striking performance, it is evident that Tommy and Fiona will somehow end up together, and it is equally evident that these lovers are acting out their love in a fantastic chronotope rather than in a cinematically representational one.[13] Two possible responses to living in this Never Never Land arise shortly after "The Heather on the Hill" when Jean Campbell's rejected suitor, Harry Beaton (Hugh Laing), calls Brigadoon this "cursed town," and Fiona calls it this "blessed place." Since Tommy and Fiona are destined by the plot to be lovers, Tommy must sooner or later come to share Fiona's response to her world — just as Johnny comes to embrace Yolanda's culture in the earlier film.

As in *Yolanda*, a kindly older male character helps to bring about the resolution. Mr. Lundie (Barry Jones) is not an angel like Mr. Candle — he is the village schoolmaster — but he as warm, charming and understanding as an angel. Thus, he is the perfect one to explain the mystery of Brigadoon to Tommy even though, as Fiona says, "It will be so hard for you to believe." The story Lundie tells is that Mr. Forsyth, the village pastor in the mid–1750s, fearful of the danger of witches to his innocent flock, prayed that the village might be protected from "all evils that might come to Brigadoon from the outside world after he died." His prayer, like Yolanda's, was answered — in this case by magically removing the inhabitants of Brigadoon from history except for one day every century. The day of Charlie and Jean's wedding is the second day on which Brigadoon has returned. Therefore, Fiona, who seems a perfect lover for Tommy, was actually born in 1732 rather than sometime around 1932, like Tommy's New York fiancée Jane Ashton (Elaine Stewart). This will obviously require some getting used to from Tommy but, as Mr. Lundie tells Tommy later on in the film, "If you love someone deeply enough, anything is possible, even miracles." There is, then, little to stand in the way of a happy ending except for Tommy's full acceptance of the miraculous.

To create dramatic tension, Tommy cannot make a commitment to Fiona at this point, and so other incidents follow. The wedding between Charlie and Jean takes place with bagpipes and drums, marching clans and blazing torches— a smaller scale Edinburgh Tattoo. Harry Beaton tries to escape from Brigadoon in an attempt to destroy himself, the town and the whole miracle. Jeff accidentally shoots Harry. Fiona and the village disappear into the mist for another century. Tommy and Jeff return to what passes for the realistic chronotope of New York City. In terms of Minnelli's recollection in his autobiography: "The modern-day segment, concentrated in a noisy bar in New York, would spell out everything that is ugly and lacking in humanity about the everyday rat race" (280). As in *Yolanda and the Thief*— and as also in *Finian's Rainbow* and *Xanadu*— the fantastic chronotope of Never Never Land called Brigadoon functions as a more desirable alternative to this "everyday rat race."

Before returning to Manhattan, Jeff has told Tommy that their experience in Brigadoon was "a fairytale ... dream stuff, boy, all made up out of broomsticks and wishing wells." After being disgusted by his return to Jane and New York, Tommy maintains, on the contrary, "Sometimes the things you believe in become more real to you than all the things you can explain away or understand." Of course, Tommy is right. When he and Jeff return to the site of Brigadoon just to touch emotional base with the place where Tommy was once happy, his love for Fiona is strong enough to call the village back from its magical sleep so that he can join her for an eternity of glorious days once a century. Although this is a slight displacement of the traditional formula for a happy ending, the idea that love conquers all is as strongly confirmed in *Brigadoon* as in any other musical comedy. By rooting this happy ending in a place and time that never were and never can be, moreover, Minnelli protects his narrative from outside criticism as surely as Brigadoon is protected by Mr. Forsyth's prayer "from all evils that might come to Brigadoon from the outside world after his death." Joseph Andrew Taylor claims about Minnelli's cinematic settings in general that they are "chosen ... to depict points in time and space which elicit in their inhabitants a reaction to escape from, transcend, or transform their particular circumstances" (74). Clearly this is what *Brigadoon* does, and for that reason, it seems to me, the film deserves a vote of thanks from all of us.

However, hardly anyone has a kind word to say for the film in which Fred Astaire made his last significant appearance as a song-and-dance man, *Finian's Rainbow* (1968), directed by Francis Ford Coppola. At the time of the film's release, Renata Adler wrote, quite harshly, in *The New York Times*: "There is something awfully depressing about seeing *Finian's Rainbow* this year,[14] this way — with Fred Astaire looking ancient, far beyond his years, collapsed and red-eyed; with film work so shoddy that the camera hardly ever includes his feet when he dances and that people who have been sopping wet in one cut are absent-mindedly dry in the next; with nobody even bothering to put the whole, cheesy, joyless thing, which is in execrable color — Technicolor and wide-screen Panavision — into synch." Around a decade later (1977), in an early book about Coppola's film work, Robert K. Johnson substantially agrees with Adler: "The plot is woeful. The acting, according to Coppola himself, is quite poor. Fred Astaire is wasted" (177). In the next decade, John Mueller continues this criticism in *Astaire Dancing* (1985): "The blame for *Finian's Rainbow* seems to rest primarily with its twenty-nine-year-old auteur, director Francis Ford Coppola, a man who had never before had anything to do with musicals" (401). It is seldom that film critics proceeding from such varied premises arrive at such a consistent conclusion about a film's overall quality — in this case, a negative conclusion. And yet, *Finian's Rainbow* does star Fred Astaire and Petula Clark; the score by Burton Lane and E.Y. Harburg is chock full of wonderful songs; the Broadway play version enjoyed a long and celebrated run; and Francis Ford Coppola eventually directed some of the most memorable films of modern times.[15] There must be something worthwhile in this film. That is to say that we may finally come to endorse one of Robert K. Johnson's other judgments: "[A]lthough the film is a failure, there are some nice things in it" (66).

One of these nice things is the film's fantastic chronotope. *Finian's Rainbow* takes place in Rainbow Valley, Missitucky, a fantastic environment located not far from Fort Knox in the United States. As the film opens, Finian McLonergan (Fred Astaire) and his daughter Sharon (Petula Clark) come to Rainbow Valley from the equally fantastic Irish landscape of Glocca Morra.[16] As the credits roll, Finian and Susan walk cheerfully along through an American landscape that includes the Statue of Liberty, the Bay Bridge in San Francisco, Mount Rushmore and the Grand Canyon. The scenery is attractive, Susan sings "Look to the Rainbow" winningly, and the Irish wanderers seem unfatigued by the distances they travel and the baggage they carry.

All of this adds up to a chronotopic signal of fantasy. Even John Mueller is willing to give the scene its due: "There is a wonderful improbability to this sequence — to cover all the territory shown, the wanderers would have to trek thousands of miles. The juxtaposition of these scenes with the fanciful Lane-Harburg ballad was exactly the right wistful touch" (404). This opening sequence is surely what led the *Variety* reviewer (Oct. 9, 1968) to call the film "a light, pastoral musical fantasy." Other elements freely contribute to this impression. Rainbow Valley itself is, despite the free-ranging chickens and running streams, obviously a studio set, not a real place.[17] Thus it is — like Patria and Brigadoon — an appropriate locale for the whimsically paranormal. In this fantastic chronotope live an interracial commune of tobacco farmers comfortably integrated into an idealistic economy, a mute, bare-footed girl who communicates through dance, a leprechaun, and a scientist who is experimenting with growing already-mentholated tobacco. When Finian decides to bury a pot of gold that he has stolen from the leprechaun within this chronotope, it seems more plausible than if he were to do so in the worlds created within *Top Hat* or *Night and Day*. Nor could even such unrealistic films as these successfully incorporate the plot development in which Sharon is falsely accused of witchcraft. While the whole incident of groundless and irrational accusation is probably intended to echo the Red Scare that haunted America in the late 1940s when the Broadway show was first produced, it can be accepted as a plausible narrative development only within the fantastic chronotope defining the whole story.

One serious flaw in *Finian's Rainbow* is Coppola's willingness to depart from this chronotope. The romance between Sharon and Woody, the head tobacco farmer (Don Francks), is fantastic enough for anyone, certainly as unrealistic as anything that happens in *Yolanda and the Thief* or *Brigadoon* — or in *Top Hat* or *Night and Day* for that matter! However, in the principal sub plot, about racism and corrupt Southern politics, events often taken on a quasi-realistic quality. Early in the film, for example, the sheriff (Dolph Sweet) and a political flunky named Buzz Collins (Ronald Colby) come to evict the happy farmers from their racial utopia. The villains sweat appropriately in the summer heat, like the fat white men in *Cat on a Hot Tin Roof* (1958) or *In the Heat of the Night* (1967). Meanwhile, the farmers look cool and collected. The two groups of characters seem to be living in different chronotopes — at least in different climates. Chronotopic conflict continues as the farmers joyfully defy and jostle the minions of the law while singing "This Time of Year." In 1968 any movie viewer would have seen enough images on television of Southern law enforcement agents beating, hosing and arresting people just as well-intentioned as these farmers to feel that singing and dancing cannot overcome armed racism, at least not without some broken heads. Part of the conflict surely arises from the fact that the Broadway show premiered in 1947, the year that Jackie Robinson integrated major-league baseball, while the film premiered in the year that Martin Luther King, Jr., was shot. Racial politics altered so radically in American between those two dates that the joyful good spirits of 1947 look preposterous in 1968. History aside, two incompatible cinematic visions often collide in this film. Another striking incident occurs near the end of the film when the district attorney (Wright King) lights the fire that will burn Sharon and Woody to death even as

Fred Astaire tries to keep up with Barbara Hancock in this publicity shot for *Finian's Rainbow*.

Finian and Og the Leprechaun (Tommy Steele) argue about pots of gold and magic wishes.[18]

Since everything works out all right, these apparent conflicts may not be as disturbing as they seem at first. After all, Johnny Riggs was going to steal Yolanda's money within the fantastic environment of Patria, and so why can't two young lovers be destined to be burned to death within the fantastic environment of Rainbow Valley? Even to ask the question is to italicize the absurdity of the chronotopic contrast that is allowed to develop in *Finian's Rainbow*. As usual, John Mueller is happy to identify the problem with this film: "What Coppola came up with was a film in which the attempted whimsy becomes leaden and the social commentary becomes trivial and self-conscious" (401). Although the *Variety* reviewer is more forgiving — "Overall, film has an ethereal quality: it's a blend of real elements, such as love, greed, compassion, prejudice, and other aspects of human nature both noble and otherwise; yet, it's also infused with mystical elements of magic, leprechauns, pixies and wishes that come true" — Mueller probably comes closer to articulating the reaction of most viewers today. Coppola has two kinds of stories, belonging to two kinds of worlds, in *Finian's Rainbow*, and he can find no convincing way to bring them together or to disguise their incompatibility.

But we are perhaps forgetting that this film is a Hollywood musical. What about the songs and dances? First of all, there is Fred Astaire. (At any rate, that's why I went to a theater to see the movie in 1968.) Mueller writes approvingly that Fred "gives one of the liveliest and most endearing performances of his career" (401) in this film. And, according to Peter Cowie's analysis of the film, "Astaire might have lost his peerless, lissome grace on the dance floor, but his timing remains as sharp and precise as ever" (42). We might naturally assume that a dancer approaching his seventieth birthday might engage in shorter solos and attempt fewer leaps and lifts than the dancer in his thirties who made those incomparable movies with Ginger, and we would be right. Fred Astaire still wears a scarf around his waist instead of a belt, and he still slants his hat at a jaunty angle, but he typically dances only a few steps per shot in *Finian's Rainbow*. Some of this is undoubtedly owing to Coppola's passion for antic cutting, but part must be owing to the fact that we all slow down with age—even Fred. Still, Fred performs a creditable solo to "When the Idle Poor Become the Idle Rich." After singing the lyric—which is often literalized by Coppola, as when two kids ride by on horses after the lyric refers to losing money on a horse race—Fred essays a few steps alone and with Petula Clark as part of a grand production number. Then he dances alone on a platform equipped with crates, boxes and a suspended bale of hay. As might be expected from a performer his age, the solo is much shorter than, say, "Slap that Bass" from *Shall We Dance* (1937). It is more surprising that Fred punctuates his dance with shouts of "Hey," in the manner of Gene Kelly, as if he is amazed at what he has just done. He repeats this "Hey" to accompany a few dance steps just before he exits the film at the end. Mueller writes that "[t]he final images in Astaire's last film musical show him frolicking down the road, and far away" (407). It is rather a shame that a syrupy chorus is singing "How Are Things in Glocca Morra" as he is doing so.

Most of the dancing slack created by Fred's advanced years is taken up by Tommy Steele. One of Steele's featured numbers, "Something Sort of Grandish," involves a duet with Petula Clark and a manic over-production by Coppola. Mueller writes that "Coppola obviously viewed [the show's songs] with impatience, distrust, and incomprehension" (401), and this number definitely supports Mueller's judgment. The diegetic premise is that Og has fallen in love with Sharon, and that the unfamiliar sensation of human love has made him wax poetic in a brilliant Harburg lyric teeming with ingenious rhymes such as "givinish" and "beginnish." To support what needs no support, Coppola fills the screen with floating laundry—and a floating Og. Even so, the song is irresistible, lyrically and musically, and Steele's often-distracting effervescence turns into an asset. Steele's other triumph occurs in "When I'm Not Near the Girl I Love," a duet with Silent Susan (Barbara Hancock), who has replaced Sharon in Og's affections. This number is oddly reminiscent of *Brigadoon*, perhaps because what is patently a studio set intended to represent a natural setting encloses two dancers who perform very well. Whatever the cause, Steele and Hancock come across as likable lovers, especially when each perches momentarily on a series of hillocks while dancing through the scene. The number is—as one might expect—weakened by Coppola's excessive cutting and by his absurd fondness for the stream of running water that he features in all outdoor scenes. One is amazed, too, to learn that Hermes Pan was fired as choreographer partway through the filming of the picture. His steadying hand is much missed in most dance numbers.[19]

Another musical highlight is "That Great Come and Get It Day," which begins as a solo for Woody and then expands to include the whole cast. Weirdly enough, Don Francks starts the number in a voice obviously recorded in a studio even though the scene is set in the supposed outdoors. As one would expect in a Coppola musical production number, the scene rapidly shifts from this outdoor setting to an outdoor church, then to some fields, then to a ruined Southern Gothic mansion, then to the town square. Everyone dances and sings along in this song about discarding your old possessions in expectation of getting new ones. The number is followed by a card that says "INTERMISSION," which is followed in turn by a card that says "ENTR'ACT." This intermission is followed by a full-screen close-up of Fred singing "When the Idle Poor Become the Idle Rich." What this all goes to show is that *Finian's Rainbow* was intended to be a very grand event indeed. Richard K. Johnson reports Coppola's memory of how the production grew to such gargantuan proportions. According to Coppola, the studio heads "decided to blow the picture up to 70 and make it a roadshow picture. And when they did that, they blew the feet off Fred Astaire when he was dancing" (64). Thus, some criticism of what seems to be Coppola's shot selection might be softened by accepting that some of what we see on the screen resulted from a business decision by others, not from Coppola's own artistic vision. This kind of financial decision is probably responsible for the film's excessive length, for the intermission, and for the distorted length-height proportions that make several scenes look so weird.

Other weird elements must be laid at Coppola's door. It is clearly Coppola, for example, who decided that during "That Old Devil Moon," Woody and Sharon should kiss passionately and roll around together in the grass instead of merely suggesting sexuality, as in older numbers such as "Pettin' in the Park," and this despite the fact that "Pettin' in the Park" was filmed before full implementation of the Hays Code. In 1968, apparently, mere suggestion was deemed to be too subtle, at least by Coppola. The year 1968 is also signaled — irrelevantly — by the brief scene in which Howard, the tobacco chemist (Al Freeman), sits in on the floor of the barn when the sheriff and district attorney come to arrest Sharon and Woody. Since the film has already removed Rainbow Valley from the historical realities of 1968 through its earlier, fantastic treatment of Southern law-and-order officials, the scene makes no sense. Howard's action has no effect anyway — except perhaps to ridicule actual sit-ins by actual educated African Americans. Less politically and morally significant, but perhaps as irrelevant, is the scenery for the massive production number, "If This Isn't Love." As usual in this film, the song takes second place to camera tricks as the voices of the principal lovers sing this lyric on the soundtrack while their bodies engage in all sorts of strenuous outdoor activities. Everything on screen seems to be taking place in a late '60s commune, especially when Sharon rides a horse bareback and the residents of Rainbow Valley innocently play children's games as if they were acting in *Hair* instead of *Finian's Rainbow*.[20]

The last item on this bill of particulars has little to do with history, but it points equally to the director's questionable choices. After Finian and Og reach a compromise concerning the pot of gold that saves the lives of Sharon and Woody, the fire that was to have burned them to death still needs to be put out. When everyone pitches in to douse the fire, the film's message of brotherhood is once more affirmed. Another familiar element reappears as Senator Billboard Rawkins (Keenan Wynn) is repeatedly struck by gushing water from the fire hose. Wynn has been one of the few bright spots in the film to this point, and so we cannot imagine his objecting to this broad comedy device. What we can imagine, though, is someone wondering, what is it with Coppola and water? Aside from the stream that floats through almost every scene, there is Silent Susan's interpretive dance in the rain just before she stumbles upon Finian's pot of gold. One clearly positive effect is to make Susan's dress cling provocatively to her body, as will happen in dozens of country music videos in years to come. What other purpose might be served is less apparent. It seems that Coppola just thinks water is cool. Thus, if we want to get in one last jab at racism, segregation and corrupt politicians before the movie ends, why not repeatedly spray Senator Rawkins with a fire hose? When William Asher desperately uses custard pies to bring an unmerited air of screen comedy to *Beach Party*, we may justifiably suspect a failure of directorial imagination. Coppola's use of water in *Finian's Rainbow* deserves the same judgment.

Coppola has lamented that when he was brought on board the *Finian's Rainbow* project, principal casting was already completed by the studio.[21] The studio heads' desire to milk Fred Astaire's Hollywood musical reputation for all the box office appeal it was worth is therefore apparent, if not artistically responsible. The same may be said for *Xanadu* (1980), starring Gene Kelly and Olivia Newton-John. Although Newton-John gets top billing in the later film, while Fred is billed first in *Finian's Rainbow*, the casting pattern in which a revered song-and-dance man and a currently hot pop star are combined to appeal to moviegoers of all ages holds true. Another line of continuity between the two films is that *Xanadu* is — like *Finian's Rainbow* — a pathetic final act to a great musical screen career. As Alvin Yudkoff writes about the film, it is "[a] hell of a sad way [for Gene Kelly] to go out" (163). The final preliminary point to be recognized is that *Xanadu* is also set in Never Never Land.

This film obviously derives its title from Samuel Taylor Coleridge's famous incomplete poem "Kubla Khan, or, A Vision in a Dream, A Fragment" (1798). Gene Kelly and Olivia Newton-John even trade lines from the poem in one scene just in case anyone might miss the significance of the title. Since the opening lines of the poem —"In Xanadu did Kubla Khan / A stately pleasure-dome decree"[22] — are among the few literary memories that even non–English majors are likely to carry away from their educational experience, the term *Xanadu* can be counted on to conjure up exotic, otherworldly associations for most viewers.[23] Within the plot, Xanadu is the name of the club that Danny McGuire (Kelly) opens in partnership with Sonny Malone (Michael Beck) under the inspiration of a Greek muse incarnated as a young, blonde charmer, Kira (Newton-John). Since this club looks like no place on Earth, its diegetic function also works consistently with the preternatural aura of its name. This preternatural impression is established early on by the Gothic, comic-book script in which the film's title is presented, as well as by its preternatural plot. Finally, the diegetic setting of the plot, Venice Beach, California, is presented on screen as nearly as otherworldly as Patria or Rainbow Valley. Thus, no matter what his diegetic nightclub is called, Gene Kelly is just as much in Never Never Land in *Xanadu* as he was years earlier in *Brigadoon*.

Of course, *Xanadu* was produced many years after *Brigadoon*, and Gene Kelly was a quarter-century older. Creating a film in 1980 starring, or co-starring, Kelly might therefore seem something of a stretch — perhaps as much of a stretch as creating a film starring Fred Astaire in 1968. *Xanadu* deals with this problem mostly through self-conscious, self-referential devices. Sonny, first of all, works in show business as an artist for the sort of pop music label that might market albums by Olivia Newton-John — or by the Electric Light Orchestra, who did half the songs on the soundtrack. Then, too, Danny McGuire tells Sonny at their first meeting, "I used to be in the music business, but now I'm what you might call retired."[24] Any viewer who fails to apply this speech to Kelly's own career just isn't paying attention. After Danny and Sonny form a bond, Danny says, "Malone and Maguire — sounds like a vaudeville team." While it is certain that Michael Beck (b. 1949) never appeared in vaudeville, and unlikely that he knew very much about it, Gene Kelly (b. 1912) played a vaudevillian in *Take Me Out to the Ball Game* (1949) and *Singin' in the Rain* (1952), among other films, and so this reference can refer only to his on-screen persona. Kelly's long career is invoked also through various references to his advanced age. After dancing with Kira to "Whenever You're Away from Me," Danny pulls his face this way and that in front of a mirror to show how old he has gotten since the last time he danced like that. Later on, the production number "All Over the World" requires Danny to change repeatedly into inappropriately hip costumes to emphasize how out-of-date Gene Kelly really is.

Danny and Sonny are connected in the film not only by their supposed potential as a vaudeville team, but also by their shared fondness for Glenn Miller's music. It is probable that Glenn Miller functioned in the minds of the writers (Richard Christian Danus and Marc Rubel) as a shorthand reference to the whole Big Band era that coincided with the heyday of the Hollywood musical, just as *Xanadu* functioned as shorthand for everything mysterious and exotic. In any case, Glenn Miller is an important device by which the film seeks to bridge the generation gap through self-referential devices. In Danny's mansion — which, self-referentially, formerly belonged to a silent film star — a band like Glenn Miller's plays "You're Never Far Away from Me," and a singer like Olivia Newton-John joins in. She is wearing a quasi-military outfit like the ones used by Bette Midler and the Pointer Sisters to signify swing time, and she even dances with Gene Kelly, as other female singers might have done back in the early '40s. Newton-John does all right, and Kelly suggests some of his former energy — though much reduced, as in Astaire's solos in *Finian's Rainbow*. If performers from such widely separated generations can dance together in 1980, the scene seems to ask us, why can't Universal produce an acceptable Hollywood musical?

In 1980, it might naturally be assumed, a leading lady would not dress like Ginger Rogers or Judy Garland. Thus, Kira is seldom seen in the film without the legwarmers that so many exercise-conscious or just plain stylish young ladies were wearing in those days. (Even when wearing her white muse dress during the "Xanadu" production number, Kira is wearing leg-warmers.) In such ways, a contemporary resonance is supposedly brought to the film. Furthermore, in an attempt to have it both ways, *Xanadu* combines the historical and the contemporary by having much of the film take place on roller skates. Gene Kelly did dance on roller skates in *It's Always Fair Weather* (1955) as Fred and Ginger did in *Shall We Dance* (1937). Since rollerskating had made a strong comeback as an invigorating form of exercise in the late 1970s, it just made sense to have the principals in *Xanadu* perform on skates, simultaneously echoing the past and celebrating the present. Since Venice Beach was an actual site of roller mania, moreover, the decision seemed inevitable. The film's young lovers therefore meet for the first time when Kira skates up to Sonny. Kira shows Sonny the future site of the club Xanadu while she is practicing her skating. Roller-skating and self-referentiality combine when Sonny and Kira skate onto a sound stage where music videos are filmed. For the production number "Suddenly," the pair perform choreographed skating while the technical devices by which wind, rain, flattering lights and other cinematic enhancements are exposed as professional tricks—as they are exposed during the "You Were Meant for Me" number in *Singin' in the Rain*, featuring, of all people, Gene Kelly! When Danny and Sonny's club opens, it seems to be what the reviewer for *Variety* (Aug. 13, 1980) called "a roller-derby disco." Thus, the major production number, "Xanadu," is done primarily on skates even though some of the cinematic techniques used to film the number—overhead crane shots, for example—are borrowed from the Berkeley repertoire developed for dancers without ball bearings.[25]

Another number, not on skates, also pretends a perfect compatibility between past and present. When Danny and Sonny discuss the club they intend to open together, their conflicting musical expectations are revealed in the number "Dancin'." Danny envisions a swank club with elegantly dressed patrons dancing to swing music. Sonny wants clashing guitars, contemporary clothes and 1980s dancing. The number "Dancin'" consists of visual and aural cuts between these two visions while the two characters seem to believe that their plans are in synch. Both imagined scenes are highly stylized—the contemporary segment because "Dancin'" isn't much of a cutting-edge rocker and the '40s segment because those days really seem to be dead and gone by 1980. Apparently, jive dancing, big band music and the conventional Hollywood musical can be resurrected only through the postmodern indulgence of irony.[26]

On the other hand, historical authenticity may be irrelevant within such a fantastic chronotope. In addition to the title, and Kira's role as a muse, numerous other elements in the film point to this fact. When Danny goes to the Platinum Palace record store to pick up his long-awaited Glenn Miller recordings, the building looks like something out of the movie *Flash Gordon* (1980). The same might be said of the future site of Xanadu, even when it is badly in need of repair and its marquee reads "UDITOIUM." In buildings like this, anything can happen. Muses can become mortal, for example, as Kira eventually does in this film. It is consistent with this otherworldliness that Sonny never suspects that there is anything odd about Kira, as Tommy never suspects anything odd about Fiona in *Brigadoon*. Since both women are centuries older than their lovers—in Kira's case, many centuries—perhaps this is just as well. Another fantastic element enters the film when Sonny and Kira first kiss, and the scene goes into cartoon animation for "Don't Walk Away." Putting aside the question of whether the animated figures dance better than Michael Beck and Olivia Newton-John, their very presence in the film reinforces the fantastic chronotope. This chronotope takes on diegetic force when Kira breaks the news to Sonny that she isn't really mortal. First, Sonny finds a reference to Kira in the dictionary as part of the definition of *muse*. Then characters in a black-and-white film on television refer to Kira's situation, and one addresses Sonny directly. Muses are clearly not part of the worlds represented in *Oklahoma!* and *West Side Story*. On the other hand, muses could conceivably pop up in *Yolanda and the Thief* or *Finian's Rainbow*. That is to say that muses belong to the chronotope of fantasy — as does the film *Xanadu*.

This fact seems not to have swayed most commentators on the film. In his Internet Movie Database biography, for example, Michael Beck testifies: "*The Warriors* [1979] opened up a lot of doors in film, for me, which *Xanadu* then closed." In *Variety* (Aug. 13, 1980), the reviewer anticipates Beck's negative experience by calling *Xanadu* "truly a stupendously bad film." In his book on Gene Kelly, Alvin Yudkoff calls the movie "the worst musical positively! The Pits!" (163). One is inclined to say "Ouch!" in sympathy, but one is also inclined to agree. In fact, *Xanadu*, *Finian's Rainbow* and *Yolanda and the Thief* are all pretty awful movies. Of the films treated in this chapter, only *Brigadoon* seems to me worth watching repeatedly, and even *Brigadoon* was largely repudiated by its director. All of this may just go to show what Robert K. Johnson asserts in his book on Francis Ford Coppola: "Fantasy can be successfully offered to a movie audience, but it must be presented within a very clearly defined framework, and with enormous skill" (66).

On the other hand, it may all go to show that the Hollywood musical is always already fantastic enough for anybody and thus in no need of Patrias, or Brigadoons, or Rainbow Valleys. And yet, without these fantastic settings, we would be deprived of at least four opportunities to watch Fred Astaire and Gene Kelly perform on the screen. Even acknowledging the harshest judgments of their critics, therefore, we may still agree with Bing Crosby's song for Thanksgiving in *Holiday Inn* and say that these films give us plenty to be thankful for.

7

Musical Biopics

The cinematic biographies (or biopics) of well-known musical entrepreneurs or composers immediately solve one intrinsic problem of the Hollywood musical — how to provide narrative justification for performance numbers in which people like Oklahoma cowboys or New York street punks burst into song or dance. Since theatrical showmen and composers are surrounded by music in their daily lives, a biographical film based on these lives must necessarily involve singing and dancing. Audience members can thus experience both a biographical narrative and a musical entertainment in the same film. As Jane Feuer explains, "The biopic could use the writing of the numbers for its narrative with the performance of those same numbers as the spectacle..." (96). Feuer also says, "It would seem that at one time or another, every composer, bandleader and entertainer who ever graced the stage or screen has had his or her life immortalized in a Hollywood musical biopic" (96).

For purposes of manageability, therefore, I have decided to confine my discussion in this chapter to a mere six musical biopics. The cinematic lives of the legendary impresarios Florenz Ziegfeld, Jr., and George M. Cohan will serve to represent the category of showmen and producers. *Words and Music* (1948) and *Three Little Words* (1950), films purporting to represent the lives of composing teams Richard Rodgers & Lorenz Hart and Bert Kalmar & Harry Ruby, will suffice to show how the supposedly built-in tensions of any creative partnership can be turned into a Hollywood musical. *Night and Day* (1946), based on the life of Cole Porter, and *Till The Clouds Roll By* (1946), based on the life of Jerome Kern, will serve to illustrate the problems attending the cinematic representation of an individual composer's life. In each case, moreover, how songs and production numbers are incorporated into the film will be discussed.

As far as pure narrative goes, *The Great Ziegfeld* (1936) is — as contemporaneous reviewers attest — more or less biographically faithful to the life and times of the man who invented the Ziegfeld Follies, Florenz Ziegfeld, Jr. (1869–1932). The reviewer for *Variety* (Apr. 15, 1936), for example, found the book by William Anthony McGuire to be "almost faithful biography save for logical or necessary theatrical license." In *The Commonweal* (Apr. 17, 1936), James P. Cunningham wrote that, in the nearly three hours' running time of the film, "there is real value in the interesting authentic biographical relation to the theatre's history of the past quarter century." Such praise is more than in keeping with the modest title card proclaiming that the film was "suggested by romances and incidents in the life of America's greatest showman, Florenz Ziegfeld, Jr." In practice, this means that the film's story begins with the young Ziegfeld promoting Sandow, the world's strongest man, at the 1893 Chicago World's Fair, follows Ziegfeld's subsequent theatrical successes and his marriages to Anna Held and Billie Burke, and concludes with his death in the Warwick Hotel in 1932.[1] Since so many shows, so many songs, and so many beautiful girls figured significantly in Ziegfeld's life during these four tumultuous decades, it is no wonder that the film runs so long! Since Ziegfeld is played brilliantly and dashingly by William Powell, however, the viewing time may seem somewhat shorter than it actually is.[2]

Powell is especially effective in several scenes intended to flesh out his Ziegfeld persona. One of these segments seems precisely designed to illustrate Rick Altman's observation that musical biopics must inflect — or distort — "biographical effects ... to make the semantic givens of the biopic conform to the syntax of the show musical" (238). In keeping with the syntax of the musical biography, the young Ziegfeld must confront his father, who is committed to the classical music taught at the Chicago College of Music,[3] in order to become his own man, a proponent of the "new" music of America. The elder Ziegfeld first threatens never to speak to his son again if he persists in his quest for show business success, and Mr. Ziegfeld's favorite child pupil, Mary Lou, cries bitterly at the prospect of losing her friend and fantasy suitor to the outside world of show business. Soon, however, everything turns out just fine, as this narrative syntax requires. After Ziggie gives his father a William Powell smile, and the little girl a box of chocolates, both are won over. To confirm this resolution, although Mr. Ziegfeld disappears from the narrative at this point, Mary Lou turns up years later looking for work in the Follies, and Ziggie is able to find a part for her.

Ziggie's handling of these two minor human obstacles to his progress is characteristic. Charm, especially a slightly dishonest form of charm, is the key to this cinematic life — and not only in Ziggie's early years — especially in his dealings with Jack Billings, whom he first meets at the Chicago World's Fair. Throughout the film, this fictional character, played by Frank Morgan, serves as Ziegfeld's competitor and foil. For example, Ziegfeld steals his first big star — and wife — Anna Held, right from under Billings' nose in London, largely on the strength of money borrowed from Billings. Later on, whenever Ziegfeld needs money to put on even more elaborate stage spectacles, Billings reluctantly supplies the financing himself or gets his partner, A. L. Erlanger, to do so. As Ziegfeld is dying, Billings arrives to cheer him up and remind him of his past successes. Ziegfeld — at least as played by William Powell — is apparently irresistible even to his rivals.

As Cunningham recognizes in his *Commonweal* review, however, the life-and-times aspects of the film are only part of its appeal: "Aside from that the producers have built a logical, glorious musical comedy pageant that is brilliant with gay, captivating music and songs, specialties and dance, all staged and excellently performed, in the lavishness with which Ziegfeld surrounded his very life and lifework." In other words, *The Great Ziegfeld* may be a biopic, but it is essentially a *musical* biopic. How the film handles its musical numbers is therefore a crucial question for critics. *Time*'s review (Apr. 20, 1936) consists mostly of arch commentary intended to display the reviewer's cultural sophistication, but the review concludes: "Pretentious, packed with hokum and as richly sentimental as an Irving Berlin lyric, it is, as such, top-notch entertainment" (48). Even Otis Ferguson, writing in *The New Republic* (May 13, 1936)—who declares his preference for *Industrial Symphony*, a film about a Dutch radio factory—finds one production number in *The Great Ziegfeld* a "bit of gorgeous flummery standing out above all the rest." If these cultural snobs were impressed by the musical numbers in *The Great Ziegfeld*, they must be very impressive indeed. In fact, the musical numbers seem as irresistible as Ziegfeld himself.

Because of the heavy narrative burden in the early parts of the film, the first real production number does not occur until Ziggie sees Anna Held (Luise Rainer) performing "Won't You Come and Play with Me?" on stage in London. This number is significant not only for its influence on Ziegfeld's romantic and professional life but also because it raises the issue of how musical numbers are presented in films. As Jane Feuer explains in her book *The Hollywood Musical*, musical numbers can be presented as part of the narrative diegesis, in what she calls the third person, or in direct address to the audience, in what Feuer calls the first person. "Won't You Come and Play with Me?" is the first of many numbers in *The Great Ziegfeld* that require a transition between modes of address, so that viewers begin by seeing Ziegfeld watching Held and then become the spectators themselves. As Feuer explains the process: "Typically, there will be a cut to a closer view of the performance taken from the theater audience's point of view but eliminating them from the frame. In this second shot (or more properly in the effect of the cut to this shot) the spectator replaces the internal audience. The subjectivity of the spectator stands in for that of the spectral audience, rendering the performance utterly theatrical" (28). In this way, Held begins by entertaining Ziegfeld, and then Luise Rainer continues to entertain us. This practice continues after Held comes to America within the biographical narrative in order to appear on stage for Ziegfeld. Her performance of "It's Delightful to Be Married" involves the same transition from third to first person so that we can judge for ourselves why she became such a hit on stage and off.

Other first-person on-stage numbers involve characters who figure less prominently in the biographical narrative. Eddie Cantor's black-face rendition of "If You Knew Susie" in the Follies, for example, is part of the narrative of Ziegfeld's growing success as a theatrical producer. As performed by Buddy Doyle, the number remains within the frame of a proscenium stage, but by dollying in and out, the camera presents the number to us in the first person. The same may be said for the songs performed by Fanny Brice. Playing herself, Brice performs "Yidl with Your Fiddle" and "Queen of the Jungle" on stage at a burlesque theater, just as Anna Held performed "Won't You Come and Play with Me?" on a London stage. As in the earlier number, the biographical Ziegfeld is in the audience scouting for new talent; as also in the earlier number, we are soon the real audience.

Shortly after Brice joins the Follies, however, a more complicated form of presentation occurs. On stage during a rehearsal intended to represent part of Ziegfeld's biography, Brice begins to sing "My Man." After a brief first-person delivery by Brice, the scene shifts to members of the rehearsal audience, including Ziegfeld and several chorus girls. Ziegfeld exits from the scene to go to his office even as Brice is singing, and the camera follows him instead of returning to the number. Here, the biographical narrative is paramount. Consequently, this exit leads to a definitely third-person musical number when Jerome Kern joins Ziegfeld in his office. At Ziggie's request, Kern begins to play "Look for the Silver Lining" on the piano, and all the actors in the scene join in to sing the lyric. Since this song will be featured prominently throughout the remainder of the film, it obviously has great significance. That it does not receive a lavish production would seem to suggest that the song's significance is narrative rather than spectacular. Third-person address thus seems more appropriate.[4]

Musical numbers of this sort are relatively rare in *The Great Ziegfeld*, and so we should conclude this discussion by examining three all-out production numbers in which first-person address clearly dominates. One sequence, intended to illustrate Ziegfeld's Midnight Frolics, opens on a scene familiar from many other films set in that era: a rooftop nightclub, society folk in evening clothes, a fashionable orchestra, a curtained stage. The curtains then part to reveal a chorus of beautiful girls who sing "You Gotta Pull Strings." Busby Berkeley–esque production techniques soon involve the diegetic audience by means of streamers and balloons. The cinema audience is also involved whenever this diegetic audience disappears from the screen, and a first-person presentation of the number follows. This number quickly segues into a feature for Ray Bolger, in which he first appears surrounded by chorus girls onstage to sing "She's a Ziegfeld Follies Girl" and then appears before the closed curtain to do a first-person tap performance. Occasional shots of the diegetic Midnight Frolics audience from time to time in this sequence — mostly following highlights in the first-person performances — plead for the biographical relevance of these numbers. If this relevance exists, it lies in the excess that characterizes these numbers and Ziegfeld's own, similar, productions. Thus, the Bolger dance elides into a series of couples singing "You" in duet, and they in turn yield to 20 chorus girls sitting up in beds and doing half-time stunts with the shiny bedclothes. As close ups of the girls alternate with longer shots of moving sets, the influence of Berkeley is again suggested. This suggestion — or perhaps a suggestion of Berkeley's Broadway precursor, Ziegfeld — continues as Ziegfeld's featured beauty, Audrey Dane (Virginia Bruce), becomes the focus of "You Never Looked So Beautiful." The ensuing number, in which chorus girls parade in costumes designed to make them look like birds, flowers and other exotica,[5] is grandly excessive, culminating in a revolving set in which medium shots and close ups of show girls illustrate, directly into the camera, the title "You Never Looked So Beautiful" before. Pausing for only a moment to recall that these four production numbers have been presented continuously as parts of a single Midnight Frolics performance, we may begin to grasp how central musical production numbers are to the cinematic presentation of Flo Ziegfeld's life.

An equally over-the-top quality defines "A Circus Must Be Different in a Ziegfeld Show." The narrative justification here is that Ziggie and his daughter Patricia (Joan Holland) share a passion for exotic animals, and this number is his gift to her. A very odd gift it turns out to be since the singing of the lyric by chorus boys soon segues into the kind of full-screen production number that we have seen several times already, and then turns into a solo dance turn for Harriet Hoctor, who is playing herself. Although many contemporary dance critics, including Arlene Croce, are disposed to mock Hoctor's freakish performances,[6] film critics were differently disposed in 1936. The *Variety* reviewer, for example, singled out "the highly imaginative and very effective Harriet Hoctor ballet" for praise. The reviewer for *Newsweek* agreed, saying that "Harriet Hoctor dances as magnificently as she did so often for Ziegfeld." The motivation for this praise begins with Hoctor *en pointe*, as usual, accompanied by a chorus of female dancers similarly elevated. The crowning touch, though, is a group of Russian Wolfhounds who act as bored stage props. After Hoctor jumps around these dogs—on one leg—the dogs exit on cue, the chorus girls lead several ponies in and Hoctor spins maniacally. This is a different circus indeed, but it is, we should observe, a circus presented directly to us in first-person address.

The final number of this sort that we will have time and space for is the most, and most justifiably, famous. The lavish production of "A Pretty Girl Is Like a Melody" features prominently in *That's Entertainment* as a sign of all that was grand in musicals of the past. It is the number that nudged Otis Ferguson out of his proletarian funk in his *New Republic* review. It is the number that, according to Clive Hirschhorn, set "a new standard in opulence that has never been surpassed" (118). It is also a number that shifts from third- to first-person address, although it is primarily couched in the latter. The sequence begins with Dennis Morgan on stage at the Ziegfeld Follies singing the Irving Berlin lyric (with the actual singing dubbed by Allan Jones). When Morgan moves off to the side of the stage, giant curtains open to reveal a giant revolving set packed with gorgeous girls in various costumes and attitudes. Some girls dance, some sing, some wear carnival outfits, some just look glorious in glorious costumes. Meanwhile, the soundtrack plays a medley of light classical melodies to add an air of refinement to the proceedings: Dvořák's "Humoresque No. 7 in G Flat; "One Fine Day" from Puccini's *Madame Butterfly*; *Liebestraum* by Franz Liszt; *The Blue Danube Waltz* by Johann Strauss II; "On with the Motley" from Leoncavallo's *Pagliacci*; and *Rhapsody in Blue* by George Gershwin. During the last named, a male chorus sings the word *rhapsody* over and over as a transition to a reprise of the Morgan/Jones rendition of "A Pretty Girl." By my count, the stage of beautiful girls revolves for six minutes and 45 seconds, almost an eternity on screen. The number is still not over, however, as we see tiers of beautiful girls, jam-packed together like eggs in a carton. A rising circular curtain, shaped like the revolving set, rises to reveal Audrey Dane atop what looks like a giant wedding cake. Then the magnificent round curtain descends, embracing the magnificent set and all the girls. Clive Hirschhorn says that this number now lives in the hearts of many moviegoers as "a collector's item of super-opulent kitsch" (118). It is, in any case, a musical extravaganza eminently suitable to represent the life of Florenz Ziegfeld, Jr., at the same time that it directly entertains these moviegoers.

Since, as Marjorie Farnsworth attests, Ziegfeld and George M. Cohan mutually detested each other,[7] it is perhaps only appropriate that we turn from the biopic of Ziegfeld's life to *Yankee Doodle Dandy* (1942), starring Jimmy Cagney as George M. Cohan (1878–1942). Contemporaneous reviewers were, for good reason, somewhat less convinced of the biographical accuracy of this film than they were of *The Great*

Ziegfeld. The *New York Times* review, for example, explained that the scriptwriters, Robert Buckner and Edmund Joseph, "have juggled facts rather freely to construct a neat, dramatic story line, and they have let slip a few anachronisms which the wise ones will gleefully spot" (May 30, 1942). The reason for these inaccuracies may be glimpsed in the observation by *Time*'s reviewer that "[f]ew films have bestowed such loving care as this one does on beaming, buoyant, wry-mouthed George M. (for Michael) Cohan" (86). In 1942, in other words, Cohan was something of a national institution, and so his biopic might be expected, as the Jerome Kern song has it, to "Look for the Silver Lining." There is no shortage of biographical detail in the film even so; *Yankee Doodle Dandy* provides enough for anyone, reaching back to the day of Cohan's birth. The life presented on screen, however, is almost entirely without dramatic tension. Young George is so self-confident that his cockiness loses his family vaudeville bookings, but everyone soon ends up doing just fine anyhow. When George sets out as a composer and playwright, he does not win immediate acclaim, but he and Sam H. Harris are soon producing the highly successful *Little Johnny Jones*. Cohan's attempt at serious drama, *Popularity*, fails with the public, but Cohan apologizes in print and soon goes on to other successes. It seems at the beginning of the film that Franklin D. Roosevelt is annoyed with Cohan for his depiction of the President in *I'd Rather Be Right*, but F.D.R. actually wants to give Cohan the Congressional Medal of Honor for having composed the songs "Grand Old Flag" and

George M. Cohan (Jimmy Cagney) and the rest of the Four Cohans perform "It's a Grand Old Flag" in *Yankee Doodle Dandy*.

"Over There." That is to say that this film may be "based on the story of George M. Cohan," as the title card reads, but, taken as the story of any actual human being's life, it can only be regarded as greatly simplified.

Not so the musical numbers. As Philip Hartung says in his review in *Commonweal*, Cohan's "songs would be a major attraction to any show. But with the good production given them here, with the costuming, dancing and singing as scenes from the various Cohan shows are done, they are a thrill in entertainment" (June 19, 1942). Since the biographical element in *Yankee Doodle Dandy* is so lacking in tension, then we must expect these production numbers to carry the burden of engaging the audience, and they do, largely by sharing the first-person mode of address that we saw at work in *The Great Ziegfeld*. As Feuer explains, "Since the musical borrows its proscenium performances from live entertainment, the shift to direct address does not strike us as odd; it seems very natural" (35). This is true of *Yankee Doodle Dandy* even before Cohan is born. The first musical number in the picture features Walter Huston as Jerry Cohan (George's father) performing "It's Easy" as a stage Irishman, even while Mrs. Cohan (Rosemary De Camp) is delivering her son George elsewhere in town. The number is, of course, intended primarily to advance the narrative element of George's career in vaudeville, as is clear when Master Georgie (Henry Blair) performs the same number shortly afterwards in the film, thus suggesting the unchanging character of vaudeville performances. Even so, Huston originally performs the number to us in full-screen once the nature of the number is established by shots indicating a theatrical stage.

Biographical musical numbers performed in the third person carry the narrative for awhile. Josie, the fourth Cohan (played by Cagney's actual sister, Jeanne), is seen from the wings as she dances on the vaudeville stage, but we do not see her face-on. George dances in his dressing room for his bride to be, Mary (Joan Leslie), but the dance serves as part of their courtship and so is framed entirely within the diegetic dressing room. Not until the four Cohans perform "I Was Born in Virginia" does the first-person mode of address that dominates the numbers in *The Great Ziegfeld* begin to function fully in *Yankee Doodle Dandy*. The number opens with a title card announcing "The Four Cohans" and with camera shots over the heads of the audience and orchestra onto the stage.[8] Following these establishing shots, the Four Cohans perform the song for us, in the first person. When the number ends with camera shots over the diegetic audience, we realize that we are returning to the diegetic narrative. Thus, Mary's subsequent performance of "The Warmest Baby in the Bunch" is shot mostly from the wings, a sign that her performance is intended primarily to advance the story rather than to serve as a first-person production number— even though she is singing a Cohan song. When Mary and George perform another Cohan song, "Harrigan," for the producing team of Dietz and Goff in order to win their support for *Little Johnny Jones*, this number also functions primarily as a biographical event, even though the performance often fills the whole screen with only a few items of stage property in the background to remind us that this is all taking place in a business office. In the same way, George performs one chorus of "Yankee Doodle Dandy" at a piano in the back room of a saloon to convince Schwab (S.Z. Sakall) to back this show, now a joint production with Sam Harris (Richard Whorf).

When the production of *Little Johnny Jones* is finally mounted within the film, however, we are securely within the area of musical performance identified by Jane Feuer. The sequence opens in the third-person mode of address with shots of the musical conductor's score, and then the camera pans up to the stage. Immediately we enter into the first-person realm for Cagney's famous rendition of "Yankee Doodle Dandy," including the leaps and kicks off the sides of the proscenium stage that figure so prominently when the number reappears in *That's Entertainment* (1974).[9] First-person address continues even after Cohan's Little Johnny Jones exits from the stage set, because the male chorus members continue to dance for the viewing audience until Cohan returns. Within this set, male and female chorus members act as parts of a racetrack crowd, actual horses appear up stage and a track announcer reports in rhyme that Johnny Jones has lost the race. During the sequence, long shots embracing the whole stage have alternated with closeups of race fans and of Johnny Jones, signifying direct presentation to the viewing audience. Third-person address returns only at the end of the number with shots of the wildly applauding theater audience.

These shots serve as a transition to another first-person presentation of the famous "Give My Regards to Broadway." At times during this number, the stage set fills the entire screen, often with a slight rim of stage apron at the bottom of the shot to tie the production number into Cohan's biographical story. At other times, the camera dollies in for a closeup of characters within the stage play, acknowledging the first-person mode of address that is actually at work. In keeping with the latter, the number concludes with another first-person dance by Cohan, this one reprised in *That's Dancing* (1985). The sequence ends with more shots of the applauding audience, a descending curtain and comic by-play between Dietz and Goff, the producers who passed up a chance to back this hit show.

In later numbers, the Four Cohans perform in the first person in a montage intended to suggest their successes in the period following *Little Johnny Jones*, and George and Mary perform the song "Mary" in the third person in her apartment as evidence of their love for each other. A montage of Cohan's hit shows, rather like the montage that crosses the mind of the dying Ziegfeld, requires snippets from the title songs,[10] but these musical signals are so brief that their function must be considered primarily narrative. The biggest production numbers, in the sense that Feuer discusses such numbers as parts of biopics, occur in the Cohan shows *Forty-Five Minutes to Broadway* and *George Washington, Jr.*

Forty-Five Minutes to Broadway claims biographical significance because it is Cohan's first show with the much-admired Fay Templeton (Irene Manning) and because Templeton wants (*demands* is too strong a word) to sing the song that Cohan wrote especially for his Mary.[11] In the life of Ziegfeld, the presence of a stunning actress or the betrayal of a man's promise to his beloved would occasion dramatic conflict. In the life of Cohan, Mary is perfectly content to yield her song to Templeton and even suggests that they invite her over for supper. To attach Irene Manning's performances to the story of Cohan's life, however, some narrative musical events must occur. We hear the last two notes of Fay Templeton's performance in another show from the wings, for example, so that we can understand her function in the

Cohan biography. Then George performs the song "Forty-Five Minutes to Broadway" at a piano in Templeton's dressing room to lure her into his new play. In Feuer's sense, these musical events take place in the third person as part of the film's biographical narrative. After Templeton agrees to star in the show, the first-person numbers can begin.

The big production number for *Forty-Five Minutes* opens with a playbill displaying the show's title. The curtain opens within the biographical third person, and the following shots from a box in the audience continue this illusion as Templeton enters onto the stage. Then the camera moves directly to first-person address as Irene Manning delivers the song "Forty-Five Minutes to Broadway" against an obviously theatrical backdrop. First-person address is only briefly interrupted by an audience shot of George, Mary and the ever-present Sam Harris, but it is clear that Manning's performance will continue. It does, including several closeups of the star, as Templeton is joined by chorus girls until the entire screen is filled. Then the camera pulls back to reveal the whole stage set, but not the framing arch or the orchestra, so that this set can open onto another for Templeton's next number, "So Long Mary." Because of the theatrical scenery, it is always clear from a narrative perspective that these numbers form parts of a show created by George M. Cohan, but because of the way the numbers are shot, first-person address to the viewing audience takes priority over biography.

The movie audience becomes even more important in the big production number from *George Washington, Jr.* It was no secret in 1942 that Cohan was closely associated with flag-waving patriotism. (In fact, it is probably no secret today.) Anyone might expect, therefore, that his biopic would contain a generous serving of the same. Given the film's release date in the first year of World War II, moreover, patriotism might be even more easily assumed.[12] Even so, the "Grand Old Flag" number is somewhat breathtaking. Instead of a playbill, the number opens with a theater marquee advertising *George Washington, Jr.* Third-person elements include shots of a theater audience and a rising curtain. Then the number turns directly to the movie audience — particularly the audience trapped in the first months of a giant war — to praise the American flag, the American military, the American melting pot, American Boy Scouts and everything else American. Some long shots during the number include curtains at the top of the screen to indicate a proscenium stage, but this fiction is frequently abandoned, as in the first-person close-up in which an uncredited African American singer delivers "The Battle Hymn of the Republic" to an audience of mammies and field hands in front of a giant statue of Abraham Lincoln. Troops — including Rough Riders and Teddy Roosevelt — marching across the stage and occasionally into the camera also indicate that this number is aimed directly at a viewing audience in need of patriotic uplift during a trying time in history. "My Country 'Tis of Thee" thus fits into the number even though it wasn't written by George M. Cohan, and so does an artillery gun crew from the early 1940s even though the soldiers contemporary with the show's opening in 1906 would have looked quite different. The Four Cohans in Uncle Sam outfits soon join in, and the number concludes with an American flag, presented to the viewers in first-person address. Shots of a theatrical audience rising to applaud do little to affect our sense that we have just been musically inspired to go out and whip the Axis powers rather than informed about the life of an American showman.

This cinematic life is told in retrospect to President Roosevelt, supposedly during the present time in which the film is being released. To get Cohan together with F.D.R., the narrative pretends that Cohan is currently appearing in the George Kaufman–Moss Hart musical play *I'd Rather Be Right* (1937, with songs by Richard Rodgers and Lorenz Hart). At the beginning of the film, this historical latitude allows Cohan to assume that he is in trouble with the President, and toward the end it allows Cagney to perform one more sensational number in first-person address, "Off the Record." Once again, the dramatic situation is a performance on a proscenium stage, and once again the proscenium disappears so that the performer can sing and dance just for us. Cagney does so with such rare aplomb that even Manny Farber shakes off his *New Republic* proletarian collywobbles long enough to reach a mild affirmation: "It is indicative of Cagney's vitality that so much tripe could seem so fresh" (June 15, 1942). The performance also seems pretty up-to-date since Lorenz Hart's lyrics have been adapted to the current political situation. Having noted that the Axis powers have taken over France, Cohan as the President rhymes "ants" with "Japants." Since the next shot in the film shows Cohan in F.D.R.'s office, the number's relevance to the international situation in 1942 is apparent. That is why the number is presented to viewers in the first-person mode of address, and that is also why the film ends with Cohan joining a military parade on Pennsylvania Avenue to sing "Over There."

Two films based on the lives of distinguished songwriters share with *The Great Ziegfeld* and *Yankee Doodle Dandy* the ingenious device of using first-person musical production numbers to illustrate stages in the great entertainers' lives. They differ slightly from the two previously discussed biopics in that establishing the biographical elements that will serve as skeletons for the production numbers poses even greater narrative challenges in *Words and Music* (1948) and *Three Little Words* (1950) than those posed by the cinematic lives of Ziegfeld and Cohan. In particular, these biopics of the writing teams of Richard Rodgers (1902–79) & Lorenz Hart (1895–1943) and of Bert Kalmar (1884–1947) & Harry Ruby (1895–1974) lack the essential dramatic *agon* that has animated narratives since the days of the Ancient Greeks.[13]

Words and Music attempts to confront this narrative problem head on by opening with an extra-diegetic scene in which Tom Drake, who plays the role of Richard Rodgers in the film, addresses the cinema audience directly. He says that the following biopic — which is "Based on the Lives and Music of Richard Rodgers and Lorenz Hart," according to a title card — will lack "the standard trials and tribulations you'd normally expect."[14] This narrative exigency has resulted, according to Drake/Rodgers, because "we were just two lucky fellows who had success very young. From a dramatic standpoint, we didn't even have the advantage of being very poor." Then he adds winningly, "We weren't very rich either." Admittedly, there could not be much narrative interest in such a story, but the screenwriter, Fred Finklehoffe, tried to mend matters by creating a story of his own. Clive Hirschhorn notes several ways in which this was a bad idea: "As Rodgers' life wasn't particularly exciting (he simply went from one success to another) and Hart, the more complex and interesting of the two, was homosexual (a taboo cinematic subject in 1948), it would surely have been kinder to let their words and music speak for themselves, rather than to allow the pack of half-truths and downright lies perpetrated in Fred Finklehoffe's anachronistic screenplay (from a story by Guy Bolton and Jean Holloway) to be passed off as fact" (299). Hirschhorn would have preferred a film in which "the studio [had] simply paid tribute to their talents by stringing together, in a revue-type format, a collection of their songs" (299). This is also the judgment of the contemporaneous reviewer for *Newsweek*, who wrote that "*Words and Music* is a good show when it sticks to the business implied in its title" (92) instead of focusing on the lives of Rodgers and Hart. The 1948 *Time* reviewer agrees with the critics quoted already by writing that "*Words and Music* make[s] the songwriters' lives into a dull and silly story" (59). For a mere glimpse of what these reviewers are complaining about, we might note John McCarten's observation, published in *The New Yorker* at the time of the film's release: "Mr. [Mickey] Rooney plays Hart, for whom success — if you can believe Metro-Goldwyn-Mayer which made this one — turned to ashes because a lady singing in a beer joint refused to fall in love with him" (102).[15] We can at least hope that the songs will save *Words and Music* in spite of its story.

We would have to entertain the same hopes for *Three Little Words* if it is true, as the *Newsweek* reviewer claims, that cast of the film is "understandably unable to cope with a story line that virtually doesn't exist" (82). Apparently, the shortcomings of the narrative must be rather extreme because this reviewer assumes that the film is about the dance team of Bert Kalmar (Fred Astaire) and Jessie Brown (Vera-Ellen), while Philip Hamburger assumes in *The New Yorker* that the film is about the songwriting team of Kalmar and Harry Ruby (Red Skelton). My own interpretation accords with Hamburger's, but we must concede that any film that confuses professional reviewers about its actual subject has serious narrative flaws. Once again, apparently, we must rely on the songs to save the day.

Both films use easily recognizable songs by the writing duos in an attempt to establish biographical credibility early on. Rodgers plays "Mountain Greenery" on a piano in Hart's apartment, for example, while his future lyricist reads a magazine on the sofa. Then Rodgers segues into "Manhattan" on the piano while, in a feeble attempt to establish dramatic tension, Hart (Mickey Rooney) seems to ignore him. As it turns out, Hart has actually been captivated by Rodgers' melody and has gone about writing a lyric for it without informing him. Thus, when Mickey Rooney sings the newly written lyric in a following scene, we hear it for the first time along with Rodgers. This time, however, there is a full orchestral background for the song even though the scene is still Hart's apartment.[16] Kalmar and Ruby's first successful collaboration also takes place within a diegetic setting, the office of music publisher Al Masters. To establish their professional compatibility, the script stipulates that Ruby has written a melody for what he thinks of as an Arabian song but which Kalmar immediately recognizes to be a melody in need of a "Southern" lyric. After a certain amount of the supposed improvisation that usually accompanies any sort of composition in Hollywood biopics — loosened neckties, cigarette butts, crumpled papers on the floor — Kalmar comes up with the perfect lyric, and Fred Astaire and Red Skelton sing "My Sunny Tennessee" to a simple piano accompaniment.

Once the two writing teams become successful, musical production numbers from their shows, done in first-person address, usually function as they do in *The Great Ziegfeld* and *Yankee Doodle Dandy*. In *Words and Music*, "Mountain Greenery" begins with a shot of the orchestral score but soon shifts into first-person presentational style as Eddie Anders (Perry Como) and a chorus perform the song as a comic number. At the London premiere of *The Girl Friend*, stage curtains part and we see Anders/Como and Margo Grant (Cyd Charisse) in a stage set for "Blue Room." As we might expect, the opening curtains have served to move the film from the third-person, biographical, mode of address to the first-person, presentational, mode. The most interesting of these shifts in presentational mode probably occurs when Rodgers and his fiancée (Janet Leigh) go to a nightclub as part of their courtship and see Lena Horne (playing herself) performing "The Lady Is a Tramp" and "Where or When." Both numbers are shot so as to separate Horne's performance from the diegetic narrative, a few shots of the approving lovers being the only concession to biography. If Southern exhibitors wished to excise her performances in order to preserve pure racial lines, nothing could be easier.[17] Racism aside, the gaping chasm between representation and presentation is underscored by the familiar first-person mode of address that would readily allow such excisions to be made.

In *Three Little Words*, "All Alone Monday" is presented twice, with slight shifts in presentational mode. Terry Lordel (Gale Robbins) sings the song first in a nightclub setting, mostly through first-person address but with enough shots of nightclub patrons to signal its relevance to the biographical narrative. Since Terry flirts with some of the male patrons while performing her song, a signal is sent within the biography that she is not really the right girl for the romantically susceptible Ruby. When the song is done for the second time as part of *The Ramblers*, the tissue of biographical relevance is discarded, and the camera cuts from a marquee advertising the show to the stage on which Terry is performing. No shots of the curtains, orchestra or audience intrude until the scene moves to the wings where Ruby is talking to another redhead, Eileen Percy (Arlene Dahl), and it is apparent from their conversation that she *is* the right girl. Even so, the distance between Gale Robbins' number and the story represented in the following scene is stylistically patent.

While *Words and Music* and *Three Little Words* resemble each other — and other musical biopics — in stylistic terms, there are also significant thematic resemblances that set them apart from *The Great Ziegfeld* and *Yankee Doodle Dandy* and relate them to *Night and Day* and *Till the Clouds Roll By*. Significantly, these two biopics of songwriting teams share distinct attitudes toward gender, perhaps owing to their origins in post-war America. Some gendered narrative elements familiar from other Hollywood musicals are, of course, observed. In *Three Little Words*, Bert Kalmar is in love with Jessie, his dancing partner, from the beginning of the film. When Bert injures his knee and can no longer dance, his generous desire to see Jessie succeed on her own is misinterpreted as rejection, and the path of true love acquires some bumps. The two are soon reunited, however, so that they can marry, move to Pelham and live happily ever after. In the same way, Rodgers is briefly smitten with Joyce Harmon (Ann Sothern) in *Words and Music*, but he quickly gets over it, marries Dorothy Feiner (Janet Leigh), moves to the country, and the two live happily ever after, even acquiring two daughters. In keeping with the same conventions of heterosexual bonding, Harry Ruby keeps getting mixed up with the wrong girl until he finds Eileen, marries her and lives happily ever after. Lorenz Hart's problem, as cynically phrased by John McCarten, is that "a lady singing in a beer joint refuse[s] to fall in love with him." Even when we observe that the lady is a singer and actress named Peggy McNeil (Betty Garrett) and that the romantic ups and downs attending her relationship with Hart are more complicated than McCarten lets on, we can easily see that both films often operate safely within the gender assumptions that govern the genre's syntax. The fact that the principal males in these biopics interact more with each other than with the women in these stories throws a somewhat different light on how the narratives are gendered.

In the language used by contemporary scholars engaged in gender studies, we might say that both *Words and Music* and *Three Little Words* are centered on homosocial relationships.[18] What this means in practice is that Rodgers and Hart are always more interested in how things are going to affect the other (male) half of the team than either is in how these events are going to affect the women with whom they are involved, and the same may be said for Kalmar and Ruby. In fact, the key scene for understanding homosociality in both films occurs when Bert and Jessie join Ruby on the train that is supposedly taking him away from Buffalo and them. Since these dancers have just been married, Harry struggles to understand his role in the group by asking, "What about the team?"—that is, the team of Kalmar and Brown, now Kalmar and Kalmar. Jessie shows her understanding of how homosociality operates by wondering aloud whether the "team" should be billed as Ruby and Kalmar or Kalmar and Ruby. This scene really says it all about who is important to whom. Dorothy Rodgers shows her commitment to the same project when she invites Larry Hart to go along on the honeymoon that she and Dick Rodgers will be taking to California.

These homosocial issues extend throughout both narratives. When Peggy McNeil turns down Hart's overtures, at least in part because he is too short, Rodgers says in a voice-over, "That was the touch-off spark that was to affect everything Larry Hart ever did again." In keeping with this concerned observation, Larry's erratic behavior worries Dick Rodgers for much of the film, even though it is never quite established what Larry does when he disappears for extended periods. When the opening date for *A Connecticut Yankee* is rapidly approaching and Larry still has not written the lyrics, Dick becomes angry as well as worried. When he learns that Larry has been chasing Eileen all the way out to Hollywood and forgetting all about the team, Rodgers is still worried but no longer angry. Then, when Dick and Dorothy agree to marry shortly after this, the crucial question obviously is, what about Larry? Dorothy agrees to tell Larry about the wedding plans at a luncheon for two, and Larry is happy for Dick, just as he was fully supportive earlier when Dick wanted to give up collaborating with Larry in order to pursue a career in children's wear. When Larry joins the happy couple on their honeymoon, the homosocial bond is completed. Thus, it is not surprising that Larry is welcome to stay with the happy couple—and their two children—in their country home years later when some kind of unexplained dissipation[19] has ruined his health.

Whatever the problem is, it takes its toll, and Larry dies on the streets, even while a revival of *A Connecticut Yankee* is opening to rave reviews. Significantly, Larry has left a hospital bed to drag himself to the opening, even though he has demonstrated considerable professional irresponsibility in the past. Since the revival is a Rodgers & Hart show, after all, and since Dick has certainly arranged for the revival in order to benefit Larry, it is important for Hart to get to the theater even if it costs him his life.[20] Perhaps in gratitude, Dick is teary-eyed throughout the memorial concert emceed by Gene Kelly that concludes the film. This sequence, which functions in the film as a look back on the lives of Rodgers and Hart, is all Larry Hart, and appropriately so because it is all seen through the teary eyes of Richard Rodgers.

Similar homosocial patterns operate throughout *Three Little Words*. In keeping with a precept of romantic comedy that the central couple should always "meet cute," we first see Kalmar and Ruby when the latter ruins the former's vaudeville magic act. If they were a heterosexual couple — Fred and Ginger, let's say — we could comfortably wait for their second, more promising meeting. Thus, Kalmar and Ruby meet in Al Masters' office, without recognizing each other, and write a hit song. Soon, what Tom Drake/Richard Rodgers calls "the standard trials and tribulations you'd normally expect" are represented by Kalmar's warning Ruby that their partnership is only temporary. As experienced filmgoers would expect, this warning is a false signal, and so the two partners stay more or less together for the rest of the film — in the process, becoming each other's best friend and protector. Because Harry knows that Bert is yearning for his former dance partner, Jessie, he arranges for the songwriting team to journey to Buffalo to catch her act. Jessie invites the two on stage, and the three of them perform the Kalmar-Ruby song "Nevertheless." This reunion leads to Bert and Jessie's marriage and to a honeymoon for three. Bert returns the favor when his buddy becomes enamoured of the fickle Terry Lordel. At Jessie's suggestion, Bert arranges for Harry to join his friend Al Schacht at the Washington Senators' spring training site in Florida.[21] The ensuing sequence gives Red Skelton a chance to demonstrate some physical comedy and Harry Ruby a chance to escape a matrimonial trap. When Harry returns to New York, he is met by Bert alone, who tells him that Terry has married another man. The two pals then drown their sorrow together with grape juice. In gratitude for Bert's assistance, Harry works indirectly to sabotage an awful play that Kalmar has written. Even though Harry has his pal's best interests at heart in sinking this play, his intervention will eventually lead to the break-up of their partnership when it is drunkenly leaked by their manager, Charlie Kope (Keenan Wynn). Before that happens, Bert and Jessie help Harry escape another matrimonial miscue through another trip to the Senators' spring training camp — this time at Bert's suggestion — and the three go to London together for the premiere of *Five O'Clock Girl*. As when George and Mary Cohan were often shot in a threesome with Sam Harris in *Yankee Doodle Dandy*, we see Bert, Jessie and Harry sitting together, watching their show. Significantly, Bert looks across Jessie to catch Harry's eye when things seem to be going well with this performance. This is as it should be. Confused reviewers notwithstanding, *Three Little Words* is, after all, a biopic about a songwriting team. The homosocial relationship between the two same-sex partners must therefore be the heart of the story.

One other issue related to gender needs to be mentioned also. In both *Three Little Words* and *Words and Music*, the women involved with these same-sex partners often function in maternal roles.[22] It is Dorothy Rodgers, after all, who helps Larry Hart understand that Dick is getting married, and it is Dorothy who comes up with the suggestion that Larry accompany them on their honeymoon. It is only to be expected, then, that Dorothy will understand Larry's existential anguish later on in the film and invite him to stay with them in their country home. When the Rodgerses depart from California halfway between these two occasions, Dick says in a voice-over that they are leaving Hollywood with two children, and then he adds Larry as the third. Larry's childish status is reinforced by the actions of his doting mother in New York and California. In New York we see her serving strudel to one and all and tenderly covering Larry with a blanket when he has returned from a debauch.[23] In California we see her staring sadly out of a second-story window at her depressed and drunken son as he falls asleep in a lounge chair after a Hollywood gala.

Jessie Kalmar is equally maternal, despite the fact that she has no actual children in *Three Little Words*. When Bert and Harry bicker loudly over the former's fondness for magic and the latter's for baseball, Jessie smiles benignly, confident that the boys are getting along just the way boys should. When a similar argument erupts toward the end of the film, Eileen Ruby is disturbed by the rancor, but Jessie assures her, as moms from Mrs. Hardy to Mrs. Cleaver would, that the boys are getting along just fine. This argument between Kalmar and Ruby is the result of a plot hatched by Jessie and Eileen to get the boys back together again. Since Bert and Harry are too pig-headed — too male — to kiss and make up, it is up to the more mature women to solve the problem. Although it seems for a few minutes late in the film that the women's devious plan may not work out, they are proved correct when Bert writes a lyric for the tune that Harry has been trying to interest him in all through the picture. When Bert sings the title song "Three Little Words" on the Phil Regan radio program, Harry is obviously touched by this confirmation of the homosocial bond, and the women are validated as the wiser, because more maternal, sex. The final shot in the film shows Eileen, Harry, Bert and Jessie together staring at a cake intended to celebrate the famous songwriting partnership. Everyone looks happy. Significantly, Bert and Harry are in the center with their arms around each other, and this seems to be all right with their wives.

In the review in which he ridicules the plotting of *Words and Music* John McCarten writes, "It's an odd thing, but most of the American tune writers the movies show an interest in these days seem to be chaps without any difficulties about money in their lives. Since they seem to be gentlemen who get along with their girls and don't get into public scrapes, there's really not much to be said about them dramatically" (102). As we have seen, McCarten's point is well taken regarding the two biopics of songwriting teams discussed here. His objection is even more valid concerning two films released in 1946 that purport to represent the lives of individual giants of the world of popular music: *Night and Day*, based on the life of Cole Porter, and *Till the Clouds Roll By*, based on the life of Jerome Kern.

Porter and Kern both enjoyed great public adulation, wealth, and relatively happy private lives.[24] As McCarten would say, "there's really not much to be said about them dramatically." And so, the authors of both biopics must invent whatever *agon* the films contain. In terms of dramatic urgency, *Night and Day*—which the title card claims to be "based on the career of Cole Porter"—offers opposition to Cole's musical career by his grandfather, J. O. Cole, a love-at-first-sight romance between Cole and his eventual wife Linda, Cole's hazardous service with the French Foreign Legion during World War I, a series of physical ordeals resulting from a horseback riding accident and a happy ending in which a musically successful Cole is reunited with Linda despite his physical infirmities. The biographical problem is, though, that most of this urgency is invented, making the film more fiction than biography.[25] In the case of Jerome Kern, the screenwriters—Guy Bolton, George Wells, Myles Connolly and Jean Holloway—abandon any real claim of biographical tension in the life of their subject and just create the fiction that Kern's life was deeply troubled by the bad behavior of his best friend's daughter—even though this particular best friend and daughter did not exist. This time the title card claims that the film is "based on the life and music of Jerome Kern." Of course, it is the music that attracted filmmakers to these stories in the first place and drew viewers into the theaters to

Cole Porter (Cary Grant) plays "I Get a Kick Out of You" for Carole Hill (Ginny Simms) in *Night and Day*.

see them. Even so, the pretense of biographical authenticity surrounding these films' presentation of this music seems even less justifiable than in *Three Little Words* or *Words and Music*.

Cole Porter's grandfather did oppose his career choice, as most biographers agree, Cole did marry a woman named Linda, and he did undergo numerous very painful operations in an attempt to reverse the damage to his legs suffered a riding accident. On the other hand, the real Linda Porter was 36 years old and divorced from E. R. Thomas when she and Cole married; she was not a college girl fortunately visiting the Porter house one Christmas while Cole was attending Yale. Furthermore, Cole suffered his tragic riding accident at the Piping Rock Riding Club on Long Island rather than while exercising his dead grandfather's favorite horse in an act of filial piety. Cole did have something to do with the French Army in 1918, but he did not first overhear the beat of "Begin the Beguine" while undergoing artillery fire with his Negro troops. "Actually," as Porter's biographer George Eels reports, "Cole's first wartime association in France was with Duryea Relief, an organization which had been set up by an American woman, Nina Larre Smith Duryea" (53). As Eels and Wilfred Sheed both report, Cole mostly just liked to dress up in various military uniforms.[26]

Perhaps most important of all in terms of biographical accuracy, Porter was—like Lorenz Hart—gay. Given the cultural environment in which the musical biographies of both songwriters were released, however, it should probably come as no surprise that the scriptwriters dreamed up traditional heterosexual movie romances for Larry Hart and Cole Porter. As Wilfred Sheed explains, "In Porter's time, the general public didn't know a homosexual from the Father of the Bride, so [Cole Porter] was able to hide his gay self inside an even gayer persona, wrap it all up in an acceptable marriage, and pass the whole rigmarole off as a reasonable facsimile of Cary Grant, who played him in the hilarious movie *Night and Day*" (96). All the same, there end up being few resemblances between the man who wrote all those wonderful songs and the character played by Cary Grant in "the hilarious movie."

Kern also resembled Hart—not sexually but in terms of height. As Gerald Bordman reports, "[B]y manhood [Kern] stood just five foot six inches" (9). Even so, the film script does not make its subject's height a source of mental anguish, as was purportedly the case with Hart. Other biographical/fictional matters do play a role. For example, Jerome Kern did actually marry a young English woman named Eva. However, Eva Leale was helping tend bar in her father's pub when Jerry first met her in real life rather than emerging from a charming English garden just in time to hear Jerry play "They Didn't Believe Me" on the piano in her mother's charming English cottage, as she does in *Till the Clouds Roll By*. Jerry's producer Charles Frohman actually did go down on the *Lusitania*, and Kern actually had planned to sail on the same ship. However, as Bordman explains, Kern was really saved by his habitual tardiness (114); he was not detained by his best friend, James Hessler. In fact, this last detail points to the greatest gap between the life of Jerome Kern and the story told in *Till the Clouds Roll By*. As I have said already, the life story of Jerome Kern apparently seemed so lacking in traditional dramatic appeal[27] that the screenwriters concocted a parallel story involving Kern's arranger, Hessler (Van Heflin), and his adorable daughter Sally (Joan Wells and Lucille Bremer). Through the earlier stages of Kern's career, Sally is her father's constant companion and her Uncle Jerry's love and inspiration. After Sally grows up into Lucille Bremer, she becomes a stage-struck, arrogant diva, causing her father to die of a broken heart and her Uncle Jerry to go into a deep depression. Even this invented crisis is resolved, however, and everything turns out all right. After Jerry sees Sally perform "I Won't Dance" with Van Johnson in a Memphis nightclub, he shakes off his depression and goes on to write *Show Boat*. Since the film runs long —137 minutes— some dramatic tension is necessary. Since the life of Jerome Kern could not provide such, his biopic did.

The invented Hessler provides another opportunity to connect the film biography of Jerome Kern to that of Cole Porter and also to the musical biographies of Rodgers & Hart and Kalmer & Ruby. Like Dick Rodgers and Bert Kalmar, the cinematic Kern is married to a woman, but — also like those other two musical geniuses — Jerry's closest connections are to his male partner. To estimate Hessler's importance in Kern's cinematic life, we might consider Van Heflin's superior billing to that of Dorothy Patrick, who plays Eva Kern. However, the diegetic narrative provides evidence enough of Hessler's centrality even apart from the many scenes in which he encourages Jerry about his music and advises Jerry about his romance with Eva. For example, when Hessler's daughter has behaved very badly after Charles Dillingham insisted that the song "Who" be given to Marilyn Miller (Judy Garland) instead of Sally, Hessler and Jerry discuss what to do about the wayward young woman as if they were her parents. "What are we going to do, Jerry?" Hessler asks, as Emily Hardy might ask the Judge. For me, though, the definitive scene occurs when Hessler is dying. Jerry goes upstairs, sits on his old friend's bed, holds his hand and promises to look after Sally. Eva waits downstairs with Hessler's housekeeper, Mrs. Muller. When the doctor breaks the news that Hessler died just after Jerry left his room, Jerry looks devastated, and Eva puts her arm around him and looks off into the distance understandingly. Eva also arranges for Jerry to meet Oscar Hammerstein, II, in order to discuss writing *Show Boat*, fully aware that he needs something to take his mind off his friend's death. In a voice-over Jerry has just said, "I was completely lost, completely helpless. Jim was gone. I had failed him.... I lost a world with Jim's passing and everywhere I walked, I walked with ghosts, reliving lost hours, facing a world of memories.... I began to feel that I might never write again." Eva clearly understands how important homosocial bonding is to her husband — perhaps to all men. Linda Porter shows a similar understanding when she entrusts Cole's welfare to Monty Woolley — "Take care of Cole!"— as she goes off to find herself. Woolley, playing himself as a college professor, is suited to take on the protector's role because he has been present through most of Porter's biopic. First Woolley is Cole's law professor at Yale.[28] Then he acts as agent, partner, director, confidant and friend as Porter's career progresses. In a slight variation on a familiar pattern, Woolley also counsels Linda when it is apparent that Cole's commitment to his career is driving the couple apart. Nevertheless, Woolley is primarily Cole's friend, as Hessler is Jerry's, and the wives in such cases are well advised to take a back seat. This is a lesson implied in most of the biopics discussed in this chapter. The differences among these quasi-fictional biographies, then, must lie in the music for which the individual subjects are renowned.

In *Noel and Cole: The Sophisticates*, Stephen Citron maintains that "Cole's classy and now classic songs provided whatever entertainment value *Night and Day* had" (214), and something similar might well be said about *Till the Clouds Roll By*. Since both films are jam-packed with musical production numbers of these classic songs, four sequences from each will have to suffice to show how these songs are presented.

Third-person address controls the first presentation of the title song in *Night and Day*. Perhaps ludicrously, a ticking grandfather clock at the military hospital where Cole is recovering from his war wound and the dripping rain outside inspire him to write *Night and Day*. As usually happens in such scenes, Cole struggles at first with the words and music and then grows increasingly fluent until he says, "You, you, you," as Linda—conveniently a nurse in the same hospital—walks into the room. The scene is fundamentally representational, intended to forward the film's romantic plot, including a kiss between the two lovers. (It is not until the end of the film that "Night and Day" receives a direct-on, first-person performance by a full orchestra and choir.) The next example also seems to be cast in the third person, representing Monty Woolley's efforts, as part of the composer's biographical story, to help sell Cole's music to a producer. As in the similar scene in which George M. Cohan and Mary attempt to interest Dietz and Goff in George's song "Harrigan," the biographical significance is slight in Woolley's version of "Miss Otis Regrets." As in the Cohan scene, the setting is a theatrical office, and as in the earlier film, occasional cuts pretend to some diegetic function for the performance. In the case of "Miss Otis," this fiction is forwarded by the producer's sour-faced secretary, who is the object of Woolley's distinctly articulated "Madam" at appropriate points in the lyric. The diegetic pretense is that this is how Porter's songs attracted the attention of Broadway producers. The presentational fact is that this is how Porter's song "Miss Otis Regrets" can be worked into *Night and Day*.

A tissue of biographical significance also underlies the "I Get a Kick Out of You" number. The diegetic premise is that Cole has invited the cast of *Anything Goes* to rehearse at the Porters' estate without asking Linda's permission. This tension in the Porters' marriage is supposedly exacerbated when Cole and Carole Hill (Ginny Simms) cast romantic glances at each other while singing this song. All of this is pretty much beside the point when a first-person rendition of the song by a full chorus of singers and dancers follows. To maintain the pretense of biographical relevance, the camera occasionally dollies back to show the rolling lawns of the estate and spectators sitting in lounge chairs, but no one is really fooled. The song is great, the singing and dancing are animated, and we get to hear another one of the songs that led us to see the movie in the first place. The staging of "Begin the Beguine" somewhat later in the film is even more obviously first person and presentational. As in numerous other production numbers in the films discussed earlier, "Begin the Beguine" takes place on stage, with a huge cast, many closeup shots and—as a bonus—pagan drums. A slight difference from the norm lies in the fact that Monty Woolley is holding a telephone up to the stage during this number so that Cole can listen from the hospital bed where he has recently undergone a twenty-seventh operation on his legs. If you'll believe that, you'll believe anything!

In Jerome Kern's biopic, the most biographical number occurs when Jerry first comes to Hessler for musical advice. To show what he can do, Jerry plays "Ka-lu-a" on the piano. Hessler finds the tune promising but uninteresting, and so he decides to show Kern how a proper arrangement can enhance a song. The technique is sophisticated, rather like the device by which Dick Rodgers' solo piano version of "Manhattan" is transformed into a full-fledged orchestral performance by Mickey Rooney. In the case of "Ka-lu-a," Kern starts to play the tune, Hessler says that strings would help, and strings come in on the sound track, even though the diegetic setting remains Hessler's living room. The number progresses as other instruments are added. Then, a representational air is added to the number when Hessler changes his mind about a bit of arrangement, and the soundtrack backs up and corrects the phrase. Perhaps because "Ka-lu-a" is not one of the Kern tunes that most members of the movie audience might be whistling on the way *into* the theater, a third-person mode of address is allowed to dominate the scene. At the opposite pole of address is Dinah Shore's version of "They Didn't Believe Me," one of many interpolations of Kern songs from Broadway shows. In the case of this song from *The Girl from Utah*, there is no pretense that a theatrical audience is watching Dinah's number. She sings the song right into the camera in front of an obviously theatrical backdrop. Anyone who truly wishes to can believe that this is what *The Girl from Utah*, one of Jerome Kern's many successful shows, looked like, but this pretense is hardly necessary. *Till the Clouds Roll By* begins with the premise, stated on an opening title card, that "[t]he story of Jerome Kern is best told in the bars and measures, the quarter notes and grace notes of his own music," and that is what the various performances by Dinah Shore, Lena Horne, Frank Sinatra, Tony Martin and many others are intended to achieve.

This is especially evident as the film opens with highlights from *Show Boat*. The diegetic premise is that this performance marks the high watermark of Kern's career and so can serve as a platform for the extended flashback that will constitute much of the film. In fact, though, these opening sequences show viewers of the film not the life of anyone, including the show's composer, but rather the musical production *Show Boat*. The usual technique whereby the camera dollies in over the orchestra into an unmitigated first-person presentation leads to performances of many famous Kern songs, including "Make Believe" by Kathryn Grayson and Tony Martin, "Life Upon the Wicked Stage" by Virginia O'Brien, "Can't Help Lovin' Dat Man" by Lena Horne and "Ol' Man River" by Caleb Peterson. If anyone was in doubt about who Jerome Kern was or why he deserved his own biopic, this sequence of songs would surely set his or her mind at ease. But, of course, it is highly unlikely that such an uninformed viewer would be seeing *Till the Clouds Roll By* in the first place. The real question, then, is—as it was in *Night and Day*—how to get as many songs as possible into the movie. This mini-version of *Show Boat* is clearly a very good answer to the question.

Another good answer differs slightly from the examples cited earlier because the collage of songs supposedly occurs in a film rather than on stage. Toward the end of *Till the Clouds Roll By*, Jerry and Eva go to a Hollywood sound stage to see how the movies will treat the life of Jerome Kern. (We can tell that many years have passed because they have gray hair.) The premise for the whole production number is that Kern's "The Land Where the Good Songs Go" will be used in a film as a frame for presenting other songs. First off, the frame song is sung by no one other than Sally, grown out of her nasty attitude, in a full-scale Busby Berkeley–style number. Other first-person numbers follow, separated only by title cards: "Yesterdays," "Long Ago and Far Away," "A Fine Romance," "All the Things You Are," "Why Was I Born" and — most egregiously — "Ol' Man River" by Frank Sinatra, with kettle drums and all.

It is perhaps appropriate that *Till the Clouds Roll By* should end with the subject's old age and with a reprise of some of his most famous songs. After all, Jerome Kern was already dead at the time of the film's release. When *Night and Day* was released, however, Cole Porter had yet to write the songs for the Broadway shows *Kiss Me Kate* (1948), *Can-Can* (1953) and *Silk Stockings* (1956) — not to mention the films *High Society* (1956) and *Les Girls* (1957). Logically speaking, the real Cole Porter's professional life wasn't over when Cary Grant and Alexis Smith embraced at the end of *Night and Day*. But, as Rick Altman has written, in *The American Film Musical*, "[W]hat use is logic in the case of a form which against all odds for twenty years survived the abuse of critics, a form which never produced anything approaching a masterpiece, and whose high point may well have been its very first example, *The Great Ziegfeld* (1936)?" (235). As we have surely seen by this point, biographical accuracy is not really what these films are about. The songs of Cohan, Rodgers & Hart, Kalmer & Ruby, Porter, and Kern are their real subjects as well as the shows mounted by producers like Ziegfeld and Cohan intended to showcase such songs. This is the true purpose of the musical biopic.

8
Intertextual Musicals

Elsewhere I have written that "intertextual encounters occur whenever an author or the author's text recognizes, references, alludes to, imitates, parodies or otherwise elicits a reader's familiarity with, other texts, however defined."[1] In specific relation to the Hollywood musical, these intertextual encounters may entail matters such as sources, generic parallels and cinematic techniques. Producers and consumers of Hollywood musicals may thus be in the position to compare and contrast a current film with a particular previous text, "however defined," or they may consider how the current film resembles and departs from the dozens, or hundreds, of other Hollywood musicals with which this rhetorical community is familiar. Even how a new film addresses an old problem such as sexuality or happy endings can be seen as an intertextual critical issue. All of this is true, moreover, whether or not any particular member of the audience "gets it." Intertextuality may be present whether a specific individual recognizes it or not, and so intertextuality is still another thing that Hollywood musicals can be "about."

Many of the musical films discussed in previous chapters are intertextual in the sense that they are filmed versions of stage musicals. *Girl Crazy* (1943; Broadway 1930), *Oklahoma!* (1955; Broadway 1943), *Finian's Rainbow* (1968; Broadway 1947), *Brigadoon* (1954; Broadway 1948), *The King and I* (1956; Broadway 1954), *Li'l Abner* (1959; Broadway 1956), *West Side Story* (1961; Broadway 1957), *Bye Bye Birdie* (1963; Broadway 1960) and *Grease* (1978; Broadway 1972) were already successful Broadway musicals before they were made into films. The people who made these films surely counted on a certain level of name recognition to pre-sell them. Some of these films' viewers had probably seen a stage version of the musical already—on Broadway, on tour, in little theater productions, or wherever. These viewers would thus be able to join a rhetorical community invented by the film makers in which everyone could see how faithfully or freely the filmed version followed the stage play. Two films discussed in this chapter—*Kiss Me Kate* (1953; Broadway 1948) and *A Funny Thing Happened on the Way to the Forum* (1966; Broadway 1962)—had already enjoyed Broadway success before being made into films, and so we may consider how the intersection of these two textual entities creates the kind of intertextuality that Hollywood musicals are often "about."

Some Hollywood musicals also have had previous textual lives that had nothing to do with Broadway musicals. *Oklahoma!* was once a play called *Green Grow the Lilacs* (1931) by Lynn Riggs. *The King and I* was based on the book *Anna and the King of Siam* (1944) by Margaret Landon, just as *Li'l Abner* was based on the successful comic strip of the same title (1934–77) by Al Capp. Nearly everyone acknowledges that *West Side Story* was based on William Shakespeare's play *Romeo and Juliet*, just as *Kiss Me Kate* was based on his *The Taming of the Shrew*. The lives of the famous performers, producers and songwriters represented in *Dixie, The Jolson Story, The Great Ziegfeld, Yankee Doodle Dandy, Words and Music, Three Little Words, Night and Day* and *Till the Clouds Roll By* perhaps do not function as viable intertexts in the biopics discussed earlier because, as we have seen, there is often little biographical accuracy involved. Famous popular songs *do* serve as intertexts, however, and so their reappearances in these biopics could receive intertextual attention.

Still another form of intertextuality occurs when Hollywood musicals refer not to specific performers or performances but to the genres in which these are so often embedded. *Golddiggers of 1933, Stand Up and Cheer, Babes in Arms, Babes on Broadway* and *Holiday Inn*—all involve the diegetic premise of putting on a show. Viewers are thus in the position of comparing diegetic and metadiegetic (the show within a show) songs, dances and production numbers.[2] In such films, viewers are involved in a classically intertextual situation. In this chapter, *The Band Wagon* (1953) and *All That Jazz* (1979) provide such opportunities for intertextual encounters and discussions. This condition is even more acute when a Hollywood musical uses Hollywood musicals as its intertext.[3] *Singin' in the Rain*, for example, takes the historical arrival of musical films as the subject of a musical film. *Pennies from Heaven* (1982) uses the musical films in which Americans blithely sang and danced their way out of the Depression as its intertext. As Albert Auster has observed: "In the traditional Hollywood screenplay, the audience watched the unfolding drama or comedy as if what was taking place on the screen was actually happening. In contrast, the film musical incorporated the audience into its fantasy world.... [T]he Hollywood musical acknowledged the fact that it was entertainment pure and simple" (280). These various forms of acknowledgement create the intertextuality that is my subject in this chapter.

Kiss Me Kate (1953) was recognized as an intertextual musical even from its first appearance on Broadway. In *Newsweek*, the reviewer wrote about this production that the authors, Sam and Bella Spewack, "Lift[ed] the general idea from William Shakespeare, as well as a few scenes and settings from his *Taming of the Shrew*" (Jan. 10, 1949). On the same day, *Time*'s reviewer expressed the same idea in these words: "Shakespeare and show business divide the burden in *Kiss Me Kate*, which has to do with the out-of-town opening of a production of *The Taming of the Shrew*" (36). Wolcott Gibbs wrote in *The New Yorker* that "Bella and Samuel Spewack ... wrote the parts of the book that Shakespeare didn't ..." (50). Finally, in a Feb. 7, 1949, story *Life* magazine called the play "a lusty marriage between the talents of Shakespeare and Songwriter Cole Porter ..." (99). Obviously, William Shakespeare's play (c. 1592), the script written by Sam and Bella Spewack and Cole Porter's score—all interact intertextually in *Kiss Me Kate* (1948). This situation only becomes more rich and complex in the film version (1953), as the reviewers' initial responses again reveal.

Beginning once again with *Newsweek*, we may note the reviewer's intertextual premise: "Cole Porter's brilliant musical-comedy fantasia on the theme of William Shakespeare's *The Taming of the Shrew* has received a handsome Technicolor film treatment …" (96). According to Philip T. Hartung's review in *The Commonweal*, the film provides "the happy combination of Cole Porter and William Shakespeare" (Nov. 20, 1953). Even a disgruntled Hollis Alpert admitted in *Saturday Review* that "[t]he movie … follows the stage norm closely enough," while objecting that "the lines of the original have been altered very much the way my cat was altered recently" (Nov. 14, 1953).[4] In other words, it is clear that critics writing both favorably and unfavorably about *Kiss Me Kate* (1953) recognize the film's intertextuality, a point established perhaps most clearly in *Time*'s review: "Based on the Broadway musical, based on Shakespeare's *Taming of the Shrew*, which was based on an Ariosto comedy based on an old folk tale, the picture is pretty far off any kind of base" (Nov. 16, 1953).

In his editorial commentary on *The Taming of the Shrew*, Charles Sisson proposes intertextual antecedents even for Shakespeare's play: "There are indications in the play of busy reading of Ovid and Plautus …" (291). Dana E. Aspinall complicates matters further by explaining that "[t]he dates surrounding *Shrew*'s early textual and

Petruchio (Howard Keel) badgers Katherine (Kathryn Grayson) as Lippy (Keenan Wynn) and Slug (James Whitmore) watch from behind a screen in *Kiss Me Kate*.

stage history create more questions than they answer, simply because we do not know whether we are piecing together the facts concerning one, two, or possibly even three different plays" (5). The later stages of this intertextual process are equally provocative, and much more obvious. Petruchio says, according to Shakespeare, "I come to wive it wealthily in Padua" (2.2.4), and Cole Porter writes a song with that title for *Kiss Me Kate*. Bianca says to Katherine in *Shrew*, "I never yet beheld that special face" (2.1.11), and so Porter writes the song "Were Thine That Special Face." When Petruchio has finally dragged Katherine to his house in the play, he sings (according to the stage directions),[5] "Where is the life that late I led?" (4.1.139). In the film, Petruchio sings a song of this title at this same point in the plot. In her last speech in the play, Katherine says, "I am ashamed that women are so simple" (5.2.161), and Porter has written a song with this title that was used in the Broadway play but not in the film. In the film, Katherine merely reads the lines, as she does in Shakespeare's original. Finally, and perhaps most significantly, Petruchio's last speech in Shakespeare's play is: "Why there's a wench! Come on, and kiss me Kate" (5.2.180). The intertextual relevance of this line to the musical play and film of the same title should be obvious.

Much of the spoken dialogue points in the same direction, as it should since the diegetic narrative about Fred Graham (Howard Keel) and Lilli Vanessi (Kathryn Grayson) contains a metadiegetic version of *The Taming of the Shrew*. Thus, many lines spoken in the film were actually written hundreds of years earlier by William Shakespeare, but not even all of the lines spoken by these characters in their roles in Shakespeare's play come from the Bard. When the curtains first go up on the metadiegetic play, Petruchio (Keel) summarizes the dramatic premises for his audience (and for us) in words that sound mildly Shakespearean but actually aren't. When Lilli, on stage in her role as Katherine, reads a note from Fred to Lois Lane (Ann Miller), she grows angry for diegetic reasons and bites Fred's finger. Her anger throws the Shakespearean scene off, and so Fred, in his role as Petruchio, must improvise Shakespeare-sounding lines to cover up the dramatic emergency. Petruchio and Baptista (Kurt Kasznar) must improvise once more when neither Lilli nor her understudy enters onto the stage in the climactic scene of *The Shrew*. Thus, we may recognize the intertextuality of *Kiss Me Kate* both when the musical closely follows *The Taming of the Shrew* and when it departs from it.[6]

When Fred/Petruchio sings the song "Were Thine That Special Face" to Lilli/Katherine — supposedly as part of *The Taming of the Shrew* — Lilli is deeply moved, taking the song as a testimony of love from Fred who she thinks has just sent her flowers. When Lilli recognizes, through the note already mentioned, that the flowers were intended for Lois, her anger spills over into Katherine — appropriately enough, since Katherine is choleric in the play anyhow. A diegetic development thus coincides with the metadiegetic intertext. Bianca (Miller) sings "Tom, Dick, or Harry," a song fitting Lois Lane's indiscriminate sexuality but not appropriate to Shakespeare's Bianca. Later on, after Bianca has married Lucentio (Tommy Rall), she sings "From This Moment On" to usher in a frantic production number that lets Ann Miller show off her dancing but that has little to do with Shakespeare's demure and obedient Bianca. The diegetic and metadiegetic texts therefore clash in places, but even these encounters are intertextual.

Other intertextual resonances result from the film's deliberate invocations of dramatic and cinematic convention. As is always the case, when a film shows diegetic actors rehearsing their parts in a metadiegetic play, intertextuality results. According to Ann C. Christensen, this kind of intertextuality is essential to *Kiss Me Kate* because "its musical-about-a-musical genre lends a unique metatheatrical complication to the discussion" (342). This is particularly evident when Fred and Lilli perform "Wunderbar," a corny song from a play they appeared in years ago. Because the lyrics of the song are so deliberately phony, Keel and Grayson have obviously been encouraged by the director, George Sidney, to ham up their performances. This bad acting indirectly draws the audience's attention to the (presumably) better acting of Keel and Grayson — or perhaps of Fred and Lilli. In a final example of a technique that could be illustrated at much greater length, two hoodlums, Lippy (Keenan Wynn) and Slug (James Whitmore), are absorbed into a scene from the metadiegetic *Shrew* that is performed on a moving stage, as the "A Couple of Swells" number is in *Easter Parade* (1948), starring Fred Astaire and Judy Garland. To emphasize the completely theatrical nature of this piece of stage business, the stage begins moving too quickly so that Lippy and Slug have to scramble to keep their footing. Confirming Jane Feuer's claim in *The Hollywood Musical* that there is always a pattern of "demystification and remystification" (43) in such films, we may note that while the theatrical device of the moving stage is demystified, the professional actors Keenan Wynn and James Whitmore are confirmed as comic gangsters.

An especially odd example of such remystification occurs at the beginning of the film. Shakespeare's play — as many may recall — begins with an Induction in which a tinker, Christopher Sly, is falsely convinced that he is a lord who has been insanely assuming that he was a tinker for several years. This induction has something to do with impersonation and assumed identities, as does the play about Petruchio and Katherine that follows, and so it may be defended organically. In George Sidney's film, the Induction involves Fred Graham, Lilli Vanessi and Cole Porter (Ron Randell). The premise of this Induction is that Lilli must be fooled into playing the female lead in a play, called *Kiss Me Kate*, for which Porter has recently completed the score. This play, according to the strangely tentative Cole, "is sort of a musical version of *The Taming of the Shrew*, Shakespeare, you know." Intertextually, this speech is right on the money. Shakespeare, Fred and Lilli are certainly going to engage one another in the film that follows this sequence. Diegetically, the speech raises the challenging question of which script Porter is describing: the musical *Taming of the Shrew* that we will see Fred and Lilli acting in or *Kiss Me Kate* itself. The question assumes greater importance as Fred and Lilli perform "So in Love"[7] and Lois Lane performs "Too Darn Hot" — two songs from *Kiss Me Kate* — in Fred's apartment. Cole explains to Lois that "there's no place" to put her number in the show he has written, but apparently there is a place for the number in George Sidney's movie. In fact, we have just seen it.

In their essay "Totally Clueless: Shakespeare Goes Hollywood in the 1990s," Linda E. Boose and Richard Burt opine that "America's best mode for film Shakespeare productions may, in fact, be the musicals *Kiss Me Kate* ... and *West Side Story*, ... where the Bard is recreated within a particular idiom that is thoroughly home-

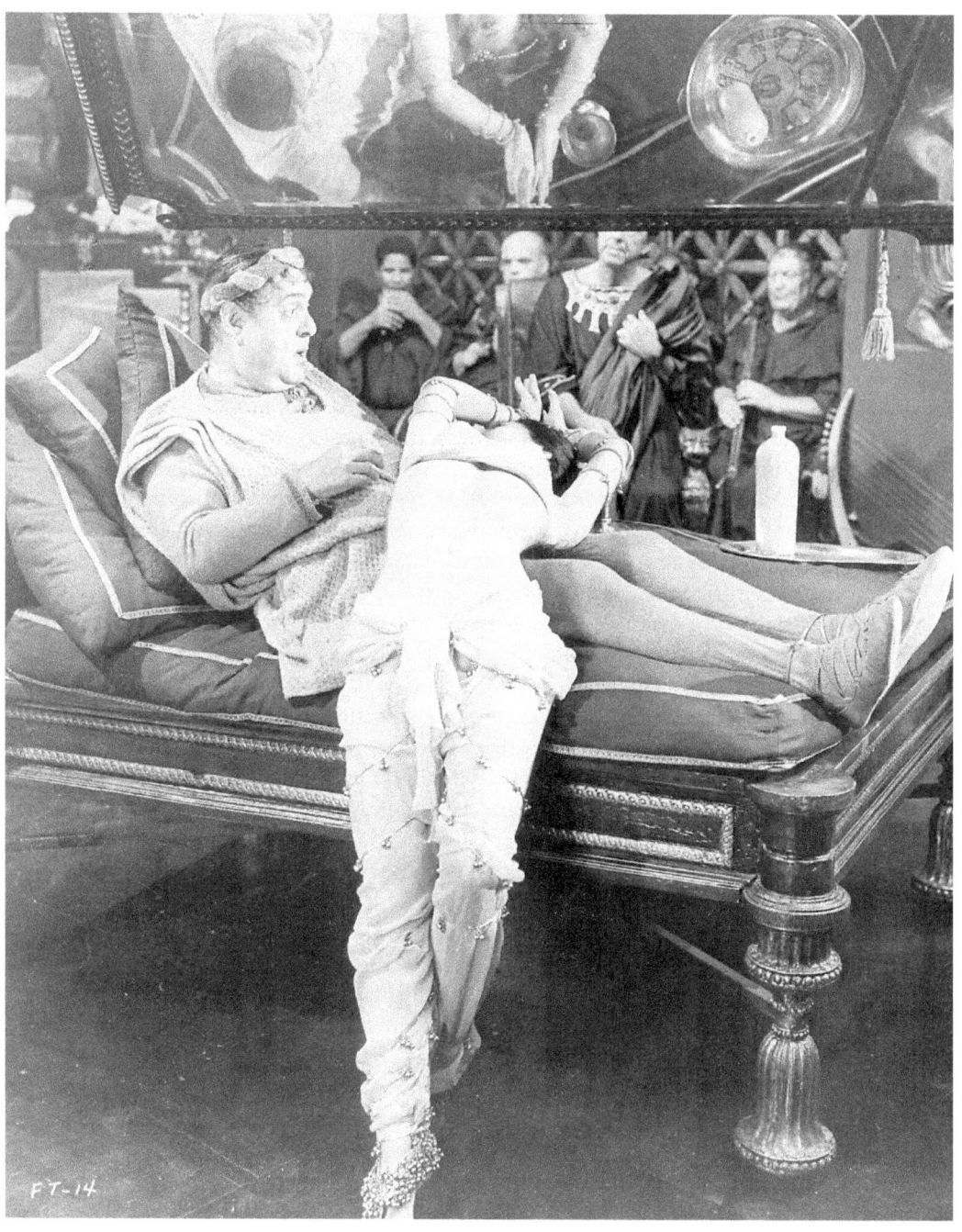

Pseudolus (Zero Mostel) checks out the female merchandise on display at the house of Marcus Lycus (Phil Silvers) in *A Funny Thing Happened on the Way to the Forum*.

grown" (13). This recreation is apparently successful in both the Broadway and Hollywood versions of *Kiss Me Kate*. As William McBrien notes in his biography of Cole Porter (318), the original Broadway production of *Kiss Me Kate* ran longer than any production of *The Taming of the Shrew* before or since. The coupling of Shakespeare and Porter in *Kiss Me Kate* obviously works in whatever form it gets cast into, and this intertextual union seems destined to endure. As a matter of fact, Joseph Papp chose the title *Kiss Me, Petruchio* for the video version (1981) of scenes from the New York Shakespeare festival's production of *The Taming of the Shrew* in Central Park.

The intertextual connections between *A Funny Thing Happened on the Way to the Forum* (1966) and its textual antecedents in the works of the Latin playwright Plautus (c. 254-c. 184 BCE) are often acknowledged, as they are in Stephen Banfield's book *Sondheim's Broadway Musicals*. As Banfield writes about the play: "[T]he chief action concerning the young man's love for the courtesan and his slave's attempts to help him out is taken from the play *Pseudolus* (though similar formulas are found elsewhere), while *Miles Gloriosus* includes the character of that name; the old man returning to find his house haunted is a motif in *Mostellaria* (*The Ghost*); and so on (95)."[8] *Time* wittily makes a similar point: "Like Shakespeare and others, authors Burt Shevelove and Larry Gelbart have rifled the plays of Titus Maccius Plautus for the stuff and nonsense that used to pack the Colosseum when the lions were lethargic and the gladiators on tour" (May 21, 1962). Banfield quotes the recollections of co-author Larry Gelbart in support: "We began the task of extracting from Plautus a character here, a scene there, and created a considerable amount of new material as connective tissue.... What treasure we found in his plays! There they were, running wild in Plautus's pages, appearing for the first time anywhere: the wily slave, the senile skirt-chaser, the henpecked husband, the domineering matron, the courtesan with the hair and heart of gold; page after page of mistaken identity and double meanings" (qtd. in Banfield 93). The result is Plautus redone for a modern audience, as Plautus often redid ancient Greek plays for his contemporaries.[9] Gordon Willis Williams (286) explains in *The Oxford Classical Dictionary* that Plautus was often criticized by Roman purists for engaging in *contaminatio* (mixing new, Latin, ingredients into established Greek plays). This sounds like classical intertextuality to me,[10] and it also sounds like what is happening in *A Funny Thing Happened on the Way to the Forum*—on stage and on screen.

The story's classical antecedents are everywhere present and readily apparent. Senex and Miles Gloriosus take their names from the Latin words for their dramatic functions: the old man and the posturing soldier. Hero's name is close enough to the Latin *heros* that no translation is required. The same is true for other characters: Domina, who browbeats her husband, Senex; Hysterium, the hysterical slave; Fertilla, the breeder slave; and the aptly named dancing courtesans: Tintinabula, Vibrata and the Geminae. Whether or not any individual viewer has read a single line of Plautus before seeing the play or watching the film, a Latin intertext is decidedly present. Gordon Willis Williams explains, for example, that in Plautus' play *Pseudolus*, a "refined Greek *hetaera* is suddenly displayed as the coarse denizen of a low Roman brothel" (844), and one immediately suspects that this development stands behind Domina's confused involvement in Miles Gloriosus' orgy in *A Funny Thing Happened on the Way to the Forum*. A classical intertext — perhaps more than one — is assuredly present in the film, but so are other intertexts. Robert Brustein observes about the Broadway play — as he might equally observe about the film — that, while the narrative "stick[s] with surprising fidelity to a number of Plautine farces[,] ... the work is also flavored with a generous seasoning of Minsky burlesque technique..." (29). In keeping with the burlesque intertext, Vincent Canby observes, about the Lycus character, that Phil Silvers is very present in the film, "without his glasses but wearing a toga and looking like Sergeant Bilko caught in a Turkish bath..." (Oct. 17, 1966). The Broadway Lycus, John Carradine, would probably be known to most viewers of the film as an actor in lugubrious features such as *Curse of the Stone Hand* (1964) and *House of the Black Death* (1965). The substitution of Silvers — at the time a well-known TV sitcom personality — clearly calls upon viewers to invoke their televiewing experience as an intertext. Contemporary farce is thereby introduced with the same confidence that other reviewers displayed in invoking Roman New Comedy.

Richard Lester's filmed version of *A Funny Thing Happened on the Way to the Forum* is, of course, intertextual in some of the same ways as George Sidney's version of *Kiss Me Kate,* since both are based on highly successful Broadway shows that were based in turn upon older literary texts. Yet, some of the differences in two equally intertextual texts may be glimpsed in Nick Roddick's essay review of the former film in *Magill's Survey of Cinema*. According to Roddick, "The film version of *A Funny Thing Happened on the Way to the Forum* is in reality two movies ... at once an adaptation of a Broadway hit and a zany film farce resembling director Dick Lester's Beatles films, *A Hard Day's Night* (1964) and *Help!* (1965)" (592). Therefore, while watching *A Funny Thing Happened on the Way to the Forum*, we need to be aware not only of the conventions of Roman New Comedy exploited in the film, as in the Broadway show, but also of the conventions of filmmaking exploited by Richard Lester. As the film opens, for example, Pseudolus (Zero Mostel) introduces the principal characters in the story as part of the number "Comedy Tonight." At one point, he looks directly into the camera and says, "Pseudolus is probably my favorite character in the piece, a role of enormous variety and nuance and played by an actor of such versatility, such magnificent strength ... Let me put it this way: I play the part." In such a flagrant violation of representational decorum, we can only recognize the presence of a camera and the assumption of an audience, a recognition only strengthened by Pseudolus' language: *character, role, actor, play the part.* This is merely a movie, in other words, a movie like many others we may have watched *without* suspecting the director's tricks.

This same message is sent in other production numbers. During the romantic ballad "I'm Lovely," sung by Hero (Michael Crawford) and Phylia (Annette Andre), Lester follows his practice in the Beatles movies by using jump cuts for comic effect, as when a fountain behind the two lovers alternately flows and runs dry as they sing or when Hero slips, slides and falls among the romantic props while the two lovers frolic in nature — sometimes in slow motion. When it is Hero's turn to sing, he holds out his hands and a lyre drops into them — a ridiculous occurrence perhaps, but no more ridiculous than other happy incidences of bricolage[11] in other Hollywood musicals. When Psudolus and Hysterium (Jack Gilford) reprise this number later in the film, the comic absurdities italicized by these jump cuts are only enhanced — in large part because Gilford is performing his romantic role in drag.[12] In "Everybody Ought to Have a Maid," the number that Clive Hirschhorn calls the film's "one cherishable musical moment" (385), Lester's camera roams with even more freedom than Busby Berkeley's. Perhaps in homage to Berkeley, Lester includes crane shots in the number, but there are also examples of trick photography, as when the low man on a totem pole walks out from under the other two and when Senex (Michael Hordern) flies off on a broomstick. As a final reminder that this is a number in a Hollywood musical, "Everybody Ought to Have a Maid" ends with a socko vaudeville finish as Pseudolus, Hysterium, Senex and Lycus dance and sing their hearts out right in front of the camera.[13]

That *A Funny Thing Happened on the Way to the Forum* is essentially a Hollywood musical is signaled throughout the film. At one point in the bizarrely tangled plot, Pseudolus and Hero race off in opposite directions in search of "a cup of mare's sweat." Hero spends about a half-hour of screen time undergoing various comic frustrations in his quest, but Pseudolus returns with the essential ingredient almost at once. Looking directly into the camera, he asks, "Would you believe it? There was a mare sweating not two streets from here." Since we have already believed that Dale Tremont confused Jerry Travers with Horace Hardwick in *Top Hat* just because she happened to see him carrying Horace's briefcase and that Eva Leale just happened to come in from her charming garden just as Jerry Kern was playing "They Wouldn't Believe Me" on her mother's piano in *Till the Clouds Roll By*, why should it be so hard to believe that a mare was conveniently sweating nearby in *A Funny Thing Happened on the Way to the Forum*? This— or something very similar — is Richard Lester's intertextual point. Why not admit the existence of conventions that we all know exist? When there is a very welcome summary of the plot's complications about halfway between "Everybody Ought to Have a Maid" and the reprise of "I'm Lovely," each character mentioned by Hysterium and Pseudolus— Senex, Hero, Philia and Domina (Patricia Jessel)— is illustrated by a full-screen closeup. We probably could recall these characters without the illustrations, but their full-screen appearances signal just what a plot summary is supposed to achieve. The same thing happens at the film's conclusion under a reprise of "Comedy Tonight." As in all good comedies, everyone is satisfactorily taken care of by the plot. And so, as the whole cast sings about what a comedy includes — lovers, liars and clowns — and excludes — tragedy, kings and crowns — we see Hero matched up with Philia, Pseudolus matched up with Gymnasia (Inga Neilsen), Senex matched up with Domina, and all the other characters awarded whatever they most desire. To emphasize the artificial nature of this resolution, Lester shows each character in closeup. Again, we probably haven't forgotten them, but, again, we apparently need to be shaken out of our representational passivity and reminded that this is merely, but certainly, a musical comedy.

Another form of intertextuality evident in the film can be traced through the *Variety* reviewer's faint praise, expressed in the judgment that the film "will probably stand out as one of the few originals of two repetition-weary genres, the film musical comedy and the toga cum scandal epic" (Sept. 20, 1966). In support of second point, the reviewer claims that "[o]ne of *Forum*'s great services is that it satirizes a 'film-myth' culture, the Romans, too long buried under homogenized and idealized unreality of laundered togas and gleaming columns." In practice, this demythologizing involves closeups of extras with wrinkled skin showing atop their togas, shots of peeling paint on Roman walls, and flies all over the place. One especially effective scene presents the triumphal entry of Miles Gloriosus (Leon Greene) into the city during the comic number "Bring Me My Bride." As the fearsome soldiers march through the city streets, they are pelted with garbage, they stumble across cobblestones and baskets, and they catch their spears on overhead laundry lines. Surely these are not the glorious Roman legions we know from *The Robe* (1953) and *Spartacus* (1960)! No, they aren't, and that — according to the perceptive *Variety* reviewer — is Lester's point. Those glorious legions exist only on screen, as seeing something else on screen is intended to remind us intertextually.

Though not so deconstructive as Lester's dismantling of the "film-myth culture" of the cinematic Romans, the film's climactic chase scene in chariots also echoes recent film history intertextually. In terms of mass entertainment, the chariot chase might be defended just as a way of "opening out" a Broadway play onto the wide screen or as a way of providing thrills and chills to a farce. In terms of the context that I am developing in this chapter, however, the (largely gratuitous)[14] chase scene in *A Funny Thing Happened on the Way to the Forum* seems designed to call upon frequent filmgoers' memories of all the other chase scenes that seemed inescapable in film comedies of the mid–1960s, most especially, perhaps, the antic go-cart chase scene in *What's New, Pussycat?* (1965). As Hollis Alpert writes disapprovingly in his review of *A Funny Thing Happened on the Way to the Forum*, "Today's chic way of being cinematic is to insert some sort of wild, insane chase episode reminiscent of silent classic comedy." In keeping with this nod toward other contemporary films, Alpert concludes that, by following the trend, "Lester spends far too much time on an idiotic chariot race, or chase" (26). The point, finally, should not be whether the chariot chase is good or bad, too long or too short, but whether Richard Lester's *A Funny Thing Happened on the Way to the Forum* is an intertextual Hollywood musical — and it most certainly is.

The Band Wagon (1953) does not call on a single literary text for its intertext, as *Kiss Me Kate* does nor on a whole literary genre, as *A Funny Thing Happened on the Way to the Forum* does, but *The Band Wagon* is just as much an intertextual Hollywood musical as either of these films. *The Band Wagon* is, diegetically, a story about putting on a musical show, and as Jane Feuer maintains in *The Hollywood Musical*, such films are always already intertextual. As Feuer writes, "What makes the musical unique among film genres is not so much that its heyday coincides with the studio years, but rather that its reflexive capability rendered it that genre whose explicit function was to glorify American entertainment while at the same time being itself a form of entertainment" (90). In the case under consideration, a musical show called *The Band Wagon* is metadiegetically embedded in a film with the same title. Viewers therefore cannot escape the task of placing the two musical entertainments side by side. *The Band Wagon* surpasses other Hollywood musicals with the same intertextual structure — *Golddiggers of 1933*, for example, or *Babes in Arms*--in that the diegetic story about the leading man, Tony Hunter, is also to some degree a real-life

Cyd Charisse and Fred Astaire perform the "Girl Hunt Ballet" in *The Band Wagon*.

story about the actor who plays Tony, Fred Astaire. As John Mueller writes in *Astaire Dancing*, "There is no ambiguity about the inspiration of the Astaire character—it was Astaire himself," and, as he amplifies: "[T]here are many references in the character to Astaire's own personality and professional approach: his sensitivity about the height of his partner, his wariness about lifts, his sometimes petulant self-consciousness about his age, his willingness to work long and hard in rehearsal, his problems in trying to match his style to that of ballet-trained partners" (351). Some of these parallels between the actor and his character would not be known by a typical viewer, but—as I have argued above—viewer awareness is not the sole basis for acknowledging the presence of intertextuality. At the same time, most viewers would recognize at least some of the intertextual references to Fred Astaire.

The film opens, for example, with a still photograph of a top hat, cane and white gloves. This photograph stands behind the credits, the second of which is "Fred Astaire." Since, as Rick Altman points out in *The American Film Musical*, this device clearly echoes the opening shots of *Top Hat*, little acuity is required to see these objects as signifiers of Fred's career. In this case, however, the top hat does not belong to a member of Horace Hardwick's stuffy London men's club—as it does in *Top Hat*—but to Tony Hunter, and it is being auctioned off (unsuccessfully), a sign that Hunter's career has reached some sort of nadir. Fred Astaire's career at the time was somewhat healthier. After all, he had recently starred in two memorable Hollywood musicals: *Easter Parade* (1948) and *Royal Wedding* (1951). On the other hand, he had also starred in *Three Little Words* (1950) and *The Belle of New York* (1952)—both opposite Vera-Ellen. So, although Fred was professionally better off than Tony in 1953, he was nowhere nearly as popular as he was back in the 1930s.[15] In any event, the 1930s were a fairly long time ago, and so when Gabrielle Gerard (Cyd Charisse) says about Tony that "[h]e's practically an historical character by now," viewers are expected to think almost the same of Fred Astaire. Furthermore, by making this historical allusion part of the diegetic representation of actors trying to put on a show, the film finesses another intertextual issue: Why is Fred Astaire (b. 1899) playing a romantic part opposite Cyd Charisse (b. 1921)? By letting Tony and Gabrielle work out this generational problem, the director, Vincente Minnelli, assumes that viewers will accept the solution for Fred and Cyd also. Astaire's professional biography is, then, most assuredly a significant intertext in this film.

This biographical intertext is repeatedly stressed, as when Tony turns out to be a good friend of Ava Gardner, who appears in a cameo early in the film, because many viewers assume that all Hollywood stars know one another. At the very beginning of the film, an auctioneer (Douglas Fowley)[16] says about the sophisticated objects that have been shown behind the opening credits that they are "perhaps the most famous top hat and stick of our generation, yes, the ones he used in *Flying Down to Panama*." Anyone who can't connect all of this to Fred's first appearance with Ginger in *Flying Down to Rio* (1933) just isn't trying. Later on, when Tony and Gabrielle dance so smoothly together in Central Park to the Howard Dietz and Arthur Schwartz tune "Dancing in the Dark," it takes very little more imagination to connect the number to the many romantic Fred Astaire-Ginger Rogers numbers in their classic musical films.[17] On the other hand, when Tony and Gabrielle fail to perform a number amid exploding fireworks and stage smoke, suitably alert viewers might recall Fred's successful negotiation of exploding fireworks in *Holiday Inn* in 1942. Fred's version of "I Love Louisa" during a cast party later in the film is based on his earlier rendition of the song in the original Broadway production of *The Band Wagon* (1931). Even viewers unequipped with this historical information can tell that "I Love Louisa" is some kind of old song, however, and not a tune suitable for the 1953 hit parade. This impression of datedness is reinforced because Lester Marton (Oscar Levant) first begs Tony to sing the old song, and then Lily Marton (Nanette Fabray) easily joins in because she knows all the words.

Outside the realm of autobiography, *The Band Wagon* is also highly intertextual. When Tony first meets Jeffrey Cordova (Jack Buchanan), the latter is exiting from the stage into the wings wearing a facial expression suitable for his role as Oedipus the King. Upon seeing Lester and Lily Marton, however, Cordova drops this expression and puts on a big smile. This is how actors put on and take off roles, apparently — including, most probably, the roles of Jeffrey Cordova and Lester and Lily Marton. Later, when Cordova begins to direct Tony and Gabrielle in a show, we see rehearsal shots of dancers making mistakes, special effects not working, actors standing on chairs to simulate a balcony, and changes in the script. Some of these botched efforts involve Tony's repeated readings of the same lines with different emphases — for example, "Did you ever try spreading ideals on a cracker?" It is thus significant intertextually that Tony (actually, Fred Astaire) gets to enact a highly dramatic blow-up at the end of the rehearsal. Tony/Fred screams at Jeffrey Cordova, "I'm not Nijinsky. I'm not Marlon Brando. I'm Mrs. Hunter's little boy, Tony, a song-and-dance man ..." and then dashes off the set. After everything has been temporarily smoothed over later on, we see another rehearsal, in New Haven, in which the stage sets won't work correctly. All such examples of demystification serve to remind viewers that they are seeing a performance — very much like the one being represented in the diegetic narrative. The crowning touch, though, probably comes in the final scene. By this point, the show is a great success. Tony has been proven right all along about what goes into a Broadway musical, and Cordova has been proven wrong in his attempts to turn a carefree musical into a modern day *Faust*. Even so, everyone is friends again. Tony and Gabrielle have sealed their love with a full-screen kiss. Therefore, the script requires a reprise of the famous show biz anthem, "That's Entertainment." In direct presentational style, the five principals sing directly into the camera about a true show's power to leave the audience radiant with happines. Since this is just what *The Band Wagon* has done, the intertextual bond is signed, sealed and delivered.

All That Jazz (1979) involves many of the same intertextual encounters as *The Band Wagon*. This time the creative genius is Joe Gideon (Roy Scheider), who is an author and choreographer rather than a performer like Tony Hunter. Since Gideon was created by Bob Fosse, who was the author, choreographer and director of *All That Jazz*, the film also resembles *The Band Wagon* in basing a fictional character on a famous show business celebrity. Since this biographical intertext is so obvious, nearly everyone who reviewed the movie arrived at some version of Clive Hirschhorn's characterization of the film as "[a] self-indulgent though undeniably effective, often brilliant, examination of the life and death of its creator Bob Fosse" (414). In addition, the film also uses the diegetic premise of putting on a show to interrogate many commonly accepted conventions of the Hollywood musical. In terms of Rick Altman's analysis in *The Hollywood Film Musical*, we may conclude that, with its "emphasis on nostalgia, intertextuality, and attempts to undermine the received ideas of a long musical tradition" (112), *All That Jazz* definitely fits the pattern I have been developing in this chapter.

Bob Fosse's biographical relations to *All That Jazz* are readily apparent. Like Joe Gideon, Fosse was a well-known smoker, drinker, workaholic and womanizer. Although he (obviously) did not die of a heart attack in 1979, he would do so in 1987. He was married to and separated from the Broadway star dancer Gwen Verdon, who often found herself in real life in the kind of awkward domestic situation in which Joe's ex-wife and star dancer Leland Palmer (Audrey Paris) finds herself in the film. Furthermore, Kate Jagger, played by Ann Reinking in the film, is obviously based on Fosse's actual lover Ann Reinking. Since Reinking followed Verdon in the role of Roxie Hart in Fosse's hit Broadway musical *Chicago* (1975), the biographical relations of these actual dancers to their fictional counterparts is only intensified. It is probably intertextually significant also that both Verdon and Reinking continued to work with Fosse even after he dumped them for other women. In the film, Leland Palmer illustrates this amazing fact by saying to Joe, after a stunning performance of "Take Off with Us," "I think it's the best work you've ever done, you son of a bitch!" In addition, Fosse departed from his specialization in musicals just once: to direct *Lenny* (1974), a film based on the life of stand-up comedian Lenny Bruce. In that film, Dustin Hoffman played Lenny. In *All That Jazz*, Cliff Gorman plays David Newman in *The Stand-Up*, a metadiegetic film modeled on *Lenny*. Since Gorman earlier played Bruce on stage, the intertextual connections between life and film multiply geometrically. Other connections of this sort also add to the film's intertextuality. Ben Vereen, who plays O'Connor Flood in *All That Jazz*, earlier starred in Fosse's Broadway hit *Pippin* (1972). Peter Allen, who wrote the song "Everything Old Is New Again" for *All That Jazz*, worked with Fosse on a number of occasions, including the Liza Minnelli[18] TV special *Liza with a "Z,"* for which Fosse won three Emmy Awards in 1973, the same year in which he won two Tony Awards for *Pippin* and an Academy Award for *Cabaret*, starring Liza Minnelli. The hyperactivity signified by all these awards is reflected in the film by Gideon's simultaneous involvement in both the Broadway show that serves as the principal metadiegetic intertext in this film and in *The Stand-Up*.

Fosse is intertextually present in *All That Jazz* in other ways also. When Joe Gideon recalls the time that he tried living with two women simultaneously, the story is illustrated with a musical number that looks like it has been lifted right out of Fosse's *Cabaret*. Clearly, it is Bob Fosse, not the diegetic Joe Gideon, who dreamed up the dance number "Take Off with Us." The hats, the snapping fingers, the mechanical steps and the erotic overtones are pure Fosse. Fosse the choreographer is intertextually present as well when Kate dances in mesh stockings and a bowler hat to the tune "There'll Be Some Changes Made" during a sequence identified as a "hospital hallucination." Kate's dance with Joe's daughter Michelle (Erzsebet Foldi) to "Everything Old Is New Again" also demonstrates the "nostalgia, intertextuality, and attempts to undermine the received ideas of a long musical tradition" that Altman identifies as central to the film and that another commentator might equally identify as Fosse's approach to choreography. Kate and Michelle wear men's hats, they snap their fingers, they strut, they parodically echo vaudeville conventions — in short, they perform a Fosse dance routine for Joe Gideon, the character based on Bob Fosse. During the film's final production number, the dancing screams "Fosse" again through the female dancers' sexy leotards, the finger-snapping by Joe and O'Connor Flood, and Flood's overt invocation of outmoded show business conventions. Joe Gideon may be dying within the film's narrative, but Bob Fosse is putting on a flashy dance number at the same time, and everyone is invited to recognize this.

All That Jazz also relies on many of the self-referential practices that have been used to increase the intertextuality of films like *Kiss Me Kate* and *The Band Wagon*. The first sequence in the film, for example, is a "cattle call" in which Gideon selects the dancers for his new show. As in all such cases, the backstage environment requires viewers to ask questions about the production methods of the film they are watching. This questioning is increased in this case by the very technical — and so very realistic — choreographic instructions given to the dancers. As we watch these dancers trying out different steps, sometimes intercut with shots of different dancers jumping across Gideon's line of vision, we are forced to realize that the seamless dancing that we see on the screen in Hollywood musicals is the result of many hours of trial and error. In terms of the film's plot, "Take Off with Us" is definitely the key musical number. To emphasize the developmental nature of musical performance, we first hear the number sung by its diegetic author, Paul Dann (Anthony Holland), so that we already know the song when it later receives its climactic performance. In a related display of self-referentiality, Joe obsessively watches the same scenes from *The Stand-Up*, looking for the directorial cuts that will make the film most effective. As viewers of *All That Jazz*, we watch these clips also. Perhaps we can tell that a minute editorial change might make the metadiegetic film better. Perhaps we don't see this at all. In either case, we are reminded of how the film that we are watching was probably put together. During the "hospital hallucination" sequence, each of the principal women in Joe's life stars in a production number based on an old song: "After You've Gone" (Audrey), "There'll Be Some Changes Made" (Kate), and "Some of These Days" (Michelle). The diegetic excuse for these numbers is that Gideon is hallucinating film sequences rather than the plain old dreams that most fictional characters (and real ones) experience. To underscore this diegetic point, each number concludes with shots clearly intended to highlight the cinematic process. We see cameras, crane shots, dollies and another version of Gideon as the film director. Even as the sequence tells viewers about Gideon's unhealthy obsession with work, it tells them even more about how movies are made.

Another reminder that this is partly a movie about making a movie occurs when Gideon watches a television review of *The Stand-Up* from his hospital bed. In the role of TV critic Leslie Perry, Irene Kane seriously pans the film, and Gideon suffers a heart seizure. Even apart from the probable reference to the obsessed director Fosse, the sequence must alert viewers to the fact that all directors worry about how their films are received by critics and paying audiences.[19] Furthermore, the obvious perspiration on the rehearsing dancers signals in another direction that this is a movie about putting on a musical show. When Leland is rehearsing her star number in front of studio mirrors with only the show's composer Paul Dann on piano, we see her painfully pulling a muscle, and then we see very visible sweat patches on her leotard. When the whole dance troupe is rehearsing "Take Off with Us," they all wear rehearsal clothes and sweat profusely, as we can tell by both their costumes and their faces. Dancing is hard work, in other words, not a joyous expression of sheer pleasure. When Joe repeatedly criticizes the performance of his sometimes lover Victoria Porter (Deborah Geffner) during one rehearsal of "Take Off with Us," Victoria breaks down in tears, as so many actors and dancers must have done during the filming of the many musicals we have discussed already.[20] This highly intertextual intersection of performer and performance is reinforced when a frustrated Joe later screams at God (or at least at the ceiling), "What's the matter? Don't you like musical comedy?" It would have to be a dull viewer indeed who would draw no connection between this line and the film in which it occurs. Equally obvious is the irony of the film's closing sequence in which the dead Joe Gideon is zipped into a body bag as Ethel Merman sings "There's No Business Like Show Business" on the sound track. While this ironic conjunction certainly serves to advance the critique of "the received ideas of a long musical tradition" that Altman recognizes in the film, it also serves as an obvious intertextual reminder that *All That Jazz* is, after all, primarily just a part of "show business."

Although it is another link in a long chain of musical entertainments, *All That Jazz* seeks to distinguish itself clearly from its predecessors. Thus, the film engages in still another form of intertextuality, the form in which a present instance invokes its predecessors through contrast rather than through imitation. Just following the cattle call that opens the film, for example, two dancers who have not been cast criticize Gideon by using the taboo term *fuck*. We need only try to imagine Fred Astaire or Ginger Rogers, or even the inhabitants of Dogpatch, saying "fuck," to see how deliberately Fosse is departing from the models with which we are all familiar. The Lenny Bruce–like obscenities sprinkled through David Newman's monologue make the same point, as does the topic of his monologue—death. As Clive Hirschhorn observes, "*All That Jazz* ... was the first musical whose subject was death" (414). Hirschhorn does not go on to note that the film did not start a trend of musicals about death. Musicals sing and dance about "Good Morning" and "Dancing in the Dark"; they don't feature comic riffs on the thanatological theories of Elisabeth Kubler-Ross. Then again, that seems to be Fosse's intertextual point. This is clear again when Victoria climbs the stairs to Joe Gideon's bedroom and we see her bare breasts. There were, after all, no bare breasts in *The Great Ziegfeld* or *Bye Bye Birdie*, but there are in *All That Jazz*—during this erotic scene and later during the full-scale production of "Take Off with Us." In fact, it is probably the presence of naked bodies, obscene language and a realistic recognition of the erotic nature of musical performances that distinguishes this film from its generic predecessors. Thus, the *double entendres* in the lyrics of "Take Off with Us"—"service you," "any seat you choose," "are you gonna come?"—are patently intentional; they are not like the hidden references in songs like "Tom, Dick and Harry." These references are right out front, like Joe Gideon's behind when he walks away from the camera in a hospital gown that is open at the back. Somehow we know that Bing Crosby would never do this.

In such large and small matters, Fosse is determined to invoke the traditional in this film intertextually, only to cancel it. When Jonesy Hecht (William LeMassina) tells the cast that the producers intend to stick by them even though Gideon has been hospitalized — "We think of you all as family" — one stagehand whispers to another, "Bullshit." This is a far cry indeed from the represented camaraderie of *Golddiggers of 1933!* The obvious insincerity displayed by Jonesy and Lucas Sergeant (John Lithgow) when discussing the possibility of Sergeant's replacing Gideon as director of the metadiegetic show provides a critique of show business, surely, but it also interrogates the level of representation usually dominant in Hollywood musicals. Jerry Travers and Alberto Beddini don't like each other much in *Top Hat*, as Jim Hardy and Ted Hanover don't in *Holiday Inn*, and yet the antagonism in both cases is shown to be just something that happens in musicals to retard the inevitable happy ending. Unlike the events that occur in real life, crises in Hollywood musicals are mere plot devices. Thus, we are surprised to see Jonesy and Sergeant first trying to manipulate each other as people do in real life and then realistically fighting over a very small check in a restaurant after their plans have been exploded. Any of this might conceivably happen in a dramatic film but not in a musical, and that is probably what Fosse is intertextually driving at. In a dramatic film, or perhaps in a contemporary comedy, a hospitalized character might say to a nurse, "I think I'm getting an erection," but Gene Kelly would never say it. Gene wouldn't sweep his bleeding forehead along a hospital wall either, or stain his dancing pants with an ejaculation induced by several over-age strippers. And yet, all these things happen in *All That Jazz*. There is a good diegetic reason for each of these occurrences, but it seems to me that the primary rationale is to distance this film from the hundreds of Hollywood musicals that preceded it, and — in this context, at least — that is what intertextuality is all about.

To most first-time viewers, of course, the film's most startling departure from the tradition is its representation of open-heart surgery. Although we see clips of *The Stand-Up*, of Leslie Perry's TV review of that film, and of O'Connor Flood's TV show as metadiegetic parts of *All That Jazz*, probably the most disturbing piece of embedded film is Joe Gideon's angiogram. Most of us are unaccustomed to seeing what people look like on the inside, and we are probably even more disturbed when we are offered such an inside view in a Hollywood musical. Our discomfort can only increase as we watch a scalpel cut through Gideon's chest and when — my most uncomfortable moment — a retractor spreads his ribs to allow surgical access to his heart. From a purely logical point of view, it should probably be more disturbing to see the hero of a Hollywood musical die, as Joe does later on in the film, than to watch heart surgery on the screen but — in terms of what we have become accustomed to from watching other Hollywood musicals — this is not the case.

As part of the production number that concludes the film, O'Connor Flood says about Joe Gideon that "he came to believe that work, show business, love, his whole life, even himself, and all that jazz, was bullshit." In this speech, we see the thematic message of Fosse's film stated, the source of its title identified, and the shocking term *bullshit* used, even before the climactic "Bye Bye Life" number is performed.[21] In this way, the speech both fits its diegetic context and epitomizes Fosse's intertextual approach in the film. The speech could not possibly be used in the musical films discussed in earlier chapters, not even to characterize George M. Cohan or Tommy Williams (*Babes on Broadway*) who were also depicted as driven to succeed in show business. To Fosse, apparently, the conventions of the genre which would make this usage previously impossible are merely "all that jazz" that must be transcended in any contemporary Hollywood musical that aspires to be truly original. By juxtaposing originality and convention in this way, Fosse creates still another form of intertextuality.

Still another form is apparent in *Singin' in the Rain* (1952), directed by Gene Kelly and Stanley Donen. In their *Lullabies of Hollywood* (1993), Richard Fehr and Frederick G. Vogel write that "[t]he praise showered on *Singin' in the Rain* over the past four decades is totally deserved" (228), a judgment shared by many — perhaps most — film critics. As we have already seen, the film slots into the American Film Institute's list of the top 100 films of all time as number ten. As we might expect, there are many reasons for this widespread approbation, including the highly intelligent script by Betty Comden and Adolph Green, the stellar performances of Gene Kelly, Debbie Reynolds, Jean Hagen and Donald O'Connor, and a brilliant exploitation of intertextuality. As Christopher Ames writes in his *Movies about the Movies*, the film's most famous production number, "Singin' in the Rain," "captures in miniature the self-referential theme of the movie: a song about singing in a musical about musicals in a Hollywood movie about Hollywood" (67). In this sense, *Singin' in the Rain* as an overall cinematic entity resembles *The Band Wagon* and other intertextual musical films we have been examining. This is James Collins' point when he notes that *Singin' in the Rain*, *The Band Wagon* and other intertextual films of that era "all contain strong self-reflexive elements that not only expose the mechanisms of production but seemingly investigate the nature of entertainment itself" (276). The very important difference is that, unlike *The Band Wagon*, for example, *Singin' in the Rain* also exploits filmmaking intertextually.

This is clear when we examine some of the film's metadiegetic intertexts. The first of these, a silent film entitled *The Royal Rascal*, is advertised by Monumental Pictures as "The Biggest Picture of 1927." A costume drama starring Don Lockwood (Gene Kelly) and Lina Lamont (Jean Hagen), *The Royal Rascal* appears on the screen early in *Singin' in the Rain* as evidence of what the movie business was like in 1927. Shots from *The Royal Rascal*—realistically shot in black-and-white—diegetically serve to familiarize viewers with Lockwood and Lamont as characters who make their living in the movie business even as the shots signal differences between the metadiegetic silent and the diegetic musical. Technicolor shots of the theater audience watching *The Royal Rascal* at its premiere performance also serve the intertextual purpose of reminding viewers that all commercial films—including *Singin' in the Rain*—depend on audience approval as a measure of their success. *The Dueling Cavalier*, another silent metadiegetic film starring Lockwood and Lamont so closely resembles *The Royal Rascal* that it serves to criticize the formulaic nature of studio film-making — presumably excluding musicals made by the Freed unit at MGM. Adjacent stages on which silent jungle pictures, college comedies and Westerns are being filmed make the same intertextual criticism. Don Lockwood is seen early in the film while he is still working as a stuntman before getting his big break. In all of these scenes, we see how different making silent formula films is from making big-budget Hollywood musicals. And yet, these scenes also send intertextual signals that the two processes are not totally unlike.

For one thing, big-budget musicals filmed in the late 1940s and early '50s always contain elaborate solos for their star male dancers. Fred Astaire performed "Limehouse Blues" with Lucille Bremer in *Ziegfeld Follies* (1946) and would dance "Girl Hunt, A Murder Mystery in Jazz" with Cyd Charisse in *The Band Wagon* (1953). Gene Kelly had already danced a famous Gershwin ballet with Leslie Caron in *An American in Paris* (1951). It only seems proper that he perform the allegorical "Broadway Ballet" with Cyd Charisse in *Singin' in the Rain* the next year. Unlike the silent movies introduced elsewhere in the film, "Broadway Ballet" is filmed in full color with an enormous cast. Like the silent films, however, "Broadway Ballet" performs a significant intertextual function. As the young dancer depicted in "Broadway Ballet" climbs the show business ladder, he successively performs the same song, "Broadway Rhythm," in the increasingly more elegant settings of burlesque, vaudeville and the Ziegfeld Follies. Echoes of Don Lockwood's professional career, depicted earlier in *Singin' in the Rain*, are surely intentional. The principal joke being made at that early point in the film involved the distance between the dreamy account provided by Lockwood to Hollywood gossip queen Dora Bailey (Madge Blake) and the gritty reality illustrated in flashbacks. As Christopher Ames points out, "*Singin' in the Rain* continues to frame the contrast between illusion and reality along the lines suggested in the opening scene: the conflict between celebrity publicity and genuine personality; the struggle between 'dignity' and folk art; the gap between sound and image; and the contrast between the duped audience and privileged audience" (60). While such contrasts are assuredly present, comparisons are also inevitable. Lockwood and his friend Cosmo Brown (Donald O'Connor) went through a lot of show business dues-paying as part of their diegetic rise to success. Surely Gene Kelly and Donald O'Connor experienced something very similar.

Part of the Lockwood-Brown initiation involved their performance of the Arthur Freed–Nacio Herb Brown tune "Fit as a Fiddle" in vaudeville. Their metadiegetic performance of the number is deliberately mannered and frantic — signaling, perhaps, their eagerness to succeed in show business at any cost but illustrating, certainly, how poorly such a number stacks up against their stunning performances in *Singin' in the Rain*. One need only compare "Fit as a Fiddle" (or "Broadway Rhythm") to O'Connor's "Make 'Em Laugh" or Kelly's "Singin' in the Rain" to grasp the intertextual point. *Singin' in the Rain* does not simply absorb metadiegetic intertexts; it also parodies them.[22] Another Freed-Brown tune, "All I Do Is Dream of You," performed by Kathy Selden (Debbie Reynolds) at a big Hollywood party thrown by studio-head R. F. Simpson (Millard Mitchell), points in the same direction. When Kathy Selden records "Would You" and "Singin' in the Rain" for the lip-synching Lina Lamont, she sounds like the star of a Hollywood musical. When she sings "All I Do Is Dream

Gene Kelly (right) views a more youthful version of the boy who's "Gotta Dance" in *Singin' in the Rain*.

of You" as part of the chorus from the Cocoanut Grove, she sounds as forced and desperate as Cosmo and Don during their days in vaudeville. By exaggerating the less attractive features of these performances, *Singin' in the Rain* intertextually invokes the superiority of the numbers contained in this film. This is true even when the earlier performances were themselves on film. As most cinema buffs know, *Singin' in the Rain* is about the coming of sound to Hollywood. As is historically appropriate, therefore, the film illustrates the hysterical rush to make "all singing, all dancing" pictures first through newspaper headlines and then through a series of parodic metadiegetic films. Once again, the songs are old numbers by Freed and Brown: "I've Got a Feeling You're Fooling"; "Wedding of the Painted Doll"; "Should I?"; and "Beautiful Girl."[23] The metadiegetic film clips that accompany each song are obviously intended to show how inferior these (allegedly) earlier production numbers are to the ones univocally associated with *Singin' in the Rain*. Flappers do the Charleston; needless overhead crane shots frame singers; dancers parade in toy soldier costumes; a Rudy Vallee look alike sings through a megaphone; an oily juvenile sings "Beautiful Girl" with trilled R's and a bevy of showgirls in dishy, high-fashion outfits. While production numbers similar to "Beautiful Girl" appear without ostensible parody in *The Great Ziegfeld* and *Easter Parade*, Comden and Green's parodic intent is revealed here through this number's absurd lyric with rhymes like "riot" and "Dye it!"— as well as through the smarmy delivery and the excessively acrobatic camera work.

The final form of intertextuality that I intend to discuss, demystification, connects *Singin' in the Rain* to a number of other films considered in this chapter, perhaps most especially to *The Band Wagon*, also written by Comden and Green. Showing how movies are made is the principal form of demystification. When Monumental Pictures first attempts to turn *The Dueling Cavalier* from a silent into a talking picture, we learn that Lina Lamont's voice must be carried from the sound stage to the recording booth through an electronic system featuring hidden microphones and cables. Lina's inability to master this technique diegetically foreshadows her decline as a film star. Aside from the cinematic plot, exposing the technique can only make viewers of *Singin' in the Rain* more conscious that they are themselves recipients of sounds delivered through a similar system. Thus, when the premiere of *The Dueling Cavalier* turns into a disaster, the causes just have to be failures of recording technique. Lina's pearls clink on the soundtrack. Don discards his staff, and it rings on the soundtrack like the crack of doom. Some sounds are indistinguishable because the actors were not originally facing the microphone when they spoke them. Lina's voice and accent are very annoying. The sound and the film get out of synch, causing lines to seem spoken by the wrong character. The movie doesn't look very good in any case, but with these sound problems it can only be viewed as a real stinker. Members of the preview audience are appropriately amused and disgusted. The film is obviously destined for the scrap heap. Any solution obviously must involve sound also.[24] Kathy dubs Lina's voice in a sound studio, so that when Lina moves her mouth on black-and-white film, Kathy's voice emerges, speaking dialogue or singing "Would You?"[25] Several scenes develop this process until we see a closeup of Lina singing the song in Kathy's perfectly matched voice in what turns out to be the studio screening room. Obviously, these shots will be part of the metadiegetic musical film now retitled *The Dancing Cavalier*— rather than *The Dueling Mammy*, as Cosmo first proposed. This is how sound is successfully matched to film, we learn, as it is (from an intertextual perspective) in the film directed by Gene Kelly and Stanley Donen. In order to remind us that films using similar sound techniques may not be all that similar after all, however, the final sequence of *The Dancing Cavalier* looks forced and artificial, even with the sound perfectly matched. Don and Lina seem to be trying too hard, more like Nelson Eddy and Jeanette MacDonald than like the Don and Kathy who will comfortably sing together and kiss at the end of *Singin' in the Rain*.

Of course, the most famous sequence of demystification in the film occurs when Don takes Kathy onto a sound stage to express his love for her through song and dance. First Don explains, as so many other characters have done in similar situations, that he is no good at putting his feelings into words. Then he turns on the cinematic special effects that might be expected in a romantic love scene in a movie: "a beautiful sunset, mist from the distant mountains, colored light in a garden." "A lady is standing on her balcony in a rose-colored spot, flooded with moonlight," he explains, as he leads Kathy up a stepladder. Then "We add 500,000 kilowatts of stardust, a soft summer breeze" and we begin to sing "You Were Meant For Me." The demystification is extreme — even down to Don's use of technical terms like *kilowatts* and *rose-colored spot*— but the remystification is extreme also — so that viewers end up seeing that Don is in love with Kathy instead of realizing that Gene Kelly has just performed a very clever musical number. But, in a sense, we do realize this, just as we realize at the end of the film that *Singin' in the Rain* has starred Gene Kelly and Debbie Reynolds rather than Don Lockwood and Kathy Selden. This realization, in the face of a billboard that says the opposite, is how this form of intertextuality operates.

Although *Pennies from Heaven* (1981), directed by Herbert Ross, is not diegetically premised on putting on a show or making movies, it is just as intertextual as the other films previously considered in this chapter. First and foremost, as I have said about *All That Jazz*, *Pennies from Heaven* "engages in ... the form [of intertextuality] in which a present instance invokes its predecessors through contrast rather than through imitation." In particular, the 1980s sensibility of Ross' film encounters the sensibility familiar from Depression musical comedies like those considered in my second chapter. *Pennies from Heaven* is indisputably a Depression musical. From its opening title card that identifies the chronotope as "Chicago.1934," through its conscientiously accurate costumes and settings, to its concluding medley of "The Glory of Love," "Love Is Good for Anything That Ails You" and "Pennies From Heaven," the film ostentatiously invokes the American Depression musically memorialized in *Golddiggers of 1933* and *Stand Up and Cheer*. As Clive Hirshhorn notes, however, this 1981 version of the Depression is "a salutary evocation of a grim period of American history" (418). Thus, no one in the film really thinks that "we're out of the red" or that "Old Man Depression" is all washed up. On the contrary, a banker (Jay Garner) tells the film's hero, Arthur Parker (Steve Martin), "The times are bad. The Depression is still with us." This gives the audience little to "stand up and cheer" about. The character known as the Accordion Man (Vernel Bagneris) hasn't eaten for days when Arthur buys him supper in Jimmy's Diner. Later on, Eileen Everson

(Bernadette Peters) finds herself in the same desperate situation just before she sells her body to Tom (Christopher Walken). The Golddiggers may have been forced to steal milk from a neighbor, but they were willing to abandon breakfast when the chance of an audition arose. The difference is the difference between the real Depression and the one usually depicted in Hollywood musicals. By the same token, even though Trixie Lorraine worries about what some of the girls might be forced to do if *Broadway Melody* doesn't open on time, none of the girls actually ends up in prostitution. Eileen does turn to hustling, however, just to feed herself—and eventually to feed Arthur. Despite the songs and dances, then, this film is not situated in the Depression familiar to audiences from earlier musicals. That's the intertextual point.

As Eileen's sexual trajectory shows, love solves nothing for the main characters. Hirschhorn also says that the film "[t]ook an extraordinarily bleak look at [the] dreary, workaday life and unsatisfactory marriage" (418) of its protagonist. In support of Hirschhorn's judgment, Arthur's wife Joan (Jessica Harper) is consistently shown as a humorless, joyless woman terrified of sex—as no one was in *Golddiggers* or in other musical films of the era. Arthur's true love interest, Eileen, does not fit the usual pattern for heroines either. She becomes impregnated by Arthur, who abandons her, she has an abortion, turns to prostitution, and eventually understands that Arthur cannot be depended on to do the right thing. In all of these ways, *Pennies from Heaven* departs from the generic norm[26] of the Depression musical comedy, and yet it intertextually echoes these norms even so.

For one thing, *Pennies from Heaven* is chock full of tunes. When Eileen reveals her erotic nature to Arthur, she sings "I Want to Be Bad." Actually, Helen Kane sings the song, and Bernadette Peters, in the role of Eileen, lip-synchs it. Peters also plays the scene very broadly, invoking Betty Boop and Shirley Temple in her dancing. The number thus simultaneously parodies the genre and adds a tune to the movie. When Arthur stands on a scaffold about to be executed for a murder he didn't commit, he first recites the verse and then sings the tune "Pennies from Heaven." Under the circumstances, the song lyric is totally inappropriate, and yet his rendition satisfies the generic requirement that musicals are built on songs. Christopher Ames recognizes the double nature of such performances when he writes that "[s]ongs such as these represent and satirize the escapist films of the depression that expressed desires for wealth and romance" (100). Even without critical commentary of this sort, the film establishes the duality of musical numbers through dialogue. Early in the film, Joan says about the songs that Arthur loves, "That's not real life." Later, Arthur tells Eileen in a diner obviously modeled on the one in Edward Hopper's painting *Nighthawks* (1942), "I don't want to live in a world where the songs don't come true. There must be someplace where the songs are for real." Brad Roberts could have said this in *Golddiggers*, or Jimmy Dugan in *Stand Up and Cheer*. If either had done so, he would not be talking to a character who has recently had an abortion, and she would not have responded, as Eileen sarcastically does, "Happy days are here again." Songs are thus presented and critiqued at the same time.

The most powerful device in this critique is the film's use of lip-synching. In *Singin' in the Rain* everyone got to see how actors on screen could be made to look as if they were singing words actually sung by someone else. In *Pennies from Heaven* this disparity is intertextually emphasized. Even before Joan tells Arthur that songs are not real life, Arthur sings "I'll Never Have to Dream Again" in the voice of Connie Boswell. Sometimes he doesn't even move his lips as the song comes pouring out. When Joan sings "It's a Sin to Tell a Lie" in the voice of Dolly Dawn, she does move her lips, but she also approaches Arthur from behind with a pair of scissors in order to stab him. Since Joan is back in bed in her nightgown when the number ends, it is apparent that this number has not advanced the action of the narrative in the manner of *Oklahoma!* or *The King and I*—even though the musical numbers in those films were surely prerecorded also. When Joan, Arthur and Eileen sing "Life Is Just a Bowl of Cherries" later on in the film, it is diegetically improbable that these three characters would ever sing together. This improbability is underlined when the trio sings in the voices of five male singers, with Joan handling the bass parts.[27] An ironic commentary on the three fictional characters' various problems emerges even so. Most significant, though, is the scene in which Arthur and Eileen go to the movies to see Fred and Ginger in *Follow the Fleet* (1936). As Fred sings "Let's Face the Music and Dance" in black-and-white on the screen, Arthur, in the full-color movie theater, is drawn farther and farther into the performance until he begins to move his lips in unison and then to sing the song in Fred's voice. Arthur is not Fred Astaire, of course — or Bake Baker, Astaire's character in that film — but the sentiment of Fred's song applies, at least ironically, to Arthur's situation.[28] In this way, recorded music is matched appropriately to the diegetic characters' situations at some times and mismatched at others. The result can only be a heightened consciousness of what is really going on up on the screen.

Other common properties of Hollywood musical comedies are also intertextually italicized in *Pennies from Heaven*. When Arthur is turned down for a bank loan, he says to the banker, "It was salesmanship that made this country great, and it'll be salesmanship that'll keep us great." In the musicals of the '30s this inspirational speech would probably lead to a loan. In this film, the banker realizes that Arthur's 30 percent commission on each ten-cent sale of sheet music is a poor basis for a $1,000 loan, and so he turns Arthur down. Arthur's dialogue parodies another cliché of Depression musicals when Eileen tells him that she doesn't love him when he acts scared. Arthur asks, "You'll stick by me if I just keep smiling, even with a rope around my neck?" The smiles are familiar from a whole line of musical comedies, including the first *Pennies from Heaven* (1936), starring Bing Crosby. Eileen's doubts and the prospective noose are inventions of the film's author, Dennis Potter.

Potter also parodies larger elements of the genre, as he does in his original *Pennies* series for British television (1978) and in his later TV miniseries *The Singing Detective* (1986). After Arthur is turned down for his bank loan, for example, he and the banker kiss and launch into a giant production number based on "Yes, Yes," sung by Sam Brown. Scads of chorus girls and supplementary dancers turn the number into a huge Berkeleyesque spectacle including enormous dimes reminiscent of the ones used in *Golddiggers of 1933*. When Arthur first sees Eileen in a music store where he has come to sell sheet music, he is struck by love at first sight. The soundtrack plays Bing Crosby's version of "Did You Ever See a Dream Walking?" The focus goes soft. Arthur and Eileen dance romantically together. Then Eileen tap dances like

Ruby Keeler, derby hat and all. Or at least that is what anyone would say who has ever seen Keeler dance on film, and Potter is clearly one such person. Potter has apparently also seen many films in which romantic scenes are shot in a heart-shaped frame. Thus, he and Herbert Ross frame Arthur's seduction/rape of Eileen on her living room sofa in such a shot. In this way, the film comments on Arthur's ethics and also invokes the cinematic tradition that makes these ethics seem so pathetic and inadequate.

The film's ending makes a similar point. The arc of the film's narrative clearly requires that Arthur die unjustly for a murder he didn't commit. Appropriately enough, he ends up standing on a scaffold singing the title song just before his death. However, as Arthur points out to Eileen, "We couldn't have gone through all of that without a happy ending. Songs ain't like that. Are they?" So, he doesn't die but instead reunites with Eileen for a happy ending. Since this ending is diegetically inappropriate, discord results, the sort of discord that forces one to reexamine other happy endings in other Hollywood musicals. As Christopher Ames argues, "The film that has preceded the hyperbolic ending makes the authenticity of such an ending impossible.... *Pennies from Heaven* uses subversive juxtaposition to make the comic resolution demanded by the genre ineffectual" (106). In this way, another intertextual point is raised through parody.

The discrepancies that emerge through parody are also apparent in the conflict of historical eras juxtaposed in the film. As in *All That Jazz* (1979), characters speak in a form of language familiar to filmgoers of the time but tabooed in Hollywood musicals about the Depression. In the first sequence of the film, for example, Arthur says, "Goddamned coffee," and Joan says, "There's no need to swear." Shortly afterwards he says, "I'm a good salesman. I can pick the right songs. Jesus Christ Almighty!," and Joan says, "Don't blaspheme, Arthur." Arthur is also criticized for his earthy language by the banker who is refusing him a loan. When he is lying to Joan about his affair with Eileen, Arthur says, "May Almighty God strike me dead on the spot [if I have been unfaithful]." Joseph Breen would have been flabbergasted! Eileen tells Tom that her assumed name, Lulu, makes her "sound cheap," and Tom replies, "Look at that big fat whore over there. That's what I call cheap." None of these speeches could have been uttered in the films considered earlier in this book, and yet they all seem diegetically appropriate in *Pennies from Heaven* because of an intentional intertextuality that is based on the collision of historical eras. This collision also involves lesser characters in the film. Just after Arthur has fallen in love with Eileen at first sight, for example, the music store owner says to Arthur, "You know what she needs, don't you?" Arthur is appropriately stunned, perhaps because he has just been singing "Did You Ever See a Dream Walking" in the voice of Bing Crosby. The viewer is probably stunned too because the remark so clearly violates the conventions of the Depression musical. This is Potter's point also when two of Arthur's sales colleagues respond to his confession of love for Eileen by asking, "Did you get your hand up her skirt, Arthur?"; "Did you lay her in the back seat?"; "She got big tits?" How would Dick Powell respond? As several of these illustrations suggest, one of the largest discrepancies exploited through this form of intertextuality is that between the two eras' generally received cultural attitudes toward sex. That is why the film opens with Arthur trying to convince Joan to have sex with him before he goes out on the road. That is why Arthur responds to the Accordion Man's grateful kissing of his hand by asking, "What are you, a goddamn pansy?"

Christopher Ames calls *Pennies from Heaven* "a nostalgic parody that subverts nostalgia" (107), and his formulation points to the dual focus maintained by all the intertextual musical films considered in this chapter. To subvert nostalgia, it is necessary for someone — the creator, the consumer, or both — to recognize a nostalgic potential. The same may be said of parody and of adaptation. Intertextual musicals arise only when a sufficient body of generic material exists to allow for this dual focus on the past and the present. This is Rick Altman's point when he writes in *The American Film Musical*, "[W]hen a filmic structure becomes so obvious, or a filmgoing community so sensitive that the film's ritual patterns can no longer pass unnoticed[,] ... instead of acquiescing to the genre's mythology simply by following and accepting the film's plot, spectators find themselves rejecting the very assumptions that underlie the film" (251). As we have seen, however, this rejection can often be compatible with another form of acceptance. Ethel Merman sings, "There's No Business Like Show Business," even as Joe Gideon's dead body is being zipped into a body bag, and in one sense we recognize the lyric to be ironically appropriate. On the other hand, death is seldom so entertaining and tuneful. That is to say that the intertextual musical allows us to have our cake and eat it, whether the cake is an arch recognition, like Joan Parker's, that musicals are "not real life," or a happy acceptance that a Broadway box office bombshell can be viewed in a local theater or at home on video or DVD. So long as someone is aware that two entertainment forms are coexisting and interacting on the screen, we can have intertextual musicals.

9

Conclusion: "How About a Nice Musical?"

As many critics have observed, the Hollywood musical always seems able to find new things to be "about" or new ways to be "about" the same old subjects. John Russell Taylor writes in *The Hollywood Musical*, "Though the musical form has been written off again and again as played out, outdated, finished, somehow it always manages to spring back as full of life as ever" (13). Along the same lines, Clive Hirschhorn observes in *his* book *The Hollywood Musical*, "In the 50 years or so since its birth, the musical has proved itself to be the phoenix of the film industry. Unlike perennials such as Westerns and war and crime films, it is the musical alone that periodically disappears, only to rise again from the ashes to prove that reports of its demise were greatly exaggerated" (11). And, as a final example of a position that could be illustrated at even greater length, we may consider Peter Gammond's statement in *The Oxford Companion to Popular Music*: "Every time the musical has seemed likely to be superseded by some new fashion it has made a strong come-back and there seems to be no reason why it should not go on doing so for ever" (406).

Finding new subjects such as gang violence is one way in which this constant renewal has been achieved—although many have recognized echoes of *Romeo and Juliet* in *West Side Story*. Another likely source of renewal is the structural avenue of demystification,[1] in which the representational claims of earlier musicals such as *Golddiggers of 1933* and *Babes in Arms* are discarded in favor of a direct avowal of the Hollywood musical's presentational nature. Surely representational musicals of the earlier sort would never, for example, have their protagonist die on the operating table as Joe Gideon does in *All That Jazz*, nor would they openly admit that musicals are ultimately about singing and dancing rather than about "life," however that might be defined. But, through these and other structural and stylistic variations, makers of Hollywood musicals have been able to make new films even as they acknowledge the difficulty or impossibility of doing so. In consequence, the Hollywood musical has repeatedly been able to make "a strong come-back," to "spring back as full of life as ever" as the "phoenix of the film industry."

One problem facing the filmmaker of today who would like to make a Hollywood musical is a widespread rejection of musical numbers, based on a literalist

O'Connor Flood (Ben Vereen) and Joe Gideon (Roy Scheider) perform "Bye Bye Life" in *All That Jazz*.

resistance to the "world is a stage" premise of many traditional musicals. In his review of *Chicago* (2002), Anthony Lane identifies this problem: "Lovers of the classic form were prepared to believe that it was natural — more of a thirsty emotional need than a luxury — for a character to break into song, whereas nowadays that perversity has to be explained" (91). Steve Daly makes a similar point in his analysis of the same film. Responding to the apparent puzzle that the coming attractions for *Chicago* frequently concealed the fact that the film was a musical, Daly writes, "The studio's afraid that despite the modest success of 2001's pop-song pastiche *Moulin Rouge* (which grossed more than $115 million overseas but only $58 million domestically), a lot of moviegoers — especially younger males — may still wince at the sound of more traditional show tunes" (22). Obviously, one challenge facing contemporary filmmakers committed to the musicals format is finding a way to free potential viewers temporarily from their suspicion of the genre itself.

Some guidance in these matters can be gathered from musicals produced for television — but not, as one might expect, from music videos. As Jane Feuer explains, "Despite the emphasis on performance ... music videos cannot be considered musicals if we define the musical by its dual levels of narrative and number. In the music video, everything is subordinated to the song, even the running time" (132). And so, the most helpful illustrations from television come not from even the most successful

9. Conclusion: "How About a Nice Musical?"

music videos but from two episodes of the musical series *Cop Rock* (1990), the "All Singing, All Dancing" (1998) episode of *The Simpsons* and the "Once More With Feeling" episode (2001) of *Buffy the Vampire Slayer*. *Cop Rock* was a short-lived television experiment combining an ongoing ensemble police drama set in Los Angeles with musical performances. As immediate ratings failures and subsequent negative critiques from televiewers attest, the combination was ineffective. In *The Simpsons* episode, Homer and Bart become disgusted while watching Lee Marvin and Clint Eastwood sing in the Hollywood musical *Paint Your Wagon* (1969), but the episode goes on to show how important singing and dancing has been to life in Springfield and in the *Simpsons* series. In "Once More With Feeling," the spookiness usually present in an episode of *Buffy* involves an evil spell that makes the characters on the show sing and dance spontaneously. In all three cases, it is evident that the conventions of "the classic form" identified by Anthony Lane have ceased to operate successfully. In particular, the potential recipients of the "classic" signals are unwilling or unable to play their parts in the generic transaction.

Cop Rock, created by Stephen Bochco and William M. Finkelstein, followed on the heels of Bochco's phenomenally successful televisions series *Hill Street Blues* (1981–87). The two shows had much in common. Both were anthology police series with a large ensemble cast. Both treated the disturbing social issues of the day: narcotics, prostitution, police brutality, government corruption and social/sexual dysfunctions. The two series differed significantly in that *Cop Rock* interspersed musical numbers within the diegetic treatment of the police drama material common to both series and — perhaps for that reason — in that *Hill Street Blues* was an enormous success, whereas *Cop Rock* is still considered by many to be one of the worst TV shows of all time.[2] While *Hill Street* had a six-season run, *Cop Rock* extended to only 11 episodes on ABC from September through December of 1990.[3] The show's shortcomings are obviously related to the producers' attempts to accommodate the demands of network television to the format of the Hollywood musical. The first episode under consideration, "Happy Mudder's Day," involves rogue detective Vincent Larusso's unorthodox police brutality and sexual aggressiveness, Mayor Plank's desire to become a United States Senator despite her physical unattractiveness, and representative police interactions with the public. The second episode, "A Three-Corpse Meal," involves Patty Spence's sale of her newborn to a baby-selling ring, LaRusso's indictment and imprisonment and romantic/emotional complications involving Detective Ruskin, his wife Officer Quinn and Quinn's wannabe suitor Officer Campo. While any of these plot elements might seem incompatible with a musical approach, none are finally considered by the series' creators to be any more incompatible with singing and dancing than, for example, life in the antebellum South or in Sun Valley, Idaho.

Some musical performances in *Cop Rock* serve to develop character — as other performances do in earlier Hollywood musicals, as when Esther Smith sings "The Boy Next Door" in *Meet Me in St. Louis* or when Tony Hunter sings "By Myself" in *The Band Wagon*. This is the case when Chief of Police Roger Kendrick (Ronny Cox) sings the old Gene Autry hit "Back in the Saddle Again" in his office while strumming a guitar in the "Happy Mudder's Day" episode. The performance is clearly intended to reinforce his character intertextually, and so in the following scene, the Chief is filmed on horseback, wearing a star and toting a carbine, singing that he wants to hear the dogies sing again as he and his horse pass through a definitely urban landscape marked by semi trailers, skyscrapers and inner-city street life. To this degree, the two musical performances—perhaps the first even more than the second—function diegetically as elements of character development. In the same way, in order to develop his character as a violent, out-of-control cop, Detective Vincent LaRusso (Peter Oronati) sings the threatening song "You Can't Keep a Good Man Down" after he is thrown in jail in "A Three-Corpse Meal" for murdering a suspect. And Mayor Louise Plank (Barbara Bosson) sings "A Face That Someone Could Love" in the same episode after plastic surgery has rendered her physically attractive to Chief Kendrick. In each case, the song is consistent with the character's diegetic function, but in each case the song merely serves to confirm what the plot has already made clear.

When an exotic dancer/mud wrestler named Nicki (Karla Tamburelli) sings "I Hate Love" in "Happy Mudder's Day," the song deepens her character rather than merely repeating what we have already gathered by watching her rolling around in the ring and interacting with Detective LaRusso. By the same token, when Detective Ralph Ruskin (Ron McLarty) sings "Their Idea of Living" in the same episode while working out in an effort to lose 35 pounds, we recognize that the repugnance for exercise expressed in the song is consistent with his narrative character, but we also get a clearer sense of exactly why he feels this way than we could have gotten through mere dialogue. McLarty's performance is also engaging musically. The song has the Randy Newman flavor that we might expect from the fact that Newman wrote and performed the series' theme song, and the number also expands to include the other cops in the gym as a chorus. In other words, this is not just a song reconfirming what has already been established by the diegetic action; it is a production number. Another striking production number is "Garbage In, Garbage Out" in "Happy Mudder's Day," during which the cops in the booking room and the alleged perpetrators whom they are booking sing as an ensemble. The song helps to establish the narrative atmosphere, as "The Farmer and the Cowman" does in *Oklahoma!*, but it also helps to establish the peculiar relationship between the forces of law and of disorder that characterizes police drama—on television, on screen, or on the page. From the same episode, the blues song "Nobody's Fault," sung by a man and woman who have just been involved in a domestic crisis, provides an insight into the situation unavailable merely from the action and dialogue. At times, that is to say, *Cop Rock* operates as a Hollywood musical even if it appeared on television.

Another category of musical presentation in the series is the number that succeeds just by itself. "Their Idea of Living" may be one of these. At least, it is conceivable that someone might end up whistling the song after viewing the episode. There is even less doubt about "Baby Merchant," sung by the criminal slime ball who engages in that reprehensible criminal activity in "A Three-Corpse Meal." Like "King Herod's Song" in *Jesus Christ Superstar* (1973), the song gets across in spite of our negative attitude toward the character associated with the song. Although viewers' attitudes toward plastic surgeons may vary more than their attitudes toward baby merchants, "Perfection," by Dr. Wattoon (Don Amendolia) with a back-up chorus of nurses in brightly colored uniforms, is also likely to please everyone. Despite its critique of conventional attitudes toward female beauty, this number from "Happy Mudder's Day" is a true Hollywood musical performance. Dr. Wattoon's character is probably more emotionally and ideologically complex than any character in *On the Town* or *Bye Bye Birdie*, but this number could slip right into either film — and into many more just like them.

Why, then, was *Cop Rock* not a hit? Why didn't this television version of the Hollywood musical find a large, appreciative viewing audience? At the time of the show's first appearance, the TV reviewer for *Variety* offered this judgment, tailored to the show's title: "The *Rock* side ... may be downright jolting for those who have trouble with the theatrical convention of characters bursting into song. After all, the current generation of tv viewers weren't exactly raised on Lerner & Loewe or Rodgers & Hammerstein" (Sept. 26, 1990). John Leonard was more encouraging in his *New York* review, even while conceding the same problem with the show's potential audience: "Some emotions almost demand to be sung, and music itself can be more than merely a kind of dramatic punctuation; it might be a whole new grammar. Why shouldn't this hoary convention of the theater, like so many others, translate to the small screen, given enough time for the viewers to get used to it?" (Sept. 10, 1990). The difficulty — at least according to these television reviewers— is that by 1990 musicals could no longer assume as part of their organic structure that the world is sometimes a stage. The problem can be viewed vividly by consulting the "user comments" on the show submitted by e-mail to the Internet Movie Database. While haljor of San Francisco confesses that "*Cop Rock* is one of my favorite shows of all time" and Phil Brady of Philadelphia says, "I remember *Cop Rock* fondly," most of the responses are far more critical, and their criticism goes right to the heart of the musical experiment. Catrandom of Los Angeles identifies the sticking point for most of those who submitted comments by writing that "someone had the ridiculous idea to have the characters continually burst into song." For this reason, Ta'Lon of Reading, England, writes that the "show was actually embarrassing to watch, even when alone," and Nick Zbu adds that the show "was a waste of time." Most critical of all is the appropriately named bubba–46, who says that the show "was so bad that it was funny ... the *Ishtar* of cop series." The problem for these viewers is that singing and dancing are not everyday activities for most people, and so performances of this sort are unacceptable even in a television musical.

This difficulty is used as an activating premise for the *Simpsons* 1998 clip show "All Singing, All Dancing." When Homer and Bart rent a video for the family, they announce that the female-oriented *Waiting to Exhale* preferred by Marge has been checked out. Instead they have rented a film starring Clint Eastwood and Lee Marvin, which they expect to be filled with violent action. As Bart says, "So prepare yourself for the bloody mayhem and unholy carnage of Joshua Logan's *Paint Your Wagon*." When this 1969 Hollywood musical plays on the Simpsons' VCR, Bart and Homer are disgusted to see their action heroes singing a song about actually painting a wagon. The number even expands to include animated cowboys, dance hall girls and female churchgoers in addition to the excellent vocal impressions of Eastwood and Marvin. Homer in particular is mightily offended. Singing is "fruity," he exclaims, and he claims further that singing is "the lowest form of communication." Soon, though, Homer is himself singing his objection that musicals are fake and phony, paving the way for Marge to develop the more moderate, pro-musical position and also for the singing that will serve as a frame to bridge the gaps between musical clips from earlier shows.

The first of these clips shows Homer singing "Baby on Board" as part of a barbershop quartet on the roof of Moe's tavern.[4] Next, Homer, Bart and the ladies from Belle's house of ill fame sing "We Put the Spring in Springfield," a song with more diegetic relevance to its original show than "Baby on Board"—notably because Homer has taken the lead in saving Belle's house from destruction.[5] The framing narrative then goes on to include Marge's reminder that Bart has "sung and danced like a girl." As the frame narrative has established, Marge is more favorably disposed toward musicals than the males in her house, but, as this speech makes clear, Marge is also inclined to accept musical performances as gendered and slightly embarrassing. In any case, the speech provides a bridge into a performance of "Springfield, Springfield" by Bart and Milhouse. This number is particularly interesting because it is a clear echo of the song "New York, New York" from *On the Town*. In case anyone misses the reference, though, we see an animated sailor searching for New York. (There is also a touring version of *Cats* starring actual felines.)

To develop the frame narrative, a heavily armed, desperate criminal arrives to take the Simpsons hostage. When he says, "[A] singing family, it's worse than I feared; for hostage purposes, you're just too weird," the story is allowed to progress, but the supposition that musicals are "just too weird" for general consumption is also licensed. Despite this generally received assumption, three musical clips featuring other cast members follow. Apu sings "Who Needs the Kwik-E-Mart?" Krusty the Clown sings "Send in the Clowns" with different lyrics than in Stephen Sondheim's original. And Mr. Burns sings "See My Vest," complete with appropriate dancing. The apparent universality of this musical impulse in Springfield surprises the criminal, who complains that now even *he* has a tune ringing in his head. Lack of ammunition makes it impossible for him to execute the Simpsons in revenge for messing with his mind musically, and so Lisa is able to sing that they might be able to "get a local law passed" that would make everybody sing "like a big Broadway cast," ushering in some new and larger production numbers.

First of all, confidence man Lyle Lanley sings "The Monorail Song" with a cast as large as the whole town, including the entire Simpson family. Prof. Harold Hill's performance in *The Music Man* (1962; Broadway 1957) is the obvious intertext, as is evident in Lanley's carnival-like costume and in the crowd's mindless acceptance of his deceitful proposal. Then, at the First Church of Springfield,[6] Bart substitutes Iron Butterfly's "In-A-Gadda-Da-Vida" (1968) for the usual hymns, and the congregation—once again, equivalent to the whole town, including the Simpsons—does a 17-minute version of the old rock tune. Finally, the Stonecutters' lodge, of which Homer is a member, performs "We Do (The Stonecutters' Song)" in an ironic endorsement of all that is wrong with America. After all of this taped evidence, Homer admits to Marge that there are "more terrible things" than musicals.

In a sense, musicals come out on top in this episode, but the victory is marginal at best. Admittedly, the parodies contained in the show demonstrate that its creators are familiar enough with various forms of musical performance to echo them and confident enough that their viewers will catch the references. At the same time—and even allowing for the fun that most episodes have with Homer's Neanderthal ideas—singing and dancing receive only very marginal, highly qualified recognition as narrative agents. They may not be the most "terrible things" that a person can think of in 1998, but they are terrible enough to invite mockery.

The *Buffy the Vampire Slayer* episode "Once More with Feeling" also mocks the general concept of musicals even as it develops a creditable version of one. Like the creators of *The Simpsons*, Joss Whedon, author of this script and creator of the series, assumes that his viewers will catch enough of the parodic references in his script to justify the undertaking. His title, for example, echoes the title of the 1960 Stanley Donen film starring Yul Brynner and Kay Kendall and the 1958 Broadway play on which it was based, with all the aura of musical show business common to both. When Anya (Emma Caulfield) and Xander (Nicholas Brendon) sing a duet about their approaching wedding, furthermore, Anya shows her familiarity with the music industry by complaining that their "number is a retro pastiche that's never going to be a breakaway pop hit."[7] Giles (Anthony Stewart Head) also reveals his awareness of how musicals operate when he tells Anya and Tara (Amber Benson) later on that Buffy needs "backup." The two characters stand by to assist Buffy (Sarah Michelle Gellar) in her diegetic battle with Sweet (Hinton Battle), but they also sing and dance behind her as she performs the song "Life." In another play on convention, one of Sweet's minions confesses his master's evil intentions in spoken dialogue even though the soundtrack has swelled with an orchestral introduction that would lead any experienced viewer to anticipate a song. In all of these ways, the episode calls upon the viewer's familiarity with the musicals format while italicizing this familiarity ironically.

Of course, the principal irony in the episode lies in the fact that the same kind of singing and dancing that liberates characters in *Singin' in the Rain* and *Babes in Arms* operates here as the source of pain, suffering and possibly damnation. Early in the episode, the cast members discuss their unexpected tendency to burst into song. In Buffy's words, "[T]here's definitely something unnatural going on here. And that doesn't usually lead to hugs and puppies." As is consistent with the show's narrative premises, the characters assume that something preternatural must be at work. Giles says, "That would explain the huge backing orchestra I couldn't see and the synchronized dancing from the room service chaps." Anya adds that she and Xander were "arguing and, and then everything rhymed and there were harmonies and the dance with cocoanuts." None of this seems too awful to Dawn (Michelle Trachtenberg), who asks, "Songs, dancing around. What's gonna be wrong with that?" Soon, we get a suitably spooky answer. A man who is tap-dancing uncontrollably bursts into flames. Sweet opens a closet door and a smoking corpse falls through it. As Xander concludes, "[W]e're sure that the things are related: the singing and dancing, and burning and dying." Or, as Sweet explains, "That's the penalty when life is but a song." The hundreds of songs in Hollywood musicals praising songs and dances as sources of joy are thus intertextually called into question.

Despite this critical perspective, "Once More with Feeling" also uses musical numbers in the familiar way. Buffy's lack of enthusiasm for anything at all is the chief component of her character in this episode, and this character is developed through her first musical number, "Alive." Tara's character is developed through "I'm Under Your Spell," the song she sings to Willow (Alyson Hannigan). We get to know more about the inner lives of Anya and Xander, especially their doubts about their upcoming wedding, through their duet "I'll Never Tell." Spike's (James Marsters') romantic feelings for Buffy are expressed in his solo, "Rest in Peace." Sweet's demonic character is also developed musically, through his solo, "That's What It's All About." In *Oklahoma!* we get to know Ado Annie when she sings "Can't Say No." In *Girl Crazy*, the "Can You Use Me" duet effectively establishes the characters of Danny Churchill and Ginger Gray. That is to say, Hollywood musicals have traditionally used songs to establish character, and in this sense "Once More with Feeling" mimics a Hollywood musical.

The tradition also sees songs as agents of plot development. And so, later in "Once More with Feeling," it emerges through the song "Life" that Buffy is dispirited over having had to leave Heaven in the previous episode. Her anomie is thus explained diegetically through song. At the end of the episode, the complicated situations in which the cast members find themselves after the events that have unfolded in this episode are revealed in the ensemble number "Where Do We Go from Here?"

Most impressive in terms of plot development, however, is the ensemble number "I've Got a Theory" early in the show. This number occurs after the individual characters have confessed to their unexpected musical experiences. Taking choruses, Giles attributes the musical developments to a demon, Willow to a child's dream, Xander to witches and Anya to "bunnies." Then the actors sing together that they can easily figure out and solve the problem if they "face it together." The song sets all of the characters in motion and even predicts the ultimate resolution because Buffy does need the help of the others to stand up to Sweet in the end.

Finally, this episode of *Buffy* can be seen in traditional terms because the show contains some full-throttle production numbers. Using the film techniques of slow motion and jump cutting familiar to viewers of music videos, Giles' number "Standing in the Way" provides action shots of Buffy, internal meditation by the mentor figure and some emotional complications that can be exploited in subsequent episodes. The number is thus functional in several ways. However, "Walk Through the Fire" is the show's equivalent of "Pettin' in the Park" or "That's Entertainment." Everybody is involved in the number. First Buffy strides through a steamy music-video set, then Spike joins in by singing his commitment to aid Buffy, then Sweet sings of his evil designs on Dawn — all to the same tune. Anya, Giles, Tara, Willow and Xander then sing their decision to help Buffy out. Cutting from Buffy, to Sweet, to Buffy's allies, the number creates musical texture, which is only intensified when Spike joins in. The sequence ends just before a commercial break when Buffy kicks down Sweet's door, and the demon intertextually cackles, "Showtime!" Of course, Buffy frustrates Sweet's designs on her sister, regains her lust for life and advances her romance with Spike. That's what we would expect from series television. What we would not expect is that so much of the characterization and action of the series would be accomplished through singing and dancing — and this despite the fact that singing and dancing are, in Buffy's own words, "definitely something unnatural."

The episode's self-conscious separation of "natural" diegesis and "unnatural" musical production numbers would seem to fulfill Bertolt Brecht's program for denaturalizing art. In Brecht's view, the apparent ease with which Fred and Ginger, for example, slide into song and dance when they get caught in the rain in *Top Hat* only strengthens the misleading propaganda by which mimesis of the prevailing system naturalizes conditions that should be perceived by the suitably enlightened as purely unnatural constructions. The solution, in his view, would be to emphasize the artificiality of art, to italicize conventions instead of passively accepting them. As Brecht writes in "The Modern Theatre is the Epic Theatre" (1930):

> [S]o long as the arts are supposed to be "fused" together, the various elements will all be equally degraded, and each will act as mere "feed" to the rest. The process of fusion extends to the spectator, who gets thrown into the melting pot too and becomes a passive [suffering] part of the total work of art. Witchcraft of this sort must of course be fought against. Whatever is intended to produce hypnosis, is likely to induce sordid intoxication, or creates fog, has got to be given up [37–38].

It seems as if — consciously or not — recent television shows have decided to engage in this sort of demystification, at least if "Once More With Feeling" may be taken as representative. It is no surprise, therefore, that successful Hollywood musicals released even after this episode of *Buffy* seem to be following a similar aesthetic strategy.

In *Moulin Rouge* (2001), for example, Baz Luhrmann distances the audience from his film in a number of ways. The very first shot shows a musical conductor in front of a grand theatrical curtain. Soon the curtain parts to reveal sepia credits[8] done in an old-fashioned typeface. From the beginning, then, we are informed that *Moulin Rouge* is a presentation — a movie — not an imitation of life. Further distancing is provided by the diegetic vocation of Ewan McGregor's character, Christian. Christian is a writer, and so the screen is often filled with words he is typing. Since these words are supposedly telling the diegetic story of the film, they often refer directly to what has been happening on screen or what is about to happen. Early in the film, for example, a tearful Christian is singing softly and typing. Soon the words he is singing appear, letter by letter, on a sheet of paper that fills the whole screen: "The greatest thing you'll ever learn is just to love and be loved in return." Since John Leguizamo, in the character of Toulouse Lautrec, has already sung these words as part of the song "Nature Boy," we assume that they have something to do with why Christian is so sad. Disappointment in love is most likely his problem. Then Christian types the phrase *Moulin Rouge*, and the camera cuts to the famous Montmartre nightclub. All of this goes to establish that, although the actors and actresses on the screen are pretending to be turn-of-the-century French bohemians, the movie overall is admitting that it is just a movie — and a musical to boot! The film ends in a similar fashion with Christian's voice arriving at the end of the story we have just seen. When he says that the story he is writing is above all "a story about love. A love that will live forever," these words also appear as if they are being typed.

Then the words "The end" appear, and the film itself ends with the closing of the grand curtains we saw at the beginning. In this way, the representational illusion is continually challenged by the film's stylistic innovations. Apparently, this was Luhrmann's intention from the outset. In the documentary "The Making of *Moulin Rouge*," which accompanies the DVD version of the film, Luhrmann says that his use of extreme cinematic techniques was meant to "remind our audience that they're watching a movie. Don't go to sleep! Don't go into a dream!" Perhaps an audience suspicious of Hollywood musicals in the first place can be disarmed in this way.

Another very effective distancing technique is the film's use of familiar popular songs to supply the *musical* dimension of this Hollywood musical. As we have seen, Toulouse Lautrec and Christian both sing the old Nat King Cole hit, "Nature Boy," in a 2001 film about life in 1900. Satine (Nicole Kidman) sings the Jule Styne-Leo Robin show tune "Diamonds Are a Girl's Best Friend" as part of her performance at the Moulin Rouge. Since Satine is made up and costumed to echo Marilyn Monroe's performance in *Gentlemen Prefer Blondes* (1953), the song is intertextually appropriate. But, just in case anyone fails to recognize this reference to the blonde movie icon, Satine's medley also includes "Material Girl," a hit by Madonna that was famously accompanied by a music video ostentatiously referring to Marilyn. Moreover, "Nature Boy" (1948), "Diamonds Are a Girl's Best Friend" (1949) and "Material Girl" (1984) are derived from historically separate eras of popular music, and so any organic illusion created by the diegetic narrative is shattered by their conjunction. This is often the point of the film's medleys. When Christian is trying to convince Satine that their love is an actual possibility, he recites a string of song titles: "Love Is Like Oxygen," "Love Is a Many-Splendored Thing," "Love Lifts Us Up Where We Belong," "All You Need Is Love." Then the two characters sing a duet in which Christian repeats familiar love lyrics and Satine sings new lyrics appropriate to her diegetic situation. The mixture of highly varied songs is intentionally illogical and unorganic. The only consistent theme is: love. At one point, Satine even echoes Paul McCartney's suspicion that people must have grown tired of "Silly Love Songs." As both McCartney's song and this medley from *Moulin Rouge* attest, people apparently have not had enough of them. Thus, Christian and Satine sing snippets from "All You Need Is Love," "I Was Made for Lovin' You," "One More Night," "Pride in the Name of Love," "Don't Leave Me This Way," "Up Where We Belong," "Heroes," "I Will Always Love You" and "Your Song." There may be some viewers who recognize all of these songs on a first hearing, but all viewers will surely recognize some of them. Hearing them in this new context makes both sorts of viewers think about the songs as songs rather than as simple musical expressions of diegetic feelings. The young males that studio executives were worried about may be reassured by this device.

This medley of love songs, performed atop the elephant-shaped building that contains Satine's living quarters, is one of the film's musical highlights. The performance of "Lady Marmalade" by the Moulin Rouge chorus[9] is another. In both cases, the performance in *Moulin Rouge* is thematically consistent with the songs' earlier lives as pieces of popular music. The love songs are performed in the film by fictional characters who are falling in love. "Lady Marmalade" is a sexy invitation in LaBelle's

1975 version: *Voulez-vous coucher avec moi, ca soir?* This sexual aura also serves effectively as an introduction to the notorious nightclub. When Harold Zidler (Jim Broadbent) performs Madonna's hit "Like a Virgin," however, the obvious aim is incongruity rather than consistency. Admittedly, there was some snide sniggering at Madonna's claim to virginity when the song was first released in 1984; this disparity is even clearer when the song is applied to Satine, a notorious courtesan. This virgin/whore dichotomy is not the principal joke, however. The real joke is that the song is being sung and danced by a portly, middle-aged male impresario with ghastly red hair and moustache. Even very limited exposure to popular music would be enough to produce a shock of ironic recognition when Zidler and a chorus of waiters perform a giant production number of this song. Little more musical knowledge is required to recognize Sting's song "Roxanne" when it is used to authorize a very impressive tango number. To put the song in context, the Argentinian (Jacek Koman) warns Christian of the dangers involved in loving a woman who sells her body. Since "Roxanne" is based on a similar narrative situation, the song's appearance here makes sense. In its previous life in 1979, though, the song was modestly mounted by The Police, a three-man band. In *Moulin Rouge*, the song requires an operatic performance, a screen full of dancers, acrobatic dance steps and an over-the-top production.[10] The contrast with the song's earlier life is striking, but it is also effective. This is what Hollywood musicals are all about, we see, whether they are staged by Busby Berkeley or by Baz Luhrmann.

Excess is as much the watchword for Luhrmann as for Berkeley. Therefore, *Moulin Rouge* is over-the-top most of the time. In some of the scenes already mentioned, Luhrmann fills the screen with singers and dancers. In others—and sometimes in the same scenes—the screen is filled with exotic architecture, sequins, confetti, neon, sparkling lights, computer graphics and animation, causing David Ansen to comment appreciatively on the "frenetic level" of "Baz Luhrnmann's deliriously energetic, promiscuously post-modern tragicomical musical" in his *Newsweek* review (May 28, 2001). Nicole Kidman's costumes are breathtaking, but the other performers at the Moulin Rouge are dressed almost as well. Because there is a play within the play, moreover, eye-catching costumes can be drawn from India and the Far East as well as from *fin de siècle* France. Toulouse Lautrec is sometimes a French boulevardier and sometimes a *commedia del arte* character. Satine lives in a building shaped like an elephant. A huge red windmill turns outside her window. As in his earlier film *William Shakespeare's Romeo & Juliet* (1996), Luhrmannn makes it just about impossible to look away from the screen. In this way, he fulfills the design that Nicole Kidman attributes to him in "The Making of *Moulin Rouge*": "His whole idea was to take the genre and sort of reinvent it." Desperate times call for desperate measures. In the judgment of many, Luhrmann's desperate measures work. Peter N. Chumo II, for example, proposes in his *Magill's Cinema Annual* article that *Moulin Rouge* "is a dizzying, heady experience—a feverish fantasia that throws all the old conventions together to create something breathtakingly original" (335). To Chumo and others, this is one way to make the Hollywood musical available to a contemporary audience.

In *Chicago* (2002), director Rob Marshall follows Luhrmann's lead to some extent[11] but also follows different demystifying strategies because of the nature of his material. For one thing, *Chicago* was in the works ever since the 1975 debut of Bob Fosse's Broadway show of the same title. Along the way, several stars and producers were convinced that they, and they alone, were ideally suited to bring Fosse's musical play to the screen. According to Steve Daly's glowing review of the 2002 film in *Entertainment Weekly*, Madonna, Goldie Hawn, Charlize Theron, Gwyneth Paltrow, Nicole Kidman and Cameron Diaz were considered for the leading female roles at one time or another. Rupert Everett, John Travolta, Kevin Kline, Kevin Spacey and Hugh Jackman were all proposed as possible Billy Flynns. Even Britney Spears was mentioned as a potential Go-to-Hell Kitty, the role eventually assigned to Lucy Liu (24–25). As Elvis Mitchell wittily observes, "[W]ith the exception of Wilma Flintstone, almost every female star of the last 20 years who ever sang a note — or dreamed of it — was mentioned as a possible star" (E42). Considerable pressure might therefore be anticipated to make *Chicago* a box office success even in a film-going climate inhospitable to Hollywood musicals.

Marshall's solution is dictated partly by the fact that he is dealing with a Fosse project and partly by his own cinematic improvisations. It is evident, first of all, that both Fosse's writing and his choreography italicize singing and dancing as show business performances and not as "the spontaneous overflow of powerful feelings."[12] In keeping with this emphasis, Velma Kelly (Catherine Zeta-Jones) performs the first number in the film "All That Jazz" on stage just after murdering her husband and sister. Despite the literal attribution of the choreography to Rob Marshall, the number is pure Fosse — lots of dancers of various genders and colors, highly stylized movements, sexy costumes, leggy women, hats. Later, when the women on murderers' row explain why they killed the men in their lives in "Cell Block Tango," Fosse-like choreography again signals that production values rather than diegetic relevance is the key. (The women's revealing costumes send the same signals.) Billy Flynn (Richard Gere) can therefore assure Roxie Hart (Renee Zelwegger) that she has nothing to worry about before being tried for the murder of her lover because the whole process of a criminal trial is "just show business." Roxie has murdered Fred Casely (Dominic West) in the first place because he has misled her about her chances of getting into show business. By the same token, Velma has killed her husband and sister, creating a serious criminal problem for herself, but by doing so she has — more importantly — also broken up a very successful sister act. While Velma and Roxie are in prison awaiting their murder trials, therefore, Velma does not sing a number about murder, guilt or repentance. In "I Can't Do It Alone," she demonstrates the act she did with her late sister. Billy Flynn mocks the criminal justice system in his big production number "Razzle Dazzle," but his singing and dancing and the antics of the chorus girls who provide back-up clearly attest that none of this is really about murder, or justice, or civil order. It is merely a production number. So is the film's finale, "Love Is a Crime," in which Roxie and Velma attain success as two singing, dancing murderesses. Fosse's characters do not sing and dance about their diegetic lives as Fred Astaire does in the "No Strings" number in *Top Hat* or as Gene Kelly does in "Almost Like Being in Love" in *Brigadoon*. Show business rather than life — even the highly romanticized version of life found in most Hollywood musicals — is Fosse's true subject. His musicals, even when adapted by someone else, are thus always already demystified.

Another form of demystification is Fosse's characteristic exploitation of show business history. As Fosse suggested in his autobiographical film *All That Jazz* (1979), everything old is new again. Thus, when Velma demonstrates the act that she formerly performed with her sister, each of the very complicated dance steps looks very old-fashioned, more like a number from *Yankee Doodle Dandy* than something from 2002. When Amos Hart (John C. Reilly) performs "Mr. Cellophane," his makeup, costume and style of performance all signal vaudeville, definitely an historical relic in 2002. Of course, *Chicago* is set in 1929, and this historical distance protects the film from the kind of disbelieving scrutiny that sank *Cop Rock*. Fosse's story—like Baz Luhrmann's—very deliberately says that this all happened a long time ago, when it was apparently more likely than it is today that fictional characters might burst into song and dance. By establishing stylistically that all the singing and dancing are presentational rather than representational, moreover, a Fosse project makes any sort of disbelief even more unlikely.

Naturally enough, Rob Marshall makes his own contributions, chiefly through his extreme use of cutting. While Velma sings and dances "All That Jazz" in a flashy nightclub, for example, her performance is marked by Fosse's characteristic sexual choreography. Consequently, Roxie watches Velma with open-mouthed wonder. The sex is not exclusively performative, however, since the developing scene alternates between Velma's on-stage antics and the represented sexual life of Roxie Hart, who is having a sordid affair with Fred Casely in her realistic apartment in the hope that Fred can arrange for her to perform on stage just like Velma. The symbolic sexuality of the dance and the diegetic sexuality of the plot thus interact through what Steve Daly calls "lots of witty crosscutting to the harsh realities of her [Roxie's] situation" (25). As far back as *Golddiggers of 1933*, we have seen chronotopic conflicts between the representational and presentational parts of the film. As James M. Collins remarks about Warner's musicals of the early '30s: "[P]erformance space and time, and narrative space and time, appeared only tangentially and intermittently related..." (273–74). In these earlier films, this conflict is an inescapable element of the genre that we are encouraged to overlook in the interest of being entertained. In the case of *Chicago*, however, this lack of relation is exaggerated as if to emphasize the artificial nature of Hollywood musicals themselves. In the same way, Roxie soon sings the song "Funny Honey" while her husband Amos tries to convince the police that Casely's murder was justifiable and committed by him. Soon shots of Roxie's singing are intercut with shots of Amos' dawning recognition that his wife has been cheating on him and of his subsequent repudiation of his earlier story. Billy Flynn's solo "All I Care About" supposedly shows us a man motivated only by his search for love while the intercut shots of Flynn's professional life show him to be a materialistic shyster. In each case, Marshall makes a presentational musical number set up an ironically discordant parallel to diegetic representation.

Even when there is no thematic contrast, musical performances are filmed so as to stand apart from the represented narrative. An especially striking example is the number "When You're Good to Mama," performed by Matron "Mama" Morton

(Queen Latifah). The sexually implicit lyrics of the song correspond to Mama's diegetic role as a prison matron in that her on-stage advice about gifts and sexual attention are intercut with her self-serving activities with the female prisoners—who are equally advised to court her good favor. Even so, there is no doubt that this number is Queen Latifah's "big solo."

As in more traditional Hollywood musicals, though, the presentational numbers often reveal attributes of the fictional characters who are performing them. Amos Hart might as well be made of cellophane as far as the plot goes, a fact signaled by Billy Flynn's inability to get his name right. Except on the witness stand, when Billy calls him Amos, the famous lawyer usually thinks Amos' name is Andy. Billy's "Razzle Dazzle" also accurately mirrors his courtroom strategy, as the number "Roxie" reveals Roxie Hart's pathetic hope for show business stardom. Although Marshall's aggressive cutting is noticeable throughout the film, it serves sometimes to underscore and sometimes to challenge the connection between presentation and representation. Viewers are thus prevented from unthinkingly adopting Homer Simpson's view that musicals are worthless because they are "fake and phony."

What this goes to show about the future is another matter.[13] *Moulin Rouge* and *Chicago* may usher in a new golden age for the Hollywood musical. *Chicago* was nominated for 13 Academy Awards in 2003 and won six, including Best Picture. This recognition may signal a return to the ways of yesteryear. On the other hand, these two successful musicals may be freakish exceptions to the general pattern of decline. I feel little inclination to predict the future, preferring to dwell on the successes and failures of the past. The careers of Fred Astaire and Gene Kelly should serve as a warning for would-be prophets in any case. Anyone seeing *Top Hat* (1935) and *Singin' in the Rain* (1952) on their initial release would probably have predicted an unending future of success for the Hollywood musical. The prediction would have been wrong. Equally wrong would have been the later prediction, based on *Finian's Rainbow* (1968) and *Xanadu* (1980), that the Hollywood musical was definitely and permanently dead. All we can say for sure is that, in the years since Al Jolson first sang on screen in *The Jazz Singer*, there has been plenty of singing and dancing, some thematic invention, and an ample supply of big production numbers. Since that is pretty much the position from which I started this book, I think I should conclude right here.

Chapter Notes

Introduction

1. Technicolor — long available in a number of processes— eventually joined sound as an indispensable ingredient of the Hollywood musical, at least in part as an effort to counter the growing popularity of television. For an economical account of these technological developments, see *Lullabies of Hollywood* by Richard Fehr and Frederick G. Vogel (22–35).

2. On Joseph Breen and the Production Code that he so rigorously enforced, see, among other sources, *The Genius of the System: Hollywood Filmmaking in the Studio Era* by Thomas Schatz (167, et passim).

3. See *An American Dilemma: The Negro Problem and Modern Democracy* by Gunnar Myrdal (1944).

4. In *Vincente Minnelli and the Musical Film*, Joseph Andrew Casper provides an economical summary of earlier, shorter experiments with musical films (21–22), none of which had the impact of *The Jazz Singer*.

5. Albert Auster writes: "Despite these honors, however, the Hollywood musical soon went into a period of serious decline. For one thing, there was a glut of them. For another, their light-heartedness— especially the echoes they evoked of Jazz Age frivolity and flapper gaiety — hardly seemed in keeping with the turmoil and despair of the early days of the Great Depression. Indeed, the years 1931 to 1933 were the nadir of the Hollywood musical" (280). John Russell Taylor also writes about this glut of musicals in *The Hollywood Musical*, one of the many books carrying a variation of this very plausible title (13).

6. According to the AFI list, these musicals ranked among the top 100 American movies of all time: *The Wizard of Oz* (1939) #6; *Singin' in the Rain* (1952) #10; *West Side Story* (1961) #41; *Snow White and the Seven Dwarfs* (1937) #49; *The Sound of Music* (1965) #55; *Fantasia* (1940) #58; *An American in Paris* (1951) #68; *American Graffiti* (1973) #77; *The Jazz Singer* (1927) #90; *My Fair Lady* (1964) #91; *Yankee Doodle Dandy* (1942) # 100.

7. In her role as journalist prophet, Wloszczyna writes, "It's true that *Chicago* with its well-tested Broadway legs may be — as columnist Martin Grove of *Hollywood Reporter* online puts it —'the next great hope' for traditional musicals to make a big-screen comeback" (13D).

8. In addition to *Grease* (Broadway, 1972; film, 1978), which I discuss in Chapter 3, several Broadway musicals were made into films during this period, including: *Tommy* (1968; 1975), *Godspell* (1971; 1973), *Jesus Christ Superstar* (1971; 1973) and *Hair* (1972; 1979).

9. See my article, "Fred Astaire as Cultural Allusion," *Studies in Popular Culture* 16.2 (1994): 9–19.

10. William H. Phillips launches a similar argument, based on different premises, when he writes in *Film: An Introduction*: "Since the 1960s, movie musicals have been scarce, and some critics have lamented the 'death of the musical.' Well, for a while. If one counts the Disney animated musicals of recent years and music videos, one could say the genre, though not in the pink of health, is far from pallid" (260).

11. Faced with a similar problem and similar doubts a decade ago, Jane Feuer added "A Postscript for the Nineties" to the second edition (1993) of *The Hollywood Musical* (123–45).

12. Albert Auster writes about all such attempts, "Unhappily for the musical, Hollywood either didn't understand this new music — most

of its executives were too old to really be in touch with it — or placed it in the unrewarding confines of the B-movie or exploitation film" (289).

13. *Lagaan: Once Upon a Time in India* (2001), directed by Ashutosh Gowanker, is the only Indian musical to have made a major impact on American audiences at the time that this chapter is being written.

Chapter 1

1. Quoted by Andrew Bergman in *We're in the Money: Depression America and Its Films* (167).

2. These are the opening sentences of, successively, "Cinderella; or, The Little Glass Slipper" by Charles Perrault; *Pride and Prejudice* by Jane Austen; and *Adventures of Huckleberry Finn* by Mark Twain.

3. See *Stagecoach* (1939), directed by John Ford; *The Wizard of Oz* (1939), directed by Victor Fleming; and *Star Wars* (1977), directed by George Lucas.

4. Sullivan discovers the uses of escapism while watching Walt Disney's animated film *Playful Pluto* after being unjustly sentenced to a chain gang.

5. On the importance of the Big White Set, see Arlene Croce, *The Fred Astaire and Ginger Rogers Book* (75–76).

6. According to Leo Braudy, "Berkeley's films show how the stylistic self-consciousness of musicals concerns the relation of their art to the everyday world outside the confines of the film. His camera presses relentlessly forward, through impossible stages that open endlessly, expanding the inner space of film and affirming the capacity of the world of style to mock the narrowness of the 'real' world outside the theater walls..." (141).

7. Keeler, Powell, Sparks and Rogers also appeared in this film's predecessor, *42nd Street* (also 1933), as did Guy Kibbee.

8. In his Introduction to *Hollywood Musicals: The Film Reader*, Steven Cohan writes, "A Berkeley show number opens on a perceivable theater stage or nightclub floor but quickly exceeds the spatial confinement of this setting..." (2).

9. Patricia Mellencamp notes both "the opulently surreal world of this film" (179) and the way in which repeated melodies cause scenes to "rhyme" (194–96).

10. John Russell Taylor writes in *The Hollywood Musical* that "it was barely noticed that what Busby Berkeley was doing was to create an entirely new, entirely cinematic form of musical extravaganza, in which the camera and its techniques played a crucial role by creating a new sort of space-time continuum which could not conceivably exist anywhere else but on a cinema screen" (79).

11. *Top Hat* (1935) and *Shall We Dance* (1937), both directed by Mark Sandrich, contain striking examples of such posh digs.

12. See Dryden's adaptation of Shakespeare's *Antony and Cleopatra*, *All for Love; or, The World Well Lost* (1678).

13. In *The Dialogic Imagination*, Bakhtin writes that what he calls "the chronotope of the threshold," or of liminality, "is always metaphorical and symbolic" (248), an explanation, perhaps, of why this backstage setting can act to legitimate such major plot developments in *Golddiggers*.

14. In "Some Warners Musicals and the Spirit of the New Deal," Mark Roth quotes Cy Caldwell's contemporary judgment of the "Forgotten Man" number published in *New Outlook*: "For downright offensiveness and bad taste, that last reel wins the Croix de Garbage..." (qtd. in Roth 55).

15. Kenneth MacKinnon is more optimistic about the possibility of intratextual resolutions in his essay "'I Keep Wishing I Were Somewhere Else': Space and Fantasies of Freedom in the Hollywood Musical": "Perhaps their [musicals'] most important message is that there is space beyond humdrum, burdensome everyday reality, and that that space belongs to the underprivileged, those who experience discrimination in the 'real world,' a world which becomes markedly less real in the musical. Within that space, another kind of space, psychical perhaps, opens out before the underrepresented and narrowly defined individual or group" (44).

16. Robert Sklar notes that *Golddiggers of 1933* is "the picture Bonnie Parker and Clyde Barrow step in to watch in Arthur Penn's 1967 film romantically evoking the violent 1930s" (178).

17. In *Shirley Temple: American Princess*, Anne Edwards reports that when Shirley was originally signed to appear in this film, its title was *Fox Movietone Follies* (54).

18. Cf. Andrew Bergman's observation that screwball comedies "created an America of perfect unity: all classes as one, the rural-urban divide breached, love and decency and neighborliness ascendant" (133).

19. On personalizing the causes of social problems in Depression films, see Bergman's *We're in the Money* (23, et passim). Note also Christopher Ames' observation about the film *Stand-In* (1937): "[T]he transformation of Atterbury Dodd is typical of Hollywood's treatment of social problems: only by framing issues in terms of individual personalities can justice be attained" (148–49).

20. "Baby Take a Bow" was also initiated back at the Department of Amusement by an exchange of dialogue between Jimmy Dugan and Cromwell, and "Broadway's Gone Hillbilly" will be initiated by Cromwell's observation — while sitting at his desk in his office — that the country needs "hillbilly tunes to make them stand up and cheer."

21. *Blacks in American Films and Television* (388).

22. Richard Fehr and Frederick G. Vogel, for example, write in *Lullabies of Hollywood* that "*Stand Up and Cheer* merits its reputation as a tacky musical largely because of its stark unrealism and excessive stereotyping" (138).

23. Nick Tosches writes that "as the quaint fantasy of the happy antebellum coon, the figment on which minstrelsy was predicated, lost its currency, the parallel fantasy of the whimsical and picturesque hillbilly simultaneously arose to take its place in the subculture of Southern show business" (180).

24. See James M. Collins' claim in "The Musical," that although (because?) musical films are "devoted shamelessly to pure entertainment," they "are based on a complicated visual-narrative style that integrates the use of space and of spectator in unparalleled fashion." *Handbook of American Film Genres*, ed. by Wes Gehring (269).

25. See Rick Altman's judgment: "Busby Berkeley ... alone among the early practitioners of the musical understood the extent to which the audio dissolve liberates the picture plane of all diegetic responsibilities" (70).

26. *The Portable Walt Whitman*, ed. Mark van Doren, rev. and enlarged ed. (150). See also James M. Collins' remark about Warners' musicals of the early '30s: "[P]erformance space and time, and narrative space and time, appeared only tangentially and intermittently related..." (273–74).

27. Fox seems to have decided that the way to end the Depression was to give everyone in Southern California a part in this picture, thus contradicting President Roosevelt, who claimed in his "Annual Message" to the American people in 1935, "The Federal Government is the only ... agency with sufficient power and credit to meet this situation" (109).

28. F. Scott Fitzgerald, *The Great Gatsby* (141).

Chapter 2

1. See also Peter Gammond's assessment in *The Oxford Companion to Popular Music*: "By the turn of the century the American minstrel show had largely retreated once again to the South, flourishing in cities like New Orleans. The black entertainer had become a part of the Broadway stage in black musicals and revues and the wholesale exploitation of jazz had supplanted the gentle notes of the minstrel stage" (390). Gammond does not stress, as Nick Tosches does (175 ff.), that many minstrel performers made an easy transition to vaudeville.

2. Arthur Knight explains that "black critics seem to have returned the favor of black displacement from these films by ignoring them..." (84–85).

3. Part of the problem is diagnosed in Knight's book when he contrasts *O Brother Where Art Thou* and *Bamboozled*, two films released in 2000 containing blackface sequences: "Blackface in *O Brother* is a throwaway effect. In *Bamboozled*, it is an obsession" (237).

4. See Bob Thomas' treatment of this marital conflict in *Astaire: The Man, the Dancer* (154–55) and Astaire's own, more politic version in *Steps in Time* (233–34).

5. In *Lullabies of Hollywood: Movie Music and the Movie Musical, 1915–1992*, Richard Fehr and Frederick G. Vogel approvingly write: "Appearing in *Swing Time* (1936) in blackface and wearing derby and spats, Astaire performs an outstanding interpretation of the Robinson style in Dorothy Fields and Jerome Kern's admirable 'Bojangles of Harlem,' It remains one of Astaire's best dance numbers" (140).

6. A possible rationalization of Robinson's roles in the Shirley Temple movies may lie in an analysis proposed by Eric Lott: "Minstrelsy's role as a mediator of northern class, racial, and ethnic conflict — all naturally grounded in a problematic of masculinity — has much to do with the equivocal character of blackface representations" (25).

7. This scene may inadvertently throw ironic light on Richard Dyer's cultural-studies premise: "Musicals typically show us space entirely occupied by white people, dancing whatever they want, singing as loudly or as

intimately as they need" (26). This is true in *Babes in Arms* even if the white people are made up to look black.

8. In *Judy*, Gerold Frank provides the following version of producer Arthur Freed's enthusiastic pitch for this film to studio head Louis B. Mayer: "Just think, a Rodgers and Hart score—I'll write a few more numbers—we'll buy 'God's Country,' which Harold and Yip wrote for *Hooray for What!*—it's great—and Roger will write additional material, we'll get Berkeley to direct..." (138).

9. In "Busby Berkeley and the Backstage Musical," Martin Rubin identifies the key elements of Berkeley's style as "large-scale chorus formations, geometric patterns, and giant props" (54).

10. Knight uses the term *veritable black musicians or comics* (30) to mark this distinction.

11. This finale is reprised in *That's Entertainment, Part II*.

12. In fact, the title makes no sense syntactically, and so we must assume that the "babes" of the title functions as the signifier of a film series, like the "angels" in *Angels with Dirty Faces* (1938) and *The Angels Wash Their Faces* (1939), starring the Dead End Kids, and like "Andy Hardy" in *Love Finds Andy Hardy* (1938) and *Andy Hardy's Private Secretary* (1941), starring Mickey Rooney.

13. Arthur Knight writes, to the contrary, that the cinematic action of blacking up is always thematically significant: "The change into blackface—either shown via an abrupt cut, as a transformation or, through a continuous shot or scene, as a process of transformation—is a crucial generic marker of the blackface film" (50).

14. Interestingly enough, when Ted Hanover and Linda Mason reprise the "Abraham" number later on for a film based on Jim Hardy's idea, they perform in evening clothes and without blackface.

15. Contrary to the position advanced in this chapter, Bob Thomas writes about the "Bojangles" number in *Astaire: The Man, The Dancer*, "The dance is totally devoid of racial stereotype and scarcely related to Robinson's style" (132).

16. Nick Tosches writes: "In the late summer of 1929, the Al G. Field Minstrels disbanded in mid-season. It was the summer that NBC began broadcasting *Amos 'n' Andy* nationally, sponsored by Pepsodent. Did minstrelsy die? Or did it simply, or subtly, undergo a metamorphosis?" (180). Mark A. Reid effectively summarizes the controversy surrounding the *Amos 'n' Andy* program in *Redefining Black Film* (20–22). Arthur Knight also raises provocative questions in *Disintegrating the Musical* (70–71), where he also calls the show "sonic blackface" (92).

17. While researching this topic, I came across *Negro Minstrels: A Complete Guide* (1902) by Jack Haverly. Haverly writes: "Nothing gives the amateur such rare opportunities for displaying talent as a negro [sic] minstrel performance. Anyone with but a little study and practice can successfully entertain an audience and keep them in roars of laughter for hours by the aid of this volume" (5).

18. See Peter Stanfield's claim that "the evocation of an American vernacular tradition inevitably leads into the fantasy world of blackness formed out of the conventions of blackface minstrelsy" (147).

19. In his study of the much admired white minstrel Emmett "Nigger" Miller, Nick Tosches reports that Miller was performing in Marion, Ohio, with the fabulously successful Field Minstrels on the very night that *The Jazz Singer* opened (91). Tosches clearly sees a thematic connection between the two events.

20. On Emmett's life, see *Dan Emmett and the Rise of Negro Minstrelsy* by Hans Nathan.

21. On the light-dark maiden conflict, see, for example, Frederick I. Carpenter, "Puritans Preferred Blondes: The Heroines of Melville and Hawthorne" (1936), and Leslie A Fiedler, *Love and Death in the American Novel* (1960, 1966), 39 ff.

22. Cf. W. J. Cash's positive characterization of the generalized Southern male in *The Mind of the South*: "Proud, brave, honorable by its lights, courteous, personally generous, loyal, swift to act, often too swift, but signally effective, sometimes terrible, in its action—such was the South at its best" (428).

23. In *Bing Crosby's Minstrel Song Folio*, featuring songs from *Dixie*, the Van Heusen–Burke songs are augmented by "Ole Dan Tucker" (2), "Dixie" (3–4) and "Swing Low, Sweet Chariot"—identified as "Negro Spiritual" (43–44)—and by stills (25–26) showing the *Dixie* actors in blackface.

24. In addition to *Dixie*, Best also appeared in *Thank Your Lucky Stars*, *The Kansan*, *Cinderella Swings It* and *Cabin in the Sky* during 1943.

25. Hans Nathan gives this account of a typical performance by the original four Virginia Minstrels in *Dan Emmett and the Rise of Early*

Negro Minstrelsy: "Their ill-assorted garments, their oddly shaped hats, and their gaudy pants and shirts were in the traditional style of the stage plantation Negro. But the effect of their costuming was heightened by almost frightening countenances which were distinguished by wide-open mouths, bulging lips, and eyes that shone like full moons" (123).

26. See Mark Twain's recollections of minstrel makeup in his *Autobiography*: "Their lips were thickened and lengthened with bright red paint to such a degree that their mouths resembled slices cut in a ripe watermelon" (60).

27. Allison McCracken reproduces an argument from Michael Rogin's *Blackface, White Noise* that throws light on this happy ending: "As Michael Rogin points out, blackface musicals of the 1930s and 1940s, like other musicals of the time, were about national unity ... rather than ethnic, generational, or romantic conflict..." (133n).

28. Jane Feuer explains this generational/musical conflict in *The Hollywood Musical* (54ff.).

29. Doug McClelland points out about the senior Joelsons, "Although Jewish family life had been dramatized on the screen before (notably in Jolson's own *The Jazz Singer*), rarely did the characters discuss their Jewishness and rarer still did they get to a synagogue" (15).

30. Hirschhorn explains Keeler's refusal to be involved (274), as does Doug McClelland (44).

31. Actually, Jolson had four wives: Henrietta Keller, Ethel Delmar, Ruby Keeler, and Erle Chennault.

32. See Peter Stanfield's claim: "Minstrelsy had become a performance style that was locked into the past, a signifier of an American musical tradition" (148).

33. Although, as Arthur Knight points out, "Jolson does not black up because he's discovered black music" (90). He has already been performing in blackface for some time at this point.

34. For a characteristic statement of this political truism, see the biographical note to Langston Hughes' poetry in *The Norton Anthology of American Literature*: "Hughes and other blacks were drawn by the American Communist party, which made racial justice an important plank in its platform, promoting an image of working-class solidarity that nullified racial boundaries" (2225).

35. See the *Newsweek* story "Larry Parks in Red Face" (April 2, 1951: 21), which includes the surprising fact that "John Wayne, president of the anti–Communist Motion Picture Alliance, quickly came to Parks's defense, asserting that the American public would 'forgive a person who is willing to admit his mistake.'"

Chapter 3

1. Many critics have pointed out that Big Band swing music was taken up first by younger Americans. See, for example, *Jazz: A History of America's Music* by Geoffrey Ward (252–54) and *Jazz in American Culture* by Burton W. Peretti (78, 85). My point is not who got where first, but the total absence of any musical generation gap.

2. Denny Martin Flinn points out that "[t]he title song is not from the show, but written for the talents of a young Swedish bombshell with one name" (504).

3. T. H. Adamowski provocatively observes, "As was often remarked in the press after his death, it was Sinatra who taught those who followed him the art of *being* a rock star" (7).

4. See the truly subversive motorcycle song "Born to be Wild" on the album *Steppenwolf* (1968).

5. Rutsky sees the use of pre-sold stars as also crucial to the overall series: "By casting ... pop-music stars in starring roles, the surfing films were clearly designed to capitalize on their preexisting appeal — and that of music, songs, and dancing — to teenaged audiences" (16). Rutsky also notes that Frankie Avalon had 13 songs in the Billboard Top 40 between 1958 and 1962 (16–17).

6. On this number, Annette sings a duet with herself while staring into a mirror, as Doris Day did in *Pajama Game* (1957).

7. Keenan Wynn was born in 1916, Martha Hyer in 1924.

8. For a complete listing of *Saturday Night Live* sketches, see http://snl.jt.org/season/index.phtml.

9. In *The Hollywood Musical*, Clive Hirschhorn explains that he has appended "a catalogue of American International and other low-budget rock 'n' roll, twist and 'beach party' musicals of the fifties and sixties" even though he does not discuss them in the main body of his text (9).

10. Here again, birth dates are relevant. John Travolta was 24 when *Grease* was released, and Olivia Newton-John was 30. Perhaps this is what led Vincent Canby to remark in his *New*

York Times review (June 16, 1978) that "the gang at Rydell High ... are all rather long in the tooth to be playing kids who'd hang around malt shops."

11. See Henley's 1984 album, *Building the Perfect Beast*.

Chapter 4

1. As Rick Altman writes in *The American Film Musical*, "From *The Merry Widow* to *The Boy Friend* and beyond, dance has often been used as a culmination, as a celebration of a love affair" (163).

2. Joseph Andrew Casper also attaches Aristotle to the Hollywood musical in *Vincente Minnelli and the Film Musical*: "The film musical, since it contains, and often attempts to unite all the elements that Aristotle deduces in his *Poetics* as constituting the full and genuine poetic experience, simultaneously and at their most intense points, thereby taxing the resources of the medium, has the theoretical potential to be the most highly developed genre of the fiction film" (9).

3. See Chapter VI of Aristotle's *Poetics* (circa 335–322 BCE).

4. Aristotle writes, also in Chapter VI, "Dramatic action, therefore, is not with a view to the representation of character; character comes in as subsidiary to the actions."

5. In his biography *Astaire: The Man, The Dancer*, Bob Thomas quotes this Astaire maxim: "Each dance ought to spring somehow out of the character or situation, otherwise it is simply a vaudeville act..." (127).

6. See *The Taming of the Shrew*, *Gone with the Wind* and many Mickey Rooney–Judy Garland musicals, perhaps most appropriately, *Girl Crazy* (1943), also featuring a Gershwin score.

7. In *The Hollywood Musical*, Jane Feuer writes, "The battle between popular and elite art was waged on every front in the Hollywood musical." And she sensibly concludes that the popular is generically selected to triumph: "The particular syntax opposing popular and elite elements arises out of the genre's overall rhetoric of affirming itself by applauding popular forms" (55–56).

8. Arlene Croce is unimpressed by all of this, maintaining, "Not even in his satin *premier danseur* tunic can Astaire be taken for a ballet dancer..." (122).

9. Leo Braudy goes even further in asserting in *The World in a Frame*: "The flip-card stills that turn into a sequence of Rogers dancing present her as a creature of the film, not the stage" (144).

10. Arlene Croce writes, "Miss Hoctor can be taken for nothing human. She was a contortionist whose specialty, a horseshoe backbend on point, was already well known to movie audiences. (In this position she would kick herself in the head.)" (122).

11. In *Generational Multiplex*, Timothy Shary notes that 1963, "the year of Kennedy's assassination ... seems to mark the division of the prosperous post–World War II '50s from the cynical Vietnam War '60s..." (290).

12. To see what the people at Kellerman's might have been listening to on the radio, we might note that Joel Whitburn lists the Top Ten selling musical artists of 1963, in descending order, as: The Beach Boys, Dion, Rick Nelson, The Four Seasons, Bobby Vinton, Brenda Lee, Peter, Paul & Mary, Chubby Checker, Steve Lawrence and Ray Charles (130). During the week including Labor Day, 1963, the Top Ten songs, in descending order, were, according to *Your Hit Parade*, "Fingertips (Part II)" by Stevie Wonder, "Hello Muddah, Hello Faddah" by Allen Sherman, "My Boyfriend's Back" by the Angels, "Blowing in the Wind" by Peter, Paul & Mary, "Candy Girl" by the Four Seasons, "If I Had A Hammer" by Trini Lopez, "Judy's Turn to Cry" by Lesley Gore, "Mockingbird" by Inez Foxx, "More" by Kai Winding and "Wipe Out" by the Surfaris (232)

13. See Laura Mulvey's "Visual Pleasure and Narrative Cinema" (1975) for an explanation and analysis of what she calls *scopophilia*, "pleasure in looking" (2184).

14. Interestingly enough, Braudy also observes in *The World in a Frame*, "Dancing isn't a euphemism for sex; in Astaire-Rogers films at least, dancing is much better" (145).

15. For a thorough treatment of the Fred and Ginger series, see *The Fred Astaire and Ginger Rogers Book* (1972) by Arlene Croce.

16. Corey K. Creekmur touches on the appeal of such nostalgic rock and roll by observing that "most compilation soundtracks ... take advantage of the historically unprecedented assumption that almost all 'popular' music is implicitly 'youth' music" (385). *American Graffiti* (1973) is, of course, the ruling example of a film that exploits this rock and roll nostalgia, but a host of other titles can be cited for the years between 1973 and 1987.

17. Northrop Frye writes in *Anatomy of Criticism*: "The plot structure of Greek New Comedy, as transmitted by Plautus and Terence,

in itself less a form than a formula, has become the basis for most comedy.... What normally happens is that a young man wants a young woman, that his desire is resisted by some opposition, ... and that near the end of the play, some twist in the plot enables the hero to have his will" (163).

18. Frye also writes that "the obstacles to the hero's desire ... form the action of the comedy, and the overcoming of them the comic resolution" (164), a plot development that he elsewhere (44) relates to Aristotle's concept of "discovery."

19. Woody Allen agrees in his *The Purple Rose of Cairo* (1985) when he lets his pathetic, unloved character Cecilia find temporary imaginative escape while viewing this number at her local movie theater. See my book *Metapop: Self-referentiality in Contemporary American Popular Culture* (85).

20. In his autobiography, Richard Rodgers says that one of the elements that first attracted him to the *Anna and the King of Siam* narrative was "the intangibility of the attraction between the teacher and king" (270).

21. As John Russell Taylor explains in *The Hollywood Musical*: "Significantly, nearly all the plots (such as they are) of Astaire-Rogers musicals are based on antagonism rather than passion between the two principals. As a rule, Astaire falls for Rogers right away, but she for some reason doesn't like him or determines to play hard to get. She devises various ways of evading, needling and generally irritating him until towards the end she succumbs and permits a happy-ever-after ending" (43).

22. According to a website dedicated to correcting Western misperceptions about Siam and about King Mongkut in particular, the King's greatest achievement was keeping Siam out of English and French colonial control. See http://www.royalty.nu/Asia/thailand/Monghut.html.

23. Contrast this narrative functionality with Mark Roth's characterization of Busby Berkeley's grandiose dance numbers: "Almost everyone (those who wait bored through the plot for Berkeley to be turned loose, and those who feel the dances slow up otherwise good comedy) agrees that the dances are removable, isolated units having little integral relation to the rest of the film" (46).

24. John Mueller writes, "Although the script is a romantic comedy, the chain of events in the boy-chases-girl structure is partly revised, and the tenor of the humor is uncharacteristically boisterous." As a result, he feels that the film "deserves better treatment" than it usually received from critics (139). Arlene Croce finds the plot structure less impressive, concluding it "clearly was never intended to support a musical" (140).

25. The other example of this un–Astaire-like technique occurs in "Steppin' Out with my Baby" in *Easter Parade* [1948]).

26. Croce calls the setting "mock pastoral" (146).

27. In his book *Richard Rodgers*, William G. Hyland explains that from their first introduction to the *Oklahoma!* narrative, "Hammerstein found the plot lacking" (137). The dream ballet solution seems, in this light, particularly ingenious.

28. According to Hyland, Agnes de Mille originally intended the "fantasized ballet to illustrate the consequences of Laurey's foolish decision to accompany Jud to the box social" (145)

Chapter 5

1. In *Popular Culture: An Introductory Text* (414 ff.), Jack Nachbar and Kevin Lause use the formula "convention plus invention" to discuss this kind of adaptation in popular cultural "texts," in which the reassuringly familiar is mixed with supposed originality.

2. In view of my arguments in Chapters 1 and 6, it would also make sense to consider "setting" in this sense as equivalent to a Bakhtinian chronotope.

3. Not everyone has been as charmed as Rose and Esther. James Naremore, for example, writes in *The Films of Vincente Minnelli*, "Set in the 'gateway to the west' at the turn of the century, [*Meet Me in St. Louis*] celebrates the foundation of an urban Eden in the wilderness—a place where capitalism makes the lawns spacious and the weather perfect, and where a giant exposition of commodities has been built on a swamp" (71–72).

4. In real life, Glenn Miller joined the United States Army in October 1942. His plane was lost over the English Channel in December 1944. John Payne went on to star with Sonja Henie in *Iceland* (1942), again under Humberstone's direction, and in *Miracle on 34th Street* (1947), among other films. Milton Berle died in March 2002 at age 93.

5. Representative "aqua musicals" featuring Esther Williams were: *Bathing Beauty* (1944), *On an Island with You* (1948), *Neptune's*

Daughter (1949) and *Million Dollar Mermaid* (1952). She also performed an aquatic specialty number in *Ziegfeld Follies* (1946).

6. The more predictable ending to such a film can be seen in the last scene in *Bathing Beauty* where Esther Williams and Red Skelton share a full-screen kiss in the pool after Esther has performed her number.

7. On the 1991 CD *Glenn Miller and His Orchestra: A Legendary Performer* we can hear W. Wallace Early, manager of record sales for Victor Records, announcing on Miller's radio program that the Glenn Miller Orchestra is receiving the first gold record ever awarded for "Chattanooga Choo Choo."

8. The contemporaneous reviewer in *The New Republic* wrote, "Whoever is responsible for the story of *Sun Valley Serenade* has the distinction of creating a heroine who is unwittingly the most unscrupulous, unsympathetic dame who ever executed a figure-eight" (20 Oct. 1941).

9. Note the same practice at work when Richard Rodgers and his fiancée hear Lena Horne perform in *Words and Music*. See Chapter 7.

10. In the end, Tom returns to the Rumford plantation and overwhelms Major Patterson and his equally evil brother. Then he breaks down the locked door to Lucy's bedroom because, as he explains, "There are some things a man has to fight for. That's why I'm here tonight." We are thus able to have our pacifist cake and eat it too.

11. Gary Giddins writes about the interpolation of "Swanee River" into the Rodgers and Hart score: "Needles to say, this galled the Broadway writers. Rodgers and Hart would not hear of it; their contract specifically mandated that they provide all the songs for *Mississippi*. The Foster song violated their contract and particularly offended them because of its theme of a former slave who longs for the old plantation" (381).

12. Charles P. Roland writes in "The South of the Agrarians," "Perhaps out of a sense of need to escape the stultifying effects of a rampant urban-industrialism, non–Southerners helped keep alive the picture of the romantic Old South — the land of moonlight, magnolias, and mint juleps" (35).

13. In *Hillbillyland*, J. W. Williamson writes, "Dogpatch is, from the git-go, a world in which proper patriarchy has become a joke.... The men in this society are presented as mere comic pawns in a ruthless female power play that makes men into mere breeders and legally hunted game on Sadie Hawkins day" (243).

14. By birth, Alfred Gerald Caplin (1909–1979).

15. The *Newsweek* reviewer writes, "Fact is, their beards don't quite fit right, their precariously leaning houses are obviously only stage properties, and anyone with a grain of sense and fair vision could tell immediately that the wildly colored hills and trees are the merest paint" (92).

16. Art direction by J. McMillam Johnson and Hal Pereira; set decoration by Sam Comer and Grace Gregory; costumes by Alvin Colt.

17. For a discussion of this problem in connection with *Finian's Rainbow*, see Chapter 6.

18. Hirschhorn points out "Apart from the casting of Leslie Parrish ... Stella Stevens ... and a few minor actors who had not appeared in the stage show, the screen version of Norman Panama and Meville Frank's *Li'l Abner* ... came to the screen in a production ... as close to the original as was possible..." (367).

19. In "Abner Unpinned: Al Capp's *Li'l Abner*, 1940–1955," Edwin T. Arnold points out that Capp also used Dogpatch as a nuclear waste dump in a series of strips in 1948 (429).

20. Some commentators have found this dancing very effective. The contemporaneous reviewer in *Time* (Dec. 21, 1959), for example, writes that "the story gallops along, and the dancing preserves the essential whomp." Bosley Crowther agrees in *The New York Times* (Dec. 12, 1959): "Michael Kidd's acrobatic dances, calculated to the new-fashioned hillbilly music of Johnny Mercer and Gene DePaul, explode with an energy that is stunning and splatter all over the place with an evidence of joy and jubilation that even gets into the static viewer's bones."

21. It has become conventional at Yankee Stadium for baseball fans from places like New Jersey and Connecticut to mimic "hick" dancing when the public address system plays "Cotton-Eyed Joe" between innings.

22. In *New Republic* (Dec. 26, 1949), Robert Hatch describes the setting as "New York in person, from Coney Island to Grant's Tomb," and adds that this is "a fine Technicolor set for the frolic." In *Time* (Jan. 2, 1950), this setting is called "the finest backgrounds yet exploited by a cinemusical: actual New York landmarks shot on location in Technicolor."

23. The three also appeared together in *Take Me Out to the Ball Game*, released in the same year.

24. Later on, Woody Allen is also accused of romanticizing New York City as a setting for his films. In a *Magill's Survey of Cinema* entry about Allen's film *Manhattan* (1979), for example, Douglas Blau comments on parallels between the film's central character, novelist Isaac Davis (Allen), and the director of the film in which Davis appears: "Isaac's novel will depict New York as 'a black and white town pulsating to the tunes of George Gershwin.' Allen's film does just that" (1067). In *Seriously Funny: The Rebel Comedians of the 1950s and 1960s*, Gerald Nachman describes Allen's New York films as "lacy film valentines to the city of his youth" (541).

25. Rick Altman writes in *The American Film Musical*, "As long as Gene Kelly and Vera-Ellen try to impress each other with their sophistication in *On the Town* they do little more than get on each other's nerves, but when they finally admit that they both grew up in the same small town (and thus had the same school teachers), their love is assured" (277).

26. In Shakespeare's *Romeo and Juliet*, on which *West Side Story* is obviously based, the two young lovers first meet at a ball held in the house of Juliet's father. For Romeo, the rest of the world disappears when he sees Juliet: "So shows a snowy dove trooping with crows, / As yonder lady o'er her fellows shows" (1.5.50–51). In Baz Luhrmann's *William Shakespeare's Romeo + Juliet* (1996), Leonardo DiCaprio, as Romeo, has fled the loud, eroticized party given by Capulet (Paul Sorvino) when he first encounters Juliet (Claire Danes) through the calming environment of an aquarium while the ballad "Kissing You" plays. In each case, the two lovers meet in a romantic space outside of normal time.

27. In fact, experimenting with such alterations in setting can only produce comedy or satire, as in *The Beverly Hillbillies*.

Chapter 6

1. See *Oklahoma!* (1955), directed by Fred Zinnemann; *Damn Yankees* (1958), directed by George Abbott and Stanley Donen; and *West Side Story* (1961), directed by Jerome Robbins and Robert Wise.

2. Albert Auster agrees, writing that "the musical was generally acknowledged to be Hollywood's most escapist form of entertainment..." (279).

3. See Rick Altman's explanation of the semantic/syntactic distinction in "A Semantic/Syntactic Approach to Film Genres."

4. In *The Dialogical Imagination*, Bakhtin writes, "We will give the name *chronotope* (literally, 'time space') to the intrinsic connectedness of temporal and spatial relationships that are artistically expressed in literature.... The chronotope as a formally constitutive category determines to a significant degree the image of man in literature.... The image of man is always intrinsically chronotopic" (84–85).

5. According to Vincente Minnelli's autobiography, "Gene Kelly describes the movie version of *Brigadoon* as a singer's show on Broadway that had to be made as a dancer's show" (279).

6. Quoted by Joseph Andrew Casper in *Vincente Minnelli and the Musical Film* (45).

7. Jane Feuer writes, "The transition to the dream in *Yolanda* is one instance of a play on the boundaries between fantasy and 'reality' which informs the entire film" (79).

8. Joseph Andrew Casper points out that this scene was shot through a dull yellow filter, which he claims to be suggestive of Yolanda's money. (155).

9. According to Hirschhorn, "the only blemish" on this dream ballet is "a regrettable lyric (by Arthur Freed) which interrupted Eugene Loring's choreography and Harry Warren's music with lines like 'Let the Band Begin, Playing Lohengrin'..." (260).

10. Fred Astaire, Lucille Bremer and Eugene Loring, who choreographed this ballet, also worked together on *The Great Ziegfeld* (1936)

11. Mueller conjectures that the dream ballet is "meant to be anticipatory" (257) of later plot developments.

12. Somewhat less sympathetically, John Russell Taylor writes that "Kelly is the open, confident, brash (but not insensitively so, like Mickey Rooney), straightforward American male, with a smile on his face for the whole human race, as one of his songs puts it. The personality is not altogether appealing. There is sometimes the feeling that the charm is laid on a little too thickly, that the smile is a trifle synthetic..." (60).

13. It may be worth remarking that the set for "The Heather on the Hill" at least suggests the out of doors, while the sets for so many of Fred Astaire's dances suggest more confined spaces. Although many specious contrasts have been proposed between the two dancers, I don't recall having come across this one.

14. This review ran October 10, 1968, and Robert F. Kennedy was assassinated on June 5, Dr. Martin Luther King, Jr., on April 4.

15. Coppola's *The Godfather* (1972) was ranked #3 on the American Film Institute's list of the 100 greatest films of all time. His *The Godfather, Part II* (1974) ranked #32, and *Apocalypse Now* (1979) ranked #28.

16. At the end of the play, Woody asks Sharon, "Where *is* Glocca Morra?" And Sharon replies, "There's no such place, Woody. It's only in father's head" (76). In the film, she answers that it is "over there somewhere." Whether purely imaginary or merely remote, Glocca Morra is certainly more fantastic than actual Irish locations such as Limerick or Tralee.

17. The *Variety* reviewer disagrees, in fact asserting: "Fact that Rainbow Valley was created on the studio backlot is not apparent."

18. One is reminded of the apparent clash of chronotopes involving Rod Steiger's Jud Fry and Shirley Jones' Laurie in *Oklahoma!*

19. See Johnson's *Francis Ford Coppola* (62) and *On the Edge: The Life and Times of Francis Coppola* by Michael Goodwin and Naomi Wise (79–80) for discussions of the Hermes Pan fiasco.

20. In 1947 such activities would probably be familiar only to those who had attended Socialist summer camps.

21. For one version of this story, see Goodwin and Wise (76–77).

22. See Samuel Taylor Coleridge, "Kubla Khan," *The Norton Anthology of Poetry*. 3rd ed. (564–65).

23. According to John Livingston Lowes in *The Road to Xanadu* (1927), Coleridge deserves full credit for coining the term. As Lowes explains, Coleridge had been reading in Samuel Purchas' *Purchas His Pilgrimages* (1617) about a palace that Kubla Khan had built in Xamdu or Xaindu just before he fell asleep and dreamed his poem (328, 362). The conversion of Xamdu or Xaindu to Xanadu was performed for reasons of what Lowes calls "euphony," although metrics surely played a part. However the change was accomplished, Coleridge came up with one of the most magical place names in all of literature.

24. In *The Hollywood Musical*, Jane Feuer points out that Kelly's name, Danny McGuire, is the same as that of his character in his 1944 film, *Cover Girl*.

25. In her contemporaneous *New York Times* review (Aug. 9, 1980), Janet Maslin writes, "Unlike old-fashioned muses, Miss Newton-John does much of her work on roller skates, although the skating portions of the movie, like its musical numbers, have a desultory feel."

26. One contrast deliberately created in the number, but not thematically emphasized, is the degree of racial integration assumed in the two eras. In the 1940s set, there are at first no black dancers. In the 1980s set, black dancers occupy the roles assumed in contemporary entertainment. When the two groups mix, black entertainers jitterbug and jive in 1940s costumes. Once again, the Pointer Sisters seem relevant.

Chapter 7

1. Clive Hirschhorn agrees with the reviewers from the 1930s about the film's biographical authenticity, writing not only that *The Great Ziegfeld* "was the classiest biopic ever to emerge from Hollywood" but also that it was "one of the most successful in its recreation of the period in which Ziegfeld flourished" (118).

2. Not to the *Variety* reviewer, who felt that "[e]ven for road-showing there is a question of how much better an entertainment it would be with an hour out."

3. See Marjorie Farnsworth's book, *The Ziegfeld Follies*, on the elder Ziegfeld's actual association with this institution (137).

4. Feuer writes apropos of such situations: "[T]he backstage musical is more than just onstage performances. Only the numbers attempt to achieve an illusion of live entertainment; the plots follow the pattern of traditional Hollywood narrative in which we, the film audience, look onto the story from a position outside it. The story is told to us by the camera in a more impersonal 'third-person' mode.... During the narrative interludes, then, we are encouraged to share the point of view of the performers, but during the musical interludes, we are encouraged to actually become part of the audience of the film — a very different and much closer type of identification" (29).

5. Marjorie Farnsworth explains Ziegfeld's original inspiration as a producer in this way: "He envisioned these beauties dressed to represent the seasons, months, nations of the world, celebrated courtesans of history, grains of the field, leaves of trees, animals of the jungle, flowers of the garden—thus he first envisioned them and through the years his vision became reality" (28).

6. See Arlene Croce's harsh description of Hoctor's style in *The Fred Astaire and Ginger Rogers Book*, quoted in Chapter 5.

7. Farnsworth writes that Cohan "would not allow a tune from any Ziegfeld show to be

played in any theatre in which he was appearing" (173).

8. See Feuer's explanation: "The conventional camera location for recording an onstage performance in a backstage musical was from an imaginary third-row-center seat within the audience. The resulting shot over the backs of the first few rows of the audience onto the stage (especially when projected upon the enormous screens of the past) gave the spectators the illusion of sitting adjacent to the internal audience, perhaps in the fourth row" (28).

9. The reviewer in *Variety* (June 3, 1942) writes that "in celluloid, Cagney has immortalized Cohan for all time. There can be no more fitting climax to any career."

10. Ziegfeld's montage includes *Rio Rita, Whoopee, The Three Musketeers* and *Show Boat*. Cohan's includes *The Honeymooners, The American Idea, The Man Who Owns Broadway, Hello Broadway* and *The Little Millionaire*. While some especially well-informed viewer might recognize all the titles in either list, it is more likely that most viewers will recall only one or a few. In the way of most such extensive allusions, the people who will recognize at least one title constitute a large part of the potential audience.

11. Actually, Cohan had two wives, neither of whom was named Mary. See Ward Morehouse, *George M. Cohan: Prince of the American Theater* (85ff.).

12. Ty Burr writes about the filming of *Yankee Doodle Dandy*: "A terminally ill Cohan personally talked Cagney into taking the part, and production began on Dec. 8, 1941—the day after Pearl Harbor—in what costar Rosemary DeCamp described as 'a kind of patriotic frenzy, as though we feared we may be sending a last message to a free world'" (33).

13. In *A Handbook to Literature*, William Harmon and C. Hugh Holman write that "[i]n discussions of plot [*agon*] has come to mean any conflict. Leading characters are classified according to their relationship to this conflict, displayed by the element *agon* inside their designations: PROTAGONIST, ANTAGONIST, DEUTERAGONIST, and so on" (10).

14. When Rodgers decides to abandon songwriting after two years in which he and Hart have failed to crack the big time, for example, his father encourages him to keep plugging away instead of accepting a job in retail. Despite this encouragement—so unlike the parental opposition dictated by the "syntax" of the Hollywood musical—Rodgers resolves to become a salesman of baby goods. Hart cheerfully accepts this decision and even offers to throw a party to celebrate the occasion. The only discernible dramatic tension may lie in Rodgers' envy of people who have ordinary, everyday jobs.

15. Hart's biographer, Frederick Nolan, writes, "Any half-baked student of psychology could make a pretty accurate guess at Hart's sexual preferences—and hang ups—from the things he wrote and the things he said" (296).

16. In *The American Film Musical*, Rick Altman discusses the enlarged, orchestral arrangement used to highlight the second version of "Manhattan" (66).

17. This topic is discussed, among other places, in *Making Movies Black* by Thomas Cripps (178).

18. For a helpful distinction between *homosexual* and *homosocial* ("social bonds between persons of the same sex"), see Eve Kosofsky Sedgwick, "From *Between Men: English Literature and Male Homosocial Desire*" (2434–38).

19. In Hollywood, Larry gives a lavish party at his mansion at which Judy Garland and Mel Torme perform Rodgers and Hart songs. When the party ends at 4:00 A.M., Larry is clearly drunk, a surprise, perhaps, because he has been turning down drinks all through the party and has performed "I Wish I Were in Love Again" with Judy Garland without any sign of inebriation. In the earlier party in honor of Rodgers' departure for the world of children's wear—the occasion of his first meeting with Eileen McNeil—Larry wheels a baby carriage full of bootleg whiskey into the room. Perhaps we are supposed to translate these hints into a diagnosis that Hart is afflicted with acute alcoholism.

20. The contemporaneous reviewer in *Time* found Mickey Rooney "Outrageously cast as lyricist Hart," especially in his final moments on screen when we see him "tottering finally to a ludicrous death on a rain-pelted sidewalk" (59).

21. As was conventional at the time—even in the hagiographic *The Babe Ruth Story* (1948)—the Senator players wear unofficial, obviously bogus, uniforms in the spring training sequences, much in the way that TV commercials of the day identified products as "Brand X."

22. Regarding post-war gender construction in America, including wives' roles as moms in popular culture, see my article "Post-War Cultural Construction in *The Babe Ruth Story*."

23. Frederick Nolan writes, in a typical pas-

sage from *Lorenz Hart: A Poet on Broadway,* "From the summer of 1940, his disintegration had accelerated so alarmingly that even his closest friends, only too familiar with his alcoholic excesses, his erratic behavior, and his irresponsible way of life, were shocked. Word on the street was that Larry was drunk by noon, and that by night he was indulging in back-alley sex with anyone he could pick up" (287–88).

24. According to Stephen Citron's *Noel and Cole: The Sophisticates,* Orson Welles described the problem of writing a film script based on Cole Porter's life in this way: "The only suspense will be — will he or will he not accumulate ten million dollars?" (212).

25. George Eels quotes Porter's reaction to the script: "It ought to be good. None of it's true" (221).

26. Citron decisively says, "Although it is everywhere reported that he joined the French Foreign Legion, the truth is that this is a romantic figment of Porter's imagination" (6). Wilfred Sheed roguishly writes about the same issue, "If he could pretend to be straight, why not claim to have fought in the French Foreign Legion as well?" (99).

27. Peter Gammond would probably not be surprised at the screenwriters' efforts to punch up Kern's biography since he observes in *The Oxford Companion to Popular Music* that "[b]iographies of composers have nearly always proved to be somewhat embarrassing and of little service to their subject, the star chosen rarely managing a truthful portrait of someone as down-to-earth as a composer" (406).

28. Cary Grant, who was born January 18, 1904, was 42 at the time he played this Yale law student. In all fairness, we should acknowledge that it was Cole who wanted Grant in the starring role, just as Linda Porter chose Alexis Smith to play Linda in the film. See Eels, *The Life That He Led: A Biography of Cole Porter* (222) and Citron, *Noel and Cole: The Sophisticates* (212).

Chapter 8

1. See my *Intertextual Encounters in American Fiction, Film, and Popular Culture* (6).

2. In *A Dictionary of Narratology,* Gerald Prince follows the example of the structuralist literary critic Gerard Genette in explaining that a "metadiegetic" narrative is "a narrative embedded within another narrative, and more particularly, within the primary narrative" (50). In the current context this would mean a fictional, subsidiary, musical play or film embedded within the primary film narrative.

3. Jane Feuer writes, "Early musicals have embedded within them earlier or different versions of the same text..." (90). Obviously, the same may be said about later musicals.

4. Alpert does not list these "alterations." A few of the more obvious — all bowdlerizations of Porter's lyrics — are: the substitution of "latest report" for "*Kinsey* report" in "Too Darn Hot"; of "mother deigned" for "mother *had*" in "I Hate Men"; of "in a brawl" for "in the *dark*" in "I've Come to Wive It Wealthily in Padua."

5. Dana E. Aspinall says about one of the many plays intertextually related to *The Taming of the Shrew,* "*A Cure for a Scold* features several 'airs,' which certain characters break into at moments of crisis" (23). This, of course, does not make either Shakespeare's play or its possible source a "musical," but some justification for the modern musical adaptations may be glimpsed here nevertheless.

6. Charles Schwartz confirms the testimony of many that Cole Porter was initially very reluctant to attempt adapting Shakespeare (230–31).

7. While singing this number, Lilli looks nostalgically at photographs of herself with Fred in happier days. One photo shows them in costume for *Annie Get Your Gun.* This film (1950) starred Howard Keel — but not Kathryn Grayson — and was also directed by George Sidney.

8. Nick Roddick agrees, writing more generally, "The story ... is similar to the Roman comedies of Plautus, on which it is based..." (593).

9. See the supporting observation by Theophilus Lewis in his *America* review: "Since Plautus wrote for a coarse and lascivious audience, it comes as no surprise that the Shevelove-Gelbart script is sprinkled with prurient innuendoes..." (361).

10. See my discussion of Virgil's *Aeneid* in *Intertextual Encounters* (9–10, 19).

11. See Jane Feuer's discussion of bricolage, the theatrical activity "in which performers make use of props at hand, things perhaps intended for other ends, to create the imaginary world of the musical number" (4). She recommends especially some startlingly happy accidents in Astaire movies — in *The Hollywood Musical* (3–5).

12. In his review in *Commonweal,* Philip T. Hartung notes that the film "takes a sock at pretty musicals with its poetic shots of the hero

and heroine ... singing 'Lovely' which are lusciously satirized later by Mostel and Gifford" (104).

13. According to Gordon Willis Williams' *The Oxford Classical Dictionary*, music (*canticum*) constituted a significant part of the style in Plautus' plays (844), although it would be foolishly anachronistic to say that they were "musicals." As in the case of *A Cure for a Scold*, however, the suggestion is provocative.

14. Philip T. Hartung is generally well-disposed toward the film in his *Commonweal* review, but even he wishes that Lester and his film editor, John Victor Smith, "had shortened that long, long chariot chase." As Hartung generously explains, "Even funny slapstick chases can pall" (106).

15. In an early scene set in a club car, a male passenger says that Tony Hunter "was good 12 or 15 years ago," and Tony agrees: "He's washed up. Hasn't made a picture in three years.... That Tony Hunter's a has-been.... The funny thing about what you're saying, boys, is that it's perfectly true." In *The Hollywood Musical*, Jane Feuer perceptively observes, "In *The Band Wagon*, Astaire is demystified by being presented as a washed-out hoofer only to be remythicized by making a comeback" (115).

16. Fowley played the much-harried director in *Singin' in the Rain* the previous year.

17. John Mueller makes this point explicitly in *Astaire Dancing* (336).

18. According to the Who2 website "The Fosse Connection," Allen was still married to Liza Minnelli at the time of *Cabaret* and *Liza with a "Z,"* but the two were "separated" at the time.

19. Liza Minnelli's father, Vincente, illustrates this point cleverly in *The Band Wagon* when he follows the opening of Jeffrey Cordova's pretentious *Faust* with a full-screen cartoon illustration of an egg. Subsequent sequences show backers, performers and creators of this show in deep depression.

20. One is perhaps reminded of Tony Hunter's explosion during an equally trying rehearsal in *The Band Wagon*.

21. Based on "Bye Bye Love" by Boudleux Bryant, a 1957 hit for the Everly Brothers, this song—like "On Broadway" by Mann, Weil, Leiber and Stoller, a 1963 hit for The Drifters—shows Fosse's eagerness to incorporate rock songs as well as nostalgic tunes into the contemporary Hollywood musical.

22. In the *Princeton Encyclopedia of Poetry and Poetics,* Robert P. Falk and William Beare say that literary parody tends to "expose a certain literary school or mannerism which has hardened into conventionality" (601). The metadiegetic performances in *Singin' in the Rain* seem to have a similar intention.

23. While discussing films such as *Easter Parade* (music by Irving Berlin), *The Band Wagon* (music by Howard Dietz and Arthur Schwartz) and *Singin' in the Rain* (music by Arthur Freed and Nacio Herb Brown), Jane Feuer explains in *The Hollywood Musical*, "By inserting old songs into new narratives, the Hollywood musical could have the best of both generations" (97). She, understandably, does not connect this practice to intertextuality.

24. Christopher Ames observes that "the plot of the film is as much about dubbing as it is about singing, and the story becomes complexly implicated in the interplay between illusion and reality" (59).

25. Ames also explains: "But in one of those fine ironies of which demystifying Hollywood films always seem to be guilty, we actually hear the voice of Betty Royce dubbed for Reynolds.... Similarly, the scene that shows Kathy dubbing Lina's dialogue was actually done entirely by Jean Hagen..."(65).

26. In *The Hollywood Musical* Jane Feuer defines *genre* as "systematic intertextuality" (124).

27. Ames observes that "the songs in *Pennies from Heaven* ... make no attempt to cover up their artificiality" (98).

28. Christopher Ames writes about this absorption of Arthur into *Follow the Fleet*: "The scene shows vividly the power of movies as a medium of imaginative escape. But as a self-referential gesture, it forces us to question the larger film, *Pennies from Heaven*. Is that film endorsing the escape offered by movies and songs, the imaginative identification that puts Eileen and Arthur into the dancing shoes of Ginger and Fred? Or is the movie once again ironically framing movie as well as song to demystify that identification?" (104).

Chapter 9

1. See Jane Feuer's *The Hollywood Musical* (42–44) for an extended explanation of "demystification."

2. As David Bianculli writes in the *Dictionary of Teleliteracy*: "In the nineties, *Cop Rock* quickly attained the kind of 'flop' status accorded to few other TV series—*My Mother the Car* and *Supertrain* being two other quick ex-

amples—and that's how it's most likely to be remembered in the future" (75).

3. For an episode list and other useful information about the show, see the *Cop Rock* tv-tome web site.

4. An animated George Harrison provides an intertextual reference when he expresses boredom with this performance.

5. One helpful guide to past *Simpsons* episodes can be found at "*The Simpsons* Archive" web site.

6. The message board outside the church reads: "No Shirt, No Shoes, No Salvation."

7. For an episode list, scripts and other pertinent information concerning the show, see *Slayage: The Online International Journal of Buffy Studies*.

8. Some viewers may be reminded of George Roy Hill's use of this technique to create a turn-of-the-century atmosphere in *Butch Cassidy and the Sundance Kid* (1969).

9. Actually performed by Christine Aguilera, Li'l Kim, Mya and Pink on the soundtrack and in a very popular music video.

10. Whether viewers also choose to connect Luhrmann's version of "Roxanne" to Eddie Murphy's in *48 HRS.* (1982), is up to them.

11. See, for example, Elvis Mitchell's comment in his *New York Times* review: "This movie, choreographed by Mr. Marshall, may be accused of being inspired by Baz Luhrmann's *Moulin Rouge* (E42).

12. See William Wordsworth's "Preface to *Lyrical Ballads*" (253).

13. Carla Hay illustrates the monkey-see-monkey-do nature of the mass media when she writes, an August 29, 2003, article: "The success of the Academy Award-winning film *Chicago* has fueled a gold rush of musicals on more than just the big screen. A slew of made-for-TV musicals is set to premiere during the next year."

Works Cited

Adamowski, T. H. "Frank Sinatra: The Subject and His Music." *Journal of Popular Culture* 33.4 (Spring 2000): 1–11.
Adler, Renata. Review of *Finian's Rainbow*. *New York Times* 10 Oct. 1968: 59.
"AFI's 100 Years ... 100 Movies." http://www.afi.com/tv/movies.asp.
Alpert, Hollis. Review of *A Funny Thing Happened on the Way to the Forum*. *Saturday Review* 15 Oct. 1966: 26.
_____. Review of *Kiss Me Kate*. *Saturday Review* 14 Nov. 1953: 40.
Altman, Rick, ed. *The American Film Musical*. Bloomington: Indiana University Press, 1987.
_____. Introduction. *Genre: The Musical; A Reader*. Ed. Rick Altman. London: Routledge, 1981. 1–7.
Ames, Christopher. *Movies About the Movies: Hollywood Reflected*. Lexington: University of Kentucky Press, 1997.
Ansen, David. "Yes, *Rouge* Can, Can, Can." Review of *Moulin Rouge*. *Newsweek* 28 May 2001: 61.
Aristotle. *The Poetics. Criticism: Major Statements*. 4th ed. Ed. Charles Kaplan and William Anderson. New York: Bedford/St. Martin's, 2000. 19–46.
Arnold, Edwin T. "Abner Unpinned: Al Capp's *Li'l Abner*, 1940–1955." *Appalachian Journal* 24 (1997): 420–36.
_____. "Al, Abner, and Appalachia." *Appalachian Journal* 17 (1990): 272–75.
Aspinall, Dana E. "The Play and the Critics." *The Taming of the Shrew: Critical Essays*. Ed. Aspinall. New York and London: Routledge, 2002. 3–38.
Astaire, Fred. *Steps in Time*. New York: Harper, 1959.
Austen, Jane. *Pride and Prejudice*. Ed. James Kinsley and Frank W. Bradbrook. New York: Oxford University Press, 1980.
Auster, Albert. "The Hollywood Musical." *Political Companion to American Film*. Ed. Gary Crowdus. New York: Lakeview Press, 1994. 279–91.
Baker, Carlos. *Ernest Hemingway: A Life Story*. New York: Scribner, 1969.
Bakhtin, M. M. *The Dialogic Imagination*. Ed. Michael Holquist. Trans. Caryl Emerson and Michael Holquist. Austin: University of Texas Press, 1981.
_____. *Problems of Dostoevsky's Poetics*. Ed. and trans. Caryl Emerson. Minneapolis: University of Minnesota Press, 1984.
"Baltimore to Padua." Review of *Kiss Me Kate*. *Newsweek* 10 Jan. 1949: 72.
Banfield, Stephen. *Sondheim's Broadway Musicals*. Ann Arbor: University of Michigan Press, 1993.
Barlow, Bill. "Minstrelsy." *Encyclopedia of Southern Culture*. Ed. Charles Reagan Wilson and William Ferris. Chapel Hill: University of North Carolina Press, 1989. 1018–20.
Bawden, Liz-Anne, ed. *The Oxford Companion to Film*. New York: Oxford, 1976.
Baym, Nina, et al., eds. *The Norton Anthology of American Literature*. Shorter 5th ed. New York: Norton, 1999.

Bergman, Andrew. *We're in the Money: Depression America and Its Films*. New York: New York University Press, 1971.
Bianculli, David. *Dictionary of Teleliteracy: Television's 500 Biggest Hits, Misses, and Events*. New York: Continuum, 1996.
Bing Crosby's Minstrel Song Folio. New York: Mayfair Music, 1945.
Blau, Douglas. Review of *Manhattan*. *Magill's Survey of Cinema: English Language Films*. First series. Ed. Frank N. Magill. Englewood Cliffs NJ: Salem Press, 1980. 1067–69.
Bogle, Donald. *Blacks in American Films and Television: An Illustrated Encyclopedia*. New York: Simon & Schuster, 1988.
_____. *Toms, Coons, Mulattoes, Mammies, and Bucks: An Interpretive History of Blacks in American Films*. New York: Viking, 1973.
Boose, Linda E., and Richard Burt. "Totally Clueless: Shakespeare Goes Hollywood in the 1990s." *Shakespeare, the Movie: Popularizing the Plays on Film, TV, and Video*. Ed. Boose and Burt. London: Routledge, 1977. 8–22.
Bordman, Gerald. *Jerome Kern: His Life and Music*. New York: Oxford University Press, 1980.
Braudy, Leo. *The World in a Frame: What We See in Films*. Garden City NY: Doubleday, 1976.
Brecht, Bertolt. "The Modern Theatre Is the Epic Theatre." 1930. *Brecht on Theatre*. Trans. John Willett. New York: Hill and Wang, 1964. 33–42.
Brustein, Robert. "Vox Populi, Vox Box." Review of *A Funny Thing Happened on the Way to the Forum*. *The New Republic* 28 May 1962: 28–30.
Burr, Ty. "Life Lines." *Entertainment Weekly Special Oscar Guide 2002* 22 Feb. 2002: 30+.
Burt, Rob. *Rock and Roll: The Movies*. New York: New Orchard, 1986.
Canby, Vincent. "Fantasy of the 50's." Review of *Grease*. *New York Times* 16 June 1978: C10.
_____. Review of *A Funny Thing Happened on the Way to the Forum*. *New York Times* 17 Oct. 1966: 48.
Caplair, Larry, and Steven Englund. *The Inquisition in Hollywood: Politics in the Film Community 1930–1960*. New York: Anchor, 1980.
Carpenter, Frederick I. "Puritans Preferred Blondes: The Heroines of Melville and Hawthorne." *New England Quarterly* 9 (1936): 253–72.
Cash, W. J. *The Mind of the South*. New York: Knopf, 1940.
Casper, Joseph Andrew. *Vincente Minnelli and the Musical Film*. South Brunswick and New York: A. S. Barnes, 1977.
Cawelti, John G. *Adventure, Mystery, and Romance: Formula Stories as Art and Popular Culture*. 1976. Chicago: University of Chicago Press, 1977.
Christensen, Ann C. "Petruchio's House in Postwar Suburbia: Reinventing the Domestic Woman (Again)." *The Taming of the Shrew: Critical Essays*. Ed. Dana E. Aspinall. New York and London: Routledge, 2002. 333–50.
Chumo, Peter N., II. Review of *Moulin Rouge*. *Magill's Cinema Annual, 2002*. Ed. Christine Tomassini. Detroit: Gale, 2003. 335–37.
Citron, Stephen. *The Musical from the Inside Out*. Chicago: Elephant Paperbacks, 1997.
_____. *Noel and Cole: The Sophisticates*. New York: Oxford University Press, 1993.
Cohan, Steven. Introduction. *Hollywood Musicals: The Film Reader*. Ed. Cohan. New York: Routledge, 2002. 1–15.
"Cole Porter Tames a Shrew to Music in a Surefire Hit." *Life* 7 Feb. 1949: 99+.
Coleridge, Samuel Taylor. "Kubla Khan." *The Norton Anthology of Poetry*. 3rd ed. Ed. Alexander W. Allison et al. New York: Norton, 1983. 564–65.
Collins, James M. "The Musical." *Handbook of American Film Genres*. Ed. Wes D. Gehring. New York: Greenwood, 1988. 269–84.
Cop Rock. http://www.tvtome.com.
Cowie, Peter. *Coppola: A Biography*. New York: Da Capo, 1994.
Crane, R. S. "The Concept of Plot and the Plot of *Tom Jones*." 1952. *Critics and Criticism*. Abridged ed. Ed. Crane. Chicago: University of Chicago Press, 1957. 62–93.
Creekmur, Corey Knight. "Picturizing American Cinema: Hindi Film Songs and the Last Days of Genre." *Soundtrack Available: Essays on Film and Popular Music*. Ed. Pamela

Robertson Wojcik and Arthur Knight. Durham, NC: Duke University Press, 2001. 375–406.

Cripps, Thomas. *Making Movies Black: The Hollywood Message Movie from World War II to the Civil Rights Era.* New York: Oxford University Press, 1993.

_____. *Slow Fade to Black: The Negro in American Film, 1900–1942.* New York: Oxford University Press, 1977.

Croce, Arlene. *The Fred Astaire and Ginger Rogers Book.* New York: Outerbridge & Lazard, 1972.

Crowther, Bosley. Review of *Li'l Abner. New York Times* 12 Dec. 1959: 19.

_____. Review of *On the Town. New York Times* 9 Dec. 1949: 37.

_____. Review of *Sun Valley Serenade. New York Times* 6 Sept. 1941: sec. 6: 20.

Cunningham, James P. Review of *The Great Ziegfeld. The Commonweal* 17 Apr. 1936: 698.

Daly, Steve. "Chicago's Hope." *Entertainment Weekly* 17 Jan. 2003: 20–28.

Dempster, Elizabeth. "Women Writing the Body: Let's Watch a Little How She Dances." *Bodies of the Text: Dance as Theory, Literature as Dance.* Ed. Ellen W. Goellner and Jacqueline Shea Murphy. New Brunswick NJ: Rutgers University Press, 1995. 21–38.

Dryden, John. *All for Love; or, The World Well Lost.* Ed. Benjamin W. Griffith, Jr. Great Neck NY: Barron's, 1961.

Dunne, Michael. "Fred Astaire as Cultural Allusion." *Studies in Popular Culture* 16.2 (1994): 9–19.

_____. *Intertextual Encounters in American Fiction, Film, and Popular Culture.* Bowling Green OH: Bowling Green State University Popular Press, 2001.

_____. *Metapop: Self-referentiality in Contemporary American Popular Culture.* Jackson: University Press of Mississippi, 1992.

_____. "Postwar Cultural Construction in *The Babe Ruth Story.*" *Studies in Popular Culture* 19.1 (1996): 1–7.

Dyer, Richard. "The Colour of Entertainment." *Musicals: Hollywood and Beyond.* Ed. Bill Marshall and Robynn Stilwell. Exeter, England: intellect, 2000. 23–30.

_____. "Entertainment and Utopia." *Genre: The Musical.* Ed. Rick Altman. Boston: Routledge, 1981. 175–89.

Edwards, Anne. *Shirley Temple: American Princess.* New York: Morrow, 1988.

Eels, George. *The Life That He Led: A Biography of Cole Porter.* New York: G. P. Putnam's Sons, 1967.

Elrod, Bruce C. *Your Hit Parade and American Top Ten Hits, A Week-by-Week Guide to the Nation's Favorite Music, 1935–1994.* Ann Arbor MI: Popular Culture Ink, 1994.

Falk, R. P. "Parody." *Princeton Encyclopedia of Poetry and Poetics.* Enlarged ed. Ed. Alex Preminger et al. Princeton NJ: Princeton University Press, 1974. 600–02.

Farber, Manny. Review of *Yankee Doodle Dandy. The New Republic* 15 Jun. 1942: 831.

Farnsworth, Marjorie. *The Ziegfeld Follies.* New York: Putnam's, 1956.

Fehr, Richard, and Frederick G. Vogel. *Lullabies of Hollywood: Movie Music and the Movie Musical, 1915–1992.* Jefferson NC: McFarland, 1993.

Ferguson, Otis. Review of *The Great Ziegfeld. The New Republic* 13 May 1936: 18.

Feuer, Jane. *The Hollywood Musical.* 2nd ed. Bloomington and Indianapolis: Indiana University Press, 1993.

Fiedler, Leslie. *Love and Death in the American Novel.* New, rev. ed. New York: Dell Laurel, 1966.

Fitzgerald, F. Scott. *The Great Gatsby.* 1925. Ed. Matthew Bruccoli. *The Cambridge Edition of the Works of F. Scott Fitzgerald.* Cambridge: Cambridge University Press, 1991.

Flinn, Denny Martin. *Musical! A Grand Tour: The Rise, Glory, and Fall of an American Institution.* New York: Schirmer Books, 1997.

"The Fosse Connection." Who2.com/fosseconnection/htm.

Frank, Gerold. *Judy.* New York: Harper & Row, 1975.

Frye, Northrop. *Anatomy of Criticism: Four Essays.* 1957. Princeton NJ: Princeton University Press, 1971.

Gammond, Peter. *The Oxford Companion to Popular Music.* New York: Oxford University Press, 1993.
Gerster, Patrick, and Nicholas Cords. "Northern Mythmaking." *Encyclopedia of Southern Culture.* Ed. Charles Reagan Wilson and William Ferris. Chapel Hill: University of North Carolina Press, 1989. 1115–16.
Gibbs, Wolcott. Review of *Kiss Me Kate. The New Yorker* 8 Jan. 1949: 50–52.
Giddins, Gary. *Bing Crosby: A Pocket Full of Dreams, The Early Years, 1903–1940.* Boston: Little, Brown, 2001.
Glenn Miller and His Orchestra: A Legendary Performer. BMG, 1991.
Goodwin, Michael, and Naomi Wise. *On the Edge: The Life and Times of Francis Coppola.* New York: Morrow, 1989.
Green, Stanley. *Hollywood Musicals, Year By Year.* Milwaukee: Hal Leonard, 1990.
Hall, Mordaunt. Review of *Stand Up and Cheer. New York Times* 20 Apr. 1934: 17.
Hamburger, Philip. Review of *Three Little Words. The New Yorker* 26 Aug. 1950: 82.
Harmon, William, and C. Hugh Holman. *A Handbook to Literature.* 9th ed. Upper Saddle River NJ: Prentice Hall, 2003.
Hartung, Philip T. Review of *A Funny Thing Happened on the Way to the Forum. Commonweal* 28 Oct. 1966: 104, 106.
———. Review of *Kiss Me Kate. The Commonweal* 20 Nov. 1953: 164.
———. Review of *Yankee Doodle Dandy. The Commonweal* 19 Jun. 1942: 207.
Hatch, Robert. Review of *On the Town. New Republic* 26 Dec. 1949: 23.
Haverly, Jack. *Negro Minstrels: A Complete Guide.* 1902. Upper Saddle River, NJ: Literature House, 1969.
Hay, Carla. "Made-for-TV Musicals Aim to Build on Success of *Chicago.*" *The (Nashville) Tennessean* 29 Aug. 2003: 5D.
Henley, Don. "All She Wants to Do Is Dance." *Building the Perfect Beast.* Geffen, 1984.
Hirschhorn, Clive. *The Hollywood Musical.* New York: Portland House, 1991.
Hotchner, A. E. *Papa Hemingway: A Personal Memoir.* New York: Random House, 1966.
Hyland, William G. *Richard Rodgers.* New Haven: Yale University Press, 1998.
Inge, M. Thomas. *Comics as Culture.* Jackson: University Press of Mississippi, 1990.
"The Internet Movie Database." htttp://imdb.com.
Jameson, Fredric. *Postmodernism, Or, The Cultural Logic of Late Capitalism.* Durham NC: Duke University Press, 1991.
Johnson, Robert K. *Francis Ford Coppola.* Boston: Twayne, 1977.
"King Mongkut of Siam." http://www.royalty.nu/Asia/thailand/Monghut.html.
Knight, Arthur. *Disintegrating the Musical: Black Performance and American Musical Film.* Durham NC: Duke University Press, 2002.
Lahr, John. "Postscript: Adolph Green." *The New Yorker* 4 Nov. 2002: 49.
Landon, Margaret. *Anna and the King of Siam.* New York: John Day, 1944.
Lane, Anthony. "Fantasyland." Review of *Chicago. The New Yorker* 6 Jan. 2003: 90–91.
"Larry Parks in Red Face." *Newsweek* 2 Apr. 1951: 21.
Leonard, John. Review of *Cop Rock. New York* 10 Sept. 1990: 42–43.
Lewis, Theophilus. Review of *A Funny Thing Happened on the Way to the Forum. America* 2 June 1962: 360–61.
Lott, Eric. "Blackface and Blackness: The Minstrel Show in American Culture." *Inside the Minstrel Mask: Readings in Nineteenth-Century Blackface Minstrelsy.* Ed. Annemarie Bean, James V. Hatch and Brooks McNamara. Hanover and London: Wesleyan University Press, 1996. 3–32.
Lowes, John Livingston. *The Road to Xanadu: A Study in the Ways of Imagination.* Boston: Houghton Mifflin, 1927.
Macek, Carl. Review of *Yolanda and the Thief. Magill's Survey of Cinema: English Language Films, Second Series.* Ed. Frank N. Magill. Englewood Cliffs NJ: Salem Press, 1981. 2731–33.
MacKinnon, Kenneth. "'I Keep Wishing I Were Somewhere Else': Space and Fantasies of Freedom in the Hollywood Musical." *Musicals: Hollywood and Beyond.* Ed. Bill Marshall and Robynn Stilwell. Exeter, England: intellect, 2000. 40–46.

Mahar, William J. *Behind the Burnt Cork Mask: Early Blackface Minstrelsy and Antebellum American Culture.* Urbana and Chicago: University of Illinois Press, 1999.
Maher, James T. Introduction. *American Popular Song: The Great Innovators, 1900–1950.* By Alec Wilder. New York: Oxford University Press, 1972. xxiii–xxxix.
Marshall, Bill, and Robynn Stilwell. Introduction. *Musicals: Hollywood and Beyond.* Exeter, England: intellect, 2000. 1–4.
Martin, Wallace. *Recent Theories of Narrative.* Ithaca NY: Cornell University Press, 1986.
Maslin, Janet. Review of *Xanadu. New York Times* 9 Aug. 1980: 10.
McBrien, William. *Cole Porter: A Biography.* New York: Knopf, 1999.
McCarten, John. Review of *Words and Music. The New Yorker* 18 Dec. 1948: 102.
McClelland, Doug. *Blackface to Blacklist: Al Jolson, Larry Parks, and "The Jolson Story."* Lanham MD: Scarecrow Press, 1998.
McCracken, Allison. "Real Men Don't Sing Ballads: The Radio Crooner in Hollywood, 1929–1933." *Soundtrack Available: Essays on Film and Popular Music.* Ed. Pamela Robertson Wojcik and Arthur Knight. Durham NC: Duke University Press, 2001. 105–33.
McGee, Mark Thomas. *Faster and Furiouser: The Revised and Fattened Fable of American International Pictures.* Jefferson NC: McFarland, 1996.
Mellencamp, Patricia. "The Sexual Economics of *Gold Diggers of 1933.*" *Close Viewings: An Anthology of New Film Criticism.* Ed. Peter Lehman. Tallahassee: The Florida State University Press, 1990. 177–99.
Minnelli, Vincente, with Hector Arce. *I Remember It Well.* Foreword by Alan Jay Lerner. New York: Doubleday, 1974.
Mitchell, Elvis. "*Chicago*, Bare Legs and All, Makes It to Film." Review of *Chicago. New York Times* 27 Dec. 2002: E1, E42.
Mitchell, Robert. Review of *Bye Bye Birdie. Magill's Survey of Cinema, English Language Films, Second Series.* Ed. Frank N. Magill. Englewood Cliffs NJ: Salem Press, 1981. 375–78.
———. Review of *Grease. Magill's Survey of Cinema, English Language Films, Second Series.* Ed. Frank N. Magill. Englewood Cliffs NJ: Salem Press, 1981. 918–22.
Morehouse, Ward. *George M. Cohan: Prince of the American Theater.* 1943. Westport CT: Greenwood, 1972.
The Motion Picture Guide: E–G, 1927–1983. Ed. Jay Robert Nash and Stanley Ralph Ross. Chicago: Cinebooks, 1986.
Mueller, John. *Astaire Dancing: The Musical Films.* New York: Wings Books, 1985.
Mulvey, Laura. "Visual Pleasure and Narrative Cinema." *The Norton Anthology of Theory and Criticism.* Ed. Vincent B. Leitch et al. New York: Norton, 2001. 2181–92.
Myrdal, Gunnar, with Richard Sterner and Arnold Rose. *An American Dilemma: The Negro Problem and Modern Democracy.* New York: Harper, 1944.
Nachbar, Jack, and Kevin Lause. "Would You Repeat That — Please!: The Meaningful Delights of Formula in the Popular Arts." *Popular Culture: An Introductory Text.* Ed. Nachbar and Lause. Bowling Green OH: Bowling Green State University Popular Press, 1992. 414–29.
Nachman, Gerald. *Seriously Funny: The Rebel Comedians of the 1950s and 1960s.* New York: Pantheon, 2003.
Naremore, James. *The Films of Vincente Minnelli.* New York: Cambridge University Press, 1993.
Nathan, Hans. *Dan Emmett and the Rise of Early Negro Minstrelsy.* Norman: University of Oklahoma Press, 1962.
"Neo-Roman Holiday." Review of *A Funny Thing Happened on the Way to the Forum. Time* 21 May 1962: 85.
"New Musical in Manhattan." Review of *Kiss Me Kate. Time* 10 Jan. 1949: 36+.
Nolan, Frederick. *Lorenz Hart: A Poet on Broadway.* New York: Oxford University Press, 1994.
Osgerby, Bill. *Playboys in Paradise: Masculinity, Youth and Leisure-style in Modern America.* New York: Oxford, 2001.
Peretti, Burton W. *Jazz in American Culture.* Chicago: Ivan R. Dee, 1997.

Perrault, Charles. "Cinderella; or, The Little Glass Slipper." *Perrault's Fairy Tales*. Trans. A. E. Johnson. New York: Dover, 1969. 65–78.
Phillips, William H. *Film: An Introduction*. Boston and New York: Bedford/St. Martin's, 1999.
Porter, Cole. "Stereophonic Sound." *Silk Stockings*. RCA, 1957.
Prince, Gerald. *A Dictionary of Narratology*. Lincoln: University of Nebraska Press, 1987.
Prouty, Howard H. Review of *West Side Story*. *Magill's Survey of Cinema, English Language Films, First Series*. Ed. Frank Magill. Englewood Cliffs NJ: Salem Press, 1980. 1826–29.
Reid, Mark A. *Redefining Black Film*. Berkeley: University of California Press, 1993.
Review of *Bye Bye Birdie*. Dir. George Sidney. *New York Times* 5 Apr. 1963: 27.
Review of *Cop Rock*. 26 Sept. 1990. *Variety and Daily Variety Television Reviews*. Vol. 16. 1989-90. New York: Garland, 1992.
Review of *Finian's Rainbow*. *Variety* 9 Oct. 1968. *Variety's Film Reviews, 1968–1970*.
Review of *A Funny Thing Happened on the Way to the Forum*. *Variety* 20 Sept. 1966. *Variety's Film Reviews, 1964–1967*.
Review of *Golddiggers of 1933*. *Variety* 13 June 1933. *Variety's Film Reviews, 1930–1933*.
Review of *The Great Ziegfeld*. *New York Times* 9 Apr. 1936: 21.
Review of *The Great Ziegfeld*. *Newsweek* 18 Apr. 1936: 29.
Review of *The Great Ziegfeld*. *Time* 20 Apr. 1936: 47–48.
Review of *The Great Ziegfeld*. *Variety* 15 Apr. 1936. *Variety's Film Reviews, 1934–1937*.
Review of *Holiday Inn*. *Variety* 17 June 1942. *Variety's Film Reviews, 1938–1942*.
Review of *Kiss Me Kate*. *Newsweek* 9 Nov. 1953: 96+.
Review of *Kiss Me Kate*. *Time* 16 Nov. 1953: 106.
Review of *Li'l Abner*. *Newsweek* 21 Dec. 1959: 92+.
Review of *Li'l Abner*. *Time* 21 Dec. 1959: 57.
Review of *Mississippi*. *New York Times* 18 Apr. 1935. *New York Times Film Reviews, 1932–1938*. New York: Arno, 1970. 27.
Review of *On the Town*. *Newsweek* 19 Dec. 1949: 76.
Review of *On the Town*. *Time* 2 Jan. 1950: 64.
Review of *Stand Up and Cheer*. 24 Apr. 1934. *Variety's Film Reviews, 1934–1937*.
Review of *Sun Valley Serenade*. *Newsweek* 1 Sept. 1941: 49–50.
Review of *Sun Valley Serenade*. *The New Republic* 20 Oct. 1941: 508.
Review of *Three Little Words*. *Newsweek* 14 Aug. 1950: 82.
Review of *West Side Story*. 27 Sept. 1961. *Variety's Film Reviews, 1959–1963*.
Review of *Words and Music*. *Newsweek* 13 Dec. 1948: 91+.
Review of *Words and Music Time* 27 Dec. 1948: 5.
Review of *Xanadu*. *Variety* 13 Aug. 1980. *Variety's Film Reviews, 1978–1980*.
Review of *Yankee Doodle Dandy*. *New York Times* 30 May 1942: 9.1.
Review of *Yankee Doodle Dandy*. *Time* 6 Jun. 1942: 86–87.
Review of *Yankee Doodle Dandy*. *Variety* 3 Jun. 1942. *Variety's Film Reviews, 1938–1942*.
Roddick, Nick. Review of *A Funny Thing Happened on the Way to the Forum*. *Magill's Survey of Cinema: English Language Films, First Series*. Ed. Frank Magill. Englewood Cliffs NJ: Salem Press, 1980. 592–95.
Rodgers, Richard. *Musical Stages: An Autobiography*. New York: Random House, 1975.
Rogin, Michael. *Black Face/White Noise: Jewish Immigrants in the Hollywood Melting Pot*. Berkeley: University of California Press, 1996.
Roland, Charles P. "The South of the Agrarians." *A Band of Prophets: The Vanderbilt Agrarians After Fifty Years*. Ed. William C. Havard and Walter Sullivan. Baton Rouge: Louisiana State University Press, 1982. 19–39.
Roosevelt, Franklin Delano. "Second Inaugural Address." *Nothing to Fear: The Selected Addresses of Franklin Delano Roosevelt, 1932–1945*. Ed. B. D. Zevin. Cambridge: Houghton Mifflin, 1946. 87–92.
Roth, Mark. "Some Warners Musicals and the Spirit of the New Deal." *Genre: The Musical*. Ed. Rick Altman. Boston: Routledge, 1981. 41–56.

Rourke, Constance. *American Humor: A Study of the National Character*. New York: Harcourt Brace, 1931.
Rubin, Martin. "Busby Berkeley and the Backstage Musical." *Hollywood Musicals: The Film Reader*. Ed. Steven Cohan. New York: Routledge, 2002. 53–61.
Rutsky, R. L. "Surfing the Other: Ideology on the Beach." *Film Quarterly* (Summer 1999): 12–23.
Saidy, Fred, and E. Y. Harburg. *Finian's Rainbow: A Musical Satire*. Burton Lane, composer. *Theatre Arts* Jan. 1949: 55–76.
"*Saturday Night Live* Information & Biography Center." http://snl.jt.org/season/index.phtml.
Schatz, Thomas. *The Genius of the System: Hollywood Filmmaking in the Studio Era*. New York: Pantheon, 1988.
Schwartz, Charles. *Cole Porter: A Biography*. New York: Dial, 1977.
Sedgwick, Eve Kosofsky. "From *Between Men: English Literature and Male Homosocial Desire*." *The Norton Anthology of Theory and Criticism*. Ed. Vincent B. Leitch et al. New York: Norton, 2001. 2434–38.
Seiler, Andy. "*Chicago* Taps into Hollywood's Dreams." *USA Today* 5 Feb. 2003: 1D, 6D.
Shakespeare, William. *Romeo and Juliet*. *The Complete Works*. Ed. Charles Jasper Sisson. New York: Harper & Row, 1953. 876–909.
———. *The Taming of the Shrew*. *The Complete Works*. Ed. Charles Jasper Sisson. New York: Harper & Row, 1953. 292–321.
Shary, Timothy. *Generational Multiplex: The Image of Youth in Contemporary American Cinema*. Foreword by David Considine. Austin: University of Texas Press, 2002.
Sheed, Wilfred. "Under His Skin." *The New Yorker* 23 Nov. 1998: 96–101.
"*The Simpsons* Archive." http://www.snpp.com/.
Sklar, Robert. *Movie-Made America: A Cultural History of American Movies*. New York: Vintage, 1975.
Slayage: The Online International Journal of Buffy Studies. http://www.slayage.tv/.
Stanfield, Peter. "From the Vulgar to the Refined: American Vernacular and Blackface Minstrelsy in *Showboat*." *Musicals: Hollywood and Beyond*. Ed. Bill Marshall and Robynn Stilwell. Exeter, England: intellect, 2000. 147–56.
Steppenwolf. "Born to be Wild." *Steppenwolf*. ABC/Dunhill, 1968.
Taylor, John Russell, and Arthur Jackson. *The Hollywood Musical*. New York: McGraw-Hill, 1971.
Thomas, Bob. *Astaire: The Man, The Dancer*. New York: St Martin's, 1984.
Tosches, Nick. *Where Dead Voices Gather*. Boston: Little, Brown, 2001.
Twain, Mark. *Adventures of Huckleberry Finn*. Ed. Hamlin Hill. Centennial Facsimile Edition. New York: Harper & Row, 1987.
———. *The Autobiography of Mark Twain*. Ed. Charles Neider. New York: Harper, 1959.
Variety's Film Reviews. 20 vols. New York: R. R. Bowker, 1983.
Ward, Ed, Geoffrey Stokes, and Ken Tucker. *Rock of Ages: The* Rolling Stone *History of Rock and Roll*. Intro. Jann S. Wenner. New York: Rolling Stone Press, 1986.
Ward, Geoffrey C. *Jazz: A History of America's Music*. New York: Knopf, 2000.
Whitburn, Joel. *Joel Whitburn's Pop Singles Annual, 1955–1990*. Menomonee Falls WI: Record Research, 1991.
Whitman, Walt. "Crossing Brooklyn Ferry." *The Portable Walt Whitman*. Ed. Mark Van Doren. Rev. and enl. ed. New York: Viking, 1974. 149–56.
W[illiams], G[ordon] W[illis]. "Contaminatio." *The Oxford Classical Dictionary*. 2nd ed. Ed. N. G. L. Hammond and H. H. Scullard. Oxford: Clarendon Press, 1970. 286.
———. "Plautus." *The Oxford Classical Dictionary*. 2nd ed. Ed. N. G. L. Hammond and H. H. Scullard. Oxford: Clarendon Press, 1970. 843–45.
Williamson, J. W. *Hillbillyland: What the Movies Did to the Mountains and What the Mountains Did to the Movies*. Chapel Hill: University of North Carolina Press, 1995.
Wloszczyna, Susan. "A 'Rouge' Awakening for Movie Musicals." *USA Today* 8 Mar. 2002: 13D–14D.

Wordsworth, William. "Preface to *Lyrical Ballads*." *Criticism: Major Statements*. 4th ed. Ed. Charles Kaplan and William Anderson. New York: Bedford/St. Martin's, 2000. 241–56.

Yudkoff, Alvin. *Gene Kelly: A Life of Dance and Dreams*. New York: Back Stage Books, 1999.

Index

Adamowski, T.H. 191
Afer, Publius Terentius 73, 192
Albert, Eddie 83
All That Jazz 5, 10–11, 148, 159–163, 168, 171, 184–185
Allen, Peter 160
Allen, Woody 193, 195
Allyson, June 54
Alpert, Hollis 149, 156, 198
Altman, Rick 3–5, 15, 20, 25, 88, 90, 99, 107–108, 113, 115, 127, 146, 158, 160–162, 172, 189, 192, 195, 197
Alvarez, Carmen 100
American Film Institute 4, 164, 187, 196
American Graffiti 63, 187, 192
An American in Paris 5, 165, 187
Ames, Christopher 2, 15, 90, 111, 164–165, 169, 171–172, 189, 199
Amsterdam, Morey 60, 62
Andre, Annette 154
Anna and the King of Siam 75, 148, 193
Ann-Margaret 55–58, 65, 200
Ansen, David 183
Arden, Eve 64
Arnold, Edwin T. 99, 194
Asher, William 58, 60, 65, 122
Aspinall, Dana E. 149, 198
Astaire, Fred 1–6, 9, 11, 15, 20, 34–35, 37, 41–43, 46, 51, 53, 61, 68–69, 72, 74, 78–81, 108–112, 116–117, 120–123, 125, 136, 151, 158–159, 162, 165, 170, 184, 186–190, 192–193, 195–196, 198–199
Auster, Albert 100, 148, 187, 195
Avalon, Frankie 53, 58, 60, 62–63, 65, 191
Aykroyd, Dan 63

Babes in Arms 7, 34–35, 37, 39–40, 42–44, 47, 148, 156, 173, 179, 190
Babes on Broadway 7, 39–44, 148, 164

Bakhtin, M.M. 8, 14, 20, 24–25, 106, 188, 193, 195
Bamboozled 7, 35, 42, 189
The Band Wagon 10, 109, 115, 148, 156, 159, 161, 164–165, 167, 175, 199
Banfield, Stephen 153
Bari, Lynn 92
Barlow, Bill 34
Barneris, Vernel 168
Barty, Billy 19–20
Battle, Hinton 179
Bawden, Liz-Anne 1
Baxter, Warner 25–32, 189
Beach Party 7, 58, 60–62, 65, 122
Beare, William 199
Beatles 62
Beck, Michael 122–123, 125
The Belle of New York 87, 158
Belushi, John 63
Bemelmans, Ludwig 110
Beneke, Tex 92
Bennett, Joan 94–95
Benson, Amber 179
Bergman, Andrew 4–5, 188–189
Berkeley, Busby 2–3, 11, 15, 17, 19–22, 30, 39–40, 54, 78, 124, 129, 146, 155, 183, 188–190, 193
Berle, Milton 91, 93–94, 193
Berlin, Irving 74, 128, 130, 199
Bernstein, Leonard 101–102
Berry, Chuck 53, 55, 61
Best, Willie 46, 99, 182, 190
Bianculli, David 199
Bikini Beach 7, 60–65
Blair, Henry 132
Blau, Douglas 195
Blondell, Joan 17–19, 21–23, 64
Blue Hawaii 8
Bochco, Stephen 175
Bogle, Donald 28, 35

209

Bolger, Ray 129
Boone, Pat 57
Boose, Linda E. 151
Bosson, Barbara 176
Braudy, Leo 85–86, 188, 192
Brecht, Bertolt 181
Breen, Joseph I. 2, 171, 187
Brendon, Nicholas 179
Brigadoon 9, 108, 110, 114–118, 120, 123–125, 147, 184, 195
Broadbent, Jim 183
Brown, Nacio Herb 165, 199
Brown, Sam 170
Bruce, Virginia 129
Brustein, Robert 154
Bryant, Boudleaux 199
Brynner, Yul 75, 77, 179
Buchanan, Jack 159
Buffy the Vampire Slayer 10, 175, 179
Burr, Ty 197
Burt, Bob 57, 151, 153
Burt, Richard 151
Bye Bye Birdie 7, 55, 57–58, 60–65, 72, 147, 162, 177

Cabaret 5, 11, 160, 199
Caesar, Sid 64
Cagney, James 130, 132–133, 135, 197
Cagney, Jeanne 132
Canby, Vincent 64, 154, 191
Cantor, Eddie 36, 128
Capp, Al 88, 99–100, 148, 194
Capra, Frank 107
Carefree 7, 54, 67, 79, 81, 85, 113
Carousel 8
Carpenter, Frederick I. 190
Cash, W.J. 94–96, 100, 190
Casper, Joseph Andrew 79, 85, 108, 187, 192, 195
Caulfield, Emma 179
Cawelti, John G. 43–44, 52, 79
Chakiris, George 103
Channing, Stockard 64–65
Checker, Chubby 63, 192
Chicago 10–11, 31, 87, 127, 160, 168, 174, 183–187, 200
Chumo, Peter N. 183
Ciccone, Madonna 182–184
Citron, Stephen 1, 144, 198
Clark, Petula 117–118, 120–122, 196
Coal Miner's Daughter 5
Cohan, George M. 9, 126, 130–135, 139, 144, 146, 164, 188, 196–197
Cohan Steven 188
Colby, Ronald 118
Cole, Nat 182

Coleridge, Samuel Taylor 122, 196
Collins, James M. 3, 15, 17, 24, 118, 164, 185, 189
Comden, Betty 101–102, 164, 167
Contours 70
Cop Rock 10, 175–177, 185, 199–200
Coppola, Francis Ford 108, 117–122, 125, 196
Cords, Nicholas 96–97
Crane, R.S. 67–68
Crawford, Michael 154
Creekmur, Corey K. 192
Cripps, Thomas 37, 46, 197
Crosby, Bing 7, 29, 34–35, 40, 42, 44–46, 50–51, 94–96, 109, 125, 163, 170–171, 190
Crowther, Bosley 94, 100, 194
Cummings, Bob 60–62, 65
Curtiz, Michael 107

Daly, Steve 174, 184–185
Damn Yankees 195
Dandridge, Dorothy 93
Daniels, Henry H. 88
Davenport, Harry 90
De Camp, Rosemary 132
Demarest, William 48
de Mille, Agnes 83–84, 193
Dempster, Elizabeth 85–86
diegesis 10, 13, 17–23, 28–29, 31–32, 43, 70, 74, 81, 83–85, 92–93, 103, 106, 109, 112, 120, 122–123, 125, 129, 132, 135–137, 143–145, 148, 150–151, 156, 158–161, 163–165, 170, 175–176, 178–179, 181–182, 184–186, 189
Dietz, Howard 158, 198–199
Dirty Dancing 7, 67, 69–73, 85
Dixie 7, 44–47, 49–50, 148, 190
Donen, Stanley 100, 164, 168, 179, 195
Dorsey, Tommy 54
Doyle, Buddy 128
Drake, Tom 88, 135, 139
Drifters 199
Dryden, John 21, 109, 188
Dunn, James 26–28, 30, 169, 189
Dunne, Michael 193, 198
Durant, Jack 28–29, 31–32
Durante, Jimmie 29
Dyer, Richard 15, 17, 24, 37, 42, 189

Easter Parade 151, 158, 167, 193, 199
Eastwood, Clint 175, 177
Eddy, Nelson 168
Edwards, Anne 188
Eels, George 142, 198
Endless Summer 61
Evans, Madge 26, 30–32
Everly Brothers 199

Fabray, Nanette 159
Falk, Robert P. 199
Farnsworth, Marjorie 130, 196
Faye, Alice 1
Fehr, Richard 24, 164, 187, 189
Ferguson, Otis 128, 130
Feuer, Jane 1–4, 14–15, 26, 38, 43, 83–84, 126, 128, 132–134, 151, 156, 174, 187, 191–192, 195–199
Fiddler on the Roof 5
Fiedler, Leslie 190
Fields, Dorothy 42, 189
Fields, W.C. 1, 42, 94–96, 109, 189
Finkelstein, William M. 175
Fisher, Carrie 63
Fitzgerald, F. Scott 189
Flinn, Denny Martin 53, 64–65, 191
Flying Down to Rio 158
Foldi, Erzsebet 160
Follow the Fleet 170, 199
Foran, Nick 26, 29–31
42nd Street 3–4, 188
Fosse, Bob 10–11, 159–164, 184–185, 199
Fowley, Douglas 158
Foy, Eddie, Jr. 46
Frank, Gerold 190
Franks, Don 118, 121–122, 193, 195–196
Freed, Arthur 3–5, 11, 53, 112, 165, 167, 190, 195, 199
Freeman, Howard 54
Friday, Pat 92
Froos, Sylvia 29, 32
Frye, Northrop 85, 192–193
Fun in Acapulco 8
Funicello, Annette 58, 60–65, 154, 191
A Funny Thing Happened on the Way to the Forum 10, 147, 153–156

Gammond, Peter 11, 44, 173, 189, 198
Garland, Judy 1, 6–7, 11, 34, 37–40, 43, 51, 53, 55, 68, 71, 87–88, 90, 109, 123, 143, 151, 190, 192, 197
Garner, Jay 168
Garrett, Betty 49, 63, 101–103, 138
Gear, Luella 81
Gelbart, Larry 153, 198
Gellar, Sarah Michelle 10, 175, 179–181, 200
Genette, Gerard 198
Gentlemen Prefer Blondes 182
Gere, Richard 184–186
Gershwin, George 53–54, 69, 72, 109, 130, 165, 192, 195
Gerster, Patrick 96–97
Gibbs, Wolcott 148
Giddins, Gary 34, 44, 50, 194
Gigi 5

Gilbert, W.S. 26
Gilford, Jack 154–155
Gillingwater, Claude 94–95
Girl Crazy 7–8, 53, 55, 147, 180, 192
Les Girls 146
Gleason, James 39–40, 42, 46
Golddiggers of 1933 2, 6, 11, 15, 17, 20, 24–27, 33, 52, 95, 106, 148, 156, 163, 168–170, 173, 185, 188
Goodwin, Bill 48, 196
Gorman, Cliff 160, 162
Gowanker, Ashutosh 188
Grant, Cary 55, 142, 146, 198
Grayson, Kathryn 68, 76, 94, 96–97, 100, 145, 150–151, 198
Grease 2, 7, 54, 63–66, 147, 187, 191
The Great Ziegfeld 9, 126–128, 132, 135, 137, 146, 148, 162, 167, 195–196
Green, Adolph 17, 101–102, 111, 148, 164, 167
Green, Jane 111
Green, Stanley 17
Green Grow the Lilacs 148
Greenwald, Robert 108

Hagen, Jean 164, 199
Hall, Mordaunt 26, 28
Hamburger, Philip 136
Hannigan, Alyson 180
Harburg, E.Y. 39, 117–118, 120
Harmon, William 87–88, 137, 197
Harper, Jessica 169
Harris, Sam H. 131–132, 134, 139
Harrison, George 200
Hart, Lorenz 9, 52, 94, 96, 126, 135–136, 138–140, 142–143, 146, 160, 184–186, 190, 194, 197–198
Hartung, Philip T. 132, 149, 198–199
Hatch, Robert 194
Haverly, Jack 190
Hay, Carla 200
Hays, Will H. 13, 33, 92–93
Head, Anthony Stewart 179
Heflin, Van 142–143, 145
Held, Anna 127–128
Hello, Dolly! 5
Hemingway, Ernest 93–94
Henie, Sonja 3, 9, 88, 91–93, 193
High Society 146
Hirschhorn, Clive 3, 47–48, 87–88, 92, 100, 114–115, 130, 135–136, 155, 159, 162, 173, 191, 194–196
Hoctor, Harriet 69, 130, 192, 196
Holiday Inn 7, 35, 40–44, 46, 50, 125, 148, 159, 163
Holland, Anthony 161
Holland, Joan 129

Holman, C. Hugh 87–88, 137, 197
homosociality 138–140, 143, 197
Hordern, Michael 155
Horton, Edward Everett 68–69, 73–75, 155, 158
Hotchner, A.E. 94
Hughes, Langston 191
Hull, Henry 39, 42
Humberstone, Bruce 91, 193
Hurston, Ted 97
Huston, Walter 132
Hyer, Martha 60, 62, 191
Hyland, William G. 193

Inge, M. Thomas 99
intertextuality 9, 147, 151, 172, 198

Jameson, Fredric 2
The Jazz Singer 3–4, 44, 47, 49, 186–187, 190–191
Johnson, Robert K. 117, 125
Johnson, Van 64, 115–116, 143
Jolson, Al 3, 7, 34, 44, 47–51, 148, 186, 191
The Jolson Story 7, 44, 47, 49–51, 148

Kalmer, Bert 9, 143, 146
Kane, Irene 161
Karloff, Boris 62
Kaye, Stubby 99
Kazner, Kurt 150
Keel, Howard 68, 150–151, 153, 198
Keeler, Ruby 17–18, 47–48, 171, 188, 191
Kelly, Gene 1, 4–5, 9, 11, 53, 78, 100–102, 108–109, 115, 120, 122–125, 139, 163–165, 168, 184, 186, 195–196
Kern, Jerome 9, 42, 126, 129, 131, 140–146, 155, 189, 198
Kibbee, Guy 20–22, 55, 188
Kidd, Michael 100, 194
Kidman, Nicole 182–184
King, Wright 118
The King and I 5, 7, 11, 67, 75, 78–79, 85, 147–148, 170
Kiss Me Kate 10, 146–148
Knight, Arthur 34–35, 43, 46, 50, 71, 83, 189–191
Knight, Shirley 83–85, 193
Knight, Wayne 71
Kohler, Fred 94
Koman, Jacek 183
Kosofsky, Eve 197
Kubler-Ross, Elisabeth 162

Lamour, Dorothy 45–46
Landon, Margaret 75, 148
Lane, Anthony 174–175
Lane, Burton 42, 117–118, 150–151, 174–175

Larkin, John 96
Lause, Kevin 97, 193
Lee, Spike 7, 35, 40, 42, 49, 66, 175, 177, 192
Leguizamo, John 181–183
Leigh, Janet 48, 55, 58, 137
Lembeck, Harvey 60, 62
Leroy, Mervyn 15
Les Girls 146
Leslie, Joan 132
Lester, Richard 154–156
Levant, Oscar 159
Lewis, Theophilus 198
Linn, Bambi 83–84
Lithgow, John 163
Lott, Eric 189
Lowes, John Livingston 196
Lucas, George 107, 188
Luhrmann, Baz 181–183, 185, 195, 200
Lynde, Paul 55, 58, 64

MacDonald, Jeanette 168
Macek, Carl 113
MacKinnon, Kenneth 188
MacMahon, Aline 17–19, 21–22, 169
MacRae, Gordon 83–85
Madonna *see* Ciccone, Madonna
Mahar, William J. 35
Maher, James T. 52
Main, Marjorie 88
Malone, Dorothy 60–61, 122–123
Manning, Irene 133–134
Marks, Joe E. 100
Marshall, Bill 1
Marshall, Rob 183–186, 200
Martin, Steve 48, 168
Martin, Tony 145
Martin, Wallace 85
Marvin, Lee 175, 177
Marx Brothers 1
Maslin, Janet 196
McBrien, William 153
McCarten, John 136, 138, 140
McCartney, Paul 182
McClelland, Doug 47, 49–51, 191
McCracken, Allison 191
McCrae, Jody 60
McGee, Mark Thomas 60, 63–64
McGregor, Ewan 123, 181–183
McLarty, Ron 176
Meet Me in St. Louis 9, 11, 87–88, 90–91, 105, 111, 175, 193
Mellencamp, Patricia 188
Merman, Ethel 162, 172
metadiegesis 148, 150–151, 156, 160–161, 163–165, 167, 198–199
Mickey and Sylvia 57, 71

Miljan, John 94
Miller, Ann 101–103, 150–151
Miller, Glenn 88, 91–93, 123–124, 193–194
Minnelli, Liza 160, 199
Minnelli, Vincente 9, 85, 87–88, 91, 108, 110, 112–114, 116–117, 160, 187, 192–193, 195, 199
minstrelsy 34, 38, 40 47, 189–191
Miranda, Carmen 3, 40
Mississippi 7–8, 45, 88, 94–97, 99–100, 103, 194
Mitchell, Elvis 184, 200
Mitchell, Frank 28–29, 31–32
Mitchell, James 83
Mitchell, Millard 165
Mitchell, Robert 57, 64
Modernaires 92
Monroe, Marilyn 182
Mordente, Tony 105
Moreno, Rita 105
Morgan, Dennis 130
Morgan, Frank 110, 112, 127
Morris, Garrett 63
The Most Happy Fella 8
Mostel, Zero 154, 199
Moulin Rouge 5, 10, 174, 181–183, 186, 200
Mueller, John 2, 4–5, 7, 37, 52, 68, 73–74, 80–81, 117–120, 158, 193, 195, 199
Mulvey, Laura 192
Munshin, Jules 101
Murray, Bill 63
The Music Man 5, 178
My Fair Lady 5, 187
Myrdal, Gunnar 3, 187

Nachbar, Jack 97, 193
Nachman, Gerald 195
Naremore, James 108, 193
Nathan, Hans 190
Natwick, Mildred 111
Neilsen, Inga 155
Nesor, Al 98
Newmar, Julie 99
Newton-John, Olivia 9, 64–65, 108, 122–123, 125, 191, 196
Nicholas Brothers 93
Night and Day 9, 118, 126, 137, 140–142, 144–146, 148
Nolan, Frederick 197

O'Connor, Donald 2, 164–165
Ogersby, Bill 61
Oklahoma! 2, 7, 67, 77, 81, 83–85, 113, 125–126, 147–148, 170, 176, 180, 193, 195–196
Oliver! 5
On the Town 8, 88, 100–103, 105–106, 177–178, 195

Oronati, Peter 176
Paint Your Wagon 8, 175, 177
Palmer, Peter 97, 99
Pan, Hermes 4, 92, 120, 196
Papp, Joseph 153
Paradise, Hawaiian Style 8
Paris, Audrey 160
Parks, Larry 7, 44, 48–49, 51, 191
Parrish, Leslie 97–99, 194
Patrick, Gail 94
Payne, John 91–92, 193
Pennies from Heaven 5, 10, 171, 199
Peretti, Geoffrey W. 191
Perry, Lincoln Theodore 28–29, 31–32, 137, 161, 163
Peters, Bernadette 137–138, 140, 168–171, 197, 199
Peterson, Caleb 145
Phillips, William H. 107, 187
Plautus, Titus Maccius 10, 73, 149, 153, 192, 198–199
Police 183
Porter, Cole 9, 52, 126, 140–144, 146, 148–151, 153, 162, 198
Powell, Dick 1, 18–22, 109, 127, 169, 171, 188
Powell, Eleanor 1, 18, 109, 127, 171, 188
Presley, Elvis 3–4, 8, 53, 55
Price, Vincent 60, 62–63
Prouty, Howard H. 105

Queen Latifah (Dana Elaine Owens) 186

Radner, Gilda 63
Rafferty, Frances 54
Rainer, Luise 128
Rall, Tommy 150
Reid, Mark A. 42–43, 190
Reilly, John C. 185
Reiner, Rob 107
Reinking, Ann 160
Reynolds, Debbie 164–165, 167–168, 199
Reynolds, Marjorie 40–42, 44–46, 51, 164–165, 168, 199
Rhodes, Erik 73
Rickles, Don 60, 62
Riggs, Lynn 148
Robbins, Gale 137
Robbins, Jerome 102–103, 106, 195
Robin, Leo 182
Robinson, Bill 35, 37, 42–43, 51, 189–190
The Rocky Horror Picture Show 2
Roddick, Nick 154, 198
Rodeo 84
Rodgers, Richard 8, 51–52, 75, 83, 94, 96, 126, 135–140, 143, 145–146, 177, 193–194, 197

Rogers, Ginger 1, 3, 9, 15, 17, 20, 24–25, 35, 61–62, 68, 73–75, 78–81, 123, 155, 158, 162, 188, 190, 192–193, 196
Rogin, Michael 34–35, 44–45, 191
Roland, Charles P. 94, 194
Romeo and Juliet 148, 173, 195
Ronettes 70
Rooney, Mickey 6–7, 34, 37–40, 44, 51, 53–55, 57, 64–65, 68, 71, 109, 122–124, 136, 140, 143, 145, 163, 180, 190, 192, 195–197
Roosevelt, Franklin D. 13, 40, 131, 134–135, 189
Ross, Herbert 168, 171
Roth, Mark 2, 188, 193
Royal Wedding 158
Rubin, Martin 190
Ruby, Harry 9, 18–19, 47, 126, 135–140, 143, 146, 171, 191
Rutsky R.L. 58, 62, 191
Rydell, Bobby 53, 55–58, 65, 192

Sakall, S.Z. 132
Sandrich, Mark 15, 75, 188
Saturday Night Fever 63
Saturday Night Live 63, 191
Schatz, Thomas 17, 187
Scheider, Roy 11, 159–163, 172–173
Schwartz, Arthur 158, 198–199
Schwartz, Charles 198
Seven Brides for Seven Brothers 5, 8
Shakespeare, William 2, 10, 50, 109, 148–151, 153, 183, 188, 195, 198
Shall We Dance 7, 11, 67–73, 78–80, 85, 120, 124, 188
Shary, Timothy 69, 192
Sheed, Wilfred 142, 198
Shevelove, Burt 153, 198
Shore, Dinah 145
Sidney, George 55, 151, 154, 198
Silk Stockings 1, 146
Silvers, Phil 154
Simpson, Bart 175, 177–178
Simpson, Homer 175, 177–179, 186
Simpson, Marge 177–178
The Simpsons 10, 175, 177, 179, 200
Sinatra, Frank 57, 101–102, 145–146, 191
The Singing Detective 170
Sirk, Douglas 69
Sisson, Charles 149
Skelton, Red 109, 136, 139, 194
Sklar, Robert 107, 188
Sly, Christopher 151
Smith, Alexis 146, 198
Smith, Queenie 95
The Sound of Music 5, 8, 187
South Pacific 8, 52

Sparks, Ned 18, 25, 76, 188
Spewack, Sam and Bella 148
Stand Up and Cheer 6, 15, 25–27, 29, 31, 33, 52, 168–169, 189
Stanfield, Peter 190–191
Steiger, Rod 83, 196
Stilwell, Robynn 1
Strickland, Robert E. 54
Sturges, Preston 15
Styne, Julie 182
Sullivan, Arthur 26
Sullivan, Ed 55, 58
Sully, Robert 90
Sun Valley Serenade 9, 88, 91–92, 194
Sutherland, A. Edward 95–97
Swayze, Patrick 69–72, 119
Sweet, Dolph 118
Swing Time 7, 34–35, 41–43, 189

Take Me Out to the Ball Game 123, 194
Tamblyn, Russ 104
The Taming of the Shrew 10, 148–151, 153, 192, 198
Taurog, Norman 53
Taylor, John Russell 2, 10, 74, 96, 109–110, 117, 122, 173, 187–188, 193, 195–196
Taylor, Libby 96
Temple, Shirley 3, 26–27, 31, 37, 83, 169, 188–189, 196
Thomas, Bob 189–190, 192
Three Little Words 9, 126, 135–140, 142, 148, 158
Tiffin, Pamela 57
Till the Clouds Roll By 9, 137, 140, 142, 144–146, 148, 155
Tom Jones 57, 67
Top Hat 7, 11, 15, 20, 27, 36, 67, 72–73, 75–76, 78, 80, 85, 91, 118, 155, 158, 163, 181, 184, 186, 188
Tosches, Nick 34, 49, 51, 189–190
Trachtenberg, Michelle 179
Travolta, John 53–55, 64–65, 122–124, 180, 184, 191, 196
Twain, Mark 51, 95, 188, 191

Vallee, Rudy 29, 167
Van Dyke, Dick 55, 57
Van Heusen, James 45, 190
Vera-Ellen 101–103, 109, 136, 158, 195
Verdon, Gwen 160
Vereen, Ben 11, 160
Vogel, Frederick G. 24, 164, 187, 189

Walken, Christopher 169
Walker, Nancy 54
Ward, Ed 52, 191, 197

Index

Ward, Geoffrey 191
Warner Brothers 3, 25, 185, 189
Wells, Joan 143
West, Dominic 184
West Side Story 3, 5, 8, 52, 88, 103–106, 125, 147–148, 151, 173, 187, 195
Whitman, Walt 30, 189
Whitmore, James 151
Wilder, Alec 52
William, Warren 20–22
Williams, Esther 3, 91, 109, 193–194
Williams, Gordon Willis 153, 199
Williamson, J.W. 194
Wills, Chill 89
Wise, Robert 103, 106, 195
The Wizard of Oz 14, 44, 112, 187, 188
Wloszczyna, Susan 5, 187
Wonder, Stevie 63, 192
Wood, Natalie 103–106
Woolley, Monty 143–144

Words and Music 9, 126, 135–138, 140, 142, 148, 194
Wordsworth, William 200
Wynn, Keenan 60–61, 122, 139, 151, 191

Xanadu 5, 9, 108, 116, 122–125, 186, 196

Yolanda and the Thief 9, 108, 110, 113, 115–116, 118, 125
Yudkoff, Alvin 122, 125

Zanuck, Darryl F. 92
Zelwegger, Renee 160, 184–186
Zeta-Jones, Catherine 11, 184–185
Ziegfeld, Florenz 9, 109, 126–133, 135, 137, 146, 148, 162, 165, 167, 194–197
Ziegfeld Follies 9, 109, 126, 129–130, 165, 194, 196

www.ingramcontent.com/pod-product-compliance
Ingram Content Group UK Ltd.
Pitfield, Milton Keynes, MK11 3LW, UK
UKHW050528150426
5217IPUK00026B/1844